Republican Democracy

Republican Democracy

Liberty, Law and Politics

Edited by Andreas Niederberger
and Philipp Schink

EDINBURGH
University Press

© Editorial matter and organization Andreas Niederberger
and Philipp Schink, 2013, 2015
© The chapters their several authors, 2013

Edinburgh University Press Ltd
The Tun – Holyrood Road
12 (2f) Jackson's Entry
Edinburgh EH8 8PJ

www.euppublishing.com

First published in hardback by Edinburgh University Press 2013

This paperback edition 2015

Typeset in 11/13.5 Goudy by
Servis Filmsetting Ltd, Stockport, Cheshire,
and printed and bound in Great Britain by
CPI Group (UK) Ltd, Croydon CR0 4YY

A CIP record for this book is available from the British Library

ISBN 978 0 7486 4306 6 (hardback)
ISBN 978 1 4744 0304 7 (paperback)
ISBN 978 0 7486 7759 7 (webready PDF)
ISBN 978 0 7486 7761 0 (epub)

Contents

Contributors

Richard Bellamy is professor of political science and director of the European Institute at the University College of London (UCL), United Kingdom.

James Bohman holds the Danforth I chair in the humanities and is professor of philosophy and professor of international studies at Saint Louis University, United States.

John Ferejohn is the Samuel Tilden professor of law at the University of New York, United States and professor emeritus for political science at Stanford University, United States.

Rainer Forst is professor of philosophy and political science at the Johann Wolfgang Goethe-Universität Frankfurt am Main, Germany.

Marco Geuna is professor of philosophy at the Università degli Studi di Milano (The University of Milan), Italy.

Cécile Laborde is professor of political theory at the University College of London (UCL), United Kingdom.

John P. McCormick is professor of political science at the University of Chicago, United States.

Andreas Niederberger is professor of philosophy at the Johann Wolfgang Goethe-Universität Frankfurt am Main, Germany.

Philip Pettit is L. S. Rockefeller University professor of politics and human values in Princeton University and distinguished professor of philosophy in the Australian National University.

Jack Rakove is professor of history and American studies, of political science and, by courtesy, of law at Stanford University, United States.

Galya Benarieh Ruffer is senior lecturer of political science and director of the international studies program at Northwestern University, United States.

Philipp Schink is assistant professor of philosophy at the Johann Wolfgang Goethe-Universität Frankfurt am Main, Germany.

Introduction

Andreas Niederberger and Philipp Schink

In many histories of political thought modernity appears as the inevitable triumph of liberal ideas. However, since the 1950s the academic discourse has also continuously been engaged with republican ideas and themes in various fields. The common core of the different positions usually associated with this republican revival in political and legal philosophy, in history and political science, consists in rejecting the central tenets of liberal political thought and denying their exclusive importance for modern politics. Motivated by a profound dissatisfaction with contemporary politics in the Western world the republican agenda aims to thoroughly develop a strong normative alternative to liberalism. Liberalism, in this view, is mainly identified with a certain type of possessive individualism, secured via a system of basic rights. Most of the contributors to the republican revival of the last fifty years argued that such a normative program is oblivious to the political and legal conditions necessary for peaceful, free, just and democratic coexistence. Republican – or neo-republican, as some label it – political thought, thus puts the ideas of the common good, citizenship and a revised understanding of freedom at the center of political theory again and reconsiders the sense and importance of politics, law and statehood in light of these three points of reference.

But there is no unified school of republican political thought. Republican theorists suggest different conceptions of politics, law and democracy: For some, law and democracy serve to enhance individual freedom by offering means of controlling political actors and institutions, whereas other approaches view democracy as the field of populist fights against economic, social and cultural elites. Still others conceive of democracy as

1

a procedure to create legitimate or even reasonable obligations, thereby constituting collectives as public political units. So far there has been only a sporadic discussion between these different positions. In highlighting different problems the different strands tend to overlook the potential and insights of the alternative republicanisms – much to the detriment of all. Therefore, this volume brings together major authors in the different strands of republican theory with the task of comparing and confronting the advantages and disadvantages of the respective approaches. All contributions focus on the links and tensions between law, liberty and democracy and work out the different purposes attributed to these aspects and elements of political order.

The first part of the book shows that these different understandings of law, liberty, democracy and political order more generally are already present or foreshadowed in key historical authors in the republican traditions. Marco Geuna, Jack Rakove and James Bohman point out that the defenses of republicanism from Italian Renaissance writers to James Madison and Immanuel Kant give different priorities and nuances to law, freedom and politics, which again leads to different ideas of the republic or of the scope and form of democratic and popular self-government. Historical texts and authors present, thus, paradigmatic models of republican political orders and structures.

The second part of the book considers more closely the relationship between politics, law and democracy in different versions of republican theory. John P. McCormick and John Ferejohn argue that in Roman republicanism and its rediscovery in Machiavelli the purpose of the republic was not to solve, but to enable political struggles over social justice. Law and political order offered a framework within which political fights could take place in a more or less peaceful way. Against this background the neo-republican understanding of the republic or democracy as a just distribution of liberty protected by a system of antimajoritarian legal structures must appear as an anti-republican model. Rainer Forst, in contrast, defends a close connection between republican democracy and justice. Forst views democracy as the structure ensuring that only those laws, measures and distributions hold that can be justified to all affected persons. Against both of these "populist" and Kantian challenges Philip Pettit defends his conception of neo-republicanism. For him only such a conception can guarantee freedom for each and everyone – freedom understood as nondomination – under conditions of pluralism.

After this focus on democracy, the third part of the book concentrates on the ideas of law and the relation between a legal order and freedom in republican political theory. In his contribution Philipp Schink critically examines the neo-republican thesis of the compatibility (or even constitutive relation) between freedom and the state. Taking the neo-republican approach as an answer to the neo-liberal conception of freedom and the rule of law, the authors argue that, contrary to the intention of its proponents, taking nondomination seriously leads to a rather critical perspective on the state. Galya Ruffer depicts the different models of citizenship present in republican approaches and argues in favor of a hybrid and composite understanding of republican citizenship. In her view citizenship essentially consists of opportunities to participate in political procedures but such participation does not exhaust the rights and legal status going along with citizenship. Richard Bellamy synthesizes the considerations in the second and third part of the book by discussing more generally the role of law and rights for democracy in the republican perspective. He rejects the neo-republican defense of judicial review and its attempt to secure individual rights. Against the "adjudication" of political and social conflicts in courts Bellamy advocates civic equality and the political struggle among citizens as the core of republican democracy.

Many current republican approaches refer to ancient authors, structures and events, but the republican tradition has its origins also and probably even mostly in Europe's and North America's modernity. It is, therefore, not surprising that many of its ideas on institutions and procedures are closely tied to the Western model of the (nation-) state. This raises the question of how republicanism could continue to be important under conditions of globalization and the development of multilevel, partially fragmented political and legal orders going along with it. Liberal theories with their methodological and legitimatory individualism seem to be much more apt to respond to these new challenges than republican approaches. How can the critique of liberalism that it is oblivious to the political and legal conditions for free and peaceful coexistence be maintained given the strong attachment in many republican approaches to possibly overcome conditions?

The final part of this volume addresses these issues and considers republicanism's contribution to the theory of global justice, legitimacy and democracy. Cécile Laborde and Andreas Niederberger argue that republican theory leads to a distinct view on global political circumstances and that there is a proper republican theory of global justice and legitimacy. However, they both highlight that this view not only adds one more position to the existing philosophical conceptions on global issues, it also challenges the republican primacy of the domestic viewpoint. Taken seriously, republicanism must be a global political theory and it can only articulate criteria for legitimacy if these criteria hold globally for everyone.

This volume had its origin in a conference at the Johann Wolfgang Goethe-Universität Frankfurt am Main, Germany in 2009. All the participants of this conference felt that there was an urgent need to further explore the parallels, differences and intersections between the various republican approaches. Thus, the contributions to this book were written with the competing positions in view, and they address possible objections that the competing positions bring forward.

The editors hope that the thoughts and arguments collected in this volume will be a valuable contribution to the discussion about the potentials as well as the limits of the republican revival. We would like to thank all the contributors and Nicola Ramsey of Edinburgh University Press.

CHAPTER I

The Tension between Law and Politics in the Modern Republican Tradition

Marco Geuna

In this essay I will consider the way in which the thinkers of the modern republican tradition – from Machiavelli to the authors of *The Federalist* – conceived the relationship and inevitable tensions between politics and law. I will do this in order to show how some interpretations of the modern republican tradition proposed by contemporary neo-republican thinkers tend to be somewhat reductive.

My aim is therefore twofold. First, I wish to provide a concise, and inevitably selective, account of how modern republicans thematize the relationship between law and politics, while seeking not to betray the complexity and richness of their ideas.

Second, in the conclusions I will attempt to show how some of the questions that the modern republicans dealt with, as well as some of their assumptions, can still represent a valuable starting point for the elaboration of republican theories that might prove capable of responding to the problems of our time. I wish to suggest, albeit in a few brief remarks, that it is possible to reformulate some republican themes in a richer and more complex way than has been done so far, thereby giving greater attention to politics and its conflicting aspects. But to carry out this task – that straddles history and theory – I must make a few introductory observations on the modern republican tradition, on the various theoretical strands within it and on contemporary modern neo-republicanism, in order to define the scope of my inquiry as accurately as possible.

1. PRELIMINARY CONSIDERATIONS

1.1. The recovery of the modern republican tradition is now more than fifty years old. If the first studies by Zera Fink and Caroline Robbins date back to the 1940s and 1950s, the definitive assertion of the paradigm came, as is universally recognized, with the publication of John Pocock's *magnum opus, The Machiavellian Moment*, the subtitle of which was *Florentine Political Thought and the Atlantic Republican Tradition.*[1] In Pocock's view, it was possible to trace a common thread, a theoretical continuity between the ideas of the Florentine humanists, especially Machiavelli, and those developed by theorists of the English Interregnum, especially Harrington, and also by the Scottish Enlightenment thinkers and the American revolutionaries. It is well-known that *The Machiavellian Moment* rests on two central theses: the idea of the continuity between Aristotelianism and republicanism, and the presentation of the republican tradition as antecedent, and as alternative to, the liberal tradition. Pocock believed that "*vita activa,*" "civil life," "virtue" and "corruption" were the key terms of the republican lexicon and claimed that the key ideas of the republican tradition were derived from classical authors: first and foremost, Aristotle and Polybius. With Pocock's book, the republican tradition earned its place among objects of study alongside highly respected and better-known traditions such as natural law, constitutionalism and liberalism. Republics and republican theories came to exercise the minds not only of historians of political thought and political language, but also of political and legal philosophers,[2] in their attempts to construct normative theories for the present. It is worth noting that many critics of John Rawls's theory of justice, thinkers soon labeled "communitarians," such as Michael Sandel (1988) and Charles Taylor (1989), took up Pocock's theses in philosophical and political debates. And this is not at all surprising since Pocock's republicanism offered them a conception of the individual and of political society that could be widely shared and used in the polemic against Rawls and, more generally, against liberal theories. Thus, the notion of a theoretical continuity between Aristotelianism, republicanism and communitarianism had become established by the end of the 1970s.

1.2. But precisely this theoretical continuity was the subject of a radical critique by Quentin Skinner. In a series of essays dating from the 1980s, from the seminal essay "Machiavelli on the Maintenance of Liberty" (1983) to "The Paradoxes of Political Liberty" (1986) and "The Republican Ideal of Political Liberty" (1990b), he had advanced an interpretation of republicanism that was radically opposed to the one advanced by Pocock's. Skinner's essays (1983, 1984, 1986, 1990b) operated on a number of levels both in terms of the historical account, expanding and elaborating Pocock's reconstruction, and on the purely interpretative level by focusing attention on the concept of liberty used by Machiavelli and other writers. From a historiographical point of view, Skinner pointed out that the development of a republican ideology did not depend on the rediscovery of Aristotle. Taking into account the numerous treatises of *ars dictaminis*, written by the masters of rhetoric, and the treatises on the government of the city, which were meant to serve as a guide of action for the *podestà*, he showed how an ideology of citizen self-government based essentially on Roman sources – Cicero's philosophical works and the works of the great historians, specifically Sallust – was proposed. In this way, he tried to break or at least to greatly reduce the importance of the continuity between Aristotelianism and republicanism for which Pocock had argued. Since then, Skinner has never ceased to emphasize that the language of the modern republican tradition owed a huge debt to Roman philosophical and historical ideas. From a strictly interpretative point of view, opposing the claims by MacIntyre (1981) that the philosophical choice to be made is between liberal individualism and some version of Aristotelianism, Skinner attempted to define an autonomous identity for republicanism, releasing it from the grasp of old and new Aristotelians. In his opinion, republicanism is not a form of Aristotelian politics. The freedom theorized by republicans is not positive liberty, but a specific form of negative liberty. The individual participates in the affairs of his *res publica* not because this is his natural destination, but in order to prevent the government from degenerating into a hateful tyranny while in the hands of others, thus endangering his security and private property. Political participation is not an ultimate end, but a means or an intermediate end.[3] Skinner thus conferred theoretical autonomy to republicanism by freeing it from the metaphysical assumptions present in the teleological Aristotelian politics, and reconfigured republicanism as political theory that could still be relevant in our own time, a possible third way between liberal individualism and Aristotelian communitarianism. Accordingly, he emphasized that a reformulation of the republican theory of liberty would make possible an interesting and innovative theory of citizenship.

The interpretation of republicanism offered by Skinner has quickly become influential.[4] Historians and theorists were increasingly aware of the existence of radically different interpretations of republicanism in

7

the scholarly community. If for many years the phrase "civic humanism" coined by Hans Baron, and the phrase "classical republicanism" preferred by Felix Gilbert had been used relatively freely, often interchangeably, from the early 1990s onwards they have been more frequently used to denote radically different conceptual frameworks. It was John Rawls who, in *Political Liberalism*, used the phrase "classical republicanism" to indicate an interpretation of republicanism *à la* Skinner, while he used the phrase "civic humanism" to denote a "form of Aristotelianism," or an interpretation of republican themes *à la* Pocock. Rawls showed that there was no substantial incompatibility between classical republicanism so understood and his political liberalism, whereas there was a radical incompatibility, a "fundamental opposition," between his views and those of civic humanism defined in this way.[5] The terminology used by Rawls to describe the two types of republicanism has quickly become canonical in the philosophical and politico-theoretical discourse.

1.3. Over the last few decades, subtle historiographical disputes concerning the distinguishing features of the republican tradition have taken place. In particular, there have been controversies about which philosophical and political heritages merged to form the republican tradition – whether predominantly the Greek (Nelson 2004) or the Roman[6] or that emerging from the treatises of *de republica hebraeorum* (Nelson 2010; Campos Boralevi 2002) and about the key terms, or key concepts, that distinguished republican political language and set it apart from other modern political languages, particularly those of natural law and contractualism. But all of this is well known.

It is also well known that in recent decades, historians have, on the one hand, questioned some of the theses of Pocock's "tunnel history" (Sullivan 1992; Scott 1993; Wootton 1994) and, on the other, focused on specific moments of the republican tradition previously neglected. New light has been shed on pre-humanist rhetorical culture and, more generally, on the pre-humanist origins of republican ideas (Skinner 1990a); on the ideas of English classical humanists, from Sir Philip Sidney to Francis Bacon (Worden 1996; Peltonen 1995); on different theories of Dutch republicanism developed during the anti-Spanish revolt (Secretan 1990; van Gelderen 1992), as well as in the age of the brothers De la Court and Spinoza (Kossmann 1995, 2000; Blom 1995; Mijnhardt 2003); on the theological and political conceptualizations of Genevan republicanism (Kirk 1994; Rosenblatt 1997; Silvestrini 2010), an important background for Rousseau's political thought, as well as on the different republican perspectives developed in modern Switzerland (Maissen 2006; Holenstein, Maissen and Prak 2008; Campi 2002); on French Enlightenment philosophers long deemed to be of secondary importance, such as Helvétius and Mably (Wright 1997; Wootton 2000); on the Italian debates in the age of the French Revolution (Guerci 1998); and on nineteenth- and early twentieth-century French republicanism (Spitz 2005; Jennings 2006). Thus in 2002 two volumes were published with the programmatic title *Republicanism: A Shared European Heritage* (van Gelderen and Skinner 2002): republican ideas were carefully investigated in various European historical contexts, from Netherlands to early modern Germany, from Poland to Spain, from England to Switzerland, from Scotland to France.

As a result of these studies, an interpretive scenario took shape that was much more varied than expected. Attention to individual historical configurations of the republican tradition has in fact brought to light the existence of a plurality of ways of interpreting the heritage of civic humanism and of Machiavelli. At one point it seemed that one could speak only of different republicanisms, in the plural, rather than of republicanism, in the singular (Zagorin 2003; Castiglione 2005; Mijnhardt 2006).

In the scientific community there is no agreement on how to differentiate one type of republicanism from another, and on how to define the different strands of thought included in the relatively heterogeneous republican tradition.[7] Various attempts have been made, from a historical perspective, to distinguish between the theories in the broader republican tradition framework. Some scholars simply contrasted an Aristotelian republicanism with a Roman republicanism – or, "civic humanism" and "classical republicanism," to borrow the terminology made paradigmatic by Rawls. Others, such as Philip Pettit, have distinguished between an "Italian–Atlantic tradition of republicanism" (or, depending on the formulations, a "Mediterranean-Atlantic" tradition) and a "Franco–German" (or "Franco-Prussian") tradition, which would include Rousseau and Kant in particular.[8] Moreover, some historians have simply proposed to distinguish between aristocratic and democratic republicanisms, while others have emphasized the distinction between a republicanism that favors order and the ideal of harmony and one that positively evaluates the moment of conflict.

1.4. Over the past two decades the term "republicanism" has been used not only to denote a historical tradition of modern political thought, and its historiography, but also a program of research in contemporary political theory, particularly in the Anglophone world. The constellation of

contemporary republicanism is, in fact, very broad. Very different thinkers have dealt with the legacy of Machiavelli and the classical republicans, singling out in their thinking the key ideas that they believe can
potentially address the problems of our time: from Philip Pettit to Michael
Sandel in the Anglophone world, and from Claude Lefort to Miguel
Abensour in the French,[9] to name but a few. It must be recognized that
there are various forms of contemporary republicanism, distinctive from
one another in both their historiographical reconstructions and in their
basic normative contents. It is worth mentioning the fact that in recent
years various proposals have been made to distinguish between and indi-
vidualize the various forms of contemporary republicanism. Limiting the
discussion to the Anglophone theoretical formulations, it can be mentioned that to characterize Michael Sandel's or Charles Taylor's theses
some talked of a "neo-Athenian interpretation of republican liberty," or
simply of a "neo-Athenian republicanism," to be contrasted with a "neo-
Roman republicanism"[10] that finds expression in the theses of Quentin
Skinner and Philip Pettit, and in those of their followers.

In this essay, I will focus only on the research program initiated by the
studies of Quentin Skinner and Philip Pettit, and including a significant
number of scholars, from John Maynor (2003) to Cécile Laborde (2008,
2010a), from Maurizio Viroli (1999) to James Bohman (2008), from
Samantha Besson to Jorge Martí (Besson and Martí 2009b), to mention
but a few. Here two texts may represent paradigmatic watersheds: Pettit's
Republicanism: A Theory of Freedom and Government (1997),[11] and
Skinner's *Liberty before Liberalism* (1998). To characterize this research,
which has an obviously normative intent, more specific terms have been
adopted, but perhaps the more accurate term is "neo-republicanism."
As Frank Lovett and Philip Pettit (2009, 12) have recently written, the
term "neo-republicanism" is adopted to address "the attempts by current
political scientists, philosophers, historians, lawyers, and others to draw
on [this] classical republican tradition, adapting and revising its various
ideas, in the development of an attractive public philosophy intended
for contemporary purposes."[12] Over the past ten years, several areas have
been touched by this theoretical work. While the attempt to distinguish
the republican conception of freedom as absence of domination by liberal
and/or communitarian alternative conceptions was central, other issues
have also been addressed, such as the relationship between republicanism
and distributive justice, that between republicanism and the condition
of women, the relationship between republicanism and multicultural

societies, and that between republicanism and international democracy (Honohan and Jennings 2006; Laborde and Maynor 2008; Besson and Martí 2009a; Pettit 2010a, Laborde 2010b).[13] The attempt was that of developing, in these fields of inquiry, theoretical perspectives from a relatively small core of assumptions: the republican conception of freedom, the concept of a free state, and that of citizenship.[14]

To envisage a political philosophy for the present, Pettit and other contemporary theorists worked on the heritage of the modern republican tradition by making a choice that led to inevitable selections. Some ideas and concepts have been reconsidered, revised and reformulated with the intent of bringing them back into the contemporary debate. This occurred primarily with the idea of freedom,[15] and the related ideas of domination (Lovett 2010; Lazzeri 2010) and dependence, and then with the conception of the republic and its institutions, and with the ideas of republican virtue and vigilance.[16] Now we have to wonder if that which fell into shadow, eschewed by the inevitable work of selection, can still teach us something, if it can still be useful to contemporary thought. I will try to be more precise and to explain myself better.

1.5. Many contemporary scholars, including Quentin Skinner and Philip Pettit themselves, have pointed out how the ideal of the rule of law is a central tenet of modern republican theories and of their criticism of monarchical institutions.[17] These scholars, however, have not paid the same attention to the question concerning the relevance that modern republicans have accorded to politics: whether this was limited to an institutional dimension – that is, within the practice of the various councils and magistrates suggested by their theories – or whether this was understood in a more original, one might say, pre-institutional dimension. Above all, some interpreters, like Pettit himself, have at times placed the rule of law alongside the rule of virtue, without properly dwelling on the tensions between the two factors present in the same tradition: law and virtue.[18] Therefore, my contribution is dedicated to recognition of these tensions. Investigating the tensions between law and virtue, of course, entails an inquiry into the systematic tensions between law and politics; or, using a different contemporary vocabulary, between constitutionalism and democracy.

It is often assumed that included within the modern republican theories there are conceptual elements that can come together in a contemporary theory of democracy; it is also assumed that the republican commitment to rule of law is the modern analog of our current interest

11

in constitutionalism. In the theories put forward by modern republicans there are elements that would allow us to develop, or to redevelop today, a conception of democracy that respects and incorporates the requirements of constitutionalism.

The fact is that we commonly speak of "constitutional democracy" without wondering, as Jürgen Habermas (2001) once suggested, whether this expression contains "a paradoxical union of contradictory principles." The theory of the existence of an inherent connection, a necessary mutual nexus between rule of law and democracy, which Habermas has been defending since 1994, seems to have convinced many interpreters to the point that it has now become something obvious. It is taken for granted that the historical-political development of the West finds its fulfillment in a complete and peaceful reconciliation between rule of law – the implementation of the ancient ideal of the government of the laws – and democracy – the implementation of the equally ancient ideal of a people's government.[19] However, there is also a position held by a minority that insists on the existence of an unsolved tension between democracy and constitutionalism. In this essay I would like to start from the point of view that law and politics are two components that cannot be completely reduced or assimilated into each other. I do not wish to assume that the two components harmonize perfectly, without leaving anything out.

1.6. It is clear that in the contemporary debate, there exist different conceptions of democracy and of constitutionalism. Some emphasize a purely procedural notion of democracy, others a notion of deliberative democracy, and still others an agonistic approach to democracy. Some think of a "legal constitutionalism" and others of a "political constitutionalism." Some see the "judicial review" as a necessary and salutary corrective to possible majoritarian tendencies within contemporary democracies; others insist that the "judicial review" has no ultimate foundation and democratic legitimacy (Tushnet 1999; Kramer 2004; Hirschl 2004; Waldron 2006).

Among neo-republican theorists, too, there are important differences in the way of thematizing the relationship between democracy and constitutionalism (Honohan 2009). The positions of Philip Pettit (1997, 1999, 2000, 2004) and Richard Bellamy (2007, 2009, 2011b), for example, present significant differences in this regard. I cannot dwell here on these problems. Suffice to say that I assume the relationship between democracy and constitutionalism to be a setting for possible tensions. Precisely this: a setting for tensions, not for perfect harmony.[20]

1.7. Focusing on the relationship between law and politics is an indirect way of entering another problem. In the following pages I shall investigate the role acknowledged to politics by modern republican theories, and indirectly, shall investigate the role assigned to politics by the neo-republican theories of the Anglophone world. The starting hypothesis is that the modern republican theorists acknowledged a larger role for politics than is recognize by neo-republican theories. If politics has to do also with innovation and conflict, this aspect does not seem to have found adequate recognition in neo-republican theories. If politics, and democracy itself, have always necessarily to do with a world in constant flux of transformation and conflictual change, then it is not always clear how neo-republican theories can come to terms with this fundamental dimension of politics itself. Neo-republican theories that draw inspiration from the theses of Philip Pettit, perhaps, are not yet adequately equipped to conceptualize these dimensions.

1.8. I think it is important, finally, to reflect explicitly on the relationship between history and theory[21] and to say a few words about it. We need to rethink and problematize the relationship between the history of modern republicanism and contemporary neo-republican theories. I believe it is important to underline and reassert the fact that there can only exist a mediated relationship between these two perspectives or fields of inquiry. First, it should not be assumed that there is a direct, immediate, continuity between modern and contemporary concepts: on the one hand, it would be a mistake to apply concepts belonging to contemporary debate on the reflections of the Moderns, and turning the republican thinkers of the sixteenth and eighteenth century either into democrats, in a contemporary sense, or into proponents of a form of constitutionalism; on the other, we should not think that some of Machiavelli's assumptions – such as his praise for the institution of the Tribunes of the plebs or his idea of public "accusations" – are immediately translatable into the contemporary theoretical and political discourse.[22] I am convinced that only by assuming, as a methodological hypothesis, the existence of significant differences between modern and contemporary logical frameworks and assumptions can we establish a fruitful engagement between history and theory. Only once the modern republican tradition is reconstructed at a distance – so to speak, "*juxta propria principia*" – can it provide fruitful suggestions for our present, for our efforts to develop theories capable of understanding and transforming it.

1.9. With an awareness of the continuities and discontinuities between modern theories and contemporary theories, between history and theory, in the following pages I shall discuss briefly and selectively certain examples and conceptualizations of the modern republican tradition. More specifically, I will frequently dwell on certain features that are *common* to many republican theories. At other times, however, I will overtly focus *on a particular family of theories*: namely, those that remain as faithful as possible to the Machiavellian lesson. I believe, in fact, that it is possible to distinguish within the modern republican tradition, in an ideal-typical way, those theories that draw on and reformulate the legacy of Machiavelli and those theories that draw on and reformulate Harrington's views.[23]

Machiavelli and Harrington, it is well known, differ in their way of thinking about political life in a republic. The former took Rome as a political model and attributed a positive role to those political conflicts that remained within certain institutional channels; Machiavelli argued not only "that the disunion of the Plebs and the Roman Senate made that Republic free and powerful" (Machiavelli 1996a, I.4, 70; 1996b, 16), but more broadly considers the divisions – "maintained without sects and partisans" (Machiavelli 1962, VII.1, 451–2; 1988, 276) – as preconditions for the preservation of freedom in the republics. The latter flatly excluded conflicts from the physiology of the republic and did not give a positive assessment of the tumultuous Roman republic. Instead he chose Venice as a political model, the city of the narrow government. The Machiavellian defense of the role of "disunions" and "tumults" went hand-in-hand with an antiaristocratic polemic and a positive assessment of the political role of the people. In Harrington we can trace an opposite stance: Harrington believed that there is a "natural aristocracy" and had no hesitation in arguing that "the wisdom of the few may be the light of mankind" (Harrington 1992, 23–4). He argued that this aristocracy, gathered in the Senate, had the role of "debating" political issues to be submitted to the people's assembly, which in turn was responsible for deciding, for "resolving." These differences, although important, seem to me to lead to even deeper differences, in particular on how to conceive institutional practices, which I cannot discuss here. Indeed, I cannot give further space to pointing out similarities and differences between these two families, or strands, of republican theories.[24]

14

2. Second part

In modern republican theories, the republic is always considered from two perspectives: a static one and a dynamic one, so to speak. The republican theorists are not just concerned with delineating in the abstract the characters of the best republic as opposed to those of principality and monarchy but are instead devoted to the analysis of the orders and the magistracies of the republic throughout history. I will not insist on this issue, which has been repeatedly pointed out by John Pocock. Thus, for the republican thinkers politics and history are strictly connected: politics and law are conceived in time.

This element is particularly apparent when we consider the structure of their theories, and we compare it, for instance, with that of modern social contract theories. Modern social contract theorists, from Hobbes onward, start from an ideal experiment, namely, from the position of a counterfactual, such as the state of nature, which results in a fundamental annihilation of the social relations, and more generally of history. In *De cive*, Hobbes (1983a, VIII.1, 127) exhorts us "to consider men as if but even now sprung out the earth, and suddenly, like mushrooms, come to full maturity, without all kind of engagement to each other."[25] The republicans, on the other hand, do not make use of this mental experiment, this sort of *annihilatio mundi* applied to the field of the political relations, but carefully think through the problems of the republic in time. Thus, they take into account the question of the genesis of the republic, the creation and development of its institutions, as well as the decadent phase of those institutions and laws and the emergence of the corruption of orders and men, when the actve virtue of citizens fails and the very end of the republic appears to be imminent.

It appears to me that particular attention has been devoted over the last few years to the normative dimension of the republican theories: scholars tend to focus on the fundamental characteristics of the republic, and of the freedom that it allows, thus reading the republican theorists from a static or structural perspective. This has brought the aspect of the rule of law, and its prerequisites and consequences, to the fore.

Instead, in this paper I would like to draw attention to that other dimension of the republican theories: namely, to their study of the republics in time, and throughout history, and, especially, to the moments of the genesis and corruption of the republics. If one considers the pages devoted to the genesis and corruption of the republics, one clearly observes the

15

great relevance that the republican thinkers ascribed to the element of virtue – be that the virtue of the individual or of collective bodies. It is possible, therefore, to detect in their theories a tension between the rule of law[26] and the rule of virtue,[27] between law and politics, which gives way to a variety of solutions.

2.1. When the republican thinkers tackle the question of the genesis of the republican political order, they are confronted, although in different ways, with two sets of problems that I intend to analyze, namely, a) the role played by the great legislators and the question of their virtue and b) the role played by social and political conflict in the creation of good orders and good laws.

When analyzing the genesis in history of the republican orders – of the republics of Sparta, Athens or Venice – and when describing their ideal republics, most of the republican thinkers, although not all, refer to the figure of the great founders and legislators (Lycurgus, Solon, Moses). Their virtue is needed in order for the republic and its rule of law to exist. The characteristics of this virtue are worth exploring. First of all, when Machiavelli (1996a, I.9, 85–8; 1996b, 28–30) began to reflect on the experience of Rome, he dwelled upon the role of its founder, Romulus, and questioned his virtue. He pointed out that this virtue is imbued with violence: Romulus first kills Remo, his brother, and then promotes, or "consents" to, the death of Titus Tatius, the king of the Sabines. The foundation of the republic *par excellence* bears the marks of violence.[28] When taking into account the founders or the legislators ("the orderers") of other past republics, Machiavelli underlined two elements: first, the fact that the legislators can resort to "any extraordinary action," to forms of violence, in order to carry out their duty;[29] second, the fact that they are led by their virtue to pretend they are in contact with the gods in order to persuade the people to accept the systems conceived by them.[30] The legislator's virtue can entail the resort to violence as well as the strategic use of lies.

Many modern republican thinkers, from Harrington to Sidney and Rousseau, dwelled on the virtue needed to give the right legal order to a republic. In "The Commonweath of Oceana," Harrington (1992, 67) followed Machiavelli's thought to the letter, almost paraphrasing a crucial passage from chapter nine of the first book of *Discourses*. He claimed that in order for a republic to become an "empire of laws" it must be founded by a "wise legislator," and added that "any man that is master of reason [shall not] blame such extraordinary means as in that case shall be necessary, the end proving no other than the constitution of a well-ordered commonwealth."[31]

In the chapter on the "Legislator" in *The Social Contract*, Rousseau referred with approval to Machiavelli and quoted directly in Italian the passage from the eleventh chapter of the first book of *Discourses*, where Machiavelli claimed that the legislators must necessarily call upon the authority of the gods to persuade the people. As is known, for Rousseau, the legislator or the law-maker:

> is, in every respect, an extraordinary man in the State. Extraordinary not only because of his genius, but equally because of his office, which is neither that of the government nor that of the sovereign. This office, which gives the Republic its constitution has no place in that constitution. It is a special and superior function which has nothing to do with empire over men.
>
> Rousseau (1964, 382; 1968, 85)

First conclusion: when tackling the question of the birth of the republican orders, and of the origin of the republics' rule of law, the republican thinkers could not avoid focusing on the existence of exceptional figures who do not hesitate to resort to forms of violence, lie and manipulation in order to accomplish their task. The emergence of the rule of law represented a problem for the republican thinkers that is solved, in the first place, by thematizing the mythical figures of the great legislators. By describing these figures, they indirectly theorized the existence of two distinct types of men with different capacities and virtues.

In Machiavelli, as well as in various other republican thinkers, the problem of the origin of the republican order is also approached from another perspective, following a different line of reasoning. Discussing the history of Rome, Machiavelli (1996a, I.2, 68; 1996b, 14) stressed the fact that the "first" Roman orders "were defective," that is to say, they were inadequate and insufficient. The "good laws and the good orders" that characterized the Roman republic in its glorious phase were brought about thanks to disunions and tumults that had marked the republic's existence for many centuries. Social and political conflict produced good orders and good laws. Conflictual politics gave birth to the constitutional orders; "tumults" and "disunions" generated good laws.[32] From a genetic perspective, politics is a *primum* and law is a *posterum* or a *derivatum*. Or, at least, it is possible to say that there is a "perpetual recursivity between laws and conflict."[33]

Machiavelli developed his argument from a particular political anthropology: He claims that in all republics and, more generally, in all political

17

bodies, there are two types of people, or, as he calls them, two humors: the nobles who are only concerned with the acquisition of greater power and who oppress the people; and the people whose only aim, instead, is to live freely.[34]

I cannot comment upon this kind of anthropology here, but I would simply point out that the distinction between two humors is an unavoidable and insuperable reality for any political community or political form. The disunion, the discord between these two humors, is what brings good "orders" about in the first place: Machiavelli (1996a, I.2, 69, I.4, 72; 1996b, 14, 17) mentioned the Tribunes of the plebs that brought, so to speak, the Roman mixed government to a state of perfection. He then underlined the fact that, even when the Roman orders had reached perfection, the conflict between the plebs and the Senate, the people and "the Great," developing "without sects and without partisans" and gaining honors rather than property, produced good laws in benefit of public freedom.[35] Developing within particular institutional channels, conflict preserves the liberty of the republic even when this has become a form of rule of law. Thus, Machiavelli pointed out the pivotal role of the element of conflict in the genesis of the republican orders, as well as in the phase of their complete development and normal function, when a sort of constitutional balance among the parties has been reached. Liberty appears as a result of orders and laws, but in the final analysis it is the outcome of the political conflict produced by those different natures, those humors aiming at different ends. If one considers this thesis from a wide perspective, it is possible to claim that Machiavelli not only acknowledged a tension between politics and law, but also came to recognize a sort of logical priority of politics over law.[36]

It is well known that Machiavelli's "tumultuous republic" has not always been enthusiastically supported by modern republican thinkers. Important theorists, from Guicciardini (1994, 105; 1983) to Harrington (1992, 33, 160–2, 218–20) and Rousseau (1964, IV.2, 439; 1968, 151–2), did not follow Machiavelli in his attempt to keep order and conflict together, that is, in his effort to prove that conflicts can be regarded as physiological and not just as pathological. Nonetheless, I would like to stress at this point that there have been other thinkers who followed in his footsteps and who consciously reformulated his ideas: from Commonwealthmen such as Algernon Sidney (1990, 153–4) and Walter Moyle (1969), to a Scottish philosopher such as Adam Ferguson (1995), to Vittorio Alfieri (1951), to include another Italian thinker. Different approaches and priorities in these two families of theories are particularly apparent when one deals with the question of the normal operation of the republic, to which I now intend to draw my attention.

2.2. All the modern republican theorists, while belonging to very different families within the tradition, have always consistently denounced the possibility of the dissolution of republican orders and the potential rise to power of individuals who govern "without laws or constraints." They have been united by the specter of, depending on the language used, tyrannical power, absolute monarchical power, or despotic power. In order to avoid this possibility, the republican thinkers have resorted to a variety of theoretical strategies: some of them have relied exclusively on the institutional architecture of the republic, on its particular institutions, and above all those of the mixed government; others, despite recognizing the importance of the institutions and of the rule of law guaranteed by them, have insisted, in the final analysis, on the crucial role of the active virtue of the citizens and public spirit.

Scholars have dwelled extensively on the fundamental features of the republican institutions theorized by the modern thinkers and upon the forms of rule of law and the type of liberty guaranteed by them. I will not discuss their analyses here, although I would like to draw attention to the rich and complex institutional imagination of the republican thinkers. They worked on the classical models of the republics of Athens, Sparta and Rome, but they have also taken into account the institutions of that *respublica hebraeorum* brought back to light in the studies of Carolus Sigonius (1582) and Petrus Cunaeus (1617). Then, they have systematically compared these classical Greek, Latin and Judaic models with the experience of the modern republics, from Venice to the United Provinces.

Some form of mixture, or Aristotelian *mikté*, guarantees the balance between the various constitutional organs and makes possible the preservation of liberty. On this point, the claims of republicanism and the requirements of constitutionalism converge. Obviously, each thinker provides a different interpretation of the idea of mixed or balanced government – some thinkers focus on aristocratic applications, others (probably a minority) on democratic ones. As a matter of fact, Machiavelli belongs to the latter group: in his *Discourses* he emphasized the importance of a series of magistracies or institutional procedures that together formed the power of the people.

Among the other institutional remedies put forward by the republicans in order to preserve liberty, I would like to recall at least the idea of the

19

small republic and of a federation of small republics that started to circulate, for instance, in the English republicanism of the second half of the seventeenth century, from John Milton to Andrew Fletcher.

While all the republican thinkers carefully considered the institutional architecture of the republic, the differences between the various families of republican theories fully emerges in the discussion of the overall relevance and ultimate significance of the ordinary function of institutions. Theorists such as Guicciardini, Harrington or Rousseau, who valued order above conflict, placed their trust entirely on the ability of institutional architectures to guarantee the law and, through it, the liberty of the citizens. Nonetheless, within modern republicanism, there are also other thinkers and families of theories which, even when dealing with the ordinary operation of the republic, emphasized the importance of the active virtue of the citizens rather than the institutional remedies in the preservation of freedom, in this sense reformulating the lesson taught by Machiavelli. In order to give an idea of this approach, I will focus particularly on the thought of a Scottish republican theorist, Adam Ferguson.

In his *An Essay on the History of Civil Society*, Ferguson developed his argument beginning from the recognition of the institutional and political relevance of mixed governments, and cited Rome and modern England as paradigmatic examples.[37] He went so far as to declare that England, in particular, "has carried the authority and government of law to a point of perfection, which they never before attained in the history of mankind"[38] (Ferguson 1995, 159). But he immediately became critical, pointing out that liberty and justice cannot be preserved by relying exclusively on laws and institutions.

> It is not in mere laws, after all, that we are to look for the securities to justice, but in the powers by which those laws have been obtained, and without whose constant support they must fall to disuse. Statutes serve to record the rights of a people, and speak the intention of parties to defend what the letter of the law has expressed: but without the vigour to maintain what is acknowledged as a right, the mere record, or the feeble intention, is of little avail.
>
> (Ferguson 1995, 160)

Ferguson insisted on this idea in various other passages of his *An Essay on the History of Civil Society*, for instance when writing: "If forms of proceeding, written statutes, or other constituents of law, cease to be enforced by the very spirit from which they arose; they serve only to cover, not to restrain the iniquities of power" (Ferguson 1995, 249).[39] The idea that

20

liberty cannot be preserved by political institutions alone is a sort of *leit-motif* in his work. In another passage, he wrote:

> Even political establishments, though they appear to be independent of the will and arbitration of men, cannot be relied on for the preservation of freedom; they may nourish, but should not supersede that firm and resolute spirit, with which the liberal mind is always prepared to resist indignities, and to refer its safety to itself.
> (Ferguson 1995, 251)

It is worth underlining the precision of Ferguson's formulation: "political establishments, though they appear to be independent of the will and arbitration of men, cannot be relied on." His position is clear: in the final analysis, virtue, "that firm and resolute spirit," is more important than political institutions, and active political participation is more important than law. It is no coincidence that Ferguson appropriated another Machiavellian theme, eulogizing political conflict in several passages of his work: "When we seek in society for the order of mere inaction and tranquillity, we forget the nature of our subject, and we find the order of slaves, not that of free men" (Ferguson 1995, 254, note 97).[40] Or once more: "The rivalship of separate communities, and the agitations of a free people, are the principles of political life, and the school of men" (Ferguson 1995, 62–3).

2.3. The question of the corruption of institutions as well as of the citizens' active virtue is pivotal to the analysis of all the republican thinkers, whatever their time and culture. How do institutions become corrupted? And what brings about the crisis of the republic? What processes determine the weakening or dissolution of public virtue and of the citizens' devotion to the common good? These questions have led the republican thinkers to develop increasingly detailed accounts of the great historical transformations that were taking place during their respective periods.

Machiavelli devoted many pages to the analysis of the different ways in which republics become corrupted.[41] In *Discourses*, in particular, he explored the transformation of conflicts in Rome from strictly political to economic enmities: from tumults having as a stake the "honors," to disunions having as a stake the "belongings" (Machiavelli 1996a, I.37, 139–42; 1996b, 78–81).[42] He denounced the reaction of the nobles against the Gracchis' proposals for an agrarian reform that attacked their control over landed property. Furthermore, in *Florentine Histories* he carefully analyzed the way in which political conflict occurred in Florence: political contrasts gave birth to "sects and partisans" and degenerated into a series of violent acts (Machiavelli 1962, III.1, 212–3; 1988, 105–6).[43]

The English Commonwealthmen of the late seventeenth century considered the formation of standing armies as a definite cause of corruption, while in the early decades of the eighteenth century others detected clear threats to liberty as coming from patronage and, more generally, the Crown's attempts to control the parliament. Finally, other republican thinkers denounced the creation of large states, and the tendency of republics to expand, as a definite cause of corruption and a threat to republican liberty. The typologies of institutional, political and moral corruption are extremely complex. I do not wish to discuss these, but rather the solutions that the republican thinkers discovered to curb these damaging processes, because these allow us once more to see at close quarters the tension between law and politics, between rule of law and rule of virtue, which runs through their work.

The republican thinkers called for institutions, or "orders," which would hold corruption in check, such as censorship exercised over the behavior of citizens[44] or the dictatorial authority in moments of extraordinary political crisis.[45] Both of these magistracies had to be precisely determined and limited by the law, as happened in the classical Roman experience. From my point of view, these magistracies are interesting because they require, for their functioning, the existence of particularly virtuous individuals within the body of citizens. Again, many republican thinkers have called for the exercise of virtue by extraordinary individuals, or groups of individuals, in order to maintain or to fully restore the rule of law when this is put under strain.

What is even more interesting from this perspective is the possibility of considering Machiavelli's ideas on what he called the republics' "return to its beginnings." This is needed when the republics start to become corrupted, when "men begin to vary in their customs and to transgress the laws."[46] While it is true that Machiavelli believed that the return to the beginnings can either be foreseen and set in motion by the regulations of the republic itself or else can be introduced through the virtue of good people, one should not forget his assertion in the crucial opening chapter of the third book of *Discourses* that in order to bring about authentic change and a return to the beginnings the "orders have need of being brought to life by the virtue of a citizen."[47] In order to put a stop to corruption, and bring institutions back to their function and original "goodness," the virtue of remarkable individuals is necessary, even if this is exercised through the sentencing to death and execution of the "sons of Brutus," and all other enemies of the republic. Such executions may serve as examples and may in some way revive the virtue of the citizens. Machiavelli was extremely crude in this respect: the memory of punishment produces fear in those who intend to attack the republic: "Unless something arises by which punishment is brought back to their memory and fear is renewed in their spirits, soon so many delinquents join together that they can no longer be punished without danger."[48] Machiavelli repeatedly pointed out that these executions had to take place at least once every decade in order to keep fear alive and to maintain a constant respect for the law among citizens or, in other words, in order to avoid the spread of corruption.

Machiavelli raised a particular problem of unquestionable relevance, namely that of the importance of the renewal of institutions and customs for the long-term survival of the republic, as can even be seen in the title of that first chapter: "If one wishes a sect or a republic to live long, it is necessary to draw it back often toward its beginning."[49] What is at stake here is, above all, the corrupt behavior of individuals, which tends to destroy the laws and orders, and the way that such conduct may be altered by those who are interested in preserving the established republican order. Machiavelli's solutions may be extremely distant from our contemporary sensitivity, but the problem he raised nevertheless continues to be crucial. It is no coincidence that it attracted the attention of many later republican thinkers, starting, for instance, from a Commonwealthman such as Algernon Sidney.[50]

I would like to add a further remark before passing to the conclusions. When one considers the modern reflection on the republic as a whole and in the context of time and, especially, its genesis and eventual corruption, it appears that the republican thinkers appealed to virtue (of the individual or of small groups) in order to tackle extremely important questions. Thus, it is not surprising that later thinkers and people of action – I am thinking in particular of the French revolutionaries and especially the Jacobins – focused on this specific dimension of their thought. I think that Hannah Arendt's remarks in *On Revolution* (2006, 199–200) concerning the possible origin and indirect sources of Robespierre's "despotism of liberty" remain valid and evocative. I am persuaded that they still offer us much food for thought, in times that might tempt us to adopt stylized reconstructions of the history of republicanism, which select and prioritize the themes closest to our sensibility.

3. Conclusion

3.1. Looking backward to the modern republican tradition enables us to shed light on the fact that it takes into account problems and theoretical subjects that, to a large extent, have been neglected by contemporary neo-republican theories. What are these subjects? First, there is the question of the genesis of republican institutions. Second, there is the problem of the corruption of the political institutions and the customs underpinning them, a problem that Machiavelli also addressed through what he called the "return to the beginnings." Third, there is the problem of possible crises in the free life of a republic, crises that could be faced with temporary political institutions, such as a "dictatorship." It can be argued that the modern republican theorists focused on a larger number of problems and theoretical concepts than are considered by contemporary theorists. In other words, one may say that modern theories were richer and more complex than contemporary ones.

I am convinced that the problems of the Moderns remain of interest and that they deserve to be reframed in a new language. This is true for the *problems* of the Moderns, not for the *solutions* that they found for them. For example, one cannot avoid thinking that the issue of the genesis of democratic institutions remains a problem for neo-republican thinkers. We have lived through the third wave of democratization, which ended with the fall of the Berlin Wall and of the communist regimes in Eastern Europe, and the movements of the Arab Spring. One must find a way of accounting for these demands for democracy in republican terms, for demands often made in the name of a freedom that calls for the end of the domination by unpopular oligarchies. Furthermore, how can one not conclude that the issue of the crisis of political institutions – that according to modern republicans came about when partisan sects, or personal bonds with political leaders, developed within the republic – should be addressed in new terms by neo-republicans thinkers? Who can avoid dealing with the contemporary crisis of political parties and, more generally, that of political representation?[51] Finally, one cannot deny, after 9/11, that the problem of the use of emergency powers[52] – that modern republicans addressed by reshaping the classical notion of dictatorship – needs to be reconsidered from a neo-republican perspective.

Some years ago, James Bohman rightly observed:

24

By reintroducing the important deal of freedom as non-domination, the republican tradition has significantly altered the landscape of political philosophy. Despite the fruitfulness of this new vocabulary, many basic republican concepts related to it remain relatively underdeveloped.

(Bohman 2008, 190)

Part of the work on basic republican concepts still awaits conclusion.

3.2. I am convinced that a deeper reflection on the issue of the genesis of democratic institutions could help to better specify what politics is for neo-republican thinkers and what role politics plays in their theoretical perspective: in other words, whether it is conceived from a merely institutional viewpoint or, as I hope, there is also an acknowledgement of a noninstitutional dimension. If we follow Machiavelli's lesson on the Roman tumults that "made that Republic free and powerful," and if we take seriously the great popular mobilizations that led to the end of communist regimes in 1989 and triggered the Arab Spring, one cannot fail to recognize and confer, above all, a noninstitutional dimension to politics. By the adoption of either the state/civil society dichotomy or of other similar conceptual distinctions, we are in any case induced to recognize a noninstitutional dimension to politics, one that could perhaps be called existential. It is a dimension that Hannah Arendt, for example, tried to capture with the term "action."[53]

This approach to politics – this broader conceptual space – permits the examination of two key problems: a) the relationship and permanent tension between politics and law, where if the fundamental task of regulating civil and political life is entrusted to the law, one must recognize that the aspirations and problems to which the law seeks to give juridical form emerge in a different – a social and political – space, very often as a result of conflicts of different kinds; and b) the inherent and essential relation between politics and conflict. In these conclusive remarks, I will devote a few words to each of these problems.

3.3. My first point concerns the permanent and insuperable tension between law and politics. I have stressed how modern republican thinkers refer to the virtue of single individuals or small groups in order to explain the genesis of the republics and to find the solutions to their internal corruption. When considering figures such as the founders of states or legislators, or "orders" such as censorship or dictatorship, or events such as "the return to the beginnings," they indirectly point out and emphasize the limits of what we call the "rule of law." Furthermore, I have shown how those republican thinkers who follow the particular theoretical group

25

inspired by Machiavelli's teaching go even further and outline a tension between the rule of law and the "rule of virtue," between law and politics, even in times when the republic functions normally. When they continue to refer to the tumultuous and conflicting virtue of the citizens, they seem to delineate an almost logical and genetic primacy of politics over law.

I therefore believe that it is extremely important that we should remain aware of the tension between law and politics, between rule of law and rule of virtue, and that we should never forget the lesson of modern republicans: politics cannot be totally exhausted or translated into law. The law does not, nor can it, bring about a total drainage of the political *Zuiderzee*.

This applies also to the attempt to rethink the problems of contemporary constitutional democracies in neo-republican terms: the hidden tension between constitutionalism and democracy cannot be entirely circumvented or removed.

3.4. My second point concerns the possibility of fruitfully combining republic and conflict, or in contemporary terms, democracy and conflict. As I have already argued, there are various families of republican theories: on the one hand, those theories that value instances of order in the republic, and place themselves within the perspective of, for instance, Guicciardini or Harrington, and, on the other, those theories that appropriate and develop Machiavelli's thought, recognizing the role played by social and political conflict within the life of the republic. I would argue that this specific lesson of Machiavelli's thought can play an important role in reformulating a republican theory up to the challenges of the present. In other words, Machiavelli's lesson might be important in formulating an agonistic conception of democracy,[54] one that does not prioritize or focus exclusively on consensus.

I will try to express this point more clearly by explaining how I interpret Machiavelli's insights. To begin with, conflict appears to be rooted in different anthropologies, in two different "humors." There are people who are constantly concerned with increasing their power, and others who prefer to live freely without seeking either to obtain or to amass power. Furthermore, conflict seems to be rooted in society and history: there is a difference of interests, to put it mildly, or – to put it bluntly – a radical clash concerning the access to and control over property. Machiavelli did not hide the fact that in Rome conflict degenerated when it began to focus on the acquisition of "belongings," when the control of property by agrarian law was called into question. It follows that, in Machiavelli's view, conflict is a constitutive dimension of politics that cannot be discarded.

Both premises can be reformulated in contemporary language and placed at the heart of a neo-republican, or democratic, theory for the present. One can redefine a realistic anthropology, which avoids both the mythologizing of the people and the sanctification of the multitude. Thus, one can accept Machiavelli's teaching on the unsurpassable and fruitful dimension of conflict without endorsing populist conclusions. Moreover, it is possible to ground our political theory on a social premise that admits the existence of radical differences of access to and control over the wide diversity of goods (from capital to culture) in contemporary society. This political theory can be developed from the premise that society is divided from its inception, without necessarily having to accept the conclusions of a Schmittian theory of the political.

Given that society is constitutively divided along different lines that are rooted in both anthropological and social conditions, a republican theory suitable for today could recognize, on new grounds, the role of social and political conflicts in the creation of the "orders and laws in defense of liberty." That is to say, it could acknowledge the part played by such conflicts in widening the framework of existing law, and elaborating and making more meaningful the network of rights guaranteed by the rule of law. A republican theory up to the challenges of the present, a genuinely agonistic theory of democracy, should acknowledge the relevance of social and political conflict – a relevance much greater than the one accorded to it, for instance, in the contestatory democracy approach. In Philip Pettit's contestatory democracy (1997, 183–202; 1999; 2000; 2006) citizens have an "effective opportunity to contest the decisions of their representatives," that is, the actors of conflict are the citizens (without any further anthropological or social characterization) and the representatives, the government agents wielding discretionary authority. Conflict has a vertical nature, so to speak, between citizens and representatives, and it occurs after laws have been created and then applied by the government's representatives.[55] Threats to liberty come only from above, from the political representatives. The type of conflict that I am thinking about, and which should be recognized and valued in a republican theory worthy of the present, has both a horizontal and vertical dimension: it is as much a social conflict as a political one. It includes both the social conflict between citizens belonging to different social groups, and the more political conflict between citizens and representatives. Moreover, the role played by conflict should not be restricted to the moment of the application of the law, but should be traced back to the moment of its creation, elaboration and discussion. From this perspective, threats to liberty originate both from the social sphere and the political.

What I therefore would recommend is a republican political theory rooted in its historical time, a theory that addresses the problem of the incessant changes of those who live in it: a theory that deals with the reality of pluralism and pays attention to points of conflict. I do not wish merely to re-propose Machiavelli's negative anthropology or, so to speak, his social ontology, based on the existence of two "humors" in every city and every republic. What is needed is a republican theory that allows a plurality of subjects and their conflicts, conflicts that at times find legal mediation, enriching and advancing the law.

If the experience of domination is crucial, if the notion of freedom as absence of domination is an essential landmark, it is important to illustrate and thematize how subjects become aware of their condition of (relative) domination, how they move forwards the walls of domination, and how they expand the areas not subject to domination. If freedom is granted by degrees, as Pettit says, it is vital that we acquire the conceptual tools that will enable us to understand how freedom can be expanded and domination reduced. Reflecting on the dimension of conflict inherent in politics can be a step in this direction.[56]

REFERENCES

Abensour, M. (1997). *La démocratie contre l'État: Marx et le moment machiavélien*. Paris: PUF.

Abensour, M. (2009). *Pour une philosophie politique critique*. Paris: Sens & Tonka.

Alfieri, V. (1951). "Della tirannide." In: *Scritti politici e morali*, Vol. I. Ed. P. Cazzani, Asti: Casa d'Alfieri.

Ando, C. (2010). "'A Dwelling beyond Violence': On the Uses and Disadvantages of History for Contemporary Republicans." *History of Political Thought* 31: 183–220.

Arendt, H. (2006 [1963]). *On Revolution*. Harmondsworth: Penguin.

Audier, S. (2005). *Machiavel, conflit et liberté*. Paris: Vrin.

Baccelli, L. (2003). *Critica del repubblicanesimo*. Roma-Bari: Laterza.

Bellamy, R. (2003). "The Rule of Law." In: *Political Concepts*. Eds R. Bellamy and A. Mason, Manchester: Manchester University Press: 118–30.

Bellamy, R. (2007). *Political Constitutionalism: A Republican Defense of the Constitutionality of Democracy*. Cambridge: Cambridge University Press.

Bellamy, R. (2008). "Republicanism, Democracy, and Costitutionalism." In: *Republicanism and Political Theory*. Eds C. Laborde and J. Maynor, Malden, MA: Blackwell: 159–89.

Bellamy, R. (2009). "The Republic of Reasons: Public Reasoning, Depoliticization, and

Non-Domination." In: *Legal Republicanism: National and International Perspectives*. Eds S. Besson and J. L. Martí, Oxford: Oxford University Press: 102–20.

Bellamy, R. (2011a). "Constitutionalism." In: *International Encyclopedia of Political Science*, Vol. 2. Eds B. Badie, D. Berg-Schlosser and L. Morlino, Thousand Oaks: Sage: 416–21.

Bellamy, R. (2011b). "Republicanism: Non-domination and the Free State." In: *Routledge International Handbook of Contemporary Social and Political Theory*. Eds G. Dalanty and S. P. Turner, London: Routledge: 130–8.

Bentouhami, H. and C. Miqueu (eds) (2010). *Conflits et démocratie. Quel nouvel espace public?* Paris: L'Harmattan.

Berger, B. (2010). "Neo-Republicanism." In: *Encyclopedia of Political Theory*, Vol. 2. Ed. M. Bevir, Thousand Oaks: Sage: 961–4.

Berns, T. (1996). "Le retour à l'origine de l'État (Machiavelli, Discorsi sopra la prima deca di Tito Livio, livre III, ch. 1)." *Archives de philosophie* 59: 219–48.

Berns, T. (2000). *Violence de la loi à la Renaissance. L'originaire du politique chez Machiavel et Montaigne*. Paris: Kimé.

Berns, T. (2001). "L'originaire de la loi chez Machiavel." In: *L'enjeu Machiavel*. Eds G. Sfez and M. Senellart, Paris: PUF: 123–40.

Besson, S. and J. L. Martí (eds) (2009a). *Legal Republicanism: National and International Perspectives*. Oxford: Oxford University Press.

Besson, S. and J. L. Martí (2009b). "Law and Republicanism: Mapping the Issues." In: *Legal Republicanism: National and International Perspectives*. Eds S. Besson and J. L. Martí, Oxford: Oxford University Press: 3–36.

Blom, H. W. (1995). *Morality and Causality in Politics: The Rise of Naturalism in Dutch Seventeenth-Century Political Thought*. Den Haag: CIP.

Bock, G. (1990). "Civil Discord in Machiavelli's *Istorie fiorentine*." In: *Machiavelli and Republicanism*. Eds G. Bock, Q. Skinner and M. Viroli, Cambridge: Cambridge University Press: 181–201.

Bohman, J. (2008). "Nondomination and Transnational Democracy." In: *Republicanism and Political Theory*. Eds C. Laborde and J. Maynor, Malden, MA: Blackwell: 190–216.

Bourdeau, V. and R. Merrill (eds) (2007). *La République et ses démons. Essais de républicanisme appliqué*. Alfortville: Éditions Ère.

Brennan, G., R. Goodin, F. Jackson and M. Smith (eds) (2007). *Common Minds: Themes from the Philosophy of Philip Pettit*. Oxford: Clarendon.

Brett, A., J. Tully and H. Hamilton-Bleakley (eds) (2006). *Rethinking the Foundations of Modern Political Thought*. Cambridge: Cambridge University Press.

Burtt, S. (1993). "The Politics of Virtue Today: A Critique and a Proposal." *American Political Science Review* 87: 360–8.

Campi, E. (2002). "Ideali repubblicani nella Zurigo riformata dell'età protomoderna." In: *Ideali repubblicani in età moderna*. Eds F. De Michelis Pintacuda and G. Francioni, Pisa: ETS: 73–96.

Campos Boralevi, L. (2002). "Classical Foundational Myths of European Republicanism: The Jewish Commonwealth." In: *Republicanism: A Shared European Heritage*, Vol. 1. Eds M. van Gelderen and Q. Skinner, Cambridge: Cambridge University Press: 247–61.

Castiglione, D. (2005). "Republicanism and its Legacy." *European Journal of Political Theory* 4: 453–65.

Connolly, W. E. (2002). *Identity, Difference: Democratic Negotiations of Political Paradox.* Minneapolis: University of Minnesota Press.

Dagger, R. (2011). "Republicanism." In: *Encyclopedia of Political Science*, Vol. 5. Ed. G. T. Kurian, Washington, DC: CQ Press: 1470–2.

Del Lucchese, F. (2001). "«Disputare» e «combattere». Modi del conflitto nel pensiero politico di Niccolò Machiavelli." *Filosofia politica* 15: 71–95.

Del Lucchese, F. (2004). *Tumulti e indignatio. Conflitto, diritto e moltitudine in Machiavelli e Spinoza*, Milano: Ghibli.

Del Lucchese, F. (2009). *Conflict, Power and Multitude in Machiavelli and Spinoza: Tumult and Indignation.* London: Continuum.

DeLuna, D. N., P. Anderson and G. Burgess (eds) (2006). *The Political Imagination in History: Essays Concerning J. G. A. Pocock*, Baltimore: The Archangul Foundation.

Ferejohn, J. and P. Pasquino (2006). "Emergency Powers." In: *The Oxford Handbook of Political Theory*. Eds J. S. Dryzek, B. Honig and A. Phillips, Oxford: Oxford University Press: 333–48.

Ferguson, A. (1995). *An Essay on the History of Civil Society.* Ed. F. Oz-Salzberger, Cambridge: Cambridge University Press.

Flynn, B. (2005). *The Philosophy of Claude Lefort: Interpreting the Political.* Evanston: Northwestern University Press.

Gaille-Nikodimov, M. (2004). *Conflit civil et liberté. La politique machiavélienne entre histoire et médecine.* Paris: Champion.

Geuna, M. (1998). "La tradizione repubblicana e i suoi interpreti: famiglie teoriche e discontinuità concettuali." *Filosofia politica* 12: 101–32.

Geuna, M. (2002). "Republicanism and Commercial Society in the Scottish Enlightenment: The Case of Adam Ferguson." In: *Republicanism: A Shared European Heritage*, Vol. 2. Eds M. van Gelderen and Q. Skinner, Cambridge: Cambridge University Press: 177–95.

Geuna, M. (2005). "Machiavelli ed il ruolo dei conflitti nella vita politica." In: *Conflitti.* Eds A. Arienzo and D. Caruso, Naples: Libreria Dante e Descartes: 19–57.

Geuna, M. (2009). "Quentin Skinner e Machiavelli." In: *Anglo-American Faces of Machiavelli. Machiavelli e machiavellismi nella cultura anglo-americana (secoli XVI–XX).* Eds A. Arienzo and G. Borrelli, Monza: Polimetrica: 579–624.

Guerci, L. (1998). *Istruire nelle verità repubblicane. La letteratura politica per il popolo nell'Italia in rivoluzione (1796–1799).* Bologna: Il Mulino.

Guicciardini, F. (1983). *Considerazioni intorno ai Discorsi del Machiavelli.* In: N. Machiavelli. *Discorsi sopra la prima deca di Tito Livio.* Ed. C. Vivanti, Torino: Einaudi.

Guicciardini, F. (1994). *Dialogo del reggimento di Firenze.* Eds G. M. Anselmi and C. Varotti, Torino: Bollati Boringhieri.

Habermas, J. (2001). "Constitutional Democracy: A Paradoxical Union of Contradictory Principles?" *Political Theory* 29: 766–81.

Harrington, J. (1992). "The Commonwealth of Oceana." In: *The Commonwealth of Oceana and a System of Politics.* Ed. J. G. A. Pocock, Cambridge: Cambridge University Press: 1–266.

Heath, E. and V. Merolle (eds) (2008). *Adam Ferguson: History, Progress and Human Nature.* London: Pickering and Chatto.

Heath, E. and V. Merolle (eds) (2009). *Adam Ferguson: Philosophy, Politics and Society.* London: Pickering and Chatto.

Hill, L. (2001). "Eighteenth-Century Anticipations of the Sociology of Conflict: The Case of Adam Ferguson." *Journal of the History of Ideas* 62: 281–99.

Hill, L. (2006). *The Passionate Society: The Social, Political and Moral Thought of Adam Ferguson*. Dordrecht: Springer.

Hirschl, R. (2004). *Towards Juristocracy: The Origins and Consequences of the New Constitutionalism*. Cambridge, MA: Harvard University Press.

Hobbes, T. (1983a). *De cive: the English Version Entitled in the First Edition Philosophical Rudiments Concerning Government and Society*. Ed. H. Warrender, Oxford: Clarendon Press.

Hobbes, T. (1983b). *De cive: The Latin Version*. Ed. H. Warrender, Oxford: Clarendon Press.

Holenstein, A., T. Maissen and M. R. Prak (eds) (2008). *The Republican Alternative: The Netherlands and Switzerland Compared*. Amsterdam: Amsterdam University Press.

Honohan, I. (2002). *Civic Republicanism*. London: Routledge.

Honohan, I. (2009). "Republicans, Rights, and Constitutions: Is Judicial Review Compatible with Republican Self-Government?" In: *Legal Republicanism: National and International Perspectives*. Eds S. Besson and J. L. Martí, Oxford: Oxford University Press: 83–101.

Honohan, I. and J. Jennings (eds) (2006). *Republicanism in Theory and Practice*. London: Routledge.

Hutcheson, F. (1747). *Short Introduction to Moral Philosophy*. Glasgow: Foulis.

Hutcheson, F. (1755). *A System of Moral Philosophy*. London: Millar.

Jennings, J. (2006). "Two Philosophers of the French Republic: Charles Renouvier and Jules Barni." In: *Republicanism in Theory and Practice*, Eds I. Honohan and J. Jennings. London: Routledge: 53–66.

Kalyvas, A. and I. Katznelson (2008). "Agonistic Liberalism: Adam Ferguson on Modern Commercial Society and the Limits of Classical Republicanism." In: *Liberal Beginnings: Making a Republic for the Moderns*. Eds A. Kalyvas and I. Katznelson, Cambridge: Cambridge University Press: 51–87.

Kennedy, E. (2011). "Emergency and Exception." *Political Theory* 39: 535–50.

Kirk, L. (1994). "Genevan Republicanism." In: *Republicanism, Liberty, and Commercial Society, 1649–1776*. Ed. D. Wootton, Stanford: Stanford University Press: 270–309.

Kossmann, E. H. (1995). "Dutch Republicanism." In: *L'età dei lumi. Studi storici sul Settecento europeo in onore di Franco Venturi*. Naples: Jovene: 453–86.

Kossmann, E. H. (2000). *Political Thought in the Dutch Republic: Three Studies*. Amsterdam: Koninklijke Nederlandse Akademie.

Kramer, L. D. (2004). *The People Themselves: Popular Constitutionalism and Judicial Review*. Oxford: Oxford University Press.

Kupiec, A. and E. Tassin (eds) (2006). *Critique de la politique: autour de Miguel Abensour*. Paris: Sens & Tonka.

Laborde, C. (2008). *Critical Republicanism: The Hijab Controversy and Political Philosophy*. Oxford: Oxford University Press.

Laborde, C. (2010a). *Français, encore un effort pour être républicains*. Paris: Seuil.

Laborde, C. (2010b). "Republicanism and Global Justice. A Sketch." *European Journal of Political Theory* 9: 46–69.

Laborde, C. and J. Maynor (eds) (2008). *Republicanism and Political Theory*. Malden, MA: Blackwell.

Lazzeri, C. (2000). "Prendre la domination au sérieux: une critique républicaine du libéralisme." *Actuel Marx* 28: 55–68.

Lazzeri, C. (2010). "Repenser le concept républicain de domination." *Diacrítica* 24: 129–64.

Lefort, C. (1972). *Le travail de l'oeuvre. Machiavel*. Paris: Gallimard.

Lefort, C. (1992). *Écrire à l'épreuve du politique*. Paris: Calmann-Levy.

Lovett, F. (2010). *A General Theory of Domination and Justice*. Oxford: Oxford University Press.

Lovett, F. and P. Pettit (2009). "Neorepublicanism: A Normative and Institutional Research Program." *Annual Review of Political Science* 12: 11–29.

McCormick, J. P. (2011). *Machiavellian Democracy*. Cambridge: Cambridge University Press.

Machiavelli, N. (1962). *Istorie fiorentine*. Ed. G. Gaeta, Milano: Feltrinelli.

Machiavelli, N. (1985). *The Prince*. Ed. H. C. Mansfield, Chicago: The University of Chicago Press.

Machiavelli, N. (1988). *Florentine Histories*. Trans. L. F. Banfield and H. C. Mansfield, Princeton: Princeton University Press.

Machiavelli, N. (1995). *Il Principe*. Ed. G. Inglese, Torino: Einaudi.

Machiavelli, N. (1996a [1984]). *Discorsi sopra la prima deca di Tito Livio*. Ed. G. Inglese, Milano: Rizzoli.

Machiavelli, N. (1996b). *Discourses on Livy*. Trans. H. C. Mansfield and N. Tarcov, Chicago: University of Chicago Press.

MacIntyre, A. (1981). *After Virtue*, London: Duckworth

Maissen, T. (2006). *Die Geburt der Republic. Staatsverständnis und Repräsentation in der frühneuzeitlichen Eidgenossenschaft*. Göttingen: Vandenhoeck.

Maynor, J. W. (2003). *Republicanism in the Modern World*. Cambridge: Polity Press.

Ménissier, T. (1999). "*Ordini* et *tumulti* selon Machiavel: la république dans l'histoire." *Archives de philosophie* 62: 221–39.

Michelman, F. (1988). "Law's Republic." *The Yale Law Journal* 97: 1493–537.

Michelman, F. (1995). "Always under Law?" *Constitutional Commentary* 12: 227–47.

Mijnhardt, W. W. (2003). "The Construction of Silence: Religious and Political Radicalism in Dutch History." In: *The Early Enlightenment in the Dutch Republic, 1650–1750*. Ed. W. van Bunge, Leiden: Brill: 231–62.

Mijnhardt, W. W. (2006). "Franco Venturi's Dutch Republic and the Crisis of the Historiography of Republicanism." In: *Il repubblicanesimo moderno. L'idea di repubblica nella riflessione storica di Franco Venturi*. Ed. M. Albertone, Naples: Bibliopolis: 407–30.

Mouffe, C. (2000). *The Democratic Paradox*. London: Verso.

Mouffe, C. (2005). *On the Political*. London: Routledge.

Moyle, W. (1969). "Essay upon the Constitution of the Roman Government." In: *Two English Republican Tracts*. Ed. C. Robbins, Cambridge: Cambridge University Press: 242–3.

Nederman, C. J. (2005). "Republicanism." In: *New Dictionary of the History of Ideas*. Ed. M. Cline Horowitz, New York: Scribner: 2098–103.

Nelson, E. (2004). *The Greek Tradition in Republican Thought*. Cambridge: Cambridge University Press.

Nelson, E. (2010). *The Hebrew Republic: Jewish Sources and the Transformation of European Political Thought*. Cambridge, MA: Harvard University Press.

Palonen, K. (2003). *Quentin Skinner: History, Politics, Rhetoric*. Cambridge: Polity Press.

Parel, A. (1992). *The Machiavellian Cosmos*. New Haven: Yale University Press.

Patten, A. (1996). "The Republican Critique of Liberalism." *British Journal of Political Science* 26: 25–44.

Pedullà, G. (2007). "Una «tirannide elettiva». Ovvero: ciò che gli umanisti e Machiavelli possono insegnarci sulla dittatura e sullo «stato di eccezione." In: *Il governo dell'emergenza. Poteri straordinari e di guerra in Europa tra XVI e XX secolo*. Eds F. Benigno and L. Scuccimarra, Rome: Viella: 35–73.

Peltonen, M. (1995). *Classical Humanism and Republicanism in English Political Thought, 1570–1640*. Cambridge: Cambridge University Press.

Pettit, P. (1989). "The Freedom of the City: A Republican Ideal." In: *The Good Polity*. Eds A. Hamlin and P. Pettit, Oxford: Blackwell: 141–67.

Pettit, P. (1993a). "Liberalism and Republicanism." *Australian Journal of Political Science* 28: 162–89.

Pettit, P. (1993b). "Negative Liberty, Liberal and Republican." *European Journal of Philosophy* 1: 15–38.

Pettit, P. (1994). "Liberal/Communitarian: MacIntyre's Mesmeric Dichotomy." In: *After MacIntyre*. Eds J. Horton and S. Mendus, Oxford: Polity Press: 176–204.

Pettit, P. (1997). *Republicanism: A Theory of Freedom and Government*. Oxford: Clarendon.

Pettit, P. (1999). "Republican Freedom and Contestatory Democratization." In: *Democracy's Value*. Eds C. Hacker-Cordón and I. Shapiro, Cambridge: Cambridge University Press: 163–90.

Pettit, P. (2000). "Democracy, Electoral and Contestatory." *Nomos* 42: 105–44.

Pettit, P. (2001). *A Theory of Freedom: From the Psychology to the Politics of Agency*. Cambridge: Polity Press.

Pettit, P. (2002). "Keeping Republican Freedom Simple: On a Difference with Quentin Skinner." *Political Theory* 30: 339–56.

Pettit, P. (2004). "Depoliticizing Democracy." *Ratio Juris* 17: 52–65.

Pettit, P. (2006). "Democracy, National and International." *The Monist* 89: 301–24.

Pettit, P. (2008). "Republican Freedom: Three Axioms, Four Theorems." In: *Republicanism and Political Theory*. Eds C. Laborde and J. Maynor, Malden, MA: Blackwell: 102–30.

Pettit, P. (2009). "Civic Republican Theory." In: J. L. Martí and P. Pettit. *A Political Philosophy in Public Life*. Princeton: Princeton University Press: 31–68.

Pettit, P. (2010a). "A Republican Law of Peoples." *European Journal of Political Theory* 9: 70–94.

Pettit, P. (2010b). "Varieties of Public Representation." In: *Political Representation*. Eds I. Shapiro, S. C. Stokes, E. J. Wood and A. S. Kirshner, Cambridge: Cambridge University Press: 61–89.

Pocock, J. G. A. (1975). *The Machiavellian Moment: Florentine Political Thought and the Atlantic Republican Tradition*. Princeton: Princeton University Press.

Pocock, J. G. A. (2006). "Theory in History: Problems of Context and Narrative." In: *The Oxford Handbook of Political Theory*. Eds J. S. Dryzek, B. Honig and A. Phillips, Oxford: Oxford University Press: 163–74.

Portinaro, P. P. (1999). *Il realismo politico*. Roma-Bari: Laterza.

Portinaro, P. P. (2009). *Breviario di politica*. Brescia: Morcelliana.

Portinaro, P. P. (2011). "Una guida dei perplessi sul futuro della democrazia." In: *L'interesse dei pochi, le ragioni dei molti*. Ed. P. P. Portinaro, Turin: Einaudi: 5–21.

Rawls, J. (1988). "The Priority of Right and Ideas of the Good." *Philosophy and Public Affairs* 17: 151–76.

Rawls, J. (1993). *Political Liberalism*. New York: Columbia University Press.

Raz, J. (1979). "The Rule of Law and its Virtue." In: *The Authority of Law: Essays on Law and Morality*. Oxford: Clarendon Press: 210–29.

Rodgers, D. T. (1992). "Republicanism: The Career of a Concept." *The Journal of American History* 79: 11–38.

Rosenblatt, H. (1997). *Rousseau and Geneva: From the First Discourse to Social Contract, 1749–1762*. Cambridge: Cambridge UP.

Rousseau, J.-J. (1964). "Du contract social." In: *Oeuvres complètes*, t. 3. Eds B. Gagnebin and M. Raymond, Paris: Gallimard.

Rousseau, J.-J. (1968). *The Social Contract*. Ed. M. Cranston, Harmondsworth: Penguin.

Sandel, M. (1988). "The Political Theory of the Procedural Republic." *Revue de Métaphysique et de Morale* 93: 57–68.

Sasso, G. (1993). "Il conflitto sociale. Un intermezzo storico-teorico." In: G. Sasso. *Niccolò Machiavelli, II. La storiografia*. Bologna: il Mulino: 167–216.

Schaap, A. (ed.) (2009). *Law and Agonistic Politics*. Aldershot: Ashgate.

Scott, J. (1993). "The Rapture of Motion: James Harrington's Republicanism." In: *Political Discourse in Early Britain*. Eds N. Phillipson and Q. Skinner, Cambridge: Cambridge University Press: 139–63.

Secretan, C. (1990). *Les privilèges, berceau de la liberté. La révolte des Pays-Bas, aux sources de la pensée politique moderne*. Paris: Vrin.

Sellers, N. M. S. (2001). "Republicanism: Philosophical Aspects." In: *International Encyclopedia of the Social & Behavioral Sciences*, Vol. 19. Eds N. J. Smelser and P. B. Baltes, Oxford: Elsevier: 13,204–10.

Shklar, J. (1987). "Political Theory and the Rule of Law." In: *The Rule of Law: Ideal or Ideology*. Eds A. C. Hutchinson and P. Monahan, Toronto: Carswell: 1–16.

Sidney, A. (1990). *Discourses Concerning Government*. Ed. T. G. West, Indianapolis: Liberty Fund.

Silvestrini, G. (2010). *Diritto naturale e volontà generale. Il contrattualismo repubblicano di Jean-Jacques Rousseau*. Torino: Claudiana.

Skinner, Q. (1983). "Machiavelli on the Maintenance of Liberty." *Politics* 18: 3–15.

Skinner, Q. (1984). "The Idea of Negative Liberty: Philosophical and Historical Perspectives." In: *Philosophy in History*. Eds R. Rorty, J. B. Schneewind and Q. Skinner, Cambridge: Cambridge University Press: 193–221.

Skinner, Q. (1986). "The Paradoxes of Political Liberty." In: *The Tanner Lectures on Human Values* VII: 225–50.

Skinner, Q. (1990a). "Machiavelli's *Discorsi* and the Pre-humanist Origins of Republican Ideas." In: *Machiavelli and Republicanism*. Eds G. Bock, Q. Skinner and M. Viroli, Cambridge: Cambridge University Press: 121–41.

Skinner, Q. (1990b). "The Republican Ideal of Political Liberty." In: *Machiavelli and Republicanism*. Eds G. Bock, Q. Skinner and M. Viroli, Cambridge: Cambridge University Press: 293–309.

Skinner, Q. (1998). *Liberty before Liberalism*. Cambridge: Cambridge University Press.

Skinner, Q. (2000 [1981]). *Machiavelli*. Oxford: Oxford University Press.

Skinner, Q. (2002a). *Visions of Politics*, 3 vols. Cambridge: Cambridge University Press.

Skinner, Q. (2002b). "A Third Concept of Liberty." *Proceedings of the British Academy* 117: 237–68.

Skinner, Q. (2008a). *Hobbes and Republican Liberty*. Cambridge: Cambridge University Press.

Skinner, Q. (2008b). "Freedom and the Absence of Arbitrary Power." In: *Republicanism and Political Theory*. Eds C. Laborde and J. Maynor, Malden, MA: Blackwell: 83–101.

Skinner, Q. (2012). "On the Liberty of the Ancients and the Moderns." *Journal of the History of Ideas* 73: 127–46.

Spitz, J.-F. (1995). *La liberté politique. Essai de généalogie conceptuelle*. Paris: PUF.

Spitz, J.-F. (2005). *Le moment républicain en France*. Paris: Gallimard.

Spitz, J. F. (2010). *Philip Pettit: le républicanisme*. Paris: Michalon.

Sullivan, V. B. (1992). "Machiavelli's Momentary 'Machiavellian Moment:' A Reconsideration of Pocock's Treatment of the 'Discourses.'" *Political Theory* 20: 309–18.

Taylor, C. (1989). "Cross-Purposes: The Liberal-Communitarian Debate." In: *Liberalism and the Moral Life*. Ed. N. L. Rosenblum, Cambridge, MA: Harvard University Press: 159–82.

Tully, J. (2008). *Public Philosophy in a New Key. I. Democracy and Civic Freedom*. Cambridge: Cambridge University Press.

Tushnet, M. V. (1999). *Taking the Constitution away from the Courts*. Princeton: Princeton University Press.

Urbinati, N. (2011). "Republicanism: Democratic or Popular." *The Good Society* 20: 157–69.

van Gelderen, M. (1992). *The Political Thought of the Dutch Revolt, 1555–1590*. Cambridge: Cambridge University Press.

van Gelderen, M. and Q. Skinner (eds) (2002). *Republicanism: A Shared European Heritage*, 2 vols. Cambridge: Cambridge University Press.

Vatter, M. (2000). *Between Form and Event: Machiavelli's Theory of Political Freedom*. Dordrecht: Kluwer.

Viroli, M. (1998). *Machiavelli*. Oxford: Oxford University Press.

Viroli, M. (1999). *Repubblicanesimo*. Roma-Bari: Laterza.

Viroli, M. (2004). "Il repubblicanesimo di Machiavelli." In: *Libertà politica e virtù civile. Significati e percorsi del repubblicanesimo classico*. Ed. M. Viroli, Torino: Fondazione Agnelli: 1–29.

Visentin, S. (2009). "How Does 'The People' Act? Philip Pettit's Reception of Machiavelli's Republicanism." In: *Anglo-American Faces of Machiavelli: Machiavelli e machiavellismi nella cultura anglo-americana (secoli XVI–XX)*. Eds A. Arienzo and G. Borrelli, Monza: Polimetrica: 623–41.

Waldron, J. (2002). "Is the Rule of Law an Essentially Contested Concept (in Florida)?" *Law and Philosophy* 21: 137–64.

Waldron, J. (2006). "The Core Case against Judicial Review." *The Yale Law Journal* 115: 1346–406.

Walker, N. (2010). "Constitutionalism and the Incompleteness of Democracy: An Iterative Relationship." *Rechtsfilosofie & Rechtstheorie* 39: 206–33.

Weinstock, D. M. and C. Nadeau (eds) (2004). *Republicanism: History, Theory, and Practice*. London: Frank Cass.

Wootton, D. (1994). "The Republican Tradition: From Commonwealth to Common Sense." In: *Republicanism, Liberty, and Commercial Society, 1649–1776*. Ed. D. Wootton, Stanford: Stanford University Press: 1–41.

Wootton, D. (2000). "Helvétius: From Radical Enlightenment to Revolution." *Political Theory* 28: 307–36.

Worden, B. (1996). *The Sound of Virtue: Philip Sidney's Arcadia and Elizabethan Politics.* New Haven: Yale University Press.

Wright, J. K. (1997). *A Classical Republican in Eighteenth-Century France: The Political Thought of Mably.* Stanford: Stanford University Press.

Zagorin, P. (2003). "Republicanisms." *British Journal for the History of Philosophy* 11: 701–12.

NOTES

1. Pocock 1975. For a recent discussion of Pocock's works, see DeLuna, Anderson and Burgess 2006. For a classical introductory synthesis of the debates, see Rodgers 1992; for more updated summaries, see: Sellers 2001, Nederman 2005 and Dagger 2011.

2. See, for example, Michelman 1988, 1995.

3. Republicanism, as defined by Skinner in these essays, has been labeled by some of his interpreters as an "instrumental republicanism." See Patten 1996, 26. See also the remarks by Burtt 1993 and Spitz 1995, 172.

4. Philip Pettit 1989, 1993a, 1993b was one of the first scholars to systematically examine and endorse Skinner's interpretation.

5. Rawls 1993, 205–6. Rawls 1988 had already proposed a similar distinction.

6. Quentin Skinner has reshaped and strengthened his theses in a series of important works; see: 1998, 2002a, 2008a. On Skinner's research program, see Palonen 2003 and, more recently, Brett, Tully and Hamilton-Bleakley 2006.

7. See Besson and Martí 2009b, 5: "While everyone accepts that republicanism is a heterogeneous tradition that has historically grown around distinct lines of thought ... there is no agreement on how many republican streams or schools there are and what they are."

8. See Pettit 2009, 32. See also Pettit's chapter "Two Republican Traditions" in this book.

9. See, for example, Lefort 1972, 1992; on Lefort's political philosophy, see Flynn 2005; Abensour 1997, 2009; on Abensour's philosophy, see Kupiec and Tassin 2006. Among recent French works, see, for example, Bourdeau and Merrill 2007.

10. See, for example, Laborde and Maynor 2008, 3. Laborde and Maynor use the term "traditions;" Besson and Martí, more precisely, use the expressions "strands" or "interpretations of political liberty" (Besson *et al.* 2009b, 13–17).

11. On Pettit's republican philosophy, see some essays included in Brennan *et al.* 2007 and Spitz 2010.

12. See also Berger 2010.

13. See also the special issue on "Neo-republicanismo" of *Diacrítica*, 24 (2010), 2, pp. 7–212, with essays by F. Lovett, J. Maynor, J.-F. Spitz, R. Merrill and J. L. Martí, among others.

14. Many scholars have contributed to the neo-republican program, sometimes following more closely Pettit's assumptions, other times criticizing and reformulating some of his theses. Among them, see, for example, Honohan 2002, Weinstock and Nadeau 2004. For a synthetic presentation of the neo-republican program, see Bellamy 2011b.

15. Skinner's 2002b, 2008b, 2012 and Pettit's 2001, 2002, 2008 work on the concept of "freedom"/"liberty" has been of decisive importance.
16. For a critical approach to the use of the Roman sources by neo-republican thinkers, dealing with the "neo-Roman tradition" and its concepts, see Ando 2010.
17. See, for example, Pettit 1997, 39–40, 172–7: Pettit likes to express his point of view quoting Harrington's phrase "the empire of laws and not of men" (Pettit 1997, 39 and 173). See Skinner 1998: Skinner points out that Harrington, when defining a government "de jure" as "the empire of laws and not of men," was translating Livy (75); emphasizes that for Livy "a free state ... is one in which there are annual elected magistracies and an equal subjection of every citizen to the rule of law" (44–5); and quotes Livy's phrase, much echoed by the neo-Roman writers – "the imperium of the laws is greater than that of any men" (45). See also, for example, Viroli 1998, 5–6, 115–31; Viroli 2004.
18. See, for example, Pettit 1994, in particular p. 187: "[N]ot only does the republic require a rule of law, and a rule of check and balance, it also needs the rule of virtue."
19. For a recent critique of this position, see, for example, Portinaro 2009, 143–54 and Portinaro 2011, 11.
20. For a recent assessment of the tensions between constitutionalism and democracy, see, fpr example, Walker 2010 and the discussion of Walker's theses by L. F. M. Besselink, M. Goodwin, S. Rummens and W. G. Werner, in the same issue of the journal *Rechtsfilosofie & Rechtstheorie*, pp. 234–75.
21. For a recent and interesting introductory discussion, see Pocock 2006.
22. For an attempt to transfer, without mediations, these Machiavellian assumptions into a contemporary theoretical context, see, for example, McCormick 2011 and the critical discussion of McCormick's book by Urbinati 2011.
23. I have already suggested this distinction in Geuna 1998, 2002. An analogous distinction has been put forward by Lazzeri 2000, 57 and by Baccelli 2003.
24. It should be also considered that Machiavelli thinks of the republic in an "international" context of constant tension and change. He also closely relates domestic and foreign policy: the "disunion" within the republic has to be considered in relation to the conflicts surrounding it. A constant tension between "the great" and "the plebs," and between different constitutional bodies, seems to be necessary in order to cope with the tension that always exists between the political "bodies" that seek their security trying to increase their power. The constitutional structures should not be assessed, therefore, in their abstract and static perfection, but in their ability to deal with the challenges of their times, with the "quality" of the times. This kind of awareness is not traceable in Harrington's perspective. His "immortal commonwealth," first, does not seem to be placed in an international context of constant tension and change. It is emphasized that the commonwealth is destined to expand, that is, that it is a "commonwealth for increase," but we do not find the Machiavellian emphasis on the need for continual "match" ["riscontro"] with the times constantly changing.
25. See the original Latin text in Hobbes 1983b, 160: "Ut redeamus iterum in statum naturalem, consideremusque homines tanquam si essent iamiam subito e terra (fungorum more) exorti & adulti, sine omni unius ad alterum obligatione."
26. A loaded phrase as "the rule of law" is available to relatively indiscriminate use. See the classical remarks by Raz, 1979, 210–11 and Shklar 1987, 1. For a recent attempt

at definition, see Bellamy 2003. For a presentation of "the rule of law" as an essentially contested concept, see Waldron 2002.

27. I will use the concepts of "rule of law" and "rule of virtue" in a relatively broad sense, analogous to the sense attributed to them by Philip Pettit. See *supra* notes 17 and 18.

28. On this question, see, for example, Berns 2000, 2001 and Portinaro 1999, 85–93.

29. In the original: "*alcuna azione straordinaria*": Machiavelli 1996a, I.9, 86; 1996b, 29.

30. "*E veramente mai fu alcuno ordinatore di leggi straordinarie in un popolo che non ricorresse a Dio perché altrimenti non sarebbero accettate.*" Machiavelli 1996a, I.11, 93; "And truly there was never any orderer of extraordinary laws for a people who did not have recourse to God because otherwise they would not have been accepted." Machiavelli 1996b, 35.

31. Compare: "*né mai uno ingegno savio riprenderà alcuno di alcuna azione straordinaria che per ordinare un regno o constituire una repubblica usasse*": Machiavelli 1996a, I.9, 86; "Nor will a wise understanding ever reprove anyone for any extraordinary action that he uses to order a kingdom or constitute a republic": Machiavelli 1996b, 29. Harrington in the same page adds: "And whereas a book or a building hath not been known to attain perfection, if it had not had a sole author or architect, a commonwealth, as to the fabric of it, is of the like nature. And thus it may be made at once, in which there be great advantages."

32. See "*quelli tumulti che molti inconsideratamente dannano; perché chi esaminerà bene il fine di essi, non troverrà ch'egli abbiano partorito alcuno esilio o violenza in disfavore del commune bene, ma leggi e ordini in beneficio della publica libertà*": Machiavelli 1996a, I.4, 71; "those tumults that many inconsiderately damn; for whoever examines their end well will find that they have engendered not any exile or violence unfavorable to the common good but laws and orders in benefit of public freedom": Machiavelli 1996b, 16. On the role of conflict in Machiavelli's thought, among recent contributions, see Ménissier 1999, Del Lucchese 2001, 2004, 241–64, Gaille-Nikodimov 2004 and Audier 2005.

33. "This perpetual recursivity between laws and conflict is the most convincing key to interpreting all aspects of Machiavelli's reflections on the law": Del Lucchese 2009, 90. If Thomas Berns 2000, 116–18 speaks of the "circularity" of the relationship between laws and conflict, Del Lucchese prefers to adopt the concept of "recursivity" in this context, for the following reason: "The reciprocal influence between politics and law, and, ultimately, between law and conflict, is not a peaceful, linear process: it 'jerks' along continuously, unexpectedly stopping in its tracks at times, or suddenly leaping forward": Del Lucchese 2009, 177, fn 7.

34. See "*Perché in ogni città si truovono questi dua umori diversi: e nasce, da questo, che il populo desidera non essere comandato né oppresso da' grandi ed e' grandi desiderano comandare e opprimere el populo*": Machiavelli 1995, IX, 63; "For in every city these two diverse humors are found, which arises from this: that the people desire neither to be commanded nor oppressed by the great, and the great desire to command and oppress the people": Machiavelli 1985, 39. See also "*come e' sono in ogni repubblica due umori diversi, quello del popolo e quello de' grandi; e come tutte le leggi che si fanno in favore della libertà, nascano dalla disunione loro*": Machiavelli 1996a, I.4, 71; "that in every republic there are two diverse humors, that of the people and that of the great, and that all the laws that are made in favor of freedom arise from their disunion": Machiavelli 1996b, 16. On Machiavelli's theory of humors, see Parel 1992, 101–12; more recently, Gaille-Nikodimov 2004, 61–101.

35. On the importance of "tumults" and "disunions" after the Roman orders had reached their perfection, see also Geuna 2005.

36. The crisis of liberty makes the logical, as well as genetic, primacy of politics over law even more apparent. When the nobles create factions, and sects develop in the republics and when corruption spreads out in the body politic, the republican orders break down. Then the republic is replaced by principality: "an almost kingly power" should check the insolence of corrupted people. See, for example, Machiavelli 1996a, I.17–18, 106–11; 1996b, 47–52.

37. "Rome and England, under their mixed governments, the one inclining to democracy, the other to monarchy, have proved the great legislators among nations:" Ferguson 1995, 159.

38. Among recent studies on Ferguson's thought, see Hill 2006, Kalyvas and Katznelson 2008 and Heath and Merolle 2008, 2009.

39. Ferguson continues: "And the influence of laws, where they have any real effect in the preservation of liberty, is not any magic power descending from shelves that are loaded with books, but is, in reality, the influence of men resolved to be free; of men, who, having adjusted in writing the terms on which they are to live with the state, and with their fellow-subjects, are determined, by their vigilance and spirit, to make these terms observed."

40. Among recent studies on Ferguson's approach to conflict, see Hill 2001 and Geuna 2002.

41. On Machiavelli's analysis of corruption, and its prevention, see the classical pages of Skinner 2000, 76–82. On Skinner's reading of Machiavelli, see also Geuna 2009.

42. Machiavelli develops a distinction between positive and negative forms of conflict; he comes to elaborate a true typology of conflicts that I cannot consider further in these pages.

43. On Machiavelli's analysis of different types of conflict in *Florentine Histories*, see, among others, Bock 1990 and Sasso 1993.

44. On censorship, see Machiavelli 1996a, I.49, 162–3; 1996b, 100; Rousseau 1964, IV.7, 458–9; 1968, 174–6. See also, for example, Hutcheson 1747, 301: "A censorial power too would be of the highest use, to reform, or prevent the corruption of manners." Hutcheson 1755, vol. 2, 265 argues it is better to give the censorial power not to a single individual, but to a "censorial council for a set term changed by rotation."

45. On dictatorship, for example, Machiavelli 1996a, I. 34, 134–7; 1996b, 73–5; Harrington 1992, 131–2; Sidney 1990, II.13, 151; Rousseau 1964, IV.6, 455–8; 1968, 170–4. On Machiavelli's approach to dictatorship, among recent studies, see Pedullà 2007.

46. In the original: "*gli uomini cominciano a variare con i costumi e trapassare le leggi*": Machiavelli 1996a, III.1, 463; 1996b, 211.

47. "*I quali ordini hanno bisogno di essere fatti vivi dalla virtù d'uno cittadino, il quale animosamente concorra ad eseguirli contro alla potenza di quegli che gli trapassano*": Machiavelli 1996a, III.1, 463; "Such orders have need of being brought to life by the virtue of a citizen who rushes spiritedly to execute them against the power of those who transgress them": Machiavelli 1996b, 210. Among the different readings of Machiavelli's theory of "the return to the beginnings," see at least Berns 1996 and Vatter 2000, 219–76.

48. "*E se non nasce cosa, per la quale si riduca loro a memoria la pena e rinnuovisi negli animi*

loro la paura, concorrono tosto tanti delinquenti che non possono più punire sanza pericolo": Machiavelli 1996a, III.1, 463; 1996b, 211.

49. Machiavelli 1996b, 209; Machiavelli 1996a, III.1, 461.

50. Algenon Sidney 1990, 462 discussed critically the idea of "a necessity of reducing every state, once in age or two, to the integrity of its principle."

51. Neo-republican thinkers are increasingly interested in the problem of representation, its actors and its forms. See, for example, Pettit 2010b.

52. For a recent introductory discussion, see Ferejohn and Pasquino 2006. For a review essay, see Kennedy 2011.

53. If "action" – according to Arendt – is the free realm of human activity, the collective dimension of this freedom takes, for her, the name of "power."

54. In the last twenty years different agonistic conceptions of politics have been elaborated, which have reshaped some of the basic assumptions of Hannah Arendt and Michel Foucault. Contemporary political theorists such as William Connolly (2002), Chantal Mouffe (2000, 2005) and James Tully (2008) turned to agonism for an alternative vocabulary to that of deliberation and communicative rationality. See, also, the essays collected in Schaap 2009 and in Bentouhami and Miqueu 2010.

55. Not coincidentally, J.-F. Spitz 2010, 103 speaks of "institutions de contestation *a posteriori*." See, also, Visentin 2009, 640–3.

56. I would like to express my gratitude to the editors of this volume, Andreas Niederberger and Philipp Schink, for their extreme kindness and friendly support. I am greatly indebted to Benedetto Fontana for his generous help in the completion of this paper.

CHAPTER 2

Impotence, Perspicuity and the Rule of Law: James Madison's Critique of Republican Legislation

Jack Rakove

Early in the spring of 1787, James Madison drafted a memorandum that holds a high place in the annals of American constitutional thinking. He called it, "Vices of the Political System of the U. States" (knowing scholars simply call it "the Vices"). Serious students of American political thinking recognize this manuscript as a first draft of that more celebrated text, *Federalist* 10, and find in its closing eleventh item, labeled "Injustice of the Laws of States," the essential outlines of Madison's analysis of the sources of faction and the proper remedies for "the inconveniences of popular States." The argument about republican injustice culminates a set of points that Madison initiated with two prior "vices" criticizing the "multiplicity" and the "mutability of the laws of the States." Madison opened these concluding passages of the document with a remarkably understated transition. "In developing the evils which viciate the political system of the U. S.," he began item nine, "it is proper to include those which are found within the states individually, as well as those which directly affect the States collectively, since the former class have an indirect effect on the general malady and must not be overlooked in forming a compleat remedy" (Madison 1999, 74). In fact, Madison held a much stronger opinion about the significance of this problem than his language suggests. "The evils issuing from these sources contributed more to that uneasiness which produced the Convention" that proposed the Constitution, he wrote to Jefferson on October 24, 1787, a month after it adjourned, "and prepared the public mind for a general reform, than those which accrued to our national character and interest from the inadequacy of the Confederation to its immediate objects" (Madison 1999, 149). The true origin of the constitutional crisis of 1787, in other words, was a crisis in the republican rule of law.[1]

41

Here, quietly but powerfully, the grounds of American constitutional thinking were shifting. The challenge awaiting the Convention went beyond the immediate problems of federalism, essential as those were. The agenda of constitutional reform also required, in Madison's thinking, a thorough assessment of the nature of republican law-making within the individual states, and thus of republican principles more generally. The central problem, as he made explicit in item eleven of "the Vices," was that the unjust character of state legislation called "into question the fundamental principle of republican Governments, that the majority who rule in such Governments, are the safest Guardians both of public Good and of private rights." This final pairing of "public good and private rights" was emblematic of Madison's thinking through the period of constitutional formation. It identified the two fundamental goals of his political science: to create processes of deliberation and decision adequate to pursuing the collective public good; and to do so in ways mindful of the importance of protecting the essential rights of individuals and minorities. The second goal in turn exposed the novel twist in Madison's republican thinking: the recognition that allowing the people to rule might lead neither to the secure protection of the rights of the people, as republicans would suppose, nor to anarchy, as the critics of republicanism might allege, but rather to policies in which reigning coalitions among the people would erode the rights of minorities of their countrymen.

"The Vices" closes with a final subheading that has no text to accompany it: "Impotence of the laws of the States (Madison 1999, 80). The wily modern professor teaching this document can have exam-time fun challenging his students to write a Madisonian paragraph explaining what this heading may mean. One plausible answer might be that a legislature that legislates too much, or changes its laws too frequently, while enacting injustice in the process, will erode fidelity to law. Perhaps officials charged with its enforcement would lose confidence that they knew what the law really was. Or perhaps, even more seriously, the civic attachment to law that should be essential to a republican society would evaporate under these conditions. In either case, the empty heading of "impotence" sounds the tocsin over the fate of the rule of law in a republican society that legislates improperly and unjustly.

Nine months later, in January 1788, Madison sounded a different concern about law in *Federalist* 37 (the essay that later opened the second volume of the first book-length publication of these essays). Here, in a reflective essay that illuminates his understanding of the science of politics, Madison set out to explain just how difficult the task of constitution-making must be. Amid a host of arguments relating to both the epistemological as well as political difficulties the Convention faced, Madison squeezed in a concise distillation of John Locke's discussion of language in Book III of the *Essay Concerning Human Understanding*, now applied to the realms of legal and political reasoning. As Madison observed, "Perspicuity" in the realms of law and politics

> requires not only that ideas should be distinctly formed, but that they should be expressed by words distinctly and exclusively appropriated to them. But no language is so copious as to supply words and phrases for every complex idea, or so correct as not to include many equivocally denoting different ideas. Hence, it must happen, that however accurately objects may be discriminated in themselves, and however accurately the discrimination may be considered, the definition of them may be rendered inaccurate by the inaccuracy of the terms in which it is delivered.
> (Madison 1999, 198)

Disagreement and uncertainty in law and politics would therefore arise from the fallible nature of language itself. *Perspicuity*, a word we rarely use today, was a favorite subject of eighteenth-century philosophy, and the desire to attach perspicuity to language, to give ambiguous words a clarity of meaning that casual usage often muddied, was one of the inspirations that loomed behind the era's flourishing interest in dictionaries.[2]

Nor was Madison's concern with perspicuity limited to the immediate task of ratifying the Federal Constitution. Madison had reflected on the difficulty of getting legislators to use words properly back in 1785, when he counseled a college friend on the kind of constitution the Kentucky district of Virginia might write when it became a state. Rather than allow bills to be drafted by ordinary, unskilled members, Madison (1999, 40–1) speculated (to Caleb Wallace on August 23, 1785), perhaps "a standing comm[it]tee composed of a few select & skilful individuals should be appointed to prepare bills on all subjects which they may judge proper to be submitted to the Legislature at their meetings & to draw bills for them during their Sessions." Such a committee might well take the place of the executive in proposing matters for discussion, but the responsibility for drawing bills also suggests that Madison was deeply concerned with the prosaic details of legislation – with ensuring that legislation was properly framed, the better to avoid the systematic vices he indicted two years later.

The dualism expressed in these concerns suggests that Madison's thinking operated at multiple levels. The major question – the one that his modern readers emphasize most – addressed the sources and nature of political factions. Why should republican citizens obey the law at all, his heading on Impotence might have asked, when they were so troubled by its multiplicity, mutability and injustice? What kind of rule of law should they respect, if these were the governing characteristics of its legislation? But next to these big questions, Madison was also deeply concerned with what one might call technical aspects of legislative deliberation and decision. These thoughts owed less to rethinking the basic premises of republican theory than to reflecting on lessons of political experience, especially the judgments he drew from his terms of service in the Continental Congress (1780–3) and the Virginia legislature (1784–6).

The nature of legislative deliberation defined the core of Madison's innovative approach to republican constitutionalism. Moreover, his judgments were not tied to traditional Anglo-American notions of the purposes of representative government, which had long emphasized the role of the legislature in checking the arbitrary use of executive (read *royal*) power. In a republic, Madison reasoned, the executive and judiciary would form the two weaker branches of government. Legislative supremacy was not simply a way of measuring the people's consent to the laws by which they would be governed. It also identified the real locus of republican politics, the institution to which the people would turn, not merely to see that their rights were protected against the arbitrary power of the state, but as the site of decision where their demands on government – what they expected government to do – would be answered. Madison looked on the legislative power in quite modern terms, and the concerns and inspirations he drew from this analysis proved fundamental to his constitutional project.

Modern American thinking about the nature of the rule of law in our democratic culture is much less interested in the place of legislation in our political system. Two other complementary concerns dominate our analysis instead: the role of courts in the constitutional system, and the proper rules of constitutional interpretation and construction. The great problem of the countermajoritarian difficulty, as formulated most famously by Alexander Bickel (1962), takes the fact of legislation as the background condition against which judicial power is applied. But Bickel's analysis, like the vast body of constitutional scholarship it helped to inspire, makes constitutional adjudication its true and proper subject. The active study of legislation has devolved primarily to political scientists. Their concerns have little to do with legislation as a constitutional value, but focus instead on (or perhaps are obsessed with) measuring the politics of forming majorities and other strategic aspects of coalition-building.

At the outset, however, the nature of legislative deliberation and the political sources of legislative majorities were the dominant themes of American constitutional thinking. The concerns that most animate scholars today – notably the origins of judicial review as a mechanism for enforcing a constitution as supreme law – evolved as responses to those legislative facts. Understanding how the American conception of the rule of law developed amid the republican innovations of the late eighteenth century thus requires paying close attention to the ways in which Americans had to rethink the nature of legislative power. In this process, Madison's deliberative experience and his reflections upon it played a critical role. It was Madison who best realized that the conventional view of the legislature as the protector of the rights of the people would no longer apply in a polity where the active power to initiate legislation would become the dominant expression of legislative supremacy. Reconstructing his insights provides an instructive way in which we can think critically about what a republican rule of law might come to mean in a society experiencing the political changes we associate with the American revolutionary era.

The constitutional crisis of the late 1780s was, of course, only one chapter – although arguably the climactic one – in a broader set of developments in the emergence of popular government in the United States. To situate Madison's insights properly, it is essential to sketch the context within which he acted – a context reflecting underlying aspects of governance in the colonies-becoming-commonwealths of Anglophone North America, and which was then reshaped by the course of revolutionary politics. While a short essay cannot do justice to so rich a subject, it will at least provide a foundation for assessing the significance of Madison's approach.

In its origins, the American Revolution was primarily a struggle over the legal supremacy of the British Parliament. Reduced to its simplest outlines, the controversy that brought Americans to independence in 1776 pitted the claims of Parliament's authority to make law for Americans "in all cases whatsoever" against the colonists' insistence that the only laws to which they could be properly bound had to be enacted by their own elected and politically accountable representatives. As late as 1774, the essential American position called for a return to a pre-1765 *status quo ante* in which laws regulating the daily structure of colonial life remained the product of provincial representative assemblies, while the colonists would accede – but only as a conciliatory gesture, not an admission of authority – to parliamentary regulation of imperial trade. From the British perspective, this position was wholly unacceptable. In part, this was because the government refused to acknowledge the manifest political legitimacy of the Americans' extra-legal institutions of resistance, from local committees and provincial conventions up to the Continental Congress. But more fundamentally, the American denial of the sovereignty of Parliament could never balance or trump the principles of the Glorious Revolution of 1688 and the additional measures that further defined and expanded its political settlement in the decades thereafter. American ideas about representation did have merit, some British leaders recognized, not least because they contrasted so strongly with the practices of the unreformed House of Commons, but in a conflict between colonial claims and the grand principle of parliamentary sovereignty, the American argument simply had to yield.[3]

As a crisis in the rule of imperial law, conducted within the framework of Anglo-American constitutionalism, this conflict was unresolvable. Both sides appealed to doctrines that were well-grounded in theory and history, and which had the further, even decisive, advantage of being psychologically convincing to their proponents. In the absence of either a written compact of imperial governance that could be fairly interpreted or a neutral agency of interpretation, the only safe resolution of this conflict would have to be political, not legal. That is, it would require the sides to negotiate a basis of accommodation grounded on prudential calculations rather than legal assertions. That was a risk neither side was willing to take. As Abraham Lincoln observed of a similar conflict nearly a century later: And the war came.

The great anomaly in the imperial controversy was that it pitted the claims of one legislative body (Parliament in Westminster) against the rival pretensions of another set of thirteen representative assemblies in America. The more conventional view of the purpose of representative assemblies was that they existed primarily to protect the rights and interests of the people against the arbitrary power and concentrated authority of the executive (or more exactly, the Crown). The great objective of political representation was not (as we would now say) to allow the disparate interests of society to aggregate their preferences and frame public policies through collective deliberation, but rather to prevent the Crown from imposing its dictates and fiats upon a society without their effective consent. That was the great (if again oversimplified) danger that the excesses of Stuart rule in the seventeenth century had raised, notably during those periods in the 1630s and 1680s when the Stuart Crown sought to rule without Parliament entirely. Americans thus found themselves in the theoretically anomalous position of asking George III to intervene on their behalf *against* Parliament, taking the part, as Thomas Jefferson (1984, 121) nicely put it in 1774 (*A Summary View of the Rights of British America*), of acting as "the balance of a great, if well-poised empire."

Once Americans abandoned their dwindling hopes for reconciliation in the spring of 1776, they could proceed with the adoption of the new state constitutions that expressed their commitment to republican government. This process has, of course, been closely studied in recent decades, beginning with Gordon Wood's (1969) pathbreaking, indispensable work, *The Creation of the American Republic, 1776–1787*. As Wood's analysis and numerous other studies make clear, a republican consensus set the intellectual foundation for the first constitutions, and while that consensus left some points of disagreement open, it was still strong enough to make some positions almost axiomatic. For one, the principle of legislative supremacy that Americans contested when claimed for Parliament nonetheless described the authority that representative assemblies would exercise in their new commonwealths. In opposition to British practice, Americans retained and expanded the norms of accountability that tied legislators to their electoral constituents. A well-constituted representative assembly should somehow resemble or map the society at large. "It should be in miniature, an exact portrait of the people at large," John Adams (1987, 108) observed in 1776. "It should think, feel, reason, and act like them. That it may be the interest of this Assembly to do strict justice at all times, it should be an equal representation, or in other words equal interest among the people should have equal interest in it." Yet this model of legislative activity presupposed, on republican principles, that the public interest had a collective integrity that representatives were bound to seek. Legislative behavior should still abide by the norms of virtual representation – not in the sense of presupposing that law-makers spoke for the nonenfranchised, but in terms of how they conceived their essential duties of deliberation and decision. At the same time, they would serve annual terms, presumably rotate frequently in office – as the state declarations of rights urged they should do – and remain highly accountable for decisions that were bound to impinge far more onerously on their constituents' lives than anything the provincial legislatures had attempted to do before then (Wood 1969, 173–96).

Adams made his claim for the representative assembly as a "miniature" of society in his *Thoughts on Government*, published in April 1776. That important document began its intellectual life back in the fall of 1775, when colleagues in the Continental Congress pressed him to explain what form American constitutions might take, once the colonists decided to replace the extra-legal apparatus of committees, conventions and congresses with fully legal governments. Adams's *Thoughts* provided a helpful focal point for the constitutional debates into which Americans entered in the spring of 1776, when they conceded that the movement for political independence and the restoration of legal government within the states would occur simultaneously. He particularly hoped his work would have a strong effect in the southern colonies where, he worried, efforts to preserve traditional notions of mixed government might appear more attractive than they would further north. Consistent with that fear, Adams's strongest critic was the conservative Virginia planter Carter Braxton, who thought that dreams of an ascetic republican simplicity might be suitable for the inhabitants of a desert island but not the abundant environment Americans were already developing.

Adams took a different view, and his pamphlet remains a useful starting point for thinking about American conceptions of a republican rule of law, *circa* 1776. Adams cast himself as a contrarian against conventional opinions. "No small fortitude is necessary to confess that one has read" the leading republican writers whom he admired. But there was only one conclusion this knowledge could support: "that there is no good government but what is Republican. That the only valuable part of the British constitution is so; because the very definition of a Republic, is 'an Empire of Laws, and not of men'"; and that to obtain "the best of Republics," the real challenge was "to secure an impartial and exact execution of the laws" (Adams 1987, 108). This was no easy matter, however, because "Of Republics, there is an inexhaustible variety," given the numerous ways in which institutions could represent the larger society.

One reason as to why that was the case hinges on the nature of colonial governance before 1776. On occasion, colonial legislatures did make positive public law, enacting statutes that affected their provinces as a whole. Some of that impulse to legislate was naturally due to the challenge of organizing new societies. The most notable category of innovative legislation was the law of slavery, where the colonists first invented and then systematized a whole category of legislation that had no direct counterpart in either English common or statutory law. Yet scholars of American law for the colonial era seem to agree that province-wide legislation, in the modern positive sense of the term, was *not* the dominant activity of colonial representative assemblies. The great bulk of their business still depended on answering petitions from local communities, some seeking legal permission to undertake an activity, others treating legislatures as general courts for the resolution of disputes and grievances. That was one reason why colonial law-makers acted as attorneys for their communities – whether townships or counties – rather than legislators on the model of Edmund Burke's oft-cited account of members of Parliament as virtual representatives of the entire realm or the modern notion of a representative as an advocate for his citizen constituents.[4] As the New York lawyer, judge, and Loyalist William Smith, Jr. famously observed, the views of most representatives "seldom extended further than to the regulation of highways, the destruction of wolves, wildcats, and foxes, and the advancement of the other little interests of the particular counties, which they were chosen to represent" (Hulsebosch 2005, 51).

How much ordinary Americans knew of provincial legislation is an open question.[5] Most aspects of governance that affected Americans in their ordinary lives were highly decentralized to community-level institutions, particularly juries. Unlike the modern American axiom, attributed to former Speaker of the House of Representatives Thomas P. (Tip) O'Neill, that "all politics is local," colonial Americans operated in a world where competition for political advantage was primarily provincial in nature, but most governance was local and customary. Provincial governments had no bureaucracies to enforce anything. Where some provincial rule had to be administered, it fell to local institutions filled with citizen participants to do their duty, in the way their community saw fit to do it.

Perhaps this portrait is somewhat overdrawn, and in any case, it would be helpful if the nature of the production of legislation in the eighteenth-century American assemblies was a better studied subject. Still, one can sketch a portrait of the nature of the rule of law in America on the eve of the Revolution that would have at least these qualities: First, the protection of colonial legislative authority against the rival claims of parliamentary supremacy was the critical issue in the imperial quarrel with Britain, and this controversy rested significantly on the extent to which Americans grounded their notions of legislative jurisdiction on active theories of consent. But second, that commitment did not presuppose that the making of legislation was the primary duty of colonial assemblies. Americans accepted the conventional Whiggish view that representative assemblies existed less to aggregate the preferences of the people than to prevent Crown officials from acting unilaterally. Third, much of the legislation that these assemblies enacted was concerned not with general purpose public statutes, but with resolving issues referred upward by local communities; and this tendency in turn confirms that the real basis for legal enforcement in the eighteenth century lay at the community level. The decisions made by selectmen, jurors and other local officers were the real "stuff" of eighteenth-century law, and these decisions generally reflected the weight of customary practice within the community rather than the top-down dictates of statutory law-makers. Fourth, the political system within individual colonies rarely operated to create coalitions that would try to gain control of the legislature. It took exceptional issues – for example, the reaction against Benjamin Franklin's effort to have the Crown revoke the Penn family's proprietary rule of Pennsylvania[6] – to generate electoral coalitions that could reshape the composition of a legislature in an informed way. Such possibilities could exist, but they did not define the ordinary course of politics.

Yet fifth, and arguably most important, when an electorate did act in such a way, it could confirm one of the underlying constitutional values of republican politics. This was the idea that when government in general arbitrarily threatened their rights or the larger public good, "the people themselves" should be the ultimate enforcers of constitutional norms.[7] In the ordinary course of colonial politics, however, it remained difficult to imagine how the people's elected representatives could ever act against their rights. The abusers the people needed to monitor were those who held offices that made them dependent upon the dictates of the Crown rather than the will of the voters. The people would rarely have occasion to channel their protests against their own directly elected representatives. How a legislature could act arbitrarily admittedly remained something of a mystery. Yet then as now, the American mind was open to conspiratorial theories, and the people themselves should be prepared for any contingency. The notion that a people bred to liberty should act as the protectors of their own rights against any danger was a staple of American thinking. It could be directed against a legislature that ignored norms of accountability and turned into an arbitrary force within a government.

James Madison, a young man of twenty-five who sat in the convention that framed the Virginia constitution of 1776, came to depart from these judgments in critical respects, and the sources for that departure help to explain why he became the leading practicing constitutionalist of his own (or perhaps any) age.[8]

The originality that Madison demonstrated in rethinking these premises of republican government was a function of the distinctive ways in which he combined and balanced lessons from experience with a capacity to think abstractly about fundamental aspects of republican government. The empirical and theorizing faculties of Madison's eighteenth-century brain were well balanced, reflected in his capacity, nicely captured by the late political theorist Judith Shklar, to look beyond the messy tumult of ordinary politics "to see a pattern amid the confusion of men and events."[9] Most casual readers know Madison chiefly as the author of *Federalist* 10 and 51, those two canonical statements of his ideas about extended republics and the separation of powers. But too great a reliance on these published texts carries some costs, particularly if one is concerned with Madison's ideas about the rule of law in republican societies. A better approach to his thinking comes if one reconstructs his insights into the nature of legislative deliberation and decision.

The starting point for pursuing this task begins with the dual concerns for public good and private rights that preoccupied Madison after the early 1780s. In point of time, the issue of public good came first. During his uninterrupted service in the Continental Congress (from the spring of 1780 to the fall of 1783), Madison was repeatedly troubled with the fundamental problem of national governance under the Articles of Confederation, in which implementation of decisions taken by Congress depended on the good faith compliance of the state legislatures with its resolutions and requisitions. In this voluntary compliance form of federalism, the states were *not* presumed to be sovereign actors, wilfully deciding whether they should enforce national measures. The theory, rather, was that the states would have both superior judgment as to how these measures could be enforced and the formal legislative authority required to oblige citizens to comply with their decisions. But in practice, for an array of reasons, state compliance varied and was often deemed to be ineffectual and self-interested. The perception that the states were failing to perform their national duties naturally led Madison to wonder how the national public good could be left to hang on the partial, ill-informed judgment of ordinary state legislators, most of them short-time members who served a term or two and then retired from service.

That perception was also shared by George Washington and his circle of military officers, who repeatedly had to deal with state officials in order to obtain the supplies that the Continental Army often badly lacked. What gave Madison's thinking its additional critical impetus was his experience in the Virginia legislature, where he served three years (1784–6) after being term-limited out of Congress.[10] At the start of his service in Richmond, Madison was a dominant figure in the legislature. However, there came a time when his disciplined efforts to drive the legislative agenda produced a backlash among less ardent colleagues. The best way to doom a measure, some of them joked, was to persuade Madison to support it. Perhaps Gordon Wood has offered the sharpest characterization of the effect on this experience on Madison's political thinking. "Really for the first time, Madison found out what democracy in America might mean," Wood observes.

> The Virginia legislators seemed so parochial, so illiberal, so small-minded, and most of them seemed to have only 'a particular interest to serve.' They had no regard for public honor and honesty. They too often made a travesty of the legislative process and were reluctant to do anything that might appear unpopular.
>
> (Wood 1987, 74)

The proper moral for Madison to draw, Wood (1987, 74) suggests, was this awkward question: "What could he do with such clods?"

Part of Madison's frustration in Virginia echoed his dissatisfaction with the difficulty of getting the states to perform their federal duties. But the new and more telling part concerned the internal character of state lawmaking. In the mid-1780s, Madison did have some success pushing major parts of Thomas Jefferson's republican revisal of the Virginia legal code through the assembly. He managed a skillful campaign to block the adoption of a general assessment bill that would have effectively re-established religion in the state by providing public support for all "teachers" (ministers) of Christianity. He then followed that success by securing the enactment of Jefferson's great Statute for Religious Freedom, a landmark both for American legislation and the Enlightenment principle of freedom of religion. Yet even with these victories, Madison worried that the character of republican politics was turning against the protection of individual and minority rights. He was particularly alarmed by the mounting popularity of paper money measures, which, he believed, would deprive creditors of their just rights of property by forcing them to accept payment in depreciated currency. Madison's alarm over this subject may have exceeded the threat actually posed, but the example of Rhode Island, where a paper money party dominated politics, still gave his fears some credibility. It also stimulated his doubts about the conventional association of the stability of a republic with the existence of small, relatively homogeneous societies peopled by a virtuous citizenry. Rhode Island was the smallest republic in the American union, and its Baptist- and Quaker-bred commitment to principles of religious liberty – Madison's favorite personal right – indicated that its citizens were not devoid of all sound principles. Yet by the mid-1780s it was an object of political scorn and evidence of the dangers that troubled Madison.

Madison's rethinking of the premises of republican rule appears to have taken place between the summer of 1785 and the early spring of 1787. His efforts had avowedly scholarly components, based in part on the "literary cargo" of books that Jefferson shipped to him from Europe. These works formed the basis not only for his notes on ancient and modern confederacies but also, as Colleen Sheehan (2009) has argued in a valuable new monograph, for an active engagement with writings on the nature of public opinion and its formation. But the deeper source of his ideas lay in his experience within government, and particularly his efforts to make sense of the character of republican politics in his own state of Virginia. The innovative element in this analysis lay in Madison's continuing fascination with the character of republican legislation, and more particularly, with Madison's attempt to understand the nature of political authority in a regime where representative assembles would act, not as a check against the arbitrary power of the executive, but as the source and locus of the positive power of the state.

The fundamental problem in the American commonwealths, Madison (1999, 40–2) observed in August 1785 (Madison to Caleb Wallace, August 23, 1785), was the lack of "*wisdom* and steadiness in legislation" and the legislature's tendency to adopt "fluctuating and indegested [*sic*] laws." When Americans first framed their constitutions a decade earlier, he reflected, they were preoccupied with past grievances, which meant "the want of *fidelity* in the administration of power" – that is, the traditional problem of controlling the executive. A decade of self-government had proven that this concern, however natural it seemed at the time, was misplaced. Executive power had been largely eviscerated in 1776 – so much so, in fact, that the construction of the executive should now matter less to reform-minded republicans than the judiciary, which "merits every care."[11] It was the legislature that now predominated as the active force in government.

When Madison initially thought about the reform of state government, the real object of his concern was properly institutional. He believed the states needed genuine senates to serve as a check on impulsive legislation, noting that members of the lower house often interceded with their colleagues in the upper house to modify or block legislation that the more popular body had already approved. The technical deficiencies of legislation might similarly be corrected by creating a new institution, an executive-judicial council of revision, armed with a limited veto over badly drafted acts. Or perhaps assemblies should have select committees of respected and skilled members to improve the quality of their legislative product. It might help, too, to depart from the sacred republican principle of annual elections to allow members of the lower house to serve three-year terms, a proposal that was likely intended less to insulate law-makers from their constituents than to give them time to learn how to do their jobs.

Had Madison stuck to these proposals alone, however, his political ideas would not have led him past the general boundaries of constitutional reform in the mid-1780s. What drove his thinking in the months to come was a more difficult and innovative question: Did the sources of legislative misrule inhere primarily in the failings of law-makers and their institutions, or could they be traced instead "out-of-doors," to political factors working within the society as a whole? Or to put the point more simply, did the faults lie more with law-makers or with the citizens whom they represented? This was the great puzzle that Madison pondered as he drafted "the Vices" in early April 1787, and with it one detects the extent to which his creative political thinking pivoted on weighing the relative importance of institutions against the larger array of interests, opinions and passions that swirled through the body politic more generally.

One sees this clearly in the development of Madison's indictment of the "multiplicity," "mutability," and finally, the "injustice" of state law-making. He began his analysis by criticizing the "luxuriancy of legislation" that the past decade has produced. Much of this output can be ascribed, he conceded, to "the situation in which the revolution has placed us" – a situation requiring the legislatures to act far more frequently and with more burdensome consequences than any circumstances the prior century of colonization had required. But that explanation worked only "in part;" other causes must explain this legislative output. Had more sensible law-makers been involved, the recent statute books could be reduced to a tenth of their length, "and at the same time be rendered tenfold as perspicuous." The problem of "mutability" compounded the problem: "[I]t emphatically denotes a vicious legislation." Laws were often "repealed or superseded" before they could be fairly tried, or "even before a knowledge of them" could have reached outlying precincts (Madison 1999, 74–5).

The critical point, however, was the next item, devoted to the "injustice" of the laws of the states. This was "more alarming not merely because it is a greater evil in itself," but because it challenged the basic republican premise that majority rule was the best judge of public good and private rights. But which majorities troubled Madison more: those that formed within the legislature, or those which operated beyond it? Madison's analysis indicates that he was clearly shifting the responsibility away from law-makers to citizens. Item 11 of "the Vices" offered a few brief remarks about the ambitions and deceptions of law-makers, and a sympathetic reflection about how "the honest but unenlightened representative" might become "the dupe of a favorite leader." But from these quick observations, Madison moved on to his real concern: the causes of injustice that lay "among the people themselves." Here, in its first draft, was the analysis of the sources of *popular* faction that modern readers know best from *Federalist* 10. Those sources, Madison announced, were not deviations from a norm of republican virtue; they were the normal conditions of all modern societies, tied to economic factors and other sources of division. "In republican Government the majority, however composed, ultimately give the law." But where such a majority could be united by an "apparent interest or common passion" (Madison 1999, 75–6) none of the restraints that ordinarily worked on individuals privately (a prudent regard for the public good, respect for character, or religion) would be efficacious.

This analysis is familiar to historians of republican and constitutional thought, and its details need not be belabored. For the republican form to survive, Madison reasoned, it has to begin with a realistic assessment of the ordinary sources of civic behavior, not an unrealistic expectation about the continued virtue of citizens. Interest, opinion, passion: these, not virtue, are the dominant factors in politics, and any effort to make republicanism consistent with the real characteristics of citizens must begin there. What deserves greater attention, however, is the extent to which Madison's argument now presupposes that the citizens will act, not as a virtuous check on the abuses of government power, but as the direct political source of the power government would wield.

Two famous documents bear on this point in distinct but equally revealing ways. One is the paragraph in *Federalist* 10 that follows Madison's familiar recapitulation of the sources of faction; the other was written a year later, when Madison explained his cautious acceptance of the idea of adding a declaration of rights to the ratified Constitution. Together, these two statements illustrate Madison's conception of the effect of popular opinion and interest on the pursuit of public good and private rights.

Madison ended the paragraph on faction with a sentence that describes the legislative function in strikingly modern terms. "The regulation of these various and interfering interests forms the principal task of modern legislation, and involves the spirit of party and faction in the necessary and ordinary operations of the government." What strikes us as common sense, I submit, was the point of departure for Madison's creative thinking, a point that was wholly consistent with his recognition that it was not the exigencies of the Revolution alone that created the "luxuriancy of legislation" he denounced in "the Vices." What other sources of legislation could there be? The next paragraph makes clear his concern.

Madison begins with a seemingly puzzling statement. "No man is allowed to be a judge in his own cause," he observes, "because his interest would certainly bias his judgment, and, not improbably, corrupt his integrity." But what are law-makers, if not "judges and parties at the same time," he continues, and "what are many of the most important acts of legislation, but so many judicial determinations," not about individuals, but about "the rights and interests of [the] large body of citizens they represent." The equation between legislation and adjudication seems surprising until one looks at the illustrations Madison offers: laws governing creditors and debtors, subsidies for manufacturers, and taxation. All involve issues where the interests of parties will come into play, channeled into the legislature by the constituencies they represent. And all ultimately do involve rights, because any decision in the realm of economics will affect rights of property by benefiting some more, and others less. More generally, all of these illustrations presuppose what Americans, late in the colonial period, would have found strange to contemplate: that the primary business of a legislature would henceforth involve, not overseeing a distinctly localist mode of governance, but managing an array of geographically based social interests seeking to benefit from government. Embedded or implicit in Madison's formulation was the idea that the representative assembly of a republic would act less as an independent source of statist authority and more as the forum within which interests would jockey for collective advantage. American representatives, in Madison's understanding, would still serve, as perhaps they always had, as the agents-attorneys of their constituents. But the examples he offered in this paragraph, all tied to a zero-sum model of economic interests, now presupposed that their business would subsume tasks associated with a dynamic economy. Perhaps it reads too much into Madison's sketch, but one can look at this language and imagine, without great difficulty, the kind of polity that eighteenth-century Britain had already become, and that nineteenth-century America would soon be: a polity for an age of improvement, where communities and their entrepreneurs would compete with one another to acquire the legal privileges and corporate forms capable of building the infrastructure of turnpikes, canals and (later) railroads essential for their active entrance in a market economy. In such an environment, there might still be a public good that the leg-islature should conscientiously seek to discover and advance, and even if different interests could not be equally affected by all measures, a rising tide of prosperity might still lift many boats. But the challenge remained that American notions of government by consent would turn elected representatives into parties and judges at once, advancing the parochial economic interests of the communities they represented. In a geographi-cally expanding society where every crossroads town could see itself as a future commercial metropolis, with the proper boost of infrastructure, this could be a formula in which every community could look to government for the resources and legal privileges essential to development.[12]

Madison's grand project was to take these social facts as given, yet to still try to construct republican habits of governance that would improve the quality of deliberation. Whether that improvement depended more on the character of institutions or on the diversity of interests lying outside the government is one of the intriguing challenges in unpacking his thinking. It would be safe to say that he cared about both, hoped that the multiplicity of interests in an extended republic would work as he predicted, and believed that the institutions of republican government should do as much as possible to structure the course of deliberation and decision. The goal was not merely to hope that external factions would somehow nullify each other's mischievous traits, but to make it possible for better deliberation to develop.

Yet the driving force behind political deliberation, Madison assumed, would be the interests "out-of-doors," or more broadly, the people them-selves. That point is made directly in the other Madison text that merits direct mention here: his October 17, 1788 letter to Thomas Jefferson (still serving as the American minister to France), in which Madison explained why, somewhat grudgingly, he now supported the addition of a declaration of rights to the ratified Constitution. Madison made clear throughout this text that he doubted whether such amendments were essential to completing the constitutional project. The real object was to reduce or remove the misgivings of the Constitution's opponents. He summarized his ongoing reservations. First, he partially accepted the argument, first advanced by James Wilson, that the addition of amendments identifying rights deserving explicit protection may be read to imply that the national government possessed powers it had not been explicitly granted. Second, if one drafted such a text, its wording might prove weaker than the language one would wish to have, and perhaps leave rights more vulnerable to violation than they would have been otherwise. Third, the existence of the states as rivals to the national government would "afford a security" for rights that did not operate within the states alone.

But fourth, and most important, Madison continued to believe that "experience proves the inefficacy of a bill of rights on those occasions when its controul is most needed." Had the Virginia assembly discovered that a majority of their constituents favored an improper act of religious establishment, notwithstanding the restriction against one in the state's declaration of rights, they would have enacted the proposed "general assessment" bill. Even now, after the adoption of Jefferson's famous Statute for Religious Freedom, such a measure could still be adopted, if the legislators felt that public opinion had shifted. And that was the key point.

> Wherever the real power in a Government lies, there is the danger of oppression. In our Governments the real power lies in the majority of the Community, and the invasion of private rights is cheifly to be apprehended, not from acts of Government contrary to the sense of its constituents, but from acts in which the Government is the mere instrument of the major number of the constituents.
>
> (Madison 1999, 421)

"This is a truth of great importance," Madison added, "but not yet sufficiently attended to" – and not least, perhaps, by Jefferson himself, then moored in France watching the *ancien regime* stumbling toward collapse. The French people were entitled to arise, as a collective entity, against their arbitrary monarchy, but Americans faced a different problem.

Just as "the real power [lying] in the majority of the community" is a republican definition of government, so Madison's thoughts on the protection of rights offered a modern definition of how a republican rule of law must henceforth be protected. "What use," Madison skeptically asked, "can a bill of rights serve in popular Governments?" His main answer to this query harked back to traditional republican norms. "The political truths declared in that solemn manner acquire by degrees the character of fundamental maxims of free Government," he observed, "and as they become incorporated with the national sentiment, counteract the impulses of interest and passion."[13] Here as elsewhere in his writings, Madison stated a key finding in a near-epigraphic form that one laments he did not expand. Yet the essential point seems evident enough. In a republic the value of declarations of rights would lie not in giving individuals a basis for litigation, but by inculcating citizens with norms that would modify their interested or impassioned behavior, and thus prevent the formation of factions. If, for example, religious liberty was to be preserved in America, it would depend not only on the fruitful capacity of disestablished Protestants to multiply their denominational differences indefinitely, but also on the acceptance by individual believers of the values of toleration and free exercise together.

James Madison was hardly the most representative American thinker of his age, but he was, arguably, its greatest constitutionalist. His efforts to reconsider republican government began with his efforts to analyze the character of legislative deliberation as he had experienced it since 1776. Legislation in a republic would not be the work of an eminent law-giver who might need to solicit the assent of the people's representatives. It would instead be a product of collective deliberation, and as a constitutionalist preoccupied with the work of institutions, Madison thought a great deal about how those deliberations should be conducted. Yet beyond these institutional concerns lay an equally powerful set of political concerns about the forces that would swirl through the republic. In these concerns lay a new basis for thinking about a republican rule of law in terms quite different from those that had prevailed within America at the first blush of republican enthusiasm a decade earlier.

REFERENCES

Adams, J. (1987). "Thoughts on Government." In: The Founders' Constitution, Vol. I. Eds Philip Kurland and Ralph Lerner, Chicago: University of Chicago Press: 107–10.

Bailyn, B. (1968). The Origins of American Politics. New York: Knopf.

Bailyn, B. (1992 [1967]). The Ideological Origins of the American Revolution. Cambridge, MA: Harvard University Press.

Bickel, A. (1962). *The Least Dangerous Branch: The Supreme Court at the Bar of Politics*. Indianapolis: Bobbs-Merrill.

Dawson, H. (2005). "Locke on Language in (Civil) Society." *History of Political Thought* 26: 397–425.

Dawson, H. (2007). *Locke, Language, and Early-Modern Philosophy*. Cambridge: Cambridge University Press.

Edling, M. (2003). *A Revolution in Favor of Government: Origins of the U. S. Constitution and the Making of the American State*. New York: Oxford University Press.

Handlin, O. and M. Handlin (1969 [1948]). *Commonwealth: A Study of the Role of Government in the American Economy, 1774–1861*. Cambridge, MA: Harvard University Press.

Howe, J. R. (2004). *Language and Political Meaning in Revolutionary America*. Amherst and Boston: University of Massachusetts Press.

Hulsebosch, D. (2005). *Constituting Empire: New York and the Transformation of Constitutionalism in the Atlantic World*. Chapel Hill: University of North Carolina Press.

Hutson, J. H. (1972). *Pennsylvania Politics, 1746–1770: The Movement for Royal Government and Its Consequences*. Princeton: Princeton University Press.

Jefferson, T. (1984). *Writings*. Ed. M. Peterson, New York: Library of America.

Kramer, L. D. (2004). *The People Themselves: Popular Constitutionalism and Judicial Review*. New York: Oxford University Press.

Madison, J. (1999). *Writings*. Ed. J. N. Rakove, New York: Library of America.

Marshall, P. J. (2007). *The Making and Unmaking of Empires: Britain, India, and America, circa 1750–1783*. Oxford: Oxford University Press.

Morgan, E. S. (1948). "Colonial Ideas of Parliamentary Power, 1764–1766." *William and Mary Quarterly* 5: 311–41.

Rakove, J. N. (1996). *Original Meanings: Politics and Ideas in the Making of the Constitution*. New York: Knopf.

Rakove, J. N. (2010). *Revolutionaries: A New History of the Invention of America*. Boston: Houghton Mifflin.

Sheehan, C. A. (2009). *James Madison and the Spirit of Republican Self-Government*. New York: Cambridge University Press.

Shklar, J. (1998). *Redeeming American Political Thought*. Eds S. Hoffman and D. F. Thompson, Chicago: University of Chicago Press.

Wood, G. (1969). *The Creation of the American Republic, 1776–1787*. Chapel Hill: University of North Carolina Press.

Wood, G. (1987). "Interests and Disinterestedness in the Making of the Constitution." In: *Beyond Confederation: Origins of the Constitution and American National Identity*. Eds R. Beeman *et al.*, Chapel Hill: University of North Carolina Press: 69–109.

Notes

1. This "Madisonian" treatment of the origins of the Constitution, however, is not the only one possible. There is a Hamiltonian story to be told as well, which emphasizes the needs of building a nation-state over concerns with republican law-making: Edling 2003. The Madisonian view deeply informs Wood 1969 and Rakove 1996.

2. In thinking about Madison's concern with the nature of legal and political language,

and his evident debt to Locke, I have learned much from Dawson 2005, 2007. On issues relating to the American concern with political language, see Howe 2004.

3. This debate has been the subject of extensive work and commentary. Two classic sources for analyzing the American position remain the seminal article by Edmund S. Morgan (1948) and Bernard Bailyn (1992). Today we live in a scholarly age where interest in the nature of empire has literally exploded, and that is leading to a broader understanding of problems of imperial governance than was available previously – or rather, one that returns to the interests of early twentieth-century scholars. For the British perspective, a good place to begin is Marshall 2007.

4. "An assemblyman was the agent of his constituents as members of a county as much as individuals:" Hulsebosch 2005, 51.

5. "Compilations of revised statutes were rare," writes Hulsebosch 2005, 55 of colonial New York. "Consequently, practicioners had difficulty discovering which laws had been repealed or had expired."

6. For this event, see Hutson 1972.

7. For an extended discussion of this argument, see Kramer 2004.

8. Hence the title of the Madison chapter in my recent book (Rakove 2010): "The Greatest Lawgiver of Modernity."

9. Or as Shklar 1998, 96 observed more generally: Madison "had a historian's mind, which was a great intellectual advantage. It enabled him to penetrate to the logic of collective action, even when on the surface there seemed to be nothing but random irrationality and partisan wrangling. By reflecting upon previous occasions and experiences he was always able to see a pattern amid the confusion of men and events."

10. Under the Confederation, which took effect on March 1, 1781, delegates could serve only three years out of every six. It is an interesting reflection on the contemporary American fondness for term limits, at least in some states (including super-populous California), that Madison numbered among its very first victims. Provisions in the declarations of rights accompanying the early state constitutions endorsed rotation in office as a general principle of republican self-government, but without formally mandating it for legislators.

11. Italics in the original. The occasion for this letter, which was Madison's first serious discussion of republican government within the individual states, was a college friend's request for guidance on the kind of constitution the district of Kentucky could draft when it separated from Virginia.

12. I draw here on the classic monograph by Oscar and Mary Handlin (1969), which traces the political economy of Massachusetts from the Revolution to the mid-nineteenth century. There is an interesting echo of these themes in the closing pages of Bailyn 1968, 124–31.

13. Madison 1999, 421–2.

CHAPTER 3

Kant, Madison and the Problem of Transnational Order: Popular Sovereignty in Multilevel Systems

James Bohman

It may seem surprising to many that Madison and the other eighteenth-century Federalists are closely linked to the very contemporary idea of a transnational political order. But the idea that the modern state with its centralized authority and supreme power threaten liberty had already been widely discussed in the eighteenth century. The Constitution of the United States still bears traces of the ambition that it was to establish a new political order that was neither a loose federation nor itself an enlarged state but rather something quite novel. The emergence of a transnational order was, very concretely, the exact intellectual and political problem that the Framers faced. They were not alone in this preoccupation. At the very same time, the German philosopher Kant struggled with the same issues of liberty and security in his political essays. In "Perpetual Peace," Kant argues for a republic of republics that might be the means by which war could be abolished. To my knowledge no Federalist or Antifederalist ever mentions Kant, even though they shared common republican concerns with freedom, peace and security. While Kant was certainly aware of the American Revolution, he does not take it to be a momentous turning point for modern republics on a par with the French Revolution. But because both the Federalists and Kant shared a conception that was both cosmopolitan and republican, they inevitably occupied the same intellectual and political space, however much they arrived at very different conceptions of the proper transnational order.

My task is to bring these two strands of republicanism into a belated dialog, with an eye to present-day discussions of the future of democracy in a transnational and international order, for which the European Union is now the exemplar in our time. In many respects, Kant and Madison grappled with issues closely related to those discussed today, including popular sovereignty, political violence, and diversity. The possibility that Kant and Madison explored, along with many other republicans of the time, is not the contemporary idea of transnational governance without government, but rather of government without a state with supreme authority and a monopoly of the means to violence. But they did so without confining themselves to the models of small-scale, ancient republics.

In order to see why this idea was so appealing to them, it is important to see Madison (or rather Publius more generally) and Kant in the distinctive context of eighteenth-century republicanism. Prior to this period, early modern republicanism favored small republics, and Rousseau continues this tradition in arguing that Corsica was the ideal size to preserve liberty. For these republicans, "to be free is to be a citizen of a free state," where a people organized around representative government in a bounded and exclusive political community was thought to be the primary means by which liberty could be secured and shared with fellow citizens. In an age when international institutions were largely absent, many republicans during the Enlightenment argued that the result was the domination of colonial empires; instead of these extensions of states they argued in favor of large-scale institutions through which freedom could be secured and shared across borders with diverse peoples. They were acutely aware not only of the horrors of colonialism, but also of the increased capacities for political violence and the destructive nature of modern warfare that was a consequence of the false division between justice and amity at home and anarchy and violence abroad. Building a republican argument for the extension of modern republican political forms, such as representative and deliberative bodies, across political communities, Enlightenment republicans proposed the political form of a peaceful federation as the major innovation of modern forms of republicanism that had finally transcended the limits of the ancient models.

It is in the context of a distinctively anticolonial form of republicanism that we can see why cosmopolitan forms of republicanism emerged in this period and took on new transnational forms that still guide transnational political thinking even today. My argument will have four main steps. First, I want to show more precisely just how much Kant shared with the Federalists' interest in a republic of republics. However, Kant's own development of such a political order remained stymied by a number of problems related to reconciling democracy (or popular sovereignty) with nondomination, the problems of which the Federalists have a strong solution. Second, I examine these institutional alternatives. On the one hand, Kant despairs of finding any more direct cosmopolitan form of democratic republicanism and begins to look for "negative substitutes" for a world state in the form of an ever-expanding zone of peace among members of a federation of republican peoples; on the other, the Federalists opened up just the space missing in Kant and devised a form of government that stood between a weak federation and the strong form of the modern hierarchical state. Their innovative solution was dominated by the concern with popular sovereignty. But their version remains cosmopolitan by rejecting the particular version that dominated political understanding of the French republic, that of the unitary sovereign people. Third, I turn to the alternative *plural* understanding of popular sovereignty as developed by Madison and the other federalists. In light of this alternative and nonunitary conception, popular sovereignty is distributed across a variety of units and institutions at various scales. When we look to such a distributive rather than unitary account, it is clear that it has now become the basis for those existing forms of transnational polities such as the European Union, which is neither a regional superstate nor a confederation, but a polity characterized by distributed sovereignty across levels. Rather than having popular sovereignty disappear in governance without government, as critics suggest, this distinctive form allows us to see the plural popular sovereignty found in the EU as the organizing principle of government without a state, or of a States' Union. Finally, I turn to deliberative practices in the EU in order to extend notions of deliberation to plural and more direct forms of popular sovereignty not considered by the Federalists, who ultimately endorsed a more indirect conception of popular rule. The next cosmopolitan republican innovation locates distributed popular sovereignty within more direct forms of deliberative self-rule. This particular institutionalization of popular sovereignty can be undermined by some of the limitations of multilevel systems, in particular the potential conflict between a juridically enforced set of liberal rights on the one hand and more republican and democratic institutions in which citizens exercise self-rule on the other.

Before turning to debates among republican cosmopolitans concerning the proper form of the republic, it is necessary to clarify the type of enduring form of political order that is at stake in this discussion. In their desire to get beyond the domination inherent in the nation-state, cosmopolitan republics sought to develop a form of political order based on a multilevel political system without the supremacy of one part over the whole. This type of self-rule captures many features of the European Union.

WHAT IS A MULTILEVEL SYSTEM?

While the EU has suffered with new political and economic difficulties, these may have less to do with its faltering project as with the type of polity that lies between a democratic state and technocratic governance. The difficulties at stake have to do with its current basic structure: That is, it is a system of multilevel government. Nick Bernard defines multilevel government as "a system of organizing public power divided into two or more layers of government, where each layer retains autonomous decision-making power vis-à-vis the others."[1] In such a multilevel structure, there is no sovereignty in the classical sense; that is, there is no supreme and final authority over a particular territory. Thus, a political unit is sovereign if it has "supreme authority." This is precisely what Bernard's definition denies, since power is instead divided, so that no other unit has final authority of the others; this means that there is no central locus of power and a clear hierarchy of levels (as there would be in a true federation). Instead, no one layer is subordinate to any other; at the same time, however, a multilevel system also can be divided up into component units or parts of each layer and a collective entity that makes up the whole, which allows us to distinguish between member states and the European Union itself. The purpose of such an order, according to Bernard, is important, since its aim is to strike a balance between "the contradictory aspirations to uniformity and diversity."[2] This same kind of order can be seen at the transnational level more generally, in which there are now many different sources of law and law-makers and in which there are many different constitutions rather than one overriding constitution as a whole.

Even if the EU has the features of a multilevel system, a common criticism of its political order is that it is more technocratic than democratic. However, the lack of supremacy and comprehensiveness in the EU works against the idea of an effectively technocratic form of multilevel governance. But when popular sovereignty is distributed, it is better to look at broader trends that are consequences of the fact that it is a multilevel system. It has also settled on various principles such as subsidiarity, in order to solve various problems of authority that often plague multilevel systems. Besides its inherent vagueness, one problem with subsidiarity is that it tends to favor older, already constituted and recognizable political forms as locations for policy making and deliberation even as the EU is creating new ones.

The EU provides the institutional structure in which to redefine the interactive relationships and overlapping memberships among the local, the national and the supranational levels of scale. If this reconstruction of the process of European political integration is correct, it also follows that a more unitary democratic structure would no longer be normatively desirable, particularly since it does not serve to enhance the capacities of citizens to exercise their sovereignty through the new and more direct practices and arrangements, including direct petition to the European Court of Human Rights (ECHR). EU-level institutions can in some instances require member states (and now even applicant states) to realize human rights better and to enhance participation by diverse actors with the overall effect of making member states more democratic.[3] This is precisely because the anomalous and often rightless persons that crossed borders into the nation-state system now have a location in which to initiate deliberation and acquire normative powers against domination. If applied to human rights policy and monitoring, novel practices such as the Open Method of Coordination (OMC) help by providing multiple pathways for publics to initiate deliberation about the rights of immigrants at various locations and on various issues. Thus, the extension of human rights in the EU to noncitizens without naturalization shows the advantages of realizing human rights across differentiated institutions.

In this way, the EU presents a different positive feedback relationship of pooled sovereignty that enables democratization to occur, in which it is precisely the transnational-level institutions that enhance democracy at the lower levels. Certainly, even in the EU the interaction can go the other way: Democracy exercised at the lower levels, in cities, regions and states can enhance the democracy of higher levels, especially as these suffer from the potentially dominating effects of juridification that could make transnational institutions so distant and alien. With such mutual interaction across levels and locations, a highly differentiated polity works not merely in policy areas, but also in creating a regime of human rights that can realize the powers of citizenship and make them more rather than less robust. This suggests that a differentiated structure best promotes peace because democracy alone is able to promote a high degree of robust interaction across its institutional levels and sites (in ways that were not technologically feasible for the Federalists). These sorts of positive and mutually enhancing interactions across borders are missing in unitary accounts of sovereignty, which is now being extended to include others who are not members of some particular republic.

This and other issues raises the question of whether or not transnational political orders should be Federalist in the now more commonly accepted meaning of the term or perhaps should even be thought of as Federal states. Given the lack of supremacy and the distributed and indirect way in which comprehensiveness is fulfilled, the latter option does not do justice to the realities of the EU system. But Federalism in a broader sense seems still to be a live possibility for the realization of popular sovereignty, at least to the extent that it identifies one type of multilevel system. Follesdal and others see Federalism as a specific kind of multilevel system characterized by the division of authority between member units and the center.[4] The normative principles that inform this sort of federalism follow Madison's dictum that "federal and State governments are in fact but different agents and trustees of the people constituted with different powers and designed for different purposes" (Hamilton, Madison and Jay 2003, 228).[56] The basic test is then how well this particular design is guided by and assessed normatively "by how well it reliably secures the relevant interests of affected parties when compared to alternative institutional arrangements."[7] The allocation of authority between member units and the center raises issues related to the effectiveness of centralization on the one hand and the decentralized dispersal of deliberation and popular control on the other. Although Follesdal is opposed to its standard uses, subsidiarity in the EU is one such principle that guides the allocation of authority. Built into the Federalist tradition in this sense is a competition between the center with its constrained supremacy and the claims of the units to self-rule. One role of the center would be to protect the human rights of citizens, a role that is primarily given over to the courts. While allocation problems must be faced in any form of Federalism, this particular dualist understanding concerns the relation among levels within the same territorial boundaries.

If one of the basic functions of the center is to protect basic rights and interests, it would seem that authority would tend to flow upwards, perhaps often to the judiciary as allocator of decisional power. Such a consequentialist argument advocates for a more hierarchical conception of Federalism, one that would certainly make authority in the EU order more statelike than the one I have been defending. While it can also be that sometimes democracy can be served by distributing authority "upwards" to institutions with broader constituencies, Follesdal's more traditional forms of Federalism are more difficult to square with the decentered form of democracy, which, in the case of the EU, provides a way to redefine the interactive relationships among the local, the national and the supranational levels of scale. If this reconstruction of the process of European political integration is correct, it also follows that a more unitary democratic structure would no longer promote popular rule, particularly since it is unable to enhance the capacities of citizens to exercise their sovereignty through new and more direct practices and arrangements. These institutions have decision-making powers that do not directly pass through the center. The traditional, two-level form of Federalism of a center and its penumbra rather than overlapping and dispersed is inadequate to the task of organizing *demoi* rather than a *demos*. This is because it presupposes the traditional answer to the question of "Who is the People?" that divides the polity into either the national level or the international level, leaving aside the whole domain of the transnational in which interaction across levels and polities becomes essential for self-rule.

INSTITUTIONAL SUPREMACY AND COSMOPOLITAN REPUBLICANISM

While multilevel systems have a new salience, they are essential features of the distinctly modern and cosmopolitan form of republicanism that emerged as the hierarchical authority of the state increasingly became intertwined with the spatial expansion of states through colonialism and war. The mechanism here is clear: The colonial periphery could only remain under the control of the metropole by escalating the coercive power of the state, resulting in shifts in authority that undermined republican checks, if they existed at all, upon sovereign power at home and abroad. Given that state power had already expanded beyond its former bounds, the only viable solution was the extension of republican institutions beyond the confines of the state. From Diderot to Kant and Madison, a transnational federation was thought the best solution to the problems posed by emerging European *imperium*, including the undermining of the various constitutional rights and powers of citizens at home (Pagden 1995, 200; Muthu 2003). Indeed, the fundamental experience that informs Enlightenment republican political thought is the need to repudiate two inadequate forms of global political integration. First, like early modern republicans, cosmopolitan republicans rejected the idea of a community of humanity governed by a universal monarchy under a single Christian ruler. But more than that, they rejected all forms of despotism, particularly colonial expansion into Empires. The expansion of Europe came at the price of the domination of non-European peoples. Contrary to the Romantic attempt to divide the world into autonomous and ultimately fictive self-regulating peoples (whatever their internal structure might be), a federation based on interlocking and self-enhancing relationships across various levels of republican institutions was needed to make the accumulation of power within Empires more difficult. These limits on power cannot only be internal to the state, but must also create checks and constraints across state boundaries, if the republican form of government is to be able to promote freedom and security.

Republicans understood the consequences of colonial power in terms of a negative feedback relation: The control exercised abroad very quickly extends to control over citizens at home. The solution to which must make possible common liberty both within and across political communities. This fits well with the republican adage about shared liberty, previously applied only within communities, that each can be free only if *all* are free. The republican defense of federations that disperse powers across institutional levels, deliberative bodies, and various offices permit the transnational extension of a single republic into a union of republics, formed in order to realize freedom from domination at home and abroad.

These cosmopolitan commitments led anticolonial republicans, such as Fletcher, to argue that "mankind would be best preserved from the convolutions of misery, if instead of framing laws for a single society alone, free governments would do so together with the common interests of humanity in mind."[8] This is a republican trope employed by Madison, Kant, Fletcher and many others to distance themselves from world government in the singular, the ideal of the Achaean league of cities, a federation of distinct units that could never become "one vicious and ungovernable city."[9] As Kant put it, in such a federation every state could derive its liberty from the rule of law and thus "expect to be able to derive its security and rights not from its own power and its own legal judgment, but rather solely from this great federation."[10] This union is held together not simply by a joint commitment to democracy and human rights, but also in its consistent republican institutions at all levels, whose fundamental aim is to assure conditions for liberty and security without domination. Contrary to the democratic peace hypothesis, the mere existence of the republican form, in which each still relies "on its own power and its own legal judgments," would be insufficient to establish an order whose aim is to make domination both at home and abroad structurally impossible. In order to avoid domination, a multilevel system operates without the supremacy typical of states and instead checks the exercise of political power by distributing it across the entire institutional structure. According to this Enlightenment strand of republican thought, the republic models shared self-rule without supremacy, since supremacy leads to the loss of liberty across the system as a whole. The problem with modern republics is not size, as early modern republicans had argued, but rather unreconstructed institutional hierarchy. Above all, the hierarchy of states with the demand for supremacy led to systemic violence as an endemic feature of modern political order.

Realizing shared liberty in a "republic of republics" proved to be a difficult task and required nothing short of a new political order. Indeed, the American founders referred to a *novus ordo saeclorum*, a new order for the ages that was neither like early republican city-states nor the "bloated" states of Europe. Such a Union of States would be possible only if each were to become a republic, and if the Union itself were to overcome anarchy and develop into "an alternative to the European Westphalian system rather than an oddly constituted state within it." Madison, Hamilton and others thought of themselves in a long line of republican thinkers whose innovations aimed at overcoming the limitations of the Roman republic and other classical models while also avoiding the problem of the patterns of violence and conflict that had become regularized in the European system of states. As articulated by "Publius" (the pen name for Madison, Hamilton and Jay) in the *Federalist Papers*, the American republic offered an alternative to the Westphalian system of hierarchical states in which security can only be attained at the price of sacrificing liberty. For the international relations theorist Daniel Deudney (2007, 161), the founding of the United States in particular decisively broke institutionally and intellectually with the impasses of previous republics and "was nothing less than the climax of early modern republican security theory" with its emphasis on freedom from domination.[11]

Why do the American Federalists go farther than other European Enlightenment republicans? The dilemmas inherent in Kant's cosmopolitan republicanism help us to see why. At roughly the same time across Europe, Kant saw the balance of power as the preparation for war. In place of this system of power, Kant saw cosmopolitan order as the only way to a lasting peace through the same idea of a transnational extension of republics. Calling the founders of classical international law such as Grotius, Vatell and Puffendorf "sorry panderers," Kant rejected the Westphalian view of state sovereignty, and its claims to sovereign equality of states could be had only with the acceptance of war as a legitimate means to resolve conflicts.[12]

The Westphalian conception of international law as the law of treaties precludes the possibility of any higher legal authority higher than the states. This solution simply leaves the supremacy within states intact. As the supreme authority within its territory, each state is bound internally only by its own laws. Law cannot act as an effective shared constraint on power, even if relations within states are structured by it. Such interdependence of political power with the law is, as Habermas put it, absent at the international level, "where an asymmetrical relation between power and law persists because international legal regulations reflect underlying power relations between states without normatively transforming them."[13]

Kant drew the central republican inference from this absence of legal constraint and thus occupies much of the same republican conceptual space as Publius: "The problem of establishing a perfect constitution depends on the problem of law-governed external relations among nations and cannot be solved unless the latter is."[14] The international law of treaties is insufficient for this task of solving the problem of law-governed external relations; instead it must be superseded by the constitution of a legal community among states, where "every state, even the smallest derives its security and rights not from its own power or its own legal judgments," but rather as a certain kind of republicanism would have it, from "the united power and law governed decisions of a united will." By analogy to the civic constitution and in a rather Hobbesian fashion, Kant hopes that states will renounce "their brutish freedom and seek the calm and security within a law-governed constitution."[15] For Kant, the American and French modern republics show that this can be brought about only by an inclusive popular procedure that makes the people rather than the monarch sovereign, so that the constitution establishes the rule of law through "a republic of republics," a "republicanism of all states" or a world republic. The logic of constitutional states can thus be extended to relations among states, where power will be constrained by the legal supremacy of the united will of the People of all states over the claims of each individual state to act according to its own will.

However much this appeal to popular sovereignty marked a new step in the republican argument for states Unions, Kant thought that this particular transition to a cosmopolitan law was thought of by an analogy to the achieving of a constitutional order through revolutionary means, which institutionalizes the Idea of Republic. Only a republican order would make it possible to fulfill Article Six of the Universal Declaration of Human Rights: "Everyone has the right to recognition everywhere as a person before the law." Or, as Höffe (2005, 121) puts it, in his discussion of Kant's right to freedom, what they lack is the "right to right," or, more accurately the right to law, "the right to be reckoned with in this legal capacity and to integration in the community of persons living in a legal form."[16] It is thus a universal right to legal standing itself that is a necessary condition for external freedom. But only a republican order is able to transform and to not merely regulate relations among states through law in such a way as to achieve lasting, indeed perpetual, peace.

The point of a republic of republics is to internalize all conflicts within a common legal framework, thereby making war and the preparation for war structurally impossible. The same may be true for a universal monarchy, but this non-republican peace would simply be pacification by the "soulless despotism" of something equivalent to universal monarchy. Kant's aim is rather to overcome the structural possibility of violence contained within the international law of the Westphalian system of states by overcoming the dichotomy between the legally secured pacification within the modern state and the external anarchy between states. Even with this properly republican aim, his solution fails to give a sufficient role to popular sovereignty, precisely because Kant lacked a distributed conception of what this might mean. As a consequence, he fails to solve the problem of the supremacy of each state over other states.

After this early republican statement found in his "Idea for a Universal History with Cosmopolitan Intent," Kant's insistence on a republican model of international law does not fundamentally change, even if his attempts to defend the possibility of such a transition to a civic constitution become more and more indirect in a very gradual process of development. But why does Kant go through so many intellectual contortions to solve the problem of a world republic, eventually accepting only the weak "surrogate of a gradually expanding league of nations"? Kant seems to be left with a fundamental contradiction between the freedom that citizens enjoy as members of individual states and the peace that they would only gain by joining together into a world state that guarantees peace and legal rights. Critics of Kant, however, argue that he never fully overcame an overly concretistic conception of a "cosmopolitan condition," where constitutionalism inevitably models this order too closely on the state as a legal order, thus seeing the cosmopolitan order as a potential competitor to the state rather than complementary to its legal forms. If that is the case, then a world state could not really hold out the promise of non-domination, since it would be functionally incapable of securing shared freedom amid cultural and political diversity. For this reason that a world state would be a "soulless despotism," Kant shifts his support to the rather weak idea of an emerging and historically unintended confederation rather than a federation, despite the fact that his guiding idea remains a republic of republics.

How can we get beyond Kant? Here is where we return to Madison and the Federalists. The problem is not that Kant's first solution of a republic of republics is too strong, but rather that Kant did not go far enough. Kant is led into the false dilemma between a despotic world state and the con-tinued anarchy of peoples. The problem is with the particular conception of "indivisible" sovereignty that he took from Rousseau and the French Revolution (Habermas 2006, 128).[17] In fact, in republican constitutions the separation of powers and other procedures for voting and representa-tion suggest that popular sovereignty is possible even in the absence of direct democracy or direct popular rule. Accordingly, the republic of republics should not be thought of as having the form of unitary entity in which the *supremacy* of each is pooled, as Kant does, but as a divided mul-tilevel system in which *popular sovereignty* is distributed. In a transnational federation of republics, popular sovereignty could be distributed across many different processes and locations, some running in parallel (as when many different bodies deliberate independently about the same problem and interactively enact the best solution among all that have been tried). In fact, this very problem of the sovereignty of distinct peoples and states is already operating at various levels of organization (including states) and interdependence (where decisions made at one level will affect decisions made at other levels). This kind of distributed order is the very problem that motivates Madison's conception of a plural or "compound republic," in which sovereignty is divided and yet as Hamilton added authority still rests with the people (Hamilton, Madison and Jay 2003, 253).

In the next section, I argue that the forms of republicanism developed in the American republics secures shared liberty for all and does so by refor-mulating classic modern republicanism as a kind of government without the state that is still able to fulfill the demands of popular sovereignty. Minimally, popular sovereignty requires some republican procedure that works against the despotism of laws imposed from higher levels without the empowered deliberation of citizens divided across various levels and representative bodies. The republican bulwark against despotism is not merely procedural (as Pettit argues), but rather sees republican self-rule as the basis for constraining political violence and insecurity.

FREEDOM AND SECURITY

In the last section, I argued that there is a significant difference between Kant's unified view of sovereignty on the one hand and a "plural" conception on the other that was developed at roughly the same time in the post-revolutionary period in North America. For the Federalists, popular sovereignty is not the result of the indivisible people assembled. Rather, they saw such sovereignty distributed across the republican system in a variety of overlapping processes. Size and diversity were thought of as necessary conditions for freedom and not as impediments to popular rule. In describing this order, Thomas Paine argued that "what Athens was in miniature, America will be in magnitude" and thus clearly indicated another difference from Rousseau's view: Far from being confined to city-states (or to small islands like Corsica in Rousseau's case), the federation's size did not undermine democracy but in fact promoted it.[18]

Even more than this particular innovation in republican thinking, Madison and the Federalists thought of themselves as developing an account of a new kind of political entity that was not modeled on either a European state or a confederation. It would in fact be a Union that at first was expressed in the plural, not "We the People," but "We the Peoples." As a *novus ordo saeclorum*, it was novel enough that no less than Tocqueville, Montesquieu and Hegel all denied that the American Union was a state at all (Hamilton, Madison and Jay 2003, 36–7). It is also not based on the ancient model of the Roman republic, a past example of a large-scale republic that the federalists (like all modern republicans) admired but also thought was deeply flawed. Daniel Deudney (2007, 161) correctly points out that because of its size and diversity, it is better thought of as "an alternative to the Westphalian system" and thus as a new kind of transnational order that attempts to avoid the conflicts and competition that is inherent in the European system. Indeed, the concern with war, safety,and security would lead the Federalists to think that the twin evils of despotism and anarchy were deep problems of the emerging polity, where warfare among the different colonies was considered to be a live possibility. To avoid this kind of violence, they adopted various ways to divide and restrain power, including interacting levels of authority without a sovereign or judge. As such it is the prototype for the international institutions that emerged later in the twentieth century, in the League of Nations and the United Nations, which have the same aim of restricting the potential for violence in the system of states that becomes part of the global basic structure, without the supremacy of a hierarchical judicial structure. While many see such multilevel systems as inherently ineffective, the Federalists saw its effectiveness primarily in structural terms having to do with the advantages of a pluralist approach to the problem of order and as a solution to the problem of sovereignty (Arendt 1963, 168).

For the Federalists, avoiding violence and domination is a two-sided problem: Not only is there anarchy between the states, but conflict and war strengthens the growth of centralized, hierarchical government power within the polity. A union of states guarantees republican order by limiting unconstrained democracy and factional strife within states on the one hand; and, on the other hand, the plurality of units together with the large size of the union lessens the need for a large military force to restrain all of them at once. Further, the capacity of each state to check the centralized power is enhanced by its lack of monopoly over the means to violence, the central feature of Weber's classic sociological definition of a state. With Kant, the Federalists shared the suspicion of standing armies as a tool for popular suppression and the centralization of political authority. The theme is already present in the Declaration of Independence, where the danger of monarchical authority was that it sought to "render the Military independent of Civil Power."[19] As Publius notes "safety from external danger is the most powerful director of national conduct; even the ardent love of liberty gives way to its dictates. To be safe, they at length become willing to run the risk of being less free" (Hamilton, Madison and Jay 2003, 67).

It is important to emphasize that the structural solution offered here is not the same as the well-known and generally Kantian "democratic peace hypothesis," which underestimates the willingness of citizens to surrender liberties for the sake of security. Several such generalizations seem to favor democratic arrangements for avoiding great harms, including famines and wars. The case for democracy as the fundamental factor is well established with respect to famines and less so with respect to war. Many explanations have been offered for why democracy reduces the risk of war, and many of these do not depend on any transformative effects of democratic institutions other than that they provide channels for influence and the expression of citizens' rational interests. Seen more broadly, however, democracy may reasonably be given a more dynamic and transformative role than is usually offered: By being embedded in democratic institutions, agents acquire the normative role of citizens whose exercise of popular sovereignty may provide the means by which to avoid the ills of war.

If this is the explanation of peace, it is important to make clear why war and the preparation for war create insecurity overall. The institutional capability to wage war increases with the executive and administrative powers of the state, which often bypass democratic mechanisms of deliberation and accountability and thus work against democratization (where this is understood precisely as the widening and deepening of the institutional powers of citizens to initiate deliberation and to participate effectively in it). At the same time, participating in national self-defense paradoxically has often been accompanied by the emergence of new rights or their broader attribution to more of the population. Charles Tilly (1990) has argued that warfare may have historically been an important mechanism for the introduction of social rights, as the state became more and more dependent on the willingness of citizens to accept the obligations of military service. As modern warfare became increasingly lethal and professionalized, however, the institutional powers of the state have outstripped this and other democratic mechanisms. The institutionally embedded normative powers of citizens are no longer sufficient to check the institutional powers to initiate wars, and these arrangements have left citizens vulnerable to expanding militarization that has weakened these same freedoms. A new dialectic between the declining political and legal capacities of citizens and the increasing instrumental powers of states has not yet reached any equilibrium, so that we now witness as a common occurrence the loss of liberty for the sake of safety.

Once the institutional mechanisms of war-making shift from representative bodies toward much less accountable administrative and executive functions and thus undermine the balance of institutional powers within a democracy, the expansive effects abroad created by democratically organized institutions of domestic politics seem much less likely. Even a hegemonic powerful state such as the United States continues to face the twin problems of anarchy and despotism. We still face a basic dilemma:

76

The promotion of peace requires government, even if it could be better realized without a unitary state. Such transnational unions are beginning to take shape that are stronger than simple confederation and yet effective without supremacy and other statelike features.

Government without the state: the plural republic

With their experience of being at the periphery of a colonial power, the Federalists sought a new basis for republican self-rule that overcame many of the contradictions and impasses of previous republics. Indeed, this sort of innovation was necessary, if the constitution was to deal with the unprecedented circumstances and difficulties of the founding, including deep problems of insecurity with relation to the European powers. Because they sought to find a way out of the impasses of European republics, which did not survive long in the European state system, their model emerged out of criticisms of ancient and modern forms. It would be a mistake, on the one hand, to romanticize the founding of the United States; but it would also be a mistake to miss the relevance of its basic innovation of a Union of States, a union which is from the start fundamentally transnational and has successors in the United States of Europe, or the European Union as it is better known. Its Federalist founder, Alterio Spinelli, sought to form a union of states in Europe in response to the unprecedented violence and interstate anarchy of World War II.

Hamilton already clearly saw the Union of the States as a solution to the problem of Westphalian anarchy "between a number of independent, unconnected sovereignties," between which war would be inevitable if wider institutional structures were not created. At the same time, he argued that if this unity was too strong, it would devolve into a despotic and hierarchical state. But since the states all had similar constitutions, where each of them was a republic that was characterized by popular sovereignty, how could the Union appeal to as its principle? Madison addresses this issue in his affirmation of the extended republic, rejecting Brutus' Antifederalist and traditional republican argument that "a free republic cannot succeed over a country of immense extent" nor can it use the devices of popular rule (Hamilton, Madison and Jay 2003, 444). His well-known discussion of the mischief of factions is placed within an argument about the extended republic, which concerns not only matters of size and the need for delegation, but also that all the units be governed by popular, but nonetheless indirect, sovereignty. Here "the excellences

77

of popular government may be retained and its imperfections avoided" by having a legislature represent the people.[20] But when we look at the system as a whole we see that popular sovereignty is distributed both to the states and to the government of the whole; both are locations for the exercise of popular sovereignty, particularly in the Lockean sense that the people could overthrow the system as a whole should it fail to attain republican liberty. Often smaller units defend unitary and independent sovereignty, but risk losing their sovereignty internally through factions or conquest by larger, hierarchical states; extended republics could retain sovereignty by distributing it and thus making it plural rather than unitary.

How are we to think of distributed sovereignty? There is certainly an ongoing tension in the history of the United States, with the interpretation and location of popular sovereignty being extremely contested from the debates prior to the Civil War period, in which the North sought to locate sovereignty in one unitary location. Later, in the New Deal, sovereignty is primarily at the Federal or national level, and hence evolves toward government that is able to deal with the pressures of the modern economy and other forms of complexity grow. Before we argue for unified sovereignty, the circumstances of politics have changed radically once again, giving the idea of a distributed republic and even a republic of republics a new salience. However, many social scientists now argue that unitary Federal sovereignty, the favored interpretation at the political level, now faces challenges of globalization that it cannot meet so long as sovereignty is not once again thought of and institutionalized in a distributed and plural way. At the same time, new types of political order are emerging, such as the European Union, which have attempted to realize plural sovereignty and new forms of citizenship.

Rather than look to multination-states, the current circumstances suggest looking directly at transnational models for plural and distributed sovereignty. The European Union provides a more appropriate model for a democratic transnational polity than either intergovernmental agreement or liberal multilateralism, both of which fail to see the European Union as a polity with a plural political subject. No longer simply operating with treaty agreements among independent liberal states, the institutions of the European Union have come to regard the citizens of its member states also as citizens of the EU and thus as having claims upon other EU states. Moreover, the EU polity is not understood in terms of the self-governance of citizens as members of a single *demos*, but rather in terms of multiple and overlapping *demoi*; the regime is then not such that all must participate in the same set of institutions or suffer the consequences of a uniform policy. More than simply adding a new layer of authority, the EU provides a way to redefine the interactive relationships among the local, the national and the supranational levels of scale. If this type of reconstruction of the process of European political integration is correct, it also follows that a more unitary democratic structure would no longer be normatively desirable, particularly since it is unable to enhance the capacities of citizens to exercise their sovereignty through new and more direct practices and arrangements. Indeed, we might see the EU as a kind of extended republic.

FEDERALISM AND TRANSNATIONAL FEDERALISM

For Follesdal and others, Federalism provides a solution to the problem of divided authority in the multilevel polity, taking it to be the issue of sharing and distributing power between the center and the periphery.[21] It is also an alternative to taking the principle of subsidiarity as a way to address the democratic deficit in the EU as a matter of granting autonomous control at the appropriate level to those who are immediately concerned and most affected. Follesdal rightly argues that the principle fails to address the most pressing problem of democracy in the EU: developing forms of deliberation that operate across these various units and develop practices of democracy at what I would call the transnational level. Moreover, he argues that subsidiarity leaves the shared objectives of the EU unclear, objectives which can only be developed over time, but these possible goals fixed by deliberation in the future cannot now function to legitimate exclusive domain of competence for EU law. But this is already to conceive of the EU as the center. As Gerald Ruggie (1996, 195) puts it, acting as a member state "endogenizes" the practices in which people regard themselves both as citizens of their state and simultaneously as citizens of the EU. For such citizens, the EU is not simply some new kind of identity over and above being the national citizenship, but rather its extension with new capacities and powers so as to make their participation and influence in various sorts of arenas more effective. It is on this basis that we can say that as a multilevel system the EU extends democratic practices without which the expanding administrative capacities of the state might undermine citizenship at the EU level as offering modes of participation and novel decentralized practices of policy formation such as the Open Method of Cooperation (OMC). Such practices of citizenship cannot be adequately conceived on the two-level Federalist model, which seems to retain more of the conception of solidarity than its quite forceful critique seems to suppose.

The European Union does not seek to constitute a "People" that it is supposed to organize into a political subject. Instead, the more modest goal, as stated in the treaties that have developed its structure from a "Coal and Steel Community" to a political union, the purpose of which is explicitly stated in the Preamble as "bringing the peoples of Europe together in an ever closer Union." In the recent attempt to ratify a European constitution that would replace the various treaties, the main purpose of this democratic reform would be to address the issue of the potential losses of freedom from domination in a polity in which the political subject of democracy is plural, *demoi* rather than a *demos*. This attempt to create a democracy of *demoi* may seem paradoxical if citizens are to achieve the ideal of self-rule by becoming both authors and subjects of the laws of Europe. Yet, as Bruce Ackerman has pointed out against such a "monistic" interpretation of constitutional structures of the United States, there is no one privileged place in which the popular will is located by some naïve synecdoche that takes the part for the whole. The EU still has no distinctive popular legislative body, since its parliament does not have the authority to enact the law directly. And even if the European parliament (EP) came to have this authority, its pluralistic structure as a democracy of *demoi* undermines any simple monism as well as any claim that the EP would somehow uniquely represent the People.

The only solution is, then, as Henry Richardson[22] has put it, to generalize representation and thus to look for a way in which "the processes that form the popular will can be distributed across the various parts of the constitutional structure." The difficulty here is that in the case of the European Union, it is the executive power of the Council, as empowered in the 2001 Laeken Declaration that has the legitimate formal right to make such a constitutional proposal, independently of any exercise of the popular will. But if citizens are to be engaged both as citizens of Europe and of the member states, their will must be engaged at various stages and locations in the process. The challenge of democratic reform of the European Union is that citizens have to appeal to normative powers that are not already constituted in some institutional structure and thus to their intrinsic democratic authority to recreate those institutions that constitute their normative powers in the first place. This kind of reflexivity is the essential innovation of democracy that makes it the proper means to overcome institutional forms of domination, and in this case it would come from new kinds of decision-making powers that cut across borders and are not neatly assigned to any one specific level.

How might this kind of political subject be organized? Weiler ambiguously describes the EU as a community in first-personal terms as "*a people,*" even if he immediately adds "a people, if you wish, of others." Thus, the requirements of a differentiated institutional structure hold for the same democratic reasons, regardless of the scale of the polity: only a polity of others, a community of *demoi*. If this were the case, the solution would be to find the proper and authoritative *demos*. Indeed, according to this conception, the larger the *demos*, the more democratic authority it has to be the voice of the people. Rather, the problem of *demoi* becomes acute when the issue of sovereignty is raised: Does democracy then require, as Dahl argues, that one of the many units or *demoi* is sovereign so that this *demos* "has control over all the others"?[23] If this is the case, then the European Union may better be thought of as a new kind of state, since the locus of control would then be the place in the structure in which popular sovereignty is exercised. This would give to the Union not only legal supremacy, but also make policies as uniform as possible across the EU, something which is not the case for a pure plural union. As we saw in the criticism of Follesdal's two-level Federalism, subsidiarity excludes the benefits not only of political interaction across levels, but also of dispersed popular sovereignty.

It might seem that from a Madisonian perspective, something like a representative legislature would be sufficient for such a large and extended republic. However, simply giving the EP as a body of representative member states greater powers than it currently has is insufficient to distribute decision-making power and hence popular sovereignty in the Union. Although for Madison "all authority proceeds from the people," such authority is distributed across many different locations. This means that the people do not rule directly, but through a variety of bodies and processes. Popular sovereignty is thus understood here in a procedural sense that was also distributed across a variety of forms, so that in a non-hierarchical Federal form of a multilevel states union, it is possible for popular sovereignty to be compatible with the corresponding "chains of legitimation" that unfold in parallel within and across the member states. This issue concerns the distributed form of inquiry that transnational institutions take to be necessary to inform their decision-making processes. Here Madison's rejection of a unicameral legislature lead him to defend

81

a bicameral legislature as representing different locations for popular sovereignty and whose deliberations ran in parallel with each other. Once again this kind of divided popular sovereignty had the purpose of preventing the domination and insecurity of the smaller states by the larger ones that would collapse the new order into a "simple republic." The equal votes of each state regardless of size are "a constitutional recognition of the portion of sovereignty remaining in the individual states" (Hamilton, Madison and Jay 2003, 301).[24] Accordingly, the Senate represented "the states," while the House represented "the people," so that no law is passed unless tested by different deliberative bodies and distinct forms of representation: the majority of people and the majority of states, each of which has its own perspectives and which retain a part of distributed sovereignty across units (*ibid.*).

Even with such constitutional provisions as entrenched plural sovereignty and parallel deliberative processes, multilevel polities inevitably encounter various jurisdictional and boundary problems that come with maintaining such a pluralism of *demoi*. In the EU thus far, such conflicts are dealt with through adjudication in various courts (or by a constitutional court in polities with a constitutional settlement). This model has its force precisely because functions cannot be neatly dispersed to specific institutions and thus must permit a wide range of different organizational forms and institutions interacting with one another in cases of conflict. If multilevel systems are formed in such a way as to distribute functions to various levels and that level alone, this kind of conflict is overcome, but at the cost of what is interesting about transnational political orders such as the European Union. But if courts take over too many political functions by being arbiters of jurisdictional conflicts in the multilevel system, the supremacy of Community could undermine the dispersed form of popular sovereignty and "lead to a hierarchical relationship between Community and national law, which is at the same time a hierarchical relationship between liberal and republican constitutional principles" (Scharpf 2009, 193). In the long run this solution is unstable to the extent that it cannot make room for legitimate democratic demands for self-rule, where juridification could lead to "the extreme case of a polity conforming to liberal principles which, at the same time, lacks practically all republican credentials" (Scharpf 2009, 176). This is evidenced in the way that courts have interpreted national wage standards for workers as violations of freedom of trade in the Union. Either too much centralization or too much decentralization creates the potential for boundary disputes that result in increased potential for domination in multilevel systems.

How might this tendency be overcome in the EU's multilevel system? While I cannot fully answer this question here, it is important for multilevel systems to develop a range of intermediaries beyond the courts, including the EP and various citizen bodies to address such cases of jurisdictional conflict deliberatively. In considering possible institutional designs that enhance and democratize deliberation, it is necessary to see that different institutional arrangements can function best at different levels and scales, and distribute decisional authority across the local, the national, the regional and the transnational levels. This will require different forms of representation at various levels, with different modes of constituency and legitimacy. Legitimacy in this context primarily concerns issues related to binding decisions, even if the exercise of communicative freedom continues to influence the generation of communicative power.

While we can look at various types of institutions, it is important to put all of this in the context of a larger whole, which Mansbridge, Dryzek and others have called "a deliberative system."[25] Such an account checks the tendency to see only one sort of representative body as distinctively democratic or closer to some particular democratic ideal. Or, as Dryzek argues, we might see interactive effects, where weaknesses in one part of the deliberative system is compensated for by developments in another part, say the informal public sphere compensating for poor deliberation in the formal bodies such as legislatures. The effects could go the other way, where the presence of deliberative institutions like a constitutional court could permit legislatures to propose bad laws simply to appeal to voters, expecting them to be struck down. Currently, different forms of democracy are often discussed, such as corporatist or consociational democracy, and we might see such variety in deliberative systems. This suggests that we do not need to idealize deliberation in each dimension (or that a particular part must be maximally deliberative according to its type), but must rather test the deliberative system as a whole and how it functions overall according to a basic list of democratic functions, including representation. A clear methodological advantage of the deliberative system approach is that it permits not just various sites for deliberation, but also relations across levels. Here I want to focus on the ways in which deliberative representation can be extended across various scales and levels, as well as develop procedures that do not require the use of electoral bodies. Rather, representative bodies of citizens can instead be used to settle many issues through deliberation.

CONTEMPORARY MULTILEVEL SYSTEMS

There are of course a variety of other justifications for such a transnational order. One returns to the republican idea of security. Transnational political orders such as the European Union have been able to extend the normative powers of citizens and create conditions in which non-citizens can take up such active powers in order to transform their circumstances of domination. Expanding republican security as Madison and others did in their day now requires creating conditions for active citizenship as a means for democratization at the transnational level, and in this way institutionalizes stronger connections between democratic institutions and nascent global publics. At a more structural level, the European Union represents the project of building a democratic polity of *demoi* necessary for the right sort of positive feedback relations between democracy at the state and transnational levels. But as security policies based on war erode the very democracy they are supposed to protect, a new kind of transnational democratization is essential to the project of an expanding peace and security in a way that is not democratically self-defeating.

This understanding of the EU also lends support to the idea of democratic security, that is, security that does not come at the cost of hierarchy. Republican and liberal ideas gave rise to a new interpretation of the international order. Indeed even prior to the New Deal Wilson and others, much as Kant did before them, saw that the same structural possibility could apply across states as a necessary condition for preserving republics as free government. In the aftermath of World War I, Wilson attempted to establish a "league of nations," to create this possibility of "making the world safe for democracy." As Daniel Deudney puts it, "the core part of Wilsonian Liberal internationalism is Madisonism in the context of global interdependence."[26] The idea here should be familiar: Democracy at home is related to peace abroad. Or to put it in republican terms: Domination abroad is inconsistent with nondomination at home. This strand of liberal-republican internationalism suggests that the idea of a hegemon striving to institute a peaceful order is a nonstarter. Perhaps by some historical amnesia, we ignore to our peril that internationalism is quite consistent with the American constitutional principles; indeed they have been used to connect democracy within the emergence of new institutions such as the United Nations and the Universal Declaration of Human Rights. But on this interpretation, a States Union is not based on shared or pooled sovereignty, distributed across various institutions, nor on popular sovereignty, but on the mutual recognition of sovereign states. It is better to pursue, as the EU does, a new form of political order that is neither national nor international. Here we should more clearly distinguish between an international order in which state sovereignty is the ordering principle from a multilevel transnational order in which *citizens* can exercise empowered deliberation at a much larger scale.

The biggest difference between the EU and delegative and international institutions such as the World Trade Organization (WTO) is precisely that the EU is not an organization established around particular targeted interests, but a polity, and thus already has an established framework for accountability through open and multiperspectival deliberative inquiry. The EU's explicit recognition of political rights as human rights empowers all those affected by authoritative decisions with normative powers and opportunities to exercise voice, including rights of participation. This makes it possible for citizens of the EU to make claims rather than simply challenge decisions; that is, they may appeal not only to basic principles of democracy and human rights, but also to political institutions that should be responsive to their claims. To be truly democratic and reflexive, however, participants must be empowered to change the normative framework as well, and this capacity requires a constitution. Calls for greater transparency or for participation by civil society are not really the answer, however, since the weaknesses here are more structural. The transnational principle of institutional differentiation along with a complex separation of powers requires multiple, cross-cutting and intersecting processes of public deliberation within a revisable framework. Multilevel systems provide the institutional framework in which to distribute the various types and forms of deliberation that make up a transnational deliberative system.

CONCLUSION

Using Kant as a foil, I have argued for the broadly Madisonian view that contemporary cosmopolitan republicanism ought to be guided by the fundamental principle of distributed popular sovereignty. In this way, Madison and the Federalists take us beyond the dilemmas of Kantian cosmopolitanism. Indeed, the Federalists thought of their conception of a States Union as an alternative to the European Wesphalian system of hierarchical states. In going beyond unified popular sovereignty even while seeing that "all authority proceeds from the People," Madison laid the groundwork for a conception of plural and distributed popular sovereignty that is still applicable to contemporary transnational orders such as the European Union. By pooling their sovereignty, such states promote their shared freedom from domination and avoid the costs of security without freedom. The solution to this problem for Madison was the States Union, in which popular sovereignty became plural and distributed across the whole entire institutional structure. While the emerging institutional order promoted by Liberal Internationalists such as Wilson and Roosevelt also bears the stamp of cosmopolitan, republican thinking, this order was about restricting sovereignty through mutual self-limitation rather than a States Union. With the emergence of the European Union, for all its flaws, a new version of such a transnational order has been realized, this time with a stronger emphasis on more directly deliberative processes than the Federalists would have allowed.

With increasing global interdependence, it is time to revive this Madisonian strand of American political thought, with its unique attempt to unite a peaceful transnational order with popular democratic rule. If this institutional form, suitably revised, was adopted it would not signal the disappearance of states, but a transformation from state to popular sovereignty as the basic principle of transnational institutions. My argument aims at affirming the superiority of the idea of a union of states as a solution to anarchy and despotism, although only in the form of a multilevel system. But this multilevel system cannot be a two-level system of center and subunits, but rather must be explicitly linked to the democratic ideal of a plural and distributed popular sovereignty and a functioning deliberative system that incorporates a variety of perspectives and cuts across the various levels. Only such a plural republic can avoid domination and insecurity.

References

Arendt, H. (1963). *On Revolution*. New York: Viking Press.

Bernard, N. (2003). *Multilevel Governance in the European Union*. Amsterdam: Kluwer.

Bowman, J. (2006). "The European Union Democratic Deficit: Federalists, Revisionists, and Skeptics." *European Journal of Political Theory* 5: 191–212.

Dahl, R. (1983). "Federalism and the Democratic Process." In: *Liberal Democracy*. Eds J. Pennock and J. Chapman, New York: New York University Press: 95–108.

Deudney, D. (2007). *Bounding Power: Republican Security Theory from the Polis to the Global Village*. Princeton: Princeton University Press.

Dryzek, J. (2010). *Foundations and Frontiers of Deliberative Governance*. Oxford: Oxford University Press.

Flikschuh, K. (2010). "Kant's Sovereignty Dilemma: A Contemporary Analysis." *The Journal of Political Philosophy* 18: 469–93.

Follesdal, A. (1998). "Survey Article: Subsidiarity." *Journal of Political Philosophy* 6: 190–219.

Follesdal, A. (2006). "Subsidiarity, Democracy, and Human Rights in the Constitutional Treaty of Europe." *Journal of Social Philosophy* 37: 61–80.

Follesdal, A. (2010). "Non-State Oriented Political Theory: A Critical Assessment." In: *Political Theory of the European Union*. Eds Jürgen Neyer and Antje Wiener, Oxford: Oxford University Press: 205–12.

Habermas, J. (2006). *The Divided West*. Cambridge: Polity Press.

Hamilton, A., J. Madison and J. Jay (2003). *The Federalist*. Ed. T. Ball, Cambridge: Cambridge University Press.

Höffe, O. (2005). *Kant's Cosmopolitan Theory of Law and Peace*. Cambridge: Cambridge University Press.

Kant, I. (1970). *Political Writings*. Cambridge: Cambridge University Press.

Mansbridge, J. (1999). "Everyday Talk in the Deliberative System." In: *Deliberative Politics*. Ed. S. Macedo, New York: Oxford University Press: 211–39.

Muthu, S. (2003). *Enlightenment against Empire*. Princeton: Princeton University Press.

Pagden, A. (1995). *Lords of All the World*. New Haven: Yale University Press.

Paine, T. (1989). "The Rights of Man." In: T. Paine. *Political Writings*. Cambridge: Cambridge University Press: 57–264.

Parkinson, J. (2006). *Deliberating in the Real World*. Oxford: Oxford University Press.

Richardson, H. (2002). *Democratic Autonomy*. Oxford: Oxford University Press.

Ruggie, G. (1996). *Constructing the World Polity*. London: Routledge.

Scharpf, F. (2009). "Legitimacy in the Multilevel European Polity." *European Political Science Review* 1: 173–204.

Tilly, C. (1990). *Coercion, Capital and European States*. London: Blackwell.

Notes

1. See Bernard 2002, 3.
2. See Bernard 2002, 3–4.
3. On the democratizing role of the European Union in recognizing and extending the normative powers entailed by human rights independent of any particular citizenship, see Bowman 2006.
4. See Follesdal 2006.
5. See Hamilton, Madison and Jay 2003, 228.
6. On the principle of subsidiarity, see Follesdal 2006, 1998.
7. See Follesdal 2010.
8. See Pagden 1995, 138.
9. Pagden 1995, 188.

10. See Kant 1970, 47.
11. Deudney 2007, 161.
12. See Kant 1970, 73.
13. Habermas 2006, 128.
14. Kant 1970, 47.
15. Kant 1970, 48.
16. The pun "*Recht auf Recht*" that Höffe employs exploits the well-known ambiguity of *Recht* as both right and law; it is thus both the right to right and the right to legal status, where the latter specifies the meaning of the former.
17. Moreover, the case can be made that Kant does not hold the dispersed view of sovereignty concerning states. For a discussion of Kant's "sovereignty dilemma" as related to the supremacy of states as enforcers of Right, see Flikschuh 2010. Hannah Arendt 1963, 166–8 argued that the Federalists found "the sole alternative to the nation-state principle" and with it the solution to the dilemmas of sovereignty. What they found, in my view, are the advantages of multilevel systems for popular sovereignty.
18. Paine 1989, 185.
19. Deudney 2007, 167–8.
20. See *Federalist 9*.
21. See Follesdal 2006, 2010.
22. See Richardson 2002, 70.
23. See Dahl 1983, 96.
24. Hamilton, Madison and Jay 2003, 301.
25. On the first use of the idea of a deliberative system see Mansbridge 1999. For recent developments, see Dryzek 2010 and Parkinson 2006.
26. Deudney 2007, 186.

CHAPTER 4

Republicanism and Democracy[1]
John P. McCormick

Democrats should worry when philosophers begin to speak the language of "republicanism." When philosophers espouse purportedly objective principles, such as the common good, the rule of law, depolitization – that is, normative standards that they claim will make democracy operate more justly – democrats should be very worried indeed. History teaches that this discourse of republicanism – of a common good not fully achievable through extensive popular participation and ultimate popular judgment – enjoys a rather dubious legacy. Republicanism, in its original forms, either prompted aristocratic coups against popular governments, or justified oligarchic consolidation once democratic regimes had been overthrown. On principle, neither of these outcomes is necessarily problematic for contemporary adherents of philosophical republicanism; after all, as I demonstrate in what follows, they value popular participation much less than they do policy outcomes that supposedly benefit the populace at large or track the common good. Minimal authorization of elite governance by common citizens, they suppose, is sufficient to promote and protect liberty.

In the first part of this paper, I show how the minimizing or narrowing of popular participation advocated by philosophical republicans of the past like Cicero, Bruni and Guicciardini led to political outcomes that did not track the common good as perceived or avowed by most citizens within their republics. In the short run, the sharp curtailing of popular participation in such contexts only served the interests of the elites consequently empowered to act on behalf of the people; and, in the long run, popular marginalization and elite empowerment invariably led to the collapse of the regimes served by these vaunted republican philosopher-statesmen. In the second part, I highlight significant affinities shared by exponents of traditional republicanism and the work of the most prominent and intellectually formidable philosopher who advances "republicanism" today, namely, Philip Pettit. In the third section, I draw on the writings of Machiavelli to argue, contra republicans traditional and contemporary, that the people are much more likely than the few to make decisions conducive to the common good within republics; and that therefore political democracy that empowers the people to deliberate and decide policy themselves is preferable on normative and empirical grounds to philosophical republicanism that empowers neutral or "depoliticized" experts and representatives to decide for the people.

I. PHILOSOPHICAL REPUBLICANISM FROM A HISTORICAL PERSPECTIVE

John Dunn (2006, 17) recently reminds us of an essential point that Moses Finley (1985, 28) made decades ago: Western philosophy emerges as a hostile response to democratic politics and society. There is no need to remind one of the enormous overlap between the oligarchic and philosophic critiques of Athens, an overlap best exemplified by Plato's and, to a lesser extent, Aristotle's writings. The critique of Athenian democracy is inextricably bound to the moral and philosophical projects of both authors, and is quite pertinent to their endorsements of the oligarchies and tyrannies that usurped or supplanted rule by the *demos* in Athens and other Greek democracies during their lifetimes.

The writings of Italian authors associated more directly with "republicanism" as such are just as antidemocratic and oligarchally inclined, and also can be situated in close proximity to subversions or usurpations of popular governments: I refer specifically here to the philosopher-statesmen Marcus Tullius Cicero, Leonardo Bruni and Francesco Guicciardini. Cicero insisted that the senate secure a monopoly over policy making within the Roman republic: He openly advocated manipulation of plebeian magistrates like the tribunes, public rather than secret ballots, and the influence of patrons over clients to ensure the compliance of common citizens with the senate's will. For Cicero, the common good is best served when the republic's wisest and most virtuous men, collected in the senate, deliberate over and decide policy. The people's participation should be confined to little more than deciding, via elections, which individuals eventually become senators, and to acclaiming as law policies made by the republic's best men.[2]

Did Cicero's aristocratic republicanism, which sought to neutralize the republic's plebeian-empowering institutions, the tribunes and the popular assemblies, serve the common good in Rome? This would be hard to argue. Cicero and fellow senators opposed attempts by the *populares* to address the economic-military crisis that was destroying the republic (Murray 1966; Seager 1972; Wood 1988, 204–5). Roman citizen-soldiers were forced into increasing poverty when senators and their clients refused to share public lands with them; in fact, they even refused to employ poor citizens to work such lands, opting to hire much cheaper slave labor instead. The more the people clamored for land redistribution, the more the senate advocated the conquest of ever more distant lands. In so doing, they hoped to acquire territory that only nobles, and not plebeians, could afford to make profitable. As a result of such policies, citizen-soldiers began to live for longer periods of time with their commanders away from Rome, and thus became economically dependent on their generals, to whom, instead of the republic, they now pledged their loyalty. These circumstances, of course, culminated in the civil wars among Rome's military commanders that cost Cicero his life and the republic its liberty (Plutarch 2005, 323–73).

In a similar vein, Bruni, whom Hans Baron (1966) identified as the founder of Florentine civic republicanism, served as intellectual spokesman for the oligarchy that replaced generations of popular rule exercised through guild corporatism in the Florentine republic (Najemy 1982). Bruni (1987, 116–26, 171–4) celebrated, in classical philosophical terms, practices of popular "participation" that, in fact, had been quite recently denuded of any significance by the oligarchy led by the Albizzi family (Hankins 2000, 1–14, 75–178). After destroying guild-republican institutions, the Albizzeans opened the magistracies of Florentine government to a wider number of citizens than ever before; *but* they reserved all consequential decisions to themselves. The Florentine patricians deliberated and decided public policy in consultative sessions (compiled in the *Consulte e Practiche*), dictating it to the magistrates for implementation (Najemy 1982). Did this dramatic narrowing of Florence's decision-making procedures produce better public policy than Florence's more popularly participatory regimes? Hardly. The leading citizens could not successfully resolve conflicts among themselves, and they corrupted the civic culture of common citizens to such an extent that circumstances were ripe for the

Medici family to emerge as tyrants of the city (Machiavelli FH IV. 2–4).

Finally, Guicciardini crystallized the aspirations of wealthy and notable citizens within republics and served as a crucial conduit between the republicanisms of Cicero and James Madison (McCormick n.d.). After the Medici's expulsion, Florence reinstated popular government: a *governo largo* characterized by a large, Athenian-style citizen assembly and, eventually, by magistrate appointment procedures that mixed lottery and election. In protest, Guicciardini proposed simple election as the proper mode of appointing magistrates and the establishment of a senate, where policy would be more substantively discussed and better decided than in the Great Council. Such reforms, he claimed, would allow the most wise, prudent and virtuous men, rather than the variable, ignorant and jealous multitude, to decide what is best for the city (Guicciardini 1998). We don't know whether Guicciardini's proposal to reform Florence as an electoral/senatorial republic would have resulted in a government that better realized the common good than did the *governo largo*; when his wealthy friends and relatives did not win such reforms, they summoned the Spanish army and placed the republic once again in Medici hands.

As I will explain further in Part 3, Niccolò Machiavelli explicitly understood himself to be arguing against the electoral/senatorial republicanism of the philosopher-statesmen mentioned above. Machiavelli's greatest work, *Discourses on Titus Livy's First Ten Books*,[3] recommended the following practices of elite accountability that transcend elections: offices or assemblies empowered with veto or legislative authority that exclude the wealthiest citizens from eligibility; magistrate appointment procedures that combine lottery and election; and political trials in which the entire citizenry acts as ultimate judge over prosecutions and appeals. Moreover, unlike republicans like Cicero, Bruni and Guicciardini, who reserved important policy decisions for a senatorial elite, Machiavelli insisted that republics afford common citizens the opportunity to discuss and vote directly on legislation. He declared that widely inclusive rather than elite-dominated fora produce better policies for regimes characterized by a "civil way of life." Put simply, Machiavelli's political theory was more popularly participatory and empowering than republicanism, generally, and, for that matter, than democracy as it is generally practiced and conceptualized today (McCormick 2010).

2. Pettit between Republicanism and Democracy

In the pathbreaking books *Republicanism* and *A Theory of Freedom*, Philip Pettit (1999a, 2001) formulates a philosophically systematic theory of republican liberty that he hopes will enable more fruitful evaluations of contemporary politics: freedom as nondomination. In these and subsequent writings, Pettit (1999b, 2004) also proposes institutional reforms through which liberty as nondomination might be more fully realized and contemporary democracy might be substantively enhanced (Pettit 2000, 105). Pettit derives this republican theory of freedom from an interpretation of the history of Anglo-European political thought that sharply, perhaps too sharply, distinguishes liberal from republican conceptions of freedom.[4] The former tradition, Pettit avers, exclusively upholds the principle of freedom as noninterference; that is, liberalism seeks to free individuals from direct forms of interference, from actual constraints, physical impediments, and so forth. Republicanism, on the contrary, upholds the broader, more robust, normative standard of freedom from domination.

For Pettit, "domination" obtains in circumstances where individuals suffer subordination, whether or not some other agent actually intervenes in their lives at any particular moment; the mere threat, either implicit or explicit, of arbitrary interference by another is sufficient to warrant the attribution of domination to such a relationship, whether social or political. Pettit defines as "arbitrary" any interference that does not comport with the perceived or expressed interest of individuals; he catalogs instances of arbitrary interference by private parties over other such parties under the term *dominium*; and he lists governmental actions that violate the "common avowable interests" of individuals under the category, *imperium*.[5]

In this section, I suggest that Pettit's account of liberty as nondomination posits two goals that actually conflict with each other: On the one hand, he takes great pains to situate liberty as nondomination within "the broad republican tradition," while, on the other, he suggests that his theory of freedom is best secured by practices that he associates with "democracy, electoral and contestatory," an institutional ensemble that Pettit promotes as a superior alternative to democracy as conventionally practiced and understood. I argue that the first effort seriously undermines the second; in fact, I demonstrate that Pettit's committed adherence to republicanism compels him to endorse some of the aspects of contemporary "democratic" politics that are least friendly to liberty, conceived in Pettit's own terms.

Election and Contestation: Through various iterations of his theory of republicanism, Pettit freely expresses suspicion of both popular judgment and majoritarian politics. Unlike, for instance, Athenian democrats, Roman *populares* and Florentine guildsmen, Pettit ascribes no superior moral status, no particular *onestà*, to wide and efficacious popular participation. As Pettit describes the intellectual legacy to which he adheres:

> [T]he writers who identify with the broad republican tradition of thinking take liberty to be defined by a status in which the evils associated with interference are avoided rather than by access to the instruments of democratic control, participatory or representative."[6]

(Pettit 1999a, 30)

Following Quentin Skinner in certain respects, Pettit (1999a, 28) credits Machiavelli with shaping a republican tradition that focused on "avoiding interference rather than on achieving participation;" moreover, he places Machiavelli alongside Cicero, Harrington, Sidney and Montesquieu as an author who does not embrace a "positive concept of liberty," who does not associate freedom with "a self-determining democracy" and who does not, first and foremost, prioritize "participation" (Pettit 1999a, 187; 1999b, 166).

To be sure, Pettit (1999a, 30) defines republican liberty in light of the "common avowable interests" of citizens, that is, the interests that citizens recognize as being shared in common with each other.[7] But, in line with his interpretation of the republican tradition, the means of participation that Pettit endorses by which citizens avow or express those interests are, in fact, quite narrow. Pettit agrees with Aristotle, Cicero, Bruni, Guicciardini and Madison that collective participation need not extend much beyond the people's choice of the specific individuals who will hold office. Participation need not transcend the politics of election. For instance, Pettit (1999a, 29) favorably invokes the English republicans, Richard Price and Joseph Priestly, who confine participation to, respectively, "choosing representatives" and "voting." As Pettit remarks in *Republicanism*:

> Electoral standing gives the collective people the power of an indirect author in relation to governmental laws and decisions. They may not be the authors of what those in government say and do, but they determine who the authors shall be or at least who the overseers of the authors shall be.

(Petit 1999a, 294)

94

Pettit (2001, 161; 2000, 125) repeatedly affirms that the people ought to act only as the "indirect" authors of public policy; they may be, in some sense, "enabled" as authors of the law, but only "imperfectly" so. In this spirit, Pettit (2000, 114, 106) defines democracy as "a system of government under which those who are governed enjoy a certain control over those who govern them," and he concedes that the idea of "a certain control" is sufficiently "vague" not to imply total or perhaps even a preponderance of control by the governed.[8] On such grounds, Pettit (2004, 52) commits himself to a form of government where real political control lies not with the people but "is left wholly or mainly to representatives in parliament, or to a government with a parliamentary majority, or to an elected administration." Consequently, representative democracy and electoral politics, according to Pettit (1999a, 168), "realize" public opinion only in a highly mediated way.

Elections, in Pettit's estimation, generally communicate to those who make policy what the "popular valuation" concerning the common good is, such that representatives can proceed to govern on that basis (Pettit 2004, 58; cf. 1999b, 173). While the people neither formulate policy themselves nor specifically instruct elected officials on how to make policy, they do nevertheless give officials a general sense of what their conception of the common good is, such that the representatives can use the wide discretion entailed by electoral politics in genuine efforts to realize that good. Unlike direct democracy, Athenian or plebiscitary, which endeavors to express the collective will of most citizens, Pettit thus espouses a form of indirect democracy, where the public deliberation accompanying electoral contests and the political authorization signaled by electoral results serve to guide policymakers in the performance of their duties.

> [T]he people should control government democratically because that is the only mode of control under which those reasons can be expected to guide government that are recognized *in common deliberation* as the valuations relevant to determining public policy. This conception represents democracy, not as a regime for the expression of the collective will, but rather as *a dispensation* for the empowerment of public valuation.
>
> (Pettit 2004, 58; italics added)

Pettit (2004, 60, n. 9) initially intimates that the main problem with the idea of a collective will is the unfeasibility of divining or expressing it under complex modern circumstances: "The core difficulty with the notion of collective will is that it presupposes collective agency, and that the existence conditions for a collective agent are too demanding for a large-scale populace or electorate to satisfy." However, Pettit (1999a, 81) does not ultimately reject the "participatory ideal" accompanying the notion of a collective will only, or even primarily, on the grounds that it is "not feasible in the modern world." As we will observe below, Pettit (1999a, 81) ultimately rejects such conceptions as "scarcely attractive" on normative grounds; that is, he considers the idea that majority rule accurately approximates popular will to be a threat, perhaps even the greatest threat, to liberty within democracies (Pettit 1999b, 177).

In any case, despite Pettit's emphasis on the overall advantages afforded by electoral mechanisms, he does not consider free elections to be unproblematic routes to justice. Even if Pettit (2001, 160–1), in a faithful Schumpeterian fashion, relies on an incentivist/consumerist model to argue that electoral politics reliably produces candidates who are likely to address the common good, it would be unfair to claim that Pettit fetishizes elections. Indeed, he acknowledges that elected representatives, like popular majorities, can themselves become agents of domination when they pursue their own interests rather than those of everyone else. In this context, Pettit (1999a, 293–4) raises the serious problem of keeping elected elites accountable to the electorate such that the former do not behave tyrannically.

> Since [elections] only allow for a very loose control of the policies eventually pursued by government, they may fail to stop those elected to power from nurturing policies that fail to answer to particular interests or from pursuing policies in a way that doesn't answer to popular interests. The electorally democratic state may be an elective despotism.
>
> (Pettit 1999a, 293–4)

In light of these considerations, it is somewhat surprising to observe Pettit (1999b, 173) argue that electoral regimes promote greater accountability than any other type of polity, more so even than those, he states explicitly, such as ancient democracies, in which most offices were distributed through lottery. This assertion is, however, somewhat misleading: While, in theory, elections may facilitate accountability in ways that lotteries, considered in isolation, do not, Pettit neglects to mention that, in practice, virtually every popular government that deployed lotteries also subjected office-holders to strict post-tenure public scrutinies where former magistrates gave account of their actions and faced serious punishment for misconduct. There is certainly no reliable evidence available demonstrating that election/re-election schemes secure greater elite accountability for citizenries than do those characterized by lottery/ scrutiny; in fact, there are serious grounds to conclude just the opposite (Ober 1993; Przeworski, Stokes and Manin 1999).

Indeed, Pettit (2000, 126) himself concedes that representative democracy's inherent indirectness allows magistrates to conduct themselves with a potentially pernicious independence from the public: Representation "means electoral control still allows governmental policy making to be influenced by factors such that it is not in the common, recognizable interest of people that [these factors] have an influence." Among the arbitrary factors that potentially undermine the efficacy of representative democracy, Pettit (2001, 162) recognizes that campaign promises are not often translated into law; policy implementers enjoy wide prerogative in carrying out their tasks; and particular lobbies can wield undue influence over the policy-making process.

To counteract representative democracy's inherent susceptibility to this kind of distortion, Pettit (2001, 154, 174) endorses "contestatory" means for challenging the policy outcomes of ordinary electoral politics. Pettit (1999a, 292–7; 2000) frequently invokes alternative institutions – judiciaries, tribunals, ombudsmen, upper houses and local boards – through which individuals, specific subsets of the citizenry and (more ambiguously) even the citizenry itself might variously contest, review or amend decisions made by elected elites. He calls this the "editorial" dimension of democratic politics that must supplement the "authorial" dimension reflected in electoral procedures (Pettit 2001, 160–3). Through the latter the people articulate the common avowable interests that the state ought to further; through the former they protest and denounce state policies that do not conform to their estimations of what constitutes interests that can be justified in terms of the commonweal (Pettit 2001, 159).[9]

However, it must be noted that Pettit understands contestatory procedures to operate in just as indirect and reactive a manner as he does electoral politics: He states unequivocally that the "procedural, consultative, and appellate measures," which constitute the contestatory dimension of his theory of democracy:

> give ordinary people *passive* rather than active control of what happens. If the measures work effectively, then they ensure not that ordinary people dictate what policies will be selected and applied but that the policies selected and applied will conform to people's common, recognizable interests.
>
> (Pettit 2000, 139–40; italics in original)

Contestation allows citizens "to raise an effective voice" concerning policies that adversely affect them, but not, Pettit (2001, 174) insists, to decide directly on their implementation or revocation.

Pettit (2001, 171) argues that, in order to facilitate contestation, however passive, democracies must allow citizens to challenge government policy on at least three grounds: "for its legality under public law; for its substantive merit; and for its general propriety." Within Pettit's framework judicial review by high or supreme courts addresses the first concern, namely, whether government action that affects citizen interests is legal or constitutional. Pettit (2000, 131) would authorize tribunals that oversee, for instance, land use, immigration and education to address whether substantive dimensions of public policy in these domains track the interests of citizens; such specialized tribunals would hold public hearings, conduct official inquiries, publish their findings and offer recommendations in "white" or "green papers."

Most intriguing among Pettit's extra-electoral institutions is the figure of the ombudsman, an agent of contestation who, at first glance, functions in a manner reminiscent of the plebeian tribunes in Rome. According to Pettit's stipulations, citizens can appeal to ombudsmen to investigate and report on government "maladministration" in the widest sense: incompetence, neglect, corruption, inattention, malfeasance, delay, arbitrariness, abuse of power and so forth (Pettit 2000, 172). While Pettit would not grant ombudsmen the "power to enforce a remedy," he understands them to serve as effective instruments for securing compensation for aggrieved parties and as catalysts for changing government practice in ways that better serve members of the public (Pettit 2000, 172; cf. 2000, 133).

However, there are significant differences between these two contestatory magistrates, the Roman tribunes and Pettit's ombudsmen. On the one hand, the former were not merely contestatory officials; the tribunes wielded authority to initiate legislation and formally prosecute prominent public and private citizens, authority that Pettit's ombudsmen obviously lack. On the other hand, Pettit doesn't attribute to the ombudsmen a group-specific character; that is, the ombudsmen are not, as were the tribunes of the plebs, necessarily members of the very groups whose interests they attempt to protect from governmental encroachment and social domination. As shall be observed below, when Pettit does endorse identity-specific officials, in the case of saved-seats for representatives of minority groups, their range of action is severely circumscribed by legislative structures and conventions.

There are, moreover, two other important differences that I wish to address at greater length. First, Pettit refuses to empower ombudsmen, or, for that matter, any contestatory principal *or* agent, with a veto authority over government policy. Second, Pettit does not conceive of common citizens, that is, the vast majority of citizens who do not belong to the ranks of socioeconomic and political elites, as a discrete group entitled to their own ombudsmen. In Pettit's account, for the most part, ombudsmen contest public policy on behalf of individuals or minority groups who claim that their avowed interests have been violated or disregarded – not on behalf of common citizens as a whole, that is, the plebeians of modern republics.

No Veto: For reasons pertaining to both plausibility and utility, Pettit rejects vetoes that enable parties prospectively affected in adverse ways by particular policies to block the implementation of such policies. The veto, according to Pettit (1999b, 178), poses little more "than an abstract, purely academic interest," and today enjoys not "the remotest chance of being instituted." More substantively, he argues that vetoes discourage compromise over public policy: With access to formal vetoes, interested parties need not negotiate outcomes (even those that might include appropriate compensation) through which benefits and costs can be distributed with some semblance of equity throughout society; such parties can simply reject certain inconvenient policies *tout court* (Pettit 1999b, 178). Pettit (2000, 118) observes that "the worst hit," if armed with a veto when confronted with onerous but socially necessary policy proposals, "would be likely to block the initiative in the hope of inducing others to bear the costs." In such circumstances, society as a whole would never benefit from advantages to be gained by, say, progressive tax arrangements, power plants, antipollution legislation or needle exchange programs.

Pettit (1999b, 178) insists that contestatory democracy should not enable people "to veto public decisions" but rather "to call them into question" by triggering reviews or appeals. Contestation of this kind is more fair and efficacious than vetoes, Pettit (1999b, 180) suggests, because "it empowers people in the assertion of their perceived interests but does not set them up as dictators with an individual capacity to negate any public decision." While Pettit certainly has a point in circumstances where minority groups or special interests may self-servingly avail themselves of formalized veto authority, it is not clear why, on the same grounds, he explicitly dismisses the tribunician veto in the Roman republic (Pettit

2001, 163). Since the tribunes exercised the veto on behalf of the majority of citizens against senatorial and consular initiatives and measures, it would be hard to claim that the tribunician veto illegitimately displaced burdens throughout society and inappropriately scuttled socially beneficial reforms. Indeed, when the tribunes exercised their veto authority in the following cases, they were ensuring that Rome's senatorial order did not impose or displace undue burdens on the majority of citizens: For instance, when the tribunes prevented consuls from proposing patrician-friendly laws before assemblies like the *comitia centuriata*, where voting was weighted in favor of the wealthy; or when they halted the levying of troops for wars initiated by the senate to quell popular protest within the republic rather than to further the latter's collective security vis-à-vis external enemies.

Pettit (2000, 118) certainly articulates good reasons for rejecting vetoes exercised by individuals or at a "group-level," but what if the veto-wielding "group" is the *demos*, that is, the poor, the many? The class-specific character of the plebeian tribunes and the majoritarian constituency they served largely obviate these concerns, or at the very least, they require Pettit to qualify his criticisms of Rome's tribunician veto. Pettit's comprehensive concern over the capacities of particular groups to shift burdens and subvert the common good through vetoes ignores a salient fact about republican politics that the Romans, especially the Roman plebeians, knew very well: The disproportionate influence of wealthy citizens and the wide discretion enjoyed by magistrates often constitute a de facto veto on policies that the majority of citizens desire to be enacted in their common interest. The de facto veto that elites exercise in such contexts combined with the disproportionate influence and discretion that elites enjoy over active policy making necessitates in response institutions through which the majority qua majority not only veto public policy in an ex post fashion but also authorize policies ex ante.

Pettit clearly rules out the use of vetoes as a form of contestation that should be available to either majorities or minorities. But does he at least afford both majorities *and* minorities other institutional avenues of contestation? Or are the latter exclusively reserved for aggrieved individuals and vulnerable minorities? Pettit often seems to suggest that majorities are generally so well served by conventional electoral politics that only individuals and minorities need recourse to contestatory practices. Let us explore Pettit's rationale for this position and the ramifications it poses for liberty as nondomination.

Contestation for Both Majorities and Minorities? Pettit often equivocates on the nature of contestation within his democratic theory: On the one hand, he states that "a government will represent a form of rule that is controlled by the people to the extent that the people individually *and collectively* enjoy a permanent possibility of contesting what government decides" (Pettit 1999a, 185; italics added); on the other, he baldly declares that contestation "cannot be exercised collectively" (Pettit 2001, 163). Pettit is clearly caught between two forms of contestation: one, reminiscent of the Roman republic, where the people, through the tribunes, collectively edited or corrected the decisions made by elected or previously elected officials, such as consuls or senators, whom the people had previously authorized to carry out or to oversee policy; the other, more reminiscent of the countermajoritarian institutions favored by post-eighteenth-century liberal constitutionalists, provides avenues through which government bodies protect minorities against potential abuses of majority rule. The former allows majoritarian contestation of the government and of whatever special interests might be hijacking democratic rule in self-serving and dominating ways; the latter facilitates minority contestation of domination that majorities exercise through elected elites, or that public officials, acting unilaterally, exercise themselves.

The preponderance of evidence afforded by Pettit's writings, despite isolated statements to the contrary, suggest that he would put contestatory institutions like the three mentioned above primarily at the disposal of individuals and minority groups. This implies that: (a) Pettit believes that electoral institutions adequately serve the majority of citizens qua majority; that is, the latter need no extra-electoral means to ensure that government is fulfilling its obligations to track the common interests of the majority of citizens; and (b) discriminatory policies that disadvantage religious, ethnic, aboriginal and other minorities are the types of domination characteristic of democratic politics that most require contestatory redress; imbalances of political and socioeconomic power that obtain between, on the one hand, common citizens and, on the other, wealthy citizens and public officials, do not, as such, require contestatory redress. An important question raised by such assumptions is whether Pettit's model provides so much recourse for individuals and minorities via countermajoritarian institutions, insulated from popular accountability, that it stymies the very possibility of democracy as popular rule in any meaningful sense of the term. Furthermore, are countermajoritarian institutions more likely to serve the interests of privileged, well-resourced and already insulated minorities rather than genuinely vulnerable minorities? The record of such institutions at actually protecting vulnerable minorities is, after all, decidedly mixed (Hirschl 2005, 2007; Rosenberg 1991; Dahl 1957).

Quite commendably, Pettit has long placed the protection of minority interests at the center of his republican theory of freedom: The "politically avowable, perceived interests" of "relevant minorities," he consistently declares, cannot be "just ignored and flouted" in democratic politics (Pettit 1999b, 178). Even on the electoral, authorial side, as opposed to the contestatory, editorial side of his model, Pettit recommends alternative, that is, not strictly electoral, means of ensuring that governmental policy takes into account social diversity.[10] For instance, Pettit advocates saved parliamentary seats for members of every minority group within society: All groups, he insists, should "achieve representation, not by grace of senatorial spokespersons, but via the presence of some of their members ... The reliably inclusive legislature will have to incorporate, in their own right, all the voices of difference that are found within the community" (Pettit 1999a, 191). Such inclusions do and should have an affect on policy formation, but there are limits to what they can achieve in this regard.[11]

Pettit, after all, intends for this diversification of voices to affect parliamentary *deliberation* primarily but legislative *decisions* only indirectly: "[A]s the assembly of law-makers debates its way towards decision, it takes account of the considerations that are salient, not just from a restricted set of privileged viewpoints, but from the full range of social perspectives" (Pettit 1999a, 191). According to Pettit, while minority voices must be heard and taken into account within this scheme, such voices have no binding effect on legislative outcomes. This scenario is, for instance, a far cry from saved-seating arrangements in the *Signoria* of the Florentine republic, where middling and lower guildsmen could collectively outvote members of the upper guilds if they felt that their interests were being threatened by particular policies favored by the latter. Occupational quotas in this case insured that perspectives from across the socioeconomic continuum of the Florentine citizenry enjoyed not only deliberative but also decisional impact.[12]

If the practice of saved parliamentary seats for members of minority groups does not replicate the empowerment of less privileged corporate groups in republican Florence, neither does it approximate the affirmative action for common citizens facilitated by the plebeian tribunes in republican Rome: In Pettit's proposal, saved parliamentary seats still leave minority representatives outnumbered among other legislators, while a particular tribune was formally answerable only to the veto of his tribunician colleagues and to the opinion of his plebeian constituency. Furthermore, the saved-seat strategy, as Pettit recommends it, is a decidedly elite-filtered affair: Party elites would have tremendous prerogative in choosing, for instance, the 40 percent of candidates that Pettit (1999a, 191) suggests should be legally mandated for women. On the one hand, the Roman plebeians themselves decided, without any senatorial imprimatur, who from among their own ranks would serve as tribunes (Pettit 1999a, 191);[13] on the other, even the consuls of the Florentine guilds, when compiling lists of potential priors to serve on the *Signoria*, did so without an eye to who was, in their estimation, "electable," since the names would be subsequently submitted not to a general election but rather to a lottery.[14]

In any case, more important for Pettit (1999a, 193) than the diversity of any particular political body is the ability of diverse types of citizens to contest the policies that such bodies issue, for instance, by writing to MPs, asking ombudsmen to conduct inquiries and appealing judicial decisions to higher courts. But the great care with which Pettit discusses the representation of minorities stands in notable contrast to his somewhat cursory treatment of traditional identity politics within republics, that is, the issue of class or, as so extensively discussed by Aristotle, material inequality. In marked contrast to his assertive, declarative and institutionally specific approach to the problem of vulnerable minorities, Pettit addresses the distorting effect of resource inequality on democratic politics in a tentatively interrogative mode. For instance, he asks, without endorsing any specific reforms, whether campaign contributions can be limited and made public, and whether electoral campaigns should be privately funded at all (Pettit 1999a, 194).

This hesitance is all the more striking once Pettit (1999a, 194) confirms the fact that economic inequality has been a perennial problem for republics and for republicanism, and that this continues to be the case: "The problem of controlling the influence of the economically powerful on politicians, and more generally on government, is at once an age-old issue ... and a pressing contemporary problem." Yet the best Pettit (1999a, 194) himself offers on this admittedly fundamental and persistent problem confronting republicanism is the following: "One of the greatest challenges for republican research must be to identify measures for effectively separating the worlds of government and business." In short, Pettit punts on the issue.

At base, Pettit's theoretical framework only indirectly addresses the principle asymmetry of power, that of wealthy citizens over poorer citizens, which has historically plagued republics. To be sure, Pettit intends for his category of "*dominium*" to cover this kind of power asymmetry: In order to minimize the dominium of, for instance, employers over employees, liberty as nondomination justifies instances where elected officials pass laws that ameliorate conditions under which the former may arbitrarily interfere with the lives of the latter. Moreover, Pettit's theory also justifies contestatory avenues through which employees, as individuals, or as members of worker organizations, can challenge the efficacy or fairness of government policy pertaining to the circumstances of their employment. Yet this approach places the burden of initiative on individuals or groups, either to mobilize behind favorable electoral candidates or to petition government actors for redress and remedy – and in both cases, to do so in competition with superiorly resourced opponents. Recognizing the disadvantages that such arrangements impose upon average citizens, advocates of traditional democracies and *governi larghi* formally structured government institutions to empower the economically disadvantaged – through lottery, class-specific institutions and direct popular judgment. On the contrary, representative governments, of the kind that Pettit advocates, effectively privatize the issue of domination by the few over the many; they, intentionally or not, put informal obstacles in the path of popular attempts at ameliorating such power asymmetries – notably by confining collective authorization and contestation to the aggrieved's capacity to elect and unelect public magistrates.

Pettit's relative inattention to wealth inequality, or, more specifically, his failure to address socioeconomic inequality through formal constitutional prescription, compounds the following problem, already mentioned above: Pettit's extra-electoral, contestatory institutions function much more like the countermajoritarian ones typifying liberal constitutionalism, namely, upper legislative chambers and supreme courts, than they do popularly contestatory ones like the Roman tribunate or the guild-specific, lottery-based practices characterizing Florentine politics. After all, elite-dominated, countermajoritarian institutions like upper houses and supreme courts, despite being charged with the protection of minorities, nevertheless have proven notoriously susceptible to capture by or collusion with entrenched, highly resourced interest groups. In the US context, one cannot help but think of the way that such institutions served the interests of, respectively, slaveholders (and their segregationist heirs) and capital for generations. To be sure, eighteenth and post-eighteenth-century aristocratic republicans like Montesquieu, Tocqueville and, to a lesser extent, Madison, hoped that such institutions would constrain if not fully thwart the will of newly enfranchized peoples in Europe and the Americas (Madison, Hamilton and Jay 1998, no. 51, 62–3; Tocqueville 2000, vol. I, chaps 15–16). In practice, however, instead of safeguarding vulnerable minorities, these countermajoritarian institutions all too often facilitated the wholesale cooptation of important government organs and functions by economic elites (Dahl 2003; Levinson 2006; Kramer 2004).

Depoliticized Institutions: The prominence of countermajoritarian institutions in Pettit's model amplifies the fact that he is not – despite some statements to the contrary, as we'll see – principally worried by the prospect that elected elites will *depart* from the will of the people when the latter request policies that advance the common avowable interests of citizens. On the contrary, Pettit seems more profoundly concerned that elected elites will be *too* responsive to popular majorities when the latter desire policies that supposedly undermine the common good or threaten the interests of minorities. Pettit (2004, 53, 55) suggests that there are policy spheres where the opinions of popular majorities, unduly swayed by their passions or "aspirational morality," ought to be only indirectly reflected in policies made by representatives – indeed, reflected *even more indirectly* than such views already are within conventional electoral politics.

For instance, Pettit (2004, 56–7) identifies criminal sentencing and the regulation of prostitution as areas where the people's emotional fervor or moral scruples might interfere with good policy making by elected officials. Pettit (2004, 56–7) worries that when the people confront issues like sentencing or prostitution, rather than "consider the overall consequences of each arrangement and make a rational choice," they instead take an unreflective "moral stand" and encourage their representatives, via the threat of punitive electoral sanction, to make bad policy. Pettit speculates that, in such circumstances, voters may use the ballot "primarily as a way of expressing their personal, often heartfelt stand on some issue of moral or religious significance;" to his mind, they are likely to "use their vote for the pleasure of expressive satisfaction" (Pettit 1999b, 177).

Pettit proposes institutional reforms that he hopes will "depoliticize democracy" in circumstances where popular irrationality or moral fastidiousness translates into deleterious policy outcomes. Pettit suggests that, in cases where the people would choose poorly themselves or might punish representatives unfairly for making sensible policies, elected officials should appoint special commissions to discuss and even effectively decide such issues. These commissions should:

> take the decisions away from the direct influence of representatives [and should themselves] make the decisions under conditions where considerations of the common good, and only such considerations, are very likely to rule ... By putting [parliamentary] control at arm's length in such a manner – by retaining only the hands-off sort of control that parliaments have over electoral commissions – [these forums] would serve the cause of deliberative democracy.
>
> (Pettit 2004, 53, 55)

Pettit recommends that these "depoliticized forums," empowered to discuss and decide especially sensitive legislative and regulatory issues, "would be able to take a long-term view, informed by sustained monitoring, of the costs and benefits of different overtures" (Pettit 2004, 56–7). These "autonomous, professionally informed" commissions would be comprised of policy experts and community leaders: representatives "of relevant bodies of expertise and opinion, as well as of the people as a whole" (Pettit 1999a, 197; 2004, 56–7, 53); Pettit anticipates that their members would "represent different sectors of popular opinion and professional expertise" (Pettit 2004, 56–7; cf. 2000, 136).

With this markedly senatorial move, Pettit entrusts policy making to wise, impartial and common good-loving elites who speak for the people, rather than entrusting it to the people themselves – or even to their conventionally elected representatives. Pettit's justifications of such institutions, based as they are on a view of the populace as too fickle, uninformed, or influenced by emotion and prejudice to make sound decisions, are strikingly reminiscent of those put forward in favor of senatorial independence by Cicero, Guicciardini and, indeed, some of the American founders, who suggested that senators be only indirectly authorized by the people through either previous popular election or by election via intermediary, elite-comprised, bodies like state legislatures. Pettit puts an exclamation point on the necessity of independence for his depoliticized commissions in cases where the people's emotional or moral proclivities too assertively come to the fore: In such circumstances, he writes, "contestatory democracy requires that the demos, and the legislative representatives of the demos, generally tie their hands and gag their mouths" (Pettit 2000, 136).

This proposal obviously raises many questions: Will elected elites regularly usurp their own authority to appoint commissions that subsequently make policy in their place? Would they appoint truly expert, impartial, virtuous and "representative" individuals to serve as commissioners? How many such persons can be found? Most importantly: Is it really possible to distinguish, on the one hand, policy spheres where the people's malevolent passions and misguided moral intuitions come into play from, on the other, spheres where their beneficial or sound ones are apposite to the issues at hand? What policy spheres, exactly, do *not* potentially fall into the former category? By failing to distinguish these spheres with more precision, Pettit runs the risk of inflating the former category in an alarmingly antidemocratic way. Pettit argues principally by example in this context, focusing on criminal sentencing, prostitution and, to a lesser extent, electoral redistricting; he does not conceptually demarcate policy spheres that ought to remain conventionally political from spheres that, in line with this scheme, ought to be depoliticized.

Pettit (2001, 169) himself flirts with a creeping expansion of policy spheres that are insulated from popular judgment when, in another instance, he identifies public prosecution as a task that ought to be depoliticized. This is, I would note, one of the primary spheres over which Machiavelli assigns the people ultimate judgment (D I.7–8; cf. McCormick 2007). Indeed, in a worryingly unspecified "variety" of cases, Pettit (1999a, 196) suggests that "popular debate" is the "worst possible" venue for democratic contestation: "In these cases, the requirement of contestatory democracy is that the complaints should be depoliticized and should be heard away from the tumult of popular discussion and away, even, from the theatre of parliamentary debate." The Machiavellian term "tumult" begs a comparison with the Florentine on the precise spheres that should be insulated from public debate and contestation: In *Discourses*, Machiavelli enumerates military strategy (devised by the Roman senate) and emergency measures (adopted by the Roman dictator) as the only matters, due to an immediately pressing need for secrecy or for expeditious action, which ought not be subject to the "tumult" of popular discussion and contestation (D I.55, D II.25, D I.34).

Pettit's attempt to depoliticize important policy spheres suggests that he largely subscribes to the traditional philosophical and historical narratives concerning the people's inability to judge political matters dispassionately and impartially that, as we'll observe below, Machiavelli explicitly criticizes (D I.58). Moreover, some of his justifications for contestatory democracy notwithstanding, Pettit expresses very little worry that small cadres of supposedly expert and public-spirited elites will abuse the policy-making authority that his model empowers them to exercise on behalf of entire citizenries.[15]

Elites, the People and "the Real Danger": In isolated instances, Pettit entertains the notion that elite prerogative is a greater threat to liberty than the arbitrary decisions of popular majorities. For example, at one point he muses that the people, acting as a majority, will be reluctant to abuse minorities for fear of depopulating the polity: "[T]he collectivity is forced, on pain of suffering mass emigration, to track the common avowable interests of its members" (Pettit 2001, 154). At another, Pettit avers, party competition in mass democracies discourages majority tyranny: Entrepreneurial politicians consistently court underrepresented groups of citizens in the hopes of enlarging their constituencies; when they do, they tend to "shame majority supporters into changing their allegiance" in ways that benefit previously vulnerable groups and individuals (Pettit 2000, 117). In the midst of these reflections that give popular majorities considerable benefit of the doubt, Pettit (2001, 162; 2000, 117) suggests that a tyranny exercised by a "democratic elite" is "probably" more dangerous to liberty than a tyranny exercised by a "democratic majority." The "probably" in this quote proves to be, however, a telling qualification: While Pettit, as he does here, sometimes gestures to the notion that elite prerogative is the greatest threat posed by contemporary democracy, he usually writes, especially when prescribing institutional reforms, as though majority tyranny is clearly the maximum political danger.

Pettit is generally much more wary of the people than he is of elites, and he frequently goes to great lengths to generate rationales for why elites can be expected to act on behalf of the common good, while he tends to accept as fact the notion that the people simply cannot. Pettit (2001, 154) insists that popular judgment is prone to "collective unreason,"[16] and he asserts definitively (that is, without the softening qualifier "probably") that majoritarian tyranny is "the real danger" posed by democracy (Pettit 1999b, 177). Indeed, to Pettit's mind, majority rule potentially replicates the arbitrary, dominating authority wielded in previous centuries by absolute monarchs: "It is quite possible that the people, understood collectively, should dominate the people, understood severally; the collective people can be as uncontrolled an agency, from the point of view of at least some individuals, as the divinely endorsed king" (Pettit 1999b, 174).

Pettit rejects the affinity between popular judgment, on the one hand,

and the maximization of liberty, social and individual, on the other, noted by authors as different as Plato (who did so with disapprobation), Machiavelli and scholars associated with the "wisdom of crowds" literature.[17] While such authors detected an empirical correlation between democracy and liberty, Pettit asserts, speaking analytically, that there is no "definitional connection" between the two (Pettit 1999a, 30). Relying instead on the patrician critique of majority rule, Pettit cites Madison and Montesquieu, and implicitly invokes Tocqueville, when he declares: "The tyranny of the majority gives the lie to any suggestion that the elective mode of democratization is bound fully to ensure the friendliness of government to freedom, in particular to freedom as non-domination" (Pettit 1999b, 176, 177).[18]

Given this view of the people, generally, and of majority rule, in particular, it is not surprising that Pettit wishes to keep important decisions away from directly expressed and even electorally indirectly expressed popular influence. Pettit recommends that his fora comprised of experts and opinion leaders should make their "judgments away from the theater of politics;" his depoliticized commissions should deliberate and decide without being "exposed to the glare and pressure of public debate" (Pettit 2000, 136; 1999, 197). Democracy, Pettit insists, lives not only in "the oxygen of public debate and participation" but also operates in "professionalized forums in which consultations are offered and negotiated, and appeals of various kinds heard and judged;" it exists in spaces "not governed by public will, and, often not opened to the public gaze" (Pettit 2000, 140).[19]

Pettit resoundingly endorses both electoral politics and expert commissions that operate, respectively, at one step removed from parliamentary politics and two steps removed from the people themselves. Both endorsements presuppose, in his own words, that "it is possible for certain bodies to be impartial on matters where the population is divided" (Pettit 2000, 120). Pettit expects that the political, professional and opinion elites who comprise legislative and, in particular, his depoliticized fora will commit themselves strictly to factual concerns and common good considerations: Such representatives and experts can, with confidence, be asked "to judge on the factual issue of whether the policy as identified and implemented is supported by common, recognizable interests and only by such interests" (Pettit 2000, 120). These actors will not, as many democrats worry (for example, Dahl 1989, 50–75 and O'Leary 2006, 5), decide matters to their own advantage, or in favor of some special interest to which they're beholden, nor will they succumb to the same ideological divisions that beset society at large: Pettit (1999b, 181) thinks it plausible to expect such elites to be "free of self-serving interests and be all the more suscep-tible to considerations of fair play." As evidence for the capacity of such bodies to generate fair-minded, well-considered and generally beneficial decisions, Pettit (1999b, 181) invokes the example of criminal juries. However, juries are, of course, comprised not of expert elites but rather of the same common people that Pettit would like to distance from impor-tant policy decisions.[20] I return to this point below.

Ultimately, what will keep expert commissioners sufficiently depo-liticized, impartial and attentive to the common good? Pettit's answer is deeply Ciceronian: Such commissioners wish to enhance "their reputa-tion," and to satisfy their "desire for esteem" (Pettit 1999b, 181; 2000, 120). They will behave appropriately, according to Pettit (2001, 165), because they "stand to win the good opinion of most of their fellows only so far as they are seen to discharge their allotted brief." This justifica-tion requires further elaboration: If a commissioner seeks reputation and esteem earned via the good opinion of fellow commissioners, then we have no reason to expect any better efforts on behalf of the common good than were afforded by the Roman senate, whose members famously vied with one another for the esteem of the entire body. Furthermore, in such circumstances, the evaluation of whether a commissioner has successfully discharged his or her allotted brief is fully determined by similarly situated colleagues, not by the public itself – hardly a standard either reflective of or, certainly, conducive to, the common good.

If, alternatively, the audience from which individual commissioners seek approval is comprised of members of parliament, then Pettit should better specify the relationship between the commissions and MPs. If we are to comprehend the full influence of parliament's estimation of com-missioners, we need to know the following: How truly "autonomous" are the former from the latter? In what sense do they operate "at arm's length" from the latter? What does it mean to say that parliament retains "ulti-mate control" in these circumstances (Pettit 2004, 53, 55–7; 1999a, 197)? Presumably, given the fact that commissioners deliberate and decide outside of public view, Pettit does not mean by "their fellows" the average people who actually are their fellow citizens. If he does, if it is the public's esteem that is meant to keep their behavior in the service of the common good, then his commissioners ought to stand for election.

These issues aside, Pettit's use of conventional juries as exemplars of rational and objective decision making – indeed, as models for the way he expects his depoliticized commissions to conduct themselves – is all the more curious since he refuses to consider the use of jury-like institutions in roles that he assigns to his depoliticized commissions. In recent years, a number of scholars and public intellectuals have theorized and even overseen experiments with institutions like citizen juries, minipublics, peoples' assemblies and deliberative polls; institutions where randomly selected or demographically representative groups of citizens gather together to discuss and vote on salient public policy issues (Dahl 1989; Fishkin 1991, 1997; Neblo 2005, n.d.; O'Leary 2006; Goodin 2008; Warren and Pearse 2008; Thompson 2008). Some of these bodies have been empowered to make decisions with legally binding authority over policy within specific jurisdictions (Baiocchi 2001, 2005; Fung 2003; Fung and Wright 2003; Goodin 2008, 11–37; Warren and Pearse 2008, xi, xii, 1–16). Pettit speaks favorably of these mini-citizen assemblies but he never entertains the notion of granting them the same political autonomy and decision-making authority that he grants to his purportedly depoliticized commissions.[21]

Perhaps Pettit has good cause to be suspicious of opinions that average people express in polls with no legally binding consequence. He draws on evidence suggesting that, when questioned for such polls, people very often express "frustration or exasperation or malice or something of the kind," since, in such contexts, they know that they are not responsible for their opinions.[22] Machiavelli offers similar observations about informally expressed and legally nonbinding popular opinion (D I.7, D I.47). Furthermore, also like Machiavelli, Pettit observes that average people are capable of arriving at well-considered conclusions when they are formally assembled to discuss and decide over policy issues (D I.18, D I.58). Citing Fishkin's work, in fact, Pettit acknowledges that groups of average people, when presented with information provided by various sources – especially, information that reflects opposing viewpoints – and when permitted to discuss this information at length, prove admirably capable of making informed decisions that may be said to advance the common good. Unlike Machiavelli, however, Pettit does not take this as a cue to further conceptualize or openly endorse institutions that formally empower the people, or some demographically representative or randomly generated subset of them, to make legally binding decisions. Stopping far short of this, Pettit would employ deliberative opinion polls or the decisions of citizen juries in a strictly consultative capacity: that is,

111

as exemplars whose decisions might change broader opinion within the wider citizenry or might affect the behavior of representatives. But Pettit (1999a, 169) would *not* assign them any direct policy impact themselves.

Why not? If such mini-publics are, in Pettit's (2000, 136) own estimation, genuinely "deliberative" and, when suitably diverse and representative, may be said to reflect the "predominant" view of a collectivity, why shouldn't they be entrusted to generate binding decisions? Or at least, why shouldn't Pettit grant them as much legislative and administrative authority as he grants to depoliticized commissions? Interestingly, Pettit (2004, 57) calls Fishkin's work on deliberative polls, "a depoliticizing proposal" – which, of course, it is by definition, since Fishkin's groups do not render political decisions. However, if groups of both elites and common citizens can function in a depoliticized way in certain circumstances, why not choose the latter, especially if Pettit still understands himself to be operating within an explicitly democratic framework? As we will observe in Part 3, from Machiavelli's perspective, such mini-publics, if legally empowered with decisional authority, possess robust political potential.

Smaller, randomly selected or demographically faithful subsets of the entire citizenry that deliberate over and ultimately decide public policy are, from a democratic perspective, an attractive alternative to institutions that further empower elites to do so. Indeed, such mini-publics are reminiscent of the popular juries, comprised of 500 citizens, which judged political trials in democratic Athens. Ultimately, with the principles of traditional democracy and *governo largo* in mind, one could ask Pettit the following question: Is it more utopian to expect, on the one hand, such mini-publics to make generally good decisions or, on the other, to expect elites to behave in a consistently impartial and depoliticized fashion?

In this spirit, Pettit (2000, 134) also probably dismisses citizen-initiated referenda too casually: They are, he claims, potentially too democratic and also too undemocratic, since they can facilitate majority mistreatment of minorities, on the one hand, as well as permit "influence by moneyed interest groups" to effect referenda results, on the other. Moreover, Pettit (2000, 134) suggests that referenda invite arbitrary and self-contradictory outcomes since, from one referendum to another, "the voting collectivity cannot be subjected to a discipline of intertemporal consistency;" and, just as he worried in the case of conventional polling, "participants in a large-scale election are often expressive rather than pragmatic in the way they vote."[23] These are perhaps valid objections to referenda as they are often conducted.[24] But citizen referenda could certainly become more reliable and efficacious if, for instance, they were not held in tandem with elections for public office, and if they were made less vulnerable to influence by publicity generated through private financing. In any case, one wishes that Pettit would work as strenuously to conceptualize conditions under which the people as a whole, or reproduced *in virtuo*, would be granted the opportunity to make decisions conducive to the common good, at least as much as he does for the experts and community leaders who comprise his purportedly depoliticized commissions.

3. MACHIAVELLI ON POPULAR PARTICIPATION AND JUDGMENT

Machiavelli severely criticizes the tradition of philosophical republicanism for denigrating popular judgment and participation, and for championing the supposedly superior governing capacities of "the one" and "the few," that is, princes and patricians. The Florentine complains that "all the writers," that is, *all* classical and medieval historians and philosophers, prefer rule by princes and oligarchs to rule by the people (D I.58). Writers, after all, face far fewer deleterious consequences when they accentuate the deficiencies and mistakes of the people than they do when they highlight the excesses of princes and nobles. The people express little interest in or lack any real recourse against writers who criticize them. Conversely, princes and patricians, on the one hand, patronize the *literati*, cut their checks as it were, and, on the other, possess harsh means of coercion and retaliation. As a result, Machiavelli suggests, philosophers and historians tend to criticize the people gratuitously and treat elites with the utmost circumspection. For each single example of the trial of Socrates, there are thousands of incidents, largely unreported, where elites have bullied *literati* into duplicity, or intimidated them into silence.

Whether motivated by sheer cowardice or more generously simple confusion, the writers, according to Machiavelli, engage in disingenuous comparisons: They compare, on the one hand, examples of the people acting without legal constraint with, on the other, princes or aristocrats who have been successfully bound by law. But Machiavelli concludes definitively that the people, when "shackled by laws," exercise better judgment than any other political actor who might actually exist in the real world (D I.58). Of course, as Machiavelli intimates, an imaginary aristocracy of philosopher kings is capable, in theory, of exercising *perfect* political judgment. But there is *no* such agent capable of exercising perfect

113

political judgment in empirical reality. Notwithstanding the people's mistakes, some of them spectacularly demonstrated by the likes of Plato, Xenophon and Thucydides, Machiavelli insists that the people will decide in a way that produces good outcomes, that is, outcomes conducive to the common good, and they will do so far more often than will similarly empowered princely or oligarchic elites.

On what grounds does Machiavelli make this claim? Machiavelli believes that the kind of people who put themselves up for election, or who gain appointment to senatorial bodies like upper houses and supreme courts, are psychologically, even physiologically, consumed by a greater desire to dominate others than to help realize the common good (D I.3–6). Magistrates, senators, judges and commissioners tend to seek elevated status over other people and endeavor to enrich themselves materially at the expense of the commonweal. Average people, on the contrary, are inclined toward security, toward keeping what they have, toward avoiding a diminution of material well-being or a demotion in social status. Thus, on the one hand, Machiavelli observes emphatically that "the judgment of free peoples is rarely pernicious to liberty" (D I.4) and, on the other, he concludes soberly that "the few always behave in the mode of the few" (D I.7).

Well-ordered republics, Machiavelli claims, structure themselves such that common people contain, contest and control the behavior of political and economic elites, and these republics place the ultimate judgment over political trials and legislation in the hands of the many and not the few. More specifically, like Rome, they establish magistracies for which wealthy and prominent citizens are ineligible, like the tribunes of the plebs, and they empower the people to veto public policies and indict individuals that threaten the common good – a common good unabashedly determined from the perspective of the people and *not* elites.

This contestatory or tribunician element in Machiavelli's politics is too often neglected in studies of the Florentine's political thought; however, the directly democratic element is completely ignored. Machiavelli recommends widely participatory, substantively deliberative procedures through which the people refine their judgments over political prosecutions and law-making. In a historically unprecedented fashion among "the writers," Machiavelli insists that republics permit common citizens to *initiate* proceedings pertaining to political trials, *propose* new legislation, formally *discuss* among themselves all the matters pertaining to political punishment and law-making, and render ultimate judgment over

114

each sphere (D I.18). Because small committees of magistrates are too susceptible to corruption by or collusion with those accused of political crimes, Machiavelli recommends bodies of "very many judges," preferably, as in Rome, the whole citizenry, formally assembled, to act as a jury that discusses and decides the guilt or innocence of magistrates or prominent citizens (D I.7–8).

Furthermore, Machiavelli thoroughly *Athenianizes* actual Roman practice when he describes law-making in the Roman assemblies as follows:

> A tribune, or *any citizen whatsoever*, could propose a law to the people, against or in favor of which every citizen was entitled to speak before a decision was reached … It was good that *anyone* who cared for the public good could propose laws, and that *everyone* could speak their mind on it so that *the assembled people could subsequently choose what was best*.
>
> (D I.18; italics added)

On the contrary, as mentioned above, Cicero affirms, and Guicciardini seeks to revive, Roman practices where the people remain mute in the assemblies where they vote on laws put to them by senatorial elites.

According to Machiavelli, the people successfully distinguish genuine accusations from spurious calumnies when they judge political criminals; moreover, they perceptively consider future benefits and ills when they discuss and formulate law. On the contrary, to Machiavelli's mind, princes or senatorial elites – because of their inherent appetite for oppression, their overall disrespect for laws, their general inclination toward corruption and collusion, conspiracy and cooptation – are constitutionally incapable, by themselves, of effectively punishing individuals who threaten a republic's liberty and of making laws conducive to the public good.

No doubt, such assertions are not likely to convince the writers, especially philosophical republicans, to forsake their suspicions of popular judgment. Philosophical republicans, as we've observed, consistently criticize the people for allowing their passions and moral intuitions to interfere with their evaluations of policy alternatives. However, Machiavelli suggests that such authors hopelessly confuse popular *opinion* with popular *judgment*. Rather than – as republicans from Cicero to Madison and beyond suggest – empowering the people's elected representatives to serve as the filter through which the people's views are "refined and enlarged," Machiavelli insists upon institutional arrangements through which the people refine and enlarge their views themselves. Let's examine a few examples.

115

For instance, when Coriolanus proposed that the Roman senate starve the plebeians into capitulating to the patricians' will, Machiavelli concedes that the people wanted to tear him to pieces in the street, which certainly would have caused a civil war (D I.7). However, once the tribunes summoned Coriolanus to stand trial before the people, formally collected in assembly, Machiavelli insists that the latter would have judged him objectively. The very same people who wanted to tear him limb from limb on the steps of the senate house would have fairly considered all the evidence and meted out an appropriate punishment within the confines of an assembly. This is borne out further by the case of Manlius Capitolinus, the people's champion against the senate on the matter of debt reform. While the people might have been willing to follow Manlius in a violent revolt against the senate, when Manlius is tried before a popular assembly for leveling false charges against the nobility, the people find him guilty and sentence him to death (D I.8). According to Machiavelli, even if the people are party to a partisan dispute, when formally empowered to render ultimate judgment, they decide more objectively than would the few.

Machiavelli's point in both these cases is that the people may often claim that they want one thing or another in taverns, in their homes or on the street, but they often choose something quite different when they are formally empowered to deliberate and decide within the bounds of an assembly. Machiavelli suggests that formal procedures of judgment compel the people to descend from the generalities of their opinions to the particulars of their true preferences (D I.47–8). Again, much more often than any prince or elites similarly empowered, the people, according to Machiavelli, will decide correctly. In all of his writings, Machiavelli perhaps criticizes no figures more harshly than leaders who deny the people the opportunity to decide the most important questions facing republics. Notably he chastizes Virginius, Valori and Savonarola for usurping popular judgment either for their own selfish purposes or because they thought they knew what was better for the people (D I.7, I.44, D I.45).

Allow me to discuss one more example posed by Machiavelli to reinforce this line of argument. Machiavelli recounts an episode from the Capuan republic, where the people, fed up with patrician oppression, espouse the opinion that they wish to kill the entire senate (D I.47). Capua's chief magistrate at the time, Pacuvius Calanus, suggests that if they wish to execute the nobles then they should do so in an orderly, formally legal fashion. Indeed, Pacuvius follows the very procedures for conducting popularly judged political trials that Machiavelli praises in many classical republics: Pacuvius calls an assembly and proceeds to draw the name of each senator, one by one, inviting the people to decide, on a case-by-case basis, whether or not a particular patrician individual should be executed or exonerated. Furthermore, he suggests that they should replace each senator whom they condemn with an individual from plebeian ranks, since, he assumes, the people do not wish to live without government. After a lively debate that includes shouting, whistling, ridicule and such – admittedly, not quite a Habermasian ideal speech situation – the people decide that they wish neither to kill any of the senators nor to replace any of them with persons from among the plebeians.

The Capuan magistrate then concludes the following about the entire episode: If the plebeians are willing to put aside their mortal hatred for the nobles and allow the latter to continue in authority, then the people must, in fact, desire good government more than they desire vengeance. Just as Machiavelli suggests elsewhere, formal procedures of judgment compel the people to descend from the generalities of opinion to the particulars of preferences. In this episode, within the formal confines of an assembly, the people weigh the tradeoffs entailed by their various preferences. They consider several options that they presumably want and decide which, in particular, they prefer: Do they want to govern themselves at the complete exclusion of the nobility, or do they want to benefit from the most optimal form of government viable at the moment? Do they really want to kill every single senator, or merely not be oppressed by the nobles as a class? On the latter point, the magistrate predicts that the fear aroused in the senators by the prospect of popularly pronounced death sentences will henceforth chasten the senate into behaving less oppressively toward the people.

Through the examples of Coriolanus, Manlius Capitolinus and the Capuan republic, Machiavelli demonstrates how arrangements that formally empower the people to make decisions themselves actually allow the people to clarify their preferences when the latter are unclear and moderate their impulses when the latter are excessive. On the contrary, it is precisely when the people are completely disempowered, or when their only recourse is to ask intermediaries to act for them, that they allow themselves to succumb to political confusion and fancy – oftentimes demanding that representatives behave more rashly and harshly than they would themselves if formally empowered to judge. Rather than placing sensitive policy decisions at one further step removed from the

117

people, as Pettit and other philosophical republicans suggest, Machiavelli implores us to theorize ways to approximate the direct judgment that the citizens of many ancient, medieval and Renaissance democratic republics and *governi larghi* exercised in assemblies. Even if we were to agree with Pettit that contemporary democracy is not a regime that expresses the collective will, but rather empowers what he calls "popular valuation" (Pettit 2004, 58), there is simply no empirical evidence supporting the claim that representative institutions perform this task any better than tribunician and/or plebiscitary ones (Pettit 2004, 57).

Pettit (2001, 170) notes correctly that under contemporary representative governments conventional "avenues of public access provide ordinary people with only very limited consultative resources," such as the capacity to petition legislators. However, I have demonstrated that the consultative measures that Pettit grants "ordinary people" within his model of "democracy, electoral and contestatory," are not much more robust. Pettit rightfully acknowledges that "democracy" played but one part within the celebrated mixed regime known as the Roman republic; but democracy, as practiced either directly through the authorial exercise of popular judgment in Rome's assemblies, or indirectly through the contestatory functions of the tribunes of the plebs, plays *no role* whatsoever in Pettit's (1999b, 167) reconstructed model of democracy. Most authors within the republican tradition with which Pettit allies himself made no effort to call a regime that excludes all direct forms of popular control a "democracy." Most republicans did not understand themselves to be democrats. Quite the contrary, Pettit, while replicating many of their criticisms of democracy, nevertheless attempts to maintain the name "democracy" for the institutional model he endorses, a model from which he excludes all directly participatory practices that one could rightfully consider democratic.

Justifying this approach, Pettit (2000, 139–40) declares that it is a fallacy to associate "democracy exclusively with the rule of the collective people: the rule of the people en masse; in a word, people power;" and, furthermore, he insists that "it would be a mistake to think that democracy exists only so far as ordinary people actively control things." Yet Pettit muddies rather than clarifies matters when he refuses to render distinct, as Machiavelli does, the likely behavior of a people formally empowered to decide in assembly from what Pettit (2000, 139) calls "unconstrained, majority rule," or, quite simply, "ochlocracy." Can one adequately base a theory of democracy on the assumption that the people acting collectively, aside from simply choosing public officials, will inevitably conduct themselves in a frivolous and rapacious manner? Even if Machiavelli did not use the word "democracy," the following definition of democracy proffered by Pettit certainly does not comport with the Florentine's reconstruction of the Roman republic as a *governo largo* in *Discourses*.

> Democracy is not inherently a collective matter ...; it is not inherently a matter of active control; and it is not inherently the sort of system that confines decision making to sites that are available to public scrutiny and influence. Democracy does not mean the reign of the collective, active will of the public or its representatives. It is a system, rather, in which things are organized so that while the people collectively have enough electoral power to guard against false negatives, the people non-collectively enjoy enough contestatory power to guard against false positives.
>
> (Pettit 2000, 141)

On the contrary, Machiavelli thought that the people collectively should guard against false negatives (that is, insure that government policies accurately reflect common avowable interests) by exercising legislative judgment themselves *and* that they should guard against false positives (that is, object to government policies that adversely affect common interests) by directly exercising judicial authority and by quasi-directly exercising contestation through the tribunician veto.

Pettit, despite certain claims to the contrary, seems at base to disagree with Machiavelli on the people's political capabilities, especially their ability to carry out tasks that are positively active (as opposed to merely negatively passive or reactive) and to do so in ways that are conducive to the common good. When explaining why "democratic" contestation ought not to be put in collective hands, Pettit sharply distinguishes majority decision making from the rule of "reason" itself: On Pettit's (1999a, 201) understanding, "the democratic process is designed to let the requirements of reason materialize and impose themselves; it is not a process that gives any particular place to will."

But Pettit poses analytically what is empirically a false dichotomy: "Reason" seldom materializes self-evidently and rarely imposes itself spontaneously in the midst of political controversy; some person or persons must decide, in such contexts, what is reasonable. In a regime organized for the purpose of minimizing domination and maximizing the common good, the people themselves must ultimately set the standard for what is reasonable. Hence, in any democracy worthy of the name the people should be institutionally empowered, wherever it is remotely efficacious logistically, to deliberate and decide public policy themselves. As Machiavelli demonstrates so well, citizens come to see their own interests most clearly and manage to avow them most articulately through political practices in which they participate directly (D I.47, I.58) and through institutional arrangements in which they discuss and decide not only the appointment of magistrates but also and especially legislation and political trials (D I.58, I.7–8).

Machiavelli compels democrats to pose the following question to critics of majoritarianism, like Pettit (1999a, 81), who fixate on the excesses and deficiencies of popular judgment: "Excessive and deficient as compared to what?" Pettit's project oftentimes seems motivated by the largely unfounded belief that decisions by the few are generally correct, that is, more often than not conducive to the common good and that they can be rendered, in Pettit's (2004, 59) sense, fully "depoliticized." In this sense, Pettit seems to approach this problem from a Platonic or Ciceronian standpoint, a standpoint that presumes that reason most likely resides among an elite few (for example, representatives elected by the people or experts appointed by the latter's representatives). Only such a Platonic perspective, according to which some enlightened, depoliticized few can justly and effectively make decisions for everyone else, could justify Pettit's much too insistent rejection of rule by the many.

As demonstrated above, Machiavelli, when arguing against "all the writers," suggests that such a perspective is woefully misguided. In this light, if Pettit and other neo-republicans wish to formulate a truly comprehensive and practically efficacious theory of liberty as nondomination, I suggest that they reconceive institutional design along Machiavellian rather than traditional republican lines. To be sure, traditional republicans espoused constitutional models that successfully allowed alliances between peoples and elites to end domination of the kind exercised by Tarquin, Bourbon and Stuart monarchs. But, in addition, Machiavelli espoused a model wherein the people could prevent domination by their erstwhile allies in such efforts: the political and socioeconomic elites who hold elected magistracies in republics and/or who sit, either literally or figuratively, in the senatorial bodies of such regimes.

CONCLUSION

I have reminded readers that the broad republican tradition was for the most part committed to a qualified form of oligarchy where socioeconomic and political elites *dominated*, according to Pettit's own definition, common citizens: The minimizing or narrowing of popular participation advocated by the founders of republican theory like Cicero, Bruni and Guicciardini, as well as by prominent English, Dutch and American proponents of republicanism,[25] led to political outcomes that did not, in Pettit's terms, "track" the common good as perceived or avowed by the vast majority of citizens. With this in mind, in conclusion I emphasize three important elements common to the republicanisms of Pettit, Cicero, Bruni and Guicciardini.

(1) Each marginalizes or constrains the place of popular participation within the politics of republics.
(2) Each advocates general election as the principle means of appointing magistrates (that is, they reject or eschew alternatives involving lottery, an election/lottery mixture, class or occupational quotas for offices).
(3) Each confers on rather senatorial sets of elites wide deliberative and decisional prerogative over policy questions concerning the common good, without formulating any clear criteria by which one could ascertain the appropriate limits to be placed upon popular judgment.

On these grounds, I've demonstrated that Pettit's adherence to the principles and, especially, the practices of traditional republicanism manifests itself in the democratically stunted and elite-empowering form of "electoral and contestatory democracy" that he subsequently espouses – one in which the people exercise both political authorization *and* extra-electoral contestation *indirectly* through representative and otherwise elite-filtered channels. Through the political prescriptions of Machiavelli, whom, *pace* the interpretations of scholars such as Pocock, Skinner and Pettit, I understand to be a self-avowed *dissenter* from the republican tradition (McCormick 2003; 2010, chap. 6), I have suggested the following. Should Pettit and progressively inclined republicans wish to elaborate a more substantive theory of democracy, they ought to: significantly qualify their relationship to traditional republicanism, which successfully championed liberty as nondomination when challenging arbitrarily wielded monarchical power, but which exhibits a manifestly poor record in ameliorating domination exercised by socioeconomic and political elites within republics; and further theorize and openly endorse institutions of political authorization and contestation that directly empower the people to decide matters of public policy, such as political trials and legislation.

After all, Machiavelli, whom Pettit and other neo-republicans

121

understand as a comrade in the cause of advancing liberty as nondomination, argues that socioeconomic and political elites, *not* common citizens, constitute the greatest threat to liberty within republics and, furthermore, that the people rather than the few are much more likely to make decisions conducive to the common good. Ultimately, I would beseech Pettit and neo-republicans to choose between democracy and republicanism on these grounds: Historically speaking, democracy politically compensates common people for their lack of material resources relative to socioeconomic elites and formally empowers the former to deliberate and decide policy themselves while republicanism, in general, safeguards elite privilege and prerogative from popular challenge and empowers representatives and purportedly neutral or "depoliticized" experts to decide, not always in good faith, on the people's behalf.

Ultimately, it doesn't matter whether one calls Machiavelli's politics republican or democratic. This is a semantic matter. The substantive point is that Machiavelli's thinking fully coincides with Pettit's indisputably imposing intellectual endeavors on the goal of liberty as nondomination. However, Machiavelli rejects the popularly marginalizing institutional arrangements characteristic of philosophical republicanism from Plato to Pettit. Machiavelli reminds us that, historically, the vast majority of citizens within republics explicitly denounced electoral and senatorial institutions as vehicles of their own domination by socioeconomic and political elites. If we are to find some semblance of objectivity and love for the common good in real world republics, it will not be in a collection of the enlightened few advocated by the philosophers – not among Plato's philosopher kings, Cicero's senatorial best men or Pettit's depoliticized experts. It will, rather, be found in the body of citizens, institutionally empowered to deliberate and decide for themselves.

References

Abramson, J. (1993). "The Jury and Democratic Theory." *Journal of Political Philosophy* 1: 45–68.

Baiocchi, G. (2001). "Participation, Activism, and Politics: The Porto Alegre Experiment and Deliberative Democratic Theory." *Politics & Society* 29: 43–72.

Baiocchi, G. (2005). *Militants and Citizens: The Politics of Participatory Democracy in Porto Alegre*. Stanford: Stanford University Press.

Baron, H. (1966). *The Crisis of the Early Italian Renaissance*. Princeton: Princeton University Press.

Brennan, G. and L. E. Lomasky (eds) (1993). *Democracy and Decision: The Pure Theory of Electoral Preference*. Cambridge: Cambridge University Press.

Bruni, L. (1987). *The Humanism of Leonardo Bruni: Selected Texts*. Eds and trans. G. Griffiths, J. Hankins and D. Thompson, Binghampton, NY: Medieval & Renaissance Texts & Studies.

Caplan, B. (2007). *The Myth of the Rational Voter: Why Democracies Choose Bad Policies*. Princeton: Princeton University Press.

Cicero, M. T. (1999 [1991]). *On the Commonwealth and On the Laws*. Ed. James Zetzel, Cambridge: Cambridge University Press.

Dahl, R. A. (1957). "Decision-Making in a Democracy: The Supreme Court as a National Policy-Maker." *Journal of Public Law* 6: 279–95.

Dahl, R. A. (1989). *Democracy and its Critics*. New Haven: Yale University Press.

Dahl, R. A. (2003). *How Democratic is the American Constitution?* New Haven: Yale University Press.

Dunn, J. (2006). *Democracy: A History*. New York: Atlantic Monthly Press.

Estlund, D. (2007). *Democratic Authority: A Philosophical Framework*. Princeton: Princeton University Press.

Farrand, M. (ed.) (1966). *The Records of the Federal Convention of 1787, vols I–III*. New Haven: Yale University Press.

Finley, M. I. (1985). *Democracy Ancient and Modern: Revised Edition*. New Brunswick, NJ: Rutgers University Press.

Fishkin, J. (1991). *Democracy and Deliberation: New Directions for Democratic Reform*. New Haven: Yale University Press.

Fishkin, J. (1997). *The Voice of the People: Public Opinion and Democracy*. New Haven: Yale University Press.

Fung, A. (2003). "Recipes for Public Spheres: Eight Institutional Choices and Their Consequences." *Journal of Political Philosophy* 11: 338–67.

Fung, A. and E. O. Wright (eds) (2003). *Deepening Democracy: Institutional Innovations in Empowered Participatory Governance*. London: Verso.

Goodin, R. (2008). *Innovating Democracy: Democratic Theory and Practice after the Deliberative Turn*. Oxford: Oxford University Press.

Guicciardini, F. (1998 [1512]). "Discorso di Logrogno" [1512]. In: *Republican Realism in Renaissance Florence: Francesco Guicciardini's Discorso di Logrogno*. Ed. and trans. A. Moulakis, Lanham, MD: Rowman and Littlefield: 117–50.

Hankins, J. (ed.) (2000). *Renaissance Civic Humanism: Reappraisals and Reflections*. Cambridge: Cambridge University Press: 143–79.

Hirschl, R. (2005). "Constitutionalism, Judicial Review, and Progressive Change." *Texas Law Review* 84: 471–507.

Hirschl, R. (2007). *Towards Juristocracy: The Origins and Consequences of the New Constitutionalism*. Cambridge, MA: Harvard University Press.

Holmes, S. (1995). *Passions and Constraint: On the Theory of Liberal Democracy*. Chicago: University of Chicago Press.

Isaac, J. C. (1988). "Republicanism vs. Liberalism? A Reconsideration." *History of Political Thought* 9: 349–77.

Kapust, D. (2004). "Skinner, Pettit, and Livy: The Conflict of the Orders and the Ambiguity of Republican Liberty." *History of Political Thought* 25: 377–401.

Kramer, L. D. (2004). *The People Themselves: Popular Constitutionalism and Judicial Review*. New York: Oxford University Press.

Larmore, C. (2001). "A Critique of Philip Pettit's Republicanism." In: *Social, Political,*

123

and Legal Philosophy: Philosophical Issues 11. Eds E. Sosa and E. Villanueva, Oxford: Blackwell Publishing: 229–43.

Larmore, C. (2008). *The Autonomy of Morality*. Cambridge: Cambridge University Press.

Landemore, H. (2007). *Democratic Reason: Politics, Collective Intelligence, and the Rule of the Many*. Dissertation: Government Department, Harvard University.

Levinson, S. (2006). *Our Undemocratic Constitution: Where the Constitution Goes Wrong (And How We the People Can Correct It)*. New York: Oxford University Press.

McCormick, J. (2003). "Machiavelli Against Republicanism: On the Cambridge School's 'Guicciardinian Moments.'" *Political Theory: An International Journal of Political Philosophy* 31: 615–43.

McCormick, J. (2007). "Machiavelli's Political Trials and the 'Free Way of Life.'" *Political Theory: An International Journal of Political Philosophy* 35: 385–411.

McCormick, J. (2010). *Machiavellian Democracy*. Cambridge: Cambridge University Press.

McCormick, J. (ed.) (n.d.). *Civic Liberty and Republican Government. Selected Political Writings of Francesco Guicciardini*. Princeton: Princeton University Press.

Machiavelli, N. (1962 [1532]). *Istorie Fiorentine*. Ed. F. Gaeta, Milan: Feltrinelli.

Machiavelli, N. (1997). "Discorsi" [c. 1513–19]. In: N. Machiavelli. *Opere I: I Primi Scritti Politici*. Ed. C. Vivanti, Torino: Einaudi-Gallimard: 193–525.

Mackie, G. (2004). *Democracy Defended*. Cambridge: Cambridge University Press.

Madison, J., A. Hamilton and J. Jay (as Publius) (1998 [1788]). *The Federalist Papers*. New York: Mentor.

Markell, P. (2008). "The Insufficiency of Non-Domination." *Political Theory: An International Journal of Political Philosophy* 36: 9–36.

Meyers, M. (ed.) (1981). *The Mind of the Founder: Sources of the Political Thought of James Madison*. Hanover, NH: University Press of New England.

Murray, R. J. (1966). "Cicero and the Gracchi." *Transactions and Proceedings of the American Philological Association* 97: 291–8.

Najemy, J. M. (1982). *Corporatism and Consensus in Florentine Electoral Politics, 1280–1400*. Chapel Hill, NC: University of North Carolina Press.

Neblo, M. (2005). "Thinking Through Democracy: Between the Theory and Practice of Deliberative Politics." *Acta Politica* 40: 1–13.

Neblo, M. (n.d.). *Common Voices: The Problems and Promise of a Deliberative Democracy*. Book manuscript.

Ober, J. (1993). *Mass and Elite Democratic Athens: Rhetoric, Ideology and the Power of the People*. Princeton: Princeton University Press.

O'Leary, K. (2006). *Saving Democracy: A Plan for Real Representation in America*. Stanford: Stanford University Press.

Page, S. (2006). *The Difference: How the Power of Diversity Creates Better Groups, Firms, Schools, and Societies*. Princeton: Princeton University Press.

Patten, A. (1996). "The Republican Critique of Liberalism." *British Journal of Political Science* 26: 25–44.

Pettit, P. (1999a). *Republicanism: A Theory of Freedom and Government*. Oxford: Oxford University Press.

Pettit, P. (1999b). "Republican Freedom and Contestatory Democratization." In: *Democracy's Value*. Eds I. Shapiro and C. Hacker-Cordon, Cambridge: Cambridge University Press: 163–89.

Pettit, P. (2000). "Democracy: Electoral and Contestatory." In: *Nomos XLII: Designing Democratic Institutions*. Eds I. Shapiro and S. Macedo, New York: New York University Press: 105–46.

Pettit, P. (2001). *A Theory of Freedom: From the Psychology to the Politics of Agency*. Oxford: Oxford University Press.

Pettit, P. (2004). "Depoliticizing Democracy." *Ratio Juris* 17: 52–65.

Phillips, A. (1995). *The Politics of Presence*. Oxford: Oxford University Press.

Plutarch (2005). "Cicero." In: Plutarch. *The Fall of the Roman Republic: Six Lives*. New York: Penguin: 323–73.

Przeworski, A., S. C. Stokes and B. Manin (eds) (1999). *Democracy, Accountability, and Representation*. Cambridge: Cambridge University Press.

Rogers, M. L. (2008). "Republican Confusion and Liberal Clarification." *Philosophy & Social Criticism* 34: 799–824.

Rosenberg, G. N. (1991). *The Hollow Hope: Can Courts Bring About Social Change?* Chicago: The University of Chicago Press.

Seager, R. (1972). "Cicero and the Word Popularis." *The Classical Quarterly* 22: 328–38.

Skinner, Q. (1998). *Liberty before Liberalism*. Cambridge: Cambridge University Press.

Sunstein, C. (2006). *Infotopia: How Many Minds Produce Knowledge*. Oxford: Oxford University Press.

Thompson, D. F. (2008). "Who Should Govern Who Governs?: The Role of Citizens in Reforming the Electoral System." In: *Designing Deliberative Democracy: The British Columbia Citizens' Assembly*. Eds M. E. Warren and H. Pearse. Cambridge: Cambridge University Press: 20–49.

Tocqueville, A. de (2000 [1840]). *Democracy in America*. Eds and trans. H. Mansfield and D. Winthrop, Chicago: University of Chicago Press.

van Gelderen, M. (2002). *The Political Thought of the Dutch Revolt, 1555–1590*. Cambridge: Cambridge University.

van Gelderen, M. (2005). "Aristotelians, Monarchomachs and Republicans: Sovereignty and respublica mixta in Dutch and German Political Thought, 1580–1650." In: *Republicanism, A Shared European Heritage: Volume 1. Republicanism and Constitutionalism in Early Modern Europe*. Eds M. van Gelderen and Q. Skinner, Cambridge: Cambridge University: 195–219.

Warren, M. E. and H. Pearse (2008). *Designing Deliberative Democracy: The British Columbia Citizens' Assembly*. Cambridge: Cambridge University Press.

Williams, M. S. (2000). *Voice, Trust, and Memory: Marginalized Groups and the Failings of Liberal Representation*. Princeton: Princeton University Press.

Wood, N. (1988). *Cicero's Social and Political Thought*. Berkeley: University of California Press.

Young, I. M. (1990). *Justice and the Politics of Difference*. Princeton: Princeton University Press.

Young, I. M. (2000). *Inclusion and Democracy*. Oxford: Oxford University Press.

125

NOTES

1. I would like to thank the conference participants, both of the fellow presenters – especially, Philip Pettit, and many members of the audience, for constructive comments and criticisms on this paper. Greg Conti provided invaluable research assistance for which I am immensely grateful.
2. Cicero 1999, 22–3 (sections I.51–2). Cf. Wood 1988, 22, 169–71, 174–5.
3. Machiavelli 1997; hereafter cited in the text as D with book and chapter numbers in parentheses.
4. On the difficulties entailed by sharply distinguishing liberalism from republicanism, see Isaac 1988; Holmes 1995, 5–6; Patten 1996; Larmore 2001, 2008, 139–95; and Rogers 2008.
5. Pettit 1999a, 55, 290–2; 2001, 156–8; or what he terms elsewhere "perceived interests": Pettit 1999b, 165, 166, 170, *passim*.
6. Cf. Pettit 1999a, 27. While Pettit states that his theorizing constitutes "a distinctively republican story," he also claims that it does not represent "slavish fidelity to the republican tradition": Pettit 2001, 173.
7. According to Pettit, a good becomes a common good when "co-operatively admissible considerations support its collective provision": Pettit 2001, 173. However, Pettit deliberately provides no list of issues that necessarily constitute democratic commonality – that is for democratic citizens to decide. He operates under the presupposition that democracies necessarily enjoy some grounds of commonality; see Pettit 2000, 108.
8. Pettit interprets the traditional standard of the common good – "What touches all ought to be considered and approved by all" – in a decidedly weak democratic sense: "This does not say that what touches all ought to be decided by all, only that what touches all ought to elicit the considered approval of all. And that is to say that what touches all ought to be controlled by all in the passive mode of control, not necessarily in the active": Pettit 2000, 140.
9. Electoral politics performs a "positive search-and-identify" function while contestatory politics performs a "negative scrutinize-and-disavow" function within Pettit's conception of democracy.
10. Even if they are not elected, Pettit insists that administrative and judicial bodies must be sociologically diverse, not "statistically dominated" by members "of one religion, one gender, one class, or one ethnicity," and so he advocates "statistical representation for the major stakeholder groupings" of society: Pettit 1999a, 193, 192.
11. On the importance of representing diversity in such contexts, see Young 1990, 2000; Phillips 1995; Williams 2000; and Goodin 2008, 233–54.
12. Williams concedes that, when it comes to affecting policy outcomes, representing groups in contemporary parliamentary contexts can only amplify voices so much; see Williams 2000, 222.
13. Pettit is more in tune with the spirit of the Roman tribunes when he recommends allotting seats to "representatives" of indigenous peoples, that is, those they choose among themselves.
14. Indeed, when considering the advantages of mixing different types of electoral systems, Pettit mentions majoritarian and proportional procedures, but he never mentions a practice that was quite prevalent in traditional republics, namely, lottery; see Pettit 2000, 135.

15. Markell 2008 suggests that Pettit's ambiguous and inconsistent use of the terms/ concepts "avowed interests" and "arbitrary" allows him to empower governments to usurp the judgment of individuals whose domination the former are supposed to alleviate.

16. For a contrary view, see Mackie 2004.

17. Contemporary theorists of "democratic reason" draw upon similar evidence correlating the cognitive diversity of large bodies with the generally optimum decisions they make; see Page 2006; Estlund 2007; and Landemore 2007. For a dissenting view, see Caplan 2007 and, more moderately, Sunstein 2006.

18. Curiously, Pettit (1999a, 182) cites Machiavelli (D I.58) on the superior judgment of the people, but he never operationalizes this insight within his framework, instead deliberately confining collective decisions with binding force to the electoral realm. In particular, he doesn't trace the institutional implications of this view that sets Machiavelli so far apart from the other republican authors with whom Pettit, following Skinner, groups him. Moreover, Pettit then uses Machiavelli to impose a strict divide between laws and orders such that the latter may be maintained beyond popular desires for change. However, Machiavelli gives many examples of the Roman people changing orders as well as laws, for better, in the case of the tribunate, and for worse, in the case of the Decemvirs.

19. Kapust suggests that, in such moments, Pettit imports the paternalism of Roman senatorial and clientelist politics into his framework; see Kaplan 2004, 397–8.

20. On the democratic ramifications of juries, see Abramson 1993.

21. Goodin summarizes cases where such mini-publics have had more than just the effect of informing public debate: mini-publics have been involved in "determining the referendum question on electoral reform in British Columbia, influencing Danish policy on irradiated food, [and] emboldening Texas utilities to invest more heavily in renewable energy even if at slightly higher prices to consumers": Goodin 2008, 37.

22. Pettit 1999a, 168, citing Brennan and Lomasky 1993.

23. Somewhat inexplicably, elsewhere Pettit condones the possibility of changing electoral rules through popular referenda; see Pettit 2001, 161.

24. Although it must be noted that any collective body, short of a life-termed senate or supreme court, is open to charges of intertemporal inconsistency.

25. Farrand 1966, vol. I, 146–7; Meyers 1981, 395; and Madison, Hamilton and Jay 1998, esp. nos 10 and 51. On the antipopular and antiparticipatory biases of the English republicans, see Skinner 1998, 31–2; on the aristocratic prejudices of Dutch republicanism, see van Gelderen 2002, especially 35, 207; 2005, especially 204, 213.

CHAPTER 5

Two Views of the City:
Republicanism and Law

John Ferejohn

Republican political theory has been thought to have distinctive implications for law and especially for constitutional institutions and practices. A
republic is supposed to pursue the common interests of its citizens and for
that reason republicans have usually opposed rule by narrow groups such
as monarchy or oligarchy, which would be tempted to pursue narrower
objectives.[1] Traditionally republicans have also usually opposed democracy, too – especially direct democracy of the kind practiced in Athens
– on the ground that rule by a majority is a form of despotic or lawless rule.
Republicans have also tended to be suspicious of liberalism because of its
emphasis on private goods rather than public projects and its deprecation
of duties and of shared or public interests. Nowadays, however, many
republicans argue that republicanism actually requires a commitment to
certain kinds of "democratic" institutions and to deliberative practices,
and they see some version of democracy as consistent with assuring robust
liberal protections for individual freedom.

Philip Pettit, for example, argues that law, even though it compels and
coerces, is or can be emancipative for individuals. By reducing the domination of some by others, it can increase the amount of liberty or freedom
enjoyed by the individuals in society. Moreover, he argues that the legal
system can be so arranged, constitutionally, as to limit domination by
governmental officials while permitting it sufficient power and purpose
to restrain private actors from dominating others. Because it offers a way
to reduce domination (on Pettit's account) republicans favor rule by law
rather than decree and that, if decrees must be used, they ought to be
regulated by law. Pettit also argues that a republican political structure
will have many democratic aspects embodying, in various ways a principle

128

of "contestability" that ensures that public policies are sensitive to the opinions (and not merely the interests) of citizens. Pettit's views, while highly distinctive in many ways, seem exemplary of modern republicanism in the assumption that republicanism, liberalism and democracy are basically compatible.[2]

Earlier modern writers also thought that freedom would be promoted by law especially if the laws were well made or were substantively good. Rousseau thought that law could increase the freedom of citizens, if laws were enacted by the people themselves using appropriate procedures. While he did not use the language of non-domination, Rousseau argued that people living under laws of their own making would not surrender any essential freedom as they would be self-governed: the laws, insofar as they reflected the general will, would not express alien commands but would embody each person's own interest and so, to be commanded by law is to be self-commanded. While their views are very different in many respects, both Rousseau and Pettit seem to exemplify a key aspect of modern republicanism, in that the law and legal institutions are justified in terms of preserving or enhancing individual freedom for the purpose of realizing value at the level of the individual.[3]

I assume that the key characteristic of republican government – classical and modern – is its commitment to pursue the public interest – an interest common to its citizens. This commits republicans to two projects. First, positively, they are committed to the need to empower a "popular" government – in which authority comes from the citizens to rule on their behalf – that is capable of effectively pursuing their shared interests. Second, republicans need to limit various kinds of corruption that can interfere with the pursuit of common interests, limiting temptations and opportunities for officials and citizens to put private concerns and interests before public ones. Republicans, therefore, have generally wanted government to be powerful and competent while being restrained from tyrannizing its citizens.

Republicans have endorsed many different kinds of institutions to achieve these ends: the use of elections to fill high offices, term limitations for high officials, combined with popular control over law-making, and sometimes a plural or collegial executive. All of these practices have been thought to encourage the choice of able officials while placing limits on their capacity to abuse public office. Other republicans have called for a strong and unified executive, law-making in elected assemblies, and a constitutional policy of separating certain governmental powers from others – singling out the judicial and legislative powers, for example, as distinct from executive authority – and building mechanisms, especially the widespread distribution of veto powers, to stabilize or protect power separations. Many republicans have also argued for the institution of a consultative or deliberative organ situated somewhere in government – sometimes as counsel to the executive or even as a kind of collective executive, and sometimes as a legislative organ – to give some kind of stability or rationality to the laws.

Some republicans have argued that a constitution ought not to provide for rigid and judicially enforceable protections for specific substantive rights, as any particular right ought to be defeasible in light of the require-ments of pursuing public purposes. This is not to say that republicans are unconcerned with rights; but they are skeptical that rights can be effec-tively guaranteed by rigid legal protections. Many believe that substantive rights would be adequately protected in a well-constructed constitutional system and agree with Alexander Hamilton when he said that a consti-tution is itself a bill of rights. However, republicans since the Romans have often supported certain specific procedural rights to restrain officials from arbitrary arrests, detentions and executions and that require legally regulated trials.[4]

In this paper I want to raise some questions about some of these diverse and sometimes contradictory prescriptions and examine what they suggest about political and legal institutions and for the nature of law. I shall argue that there are really at least two separate complexes of constitutional prescriptions that can be found in republican thought. The classical complex can be seen in various forms in Rome and Athens: there were popular or directly democratic components in both cities (the Roman comitia; the Athenian ekklesia and jury courts). Both cities also divided executive powers (in Rome there were two independent consuls; in Athens there were typically plural magistracies). Both cities also had an advisory body that was more or less aristocratic (in Rome this role was played by the Senate; in Athens, the Boule managed the agenda of the ekklesia). Of course the Athenian mix was more democratic than the Roman in affording a much greater role to direct rule by the people, either in rotating magistracies chosen by lottery, or in the *ekklesia* and the popular jury courts. But the basic elements were qualitatively similar throughout the classical world.[5]

The modern complex is different in embracing a functional division of powers: Legislative powers are usually delegated to elected assemblies; the advisory body is a part of the legislative (while it may advise the executive it has little formal role in it); the executive is unified; and probably most importantly, the judiciary is generally made independent of the other parts of government presumably to give every citizen a neutral forum to contest applications of law. There is, in other words, no longer any constitutional "recognition" of a popular vs. an aristocratic interest. Only individuals, as undifferentiated citizens, have constitutional status. The main way in which individuals come into contact with the state is through its coercive commands and, as Montesquieu argued, this makes the courts a central element in maintaining nondespotic rule.[6] Indeed, one might even argue that court procedures contain a core democratic aspect, at least if the courthouse doors are truly open to anyone. It is in a court that a person has the chance to insist that the state recognize his or her particular rights as a legal person and justify its coercive claims. To the extent the case is judged impartially it is in the courts that a person has at least some prospect of participating in self-government. Of course most people do not challenge the compulsions to which they are subject, fewer still prevail, and courts are usually difficult to access for the poor. But the presence of an impartial judiciary is a powerful inducement for state actors to contemplate the individualized affect of laws, and to adjust proposed legal rules in that light.

I argue that the reason that modern republicans endorse different institutions than their classical forbearers is that they have a different understanding of society and social conflict. While classical republicans believed that citizens had interests in common, they also saw the city as deeply divided by profound distributional conflicts and regarded political institutions as a main mechanism for regulating these conflicts. Modern republicans tend to play down this kind of structural conflict and emphasize instead common purposes. I believe that this difference is rooted in what can be called "social ontology." Classical republicanism emerged from a society made up of social orders or classes; modern republicanism sees society as fundamentally composed of individuals rather than social classes.[7] Because of their distinctive views about society, modern republicans face a different kind of justificatory challenge for state coercion, because they think it is individuals rather than social classes that have to be given reasons for allegiance. I suggest that individualist ontology leads modern republicans to make roughly similar institutional prescriptions to liberal theories and may account for controversy over how to understand some of their writings. Think, for example, of the controversies

131

over whether and to what extent James Madison (or Locke, or Kant, or Montesquieu for that matter) can be understood as a republican thinker rather than a liberal one.

My second claim is that republican institutional prescriptions depend on the nature of the common good asserted in the particular republican theory – the principal source of normative direction for citizens and officials – and in that respect are not really attributable to republicanism itself. I argue that a republican conception of the common good depends at least partly on what is seen as the greatest danger or threat to the republic. Is the greatest threat invasion? Fear of despotic rule? Corruption by the rich or well born? Or is it the threat of populism or mob rule, or the erosion of the public spiritedness and willingness to sacrifice? As republicans have differed greatly in their fears and therefore in their conceptions of the public good, one would expect them to urge different kinds of institutions capable of advancing the particular conception and being robust against the kinds of corruption to which it might be subject. Indeed, depending on the conception of common interests, republican prescriptions can approach or depart from liberal ones.

The next two sections present the main arguments: the first compares classical and modern republicanism with an eye to drawing out and explaining their different institutional choices. The second is an attempt to identify the institutional implications of alternative conceptions of the common good – again separating the classical from the modern – using roughly the same kinds of historical materials discussed in the first part.

I. CLASSICAL VS. MODERN REPUBLICANISM

I start by describing two models of republicanism. The classical republican sees "class" conflict as a central and ineliminable obstacle to social cooperation and key to devising stable republican institutions and practices.[8] Modern republicanism takes an individualist perspective that emphasizes different kinds of conflicts and different problems of cooperation. As they are versions of republicanism, both assert the existence of a common good that can be fruitfully pursued through cooperative activity. But the classical view sees the central problem of cooperation as arranging a stable class bargain whereas, for the moderns, the main problem is to incentivize individuals to pursue common interests. This difference is, of course, a matter of tendency and emphasis and both classical and modern theories exhibit variation and overlap.

132

Before beginning I need to say what the terms are supposed to refer to. I take classical republicanism to refer to governmental practices in republican Rome, Athens, Carthage and Sparta, and many lesser known states, during the fifth and fourth centuries BCE and to the views of writers describing or criticizing how those practices worked or failed. I take Cicero and Sallust – however much they may have disagreed about the kind of balance among social classes that would be desirable – to typify classical republicanism. And, insofar as he analogizes Florentine to Roman political life, I also understand Machiavelli to represent a classical viewpoint. Modern republicans are those who take a post-Hobbesian perspective, writers like Madison on the one hand, and Rousseau on the other. I would also include Kant, Madison and Pettit and many other modern writers here. I am leaving out of my account writers in between like Harrington, Hunton and Sidney and later writers in the English tradition such as Trenchard and Gordon who wrote as Cato against the Whig oligarchy. I do not really doubt that they could be discussed in this framework but the categories would get fuzzier for many reasons, not least of which is that many of them had never really experienced anything like republican rule by their own lights. Opposition republicans, especially if facing a monarchy or an oligarchy, have a natural tendency to play down internal divisions among the people and to represent the government as, in some sense, foreign to the people. This probably has nothing much to do with republicanism and everything to do with opposition to despotic rule. In any case I am already in pretty deep water as it is.

Classical republicanism

Classical republican thought rested on a characteristic ontology of the city. Aristotle and Machiavelli, if they agreed on little else, both thought that the city consisted of the rich and poor, each of which would run the city according to their class interests if they had the chance to control the government. Classical writers thought that the rich and powerful had an overwhelming temptation to dominate and bully, whereas the poor wanted protection from them as well as a chance at material well-being. Polybius and Roman writers seemed to share this view and to regard a city in a permanent state of existential crisis. Livy sometimes asked about Rome: Is this one city or two? He implied that the correct answer was not at all obvious. The point is that for classical republicans, class conflict is a primary and persistent fact of social existence and the best one can hope

133

for is to try to channel and control its effects. And one principal way this is done is to find or construct common interests that both the rich and poor can pursue. But people will inevitably disagree about the content of common interests and how the burdens of providing them shall be borne. The Romans discovered more reliable means of managing conflict – developing an institutional structure that forces the classes to cooperate with one another governing the city.

Legend had it that the Roman constitution was not actually designed but emerged from a long history of class struggle. After the aristocrats overthrew the Etruscan king in favor of a republican plural executive they needed popular (plebeian) support to keep the Etruscans from returning and to resist incursions from the surrounding hostile tribes. But the plebeian infantry, on several occasions, refused to fight or even to stay on the battlefield unless patricians conceded them some share in government by yielding institutional concessions. And many times the patricians were forced to accede to many of these demands: permitting the plebes to take part in electing magistrates, to reserve one of the consuls for the plebes,[9] to elect their own representatives (tribunes) with extensive powers to interfere with other magistrates, and to give the plebes-dominated-assemblies a monopoly on law-making.

True, the aristocrats kept certain formal privileges that were protected by arranging favorable vote-counting rules, keeping control of the assemblies in the hands of executive officials, and retaining public (rather than secret) balloting until late in republican history. But even these protections were imperfect since the people's representatives could convene legislative assemblies to enact new laws, and they could mobilize public sentiment in various ways to alter the course of policy.[10] In any case, the popular institutions and practices made it possible for an ambitious politician, from any social class, to base his career on popular rather than aristocratic support.

The timing and contexts (and even reality) of many of these events are shrouded in mystery since few events before the time of Polybius were recorded. But all these institutions were in place and well documented in the last two centuries of the republic. In any case, how much of the story is literally true may not matter; it was certainly official myth and says much about how the Romans saw their institutions. And, despite many changes in class composition and structure over time, and the vast expansion in Roman citizenship throughout Italy, these institutional concessions did not put an end to the underlying social conflict but rather domesticated

134

it into an institutional or political conflict. Class struggles remained prominent until the very end of the republican period and probably they increased in intensity over time. Endless battles over redistribution of power and wealth remained a constant preoccupation of republican politics. Of course, it was always expected that advocates of the poor would advocate redistribution as being in the public interest, and that defenders of privilege would mount their defenses in those terms as well. Such rhetoric was probably at least somewhat effective in persuading those in the middle – after all, both the poor and the rich had to appeal to some imagined unity if they were to succeed – and thus inevitable.

One way to characterize the Roman constitutional "bargain" is that elite rule was accepted but, in exchange, it would be confined and regulated by laws, and that law-making was conceded to the people's assemblies. The Senate and the executive magistrates, representing the aristocracy, could make the day-to-day policies for the state and, inevitably, some of these policies entailed coercing Roman citizens. But the tribunes, the people's representatives, not only had the authority to force executive magistrates to provide due process to individual Roman citizens (at least inside the city), they could generally block any policy action that the Senate or the executive officials tried to undertake.

The emergence of the rule of law followed the same concessionary pattern as constitutional development. As far as one can tell there seem to have been relatively few laws throughout most of the republican period (you can find a list on Wikipedia or in any number of other sources), and those laws were relatively stable (at least until the last century). And many of these laws were concerned largely with constitutional matters: creating new offices, laying out the powers of officials and classes with respect to one another, making extraordinary appointments. One of the early elite concessions to the plebes was to establish a council that combined constituent and executive powers that had the task of codifying the customary laws that were used to regulate private disputes. Ultimately this body and its successor produced the Twelve Tables that codified the main elements of (previously customary) Roman private law. Additional laws were made in the popular assemblies, initially with the Senate having a kind of proposal power or gatekeeping authority. But the Senate's gatekeeping role was abolished in the *lex Hortensia* in the third century and was only briefly and unsuccessfully restored by Sulla. So from the earliest days, legal development followed the pattern of concessions to the plebes and restricted the powers of the magistrates and the Senate. The result

135

was that, in an important sense, laws made in the assembly functioned something like the way constitutional laws do in the modern state – as limits on what the main (elite-dominated) governing bodies can do. At least this was so juridically.[11]

On the face of it, then, the constitution made policy hostage to widely distributed veto powers and, as a result, Roman institutions were probably not well suited to adopting socially divisive policies that might be necessary in confronting a crisis. Perhaps this is the reason the Romans developed the dictatorship, which offered a way to eliminate, for a short time and for a well-defined purpose, the veto powers of the tribunes and the potential for the consuls to interfere with one another. As Nippel (1995) has demonstrated, the dictatorship was very frequently used to solve intractable political problems – in both domestic and foreign affairs – and was probably best seen as a regular, if abnormal, part of Roman constitutional practice at least throughout the middle period of the republic. It is important to see that the dictatorship remained almost completely in the control of the aristocratic part of the constitution: It could be invoked only by the Senate and the dictator had to be appointed by one or both consuls. Possibly for that reason, no constitutional dictator was appointed after 200 BCE, at roughly the time that the popular part of the Roman constitution became more important in the overall institutional mix. The Senate attempted to substitute for this lack by inventing a new edict demanding that the consuls do whatever is necessary to defend the republic. But these edicts remained divisive because they were often invoked to intervene in internal class conflict.[12]

Moreover, the assemblies were not self-operating but needed to be convened by magistrates and have questions put to them for decision. But, as I have emphasized, tribunes as well as consuls and praetors had the authority to do the convening and to set the agenda. In that way, the constitution instituted elite competition over legislative agenda-setting. And since all important magistrates had to stand for election if they wanted to ascend the ladder of offices, officials had plenty of reasons to compete for popular favor. Juridically, therefore, the people had some degree of (indirect) control over the content of law, while the aristocracy (which was elected in the assemblies) controlled day-to-day policy. Of course one could doubt how well this juridical bargain described political reality. The aristocrats were generally rich and well-armed and found ways to coopt or terrify the people and their tribunes and to manipulate the assemblies. Still intra-elite competition may have restrained these efforts and, at least when Polybius wrote, it was possible to describe the republic as well-governed. But the deeper point is that it was well-governed insofar as it institutionalized and successfully channeled endemic, and irremediable, social conflict.

Later generations of Romans split over how to interpret these events and therefore held heterogeneous views of the constitution. Where Polybius saw a balanced constitution where class interests were more or less securely protected, Sulla and Cicero, and other conservatives, thought that the crucial part of the constitution was its aristocratic component and that had decayed dangerously. Sulla thought that the Senate was in decline, thanks both to natural attrition and, more significantly, to the rise of populist generals like the Gracchi and Marius whose power lay in their popularity with the people and especially the veterans. Conservatives believed that the "populares" political leaders exploited their popularity to overrun constitutional barriers despite the many institutional and social advantages the aristocrats retained. When Sulla made himself dictator he tried to reverse these trends by enlarging the Senate, reducing the legislative power of the tribunes, restoring ancient senatorial veto power over legislation and, most effectively, by killing anyone he thought to be an enemy of the republic. But most of his reforms lasted barely a decade. Cicero's initial actions to defend Roman institutions were directed against conspirators led by the rogue patrician Catiline. But after being exiled he developed a highly conservative defense of the aristocratic or pro-Senate position that was largely expressed in his writings after returning from exile.

Others blamed the decline in the republic on the blind intransigence of aristocrats who failed to recognize or appreciate growing inequalities or to pay sufficient attention to the demands by veterans in recognition of their service to the state. Others thought the problem was the general decline of the republican character or virtue. In any case the disintegration had gone far enough by the time he wrote that Livy observed that at times Rome seemed to be two cities rather than one. Distributional issues kept returning, especially concerning veterans, and were never resolved. In place of resolution, institutional concessions were given: which amount to an offer to continue class struggles. Others blamed the crisis on the great men themselves – on their hubristic insistence on dignity and their unwillingness to respect public norms. But in any case, almost everyone believed that the Polybian balance had collapsed and that Rome's institutions no longer assured either liberty or security.

To some political scientists the end of the story may not seem mysterious. Roman institutions had accumulated so many veto points by the second century that it was chronically prone to gridlock and inefficacy, especially after it became politically impossible to appoint a constitutional dictator. Indeed, from this viewpoint, the hard thing to understand is how those institutions could have lasted so long since their successful functioning would seem to rest on an implausible degree of elite consensus. Perhaps the political success of Rome in this period was because power was exercised largely outside of constitutional channels. One might instead regard Roman institutions as an equilibrium of a bilateral bargaining process between the classes in a situation of repeated play. As long as the underlying conflict at Rome retained this dualist character, and as long as the players took a long view, vetoes would rarely be exercised and would not necessarily block new laws nor prevent effective policy. On this view, the breakdown would be attributable to a collapse of the underlying bilateral structure – perhaps due to new entrants or to the rise of individuals whose interests were separable from the classes – or to an increased tendency of elites to discount the future.

I believe that both of these views are inadequate because they underestimate the creative uses that Romans made of their constitution. For one thing, the plebes developed their own aristocracy so that the interests of plebeian tribunes no longer conflicted sharply with the Senate. Ambitious tribunes would have found easy alliances throughout the upper classes. Second, increased use was made of legally commissioned magistrates – proconsuls, for example – to do things the dictators had done before. Moreover, the traditional strictures against repeated election to consular office decayed. So even if the constitution appeared rigid and unbending, there was room for maneuver and compromise.

In any case, the origins of self-conscious republican thought are located at this late period, while republican institutions were failing. Cicero formulated a nostalgic view of what the republic had been and what it may become. Having been hounded into exile by Caesar's supporters, he became an unabashed conservative, a defender of the Senate against the populares, and it is sometimes hard to see where he would have parted with Sullan constitutional ideas. Other republicans, especially Cato, took increasingly strident positions against Caesar, ultimately leading forces during the civil wars. Cicero and Cato developed an ideology of opposition offered not only in Cicero's books on the republic and the laws, but especially in more dangerous speeches against Caesar's political heir, Marc Antony. The Philippics were to become important sources of republican ideology and a demonstration of public courage, and they led to his murder.

Sallust and other writers took less pro-Senate views, arguing that the cause of Roman decline was in the unwillingness of oligarchs to curb growing exploitation of veterans and peasants. At this period, republican thinking seemed to divide along partisan lines, as did Roman politics itself. But even if the articulation of republican ideas took place late and in opposition, it seems likely to me that the various strains of republican thought drew heavily on the practical republicanism described already in Polybius. There was widespread acceptance of the basic institutions and governmental practices – but disagreement as to how these elements ought to be balanced. (Indeed, the striking unoriginality of Cicero's "ideal" constitution – that amounted to a bare redescription of Roman institutions – seems evidence of how much his theory drew from earlier governmental practice.)

Modern republicanism

Modern republicanism starts from different premises than the classical version in three ways. First, it is premised on a different social ontology and therefore a different view of social conflict. Second, until the time of the US constitutional convention, modern republican thought developed mostly as an opposition ideology and one that had been in the political wilderness for a very long time, starting with Machiavelli's exile and running through the English republicans up through the time of Cato's Letters. And this remains an aspect of much contemporary republican thought. To the extent that republicans were theorizing about correcting the evils of an existing regime, or theorizing about an ideal republic, they were largely freed from anchoring their prescriptions tightly to practical issues of how institutions would work or relate to society. They could speak of common interests or of the people, as though these were natural and undivided unities, and could thus deemphasize internal conflicts. Third, modern republicans tended to exhibit a deep aversion to any form of direct or popular rule that ran as deep as classical conservatives like Cicero.

I argue that these three features conspired to bring about a fourth change – a transformation in the nature and content of republican conceptions of law. In the classical model, the laws were concerned with principles of justice, with fundamental relations among the classes, and with the regulation of power. Day-to-day aspects of policy were carried out in other ways, largely by executive magistrates. For something to be a law rather than a decree, it had to satisfy a kind of substantive test of some kind.

I will argue that when people came to accept a functional separation of powers, distinguishing the legislative from the executive and judicial powers, for example, and as they began to think that the people cannot really be trusted to exercise any of these functions directly, it becomes natural to delegate powers to representatives and to evolve a procedural theory of law. Law then becomes whatever the legislature asserts as law, and magistrates and judges are to apply procedurally valid law. Procedural notions are found in command theories of law beginning with Hobbes, but are traceable as well in modern forms of positivism (where the legislative power becomes more institutionally distributed).

Pasquale Pasquino describes the modern post-Hobbesian world as a society without qualities – by which he means without social orders – but composed instead of atomic individuals. This does not imply the absence of conflict, but the structure of conflict is very different from the classical model. Conflict in this new world is usually invisible or latent – explicit fighting rarely occurs when the contending forces are very unequal – but is rather structural and rooted in the simple fact that each individual has his or her own distinct interests. This change shifts what counts as an adequate justification for state institutions and actions. State coercion needs to be justified to each person and not to classes. But it is important to see that this switch is central to the nature of republicanism: Individuals generally are in no position to threaten or force the state to make institutional concessions in the way that powerful and unified social classes can. The classical city needed the plebes, as a class, for defense of the city and the acquisition of new territory. The modern state does not depend on social classes in the same way. It needs to recruit enough people and resources to defend itself. Individuals, who have their own private interests, have to be induced to serve public purposes, leaving it to each of them to decide how much of any public burden she wants to take on. It is hard to organize modern individuals to pursue class interests even temporarily. Private interests can obscure their vision of what they have in common with others and limit their willingness to cooperate.

On modern views, the pursuit of private interest is not merely an obscuring nuisance that gets in the way of pursuing common projects, but is also an important and separate source of value that needs to be balanced against public interests. Classical republican institutions seem unsuited for this balancing since they barely recognize substantive individual claims. For this reason modern republicans have been led to devise theories that recognize individual interests and seek to balance them against the normative demands of common pursuits. Liberals, starting with Hobbes, have had to make room for common interests (in personal security, property, defense, economic security, environmental goods, and so forth). Modern republicans still tend to resist the liberal prescription of protecting individuals with rigidly enforceable legal rights, thinking them an impediment to common pursuits, but they have come a long way in recognizing the value of individual pursuits as well.

Rousseau and Madison, writing from very different (but recognizably republican) perspectives, saw the possibility of conflicting private interests as a primary fact that should guide us in thinking about which institutions we should have and what they should do. Rousseau argued for a small republic in which preference diversity would be naturally limited by the fact that people lived as neighbors. He favored keeping the legislative powers with the popular assembly as at Rome and in other classical republics. He thought that the need to justify state coercion required that citizens play a direct role in enacting the positive laws to which they were subject, and not delegate that choice to elected representatives. He described the institutions and practices that would facilitate the making of good (or at least justifiable) laws in the popular assembly. At the same time, he permitted magistrates a good deal of authority: Magistrates were to make legislative proposals and to control the agenda of the assembly. And they were to direct the policy of the city, subordinate to legislation. Thus, the republic that Rousseau described was hardly a democracy but resembled the classical practices at Rome: There would be voting on laws, but proposals would come from government officials and any arguments in the assembly would be conducted from the dais, by magistrates and not by ordinary citizens. Moreover, he placed no real restriction on how magistrates were to be chosen and certainly envisioned heredity, appointment and election as possibilities.

Madison took essentially the opposite approach to managing conflicting interests, which he thought were inevitable in any modern political economy. He neither hoped nor wished to extinguish private pursuits. He argued for a large and diverse republic in which majorities would be hard to form and internally unstable and argued that, in this new "compound" republic, liberties would be adequately protected against the urgent claims of faction. He thought that in such a government there would be limits on the damage any particular majority could do. Moreover, he thought that adequate justification for coercive rules could be offered to individuals without their direct participation in law-making or even elections; indeed he worried that regular popular involvement in either constitutional or ordinary politics was generally dangerous. So, he was willing to alienate both law and politics to elected elites, and to retain for the people the abstract assurance of popular sovereignty.[13] Madison's views are obviously much closer to liberal thinking and have come to seem even closer as Americans have accepted the notion of judicial protection of rights.

It is well to remember, however, that the opponents to Madison's constitution – those known to us as "anti-federalists" – were republicans, too. They had a much more classical vision, and fear, of the new national government that Madison proposed, seeing it as likely to be dominated by patricians (who dominated the Philadelphia convention) who would freeze out provincials. Many of the anti-federalists agreed on the need for constitutional reforms; they believed, however, that republican rule – and especially legislation – had to remain close to the people if it was to avoid tyranny. This implied that the new nation should be made up of small confederated republics, rather than a powerful new government imposed on the states. The anti-federalists did not insist on direct popular rule of course, but they thought elections should be very frequent, and that they should be conducted in very small constituencies so that the representatives would be accountable to the people. And they thought that the executive power should not be placed in one man but ought to be collegial, and that popular juries should continue to play the primary role in law enforcement.

Nowadays, we tend to think of these people as rural provincials who lost the contest of ideas with Madison and Hamilton. But as the historian Gordon Wood argues, and as Tocqueville saw, Federalist patricians were themselves soon swept from power to be replaced by more popular and often rambunctious local figures – essentially men who resembled the anti-federalists during the debates over the ratification of the Constitution. Madison himself played an important role in defeating the Federalist some years after the ratification, teaming with Thomas Jefferson (another Virginia oligarch) to turn the Federalists out of office in the first "popular" election campaign. The "democratic" aspects of the American constitutional experiment advanced rapidly from that time onwards.[14]

The priority that republicans place on the common good suggests that a republican constitution ought to arrange its governmental institutions in ways that assure that that good would be reliably pursued, and that decisions about public policies and laws would be resolved largely on the basis of considerations relating to common interests. Again Madison and Rousseau diverged on how this might be done: While both were concerned to limit the damage that factions and parties could do to common interests, Madison thought the best way to organize legislation was to have popularly elected representatives share in the legislative process with a more elite Senate, which he expected both to discover and to "refine and enlarge" public opinion about common interests.[15] Rousseau thought it better to keep the republic small and homogeneous so that the citizens themselves could decide whether or not to accept the legal propositions posed and deliberated by magistrates within a suitably regulated legislative process. His proposed framework was explicitly neoclassical and more or less similar to (idealized) Roman practices and probably even more similar to fourth-century Athenian institutions.[16]

How common aims can be achieved would seem to depend on some conception of the common good and some notion of how it could be reliably determined and pursued. We can imagine three alternatives. One has to do with the substance of the common good; a the second has to do with what abilities and skills are appropriate to recognizing and realizing the common good; and the third has to do with institutional arrangements that make it likely that the first two considerations will line up appropriately.

Rousseau's theory of the general will – that is the part of the common good that should be enacted as positive law – exemplifies each of these notions: He thought the substance of the general will consisted of abstract norms (which mentioned no particulars) that each of us could accept as binding laws. He thought that people were likely to be able to recognize a norm as a part of general will in the context of a suitably organized citizens' assembly once the reasons were put before them (by magistrates); and he thought that the assembly was most likely to enact appropriate laws if individual answers in the assembly were aggregated in certain ways.

Following Rousseau, many modern republicans have rejected the classical view that there is a chronic structural conflict between the rich and the poor that must be reflected in any stable political arrangement. For Rousseau the rejection goes along with his idea that everyone has the general will as part of his or her own interests and that class interests are merely factional and have no respectable role in legislation. The Polybian institutionalization of social conflict is unacceptable on such an account. Madison recognized that classes, as factions, were inevitable in a free society but thought of them mostly as nuisances and would, I guess, have been hostile to institutionalizing them in the way that the Romans had. In any case he thought that American national institutions would provide a setting in which those factional interests would be fairly impotent.[17]

2. Conceptions of the common good and constitutional design

Republicans share the notion that considerations of the common good ought to motivate citizens and officials and shape law and politics. But the Romans had diverse ideas of the common good. Polybius and, we imagine, many Romans of his era and before, thought that Roman domination of nearby parts of Italy and the Mediterranean was the principal interest that Romans had in common. He might plausibly have thought that most public policy deliberations would naturally have been structured around this objective: to keep Rome secure and free of foreign domination. This notion fits well with their early history in which Romans threw off the yoke of the Etruscan kings, who nevertheless remained a persistent threat to Roman liberty. The pursuit of security from external domination would give reasons to ensure that people were induced to defend the city, that military veterans were well-treated, that the lower classes were not too deprived, and that merit, especially military merit, was recognized and rewarded. His *Histories* placed Roman institutions and public norms in an instrumental relationship to this end.

This notion of the common good seems to lead institutional and legal design in a very specific direction: to devise institutions and laws so as to make the Romans formidable to their enemies. Polybius thought this shared objective was the best explanation for the structure of Roman institutions and laws. The institutions were devised to permit the wealthy and well-armed aristocracy to control the army where they could devise foreign (imperial) policies and control military strategy. Political institutions were arranged also in such a way as to limit competition within the elite by rotating offices. And the loyalties of the foot soldiers were won by guaranteeing them full political citizenship and sometimes a plot of land at the end of their service. Still, in the interest of maintaining conservative order, voting and other rules were rigged to keep aristocrats securely in control of policy. There were of course checks and balances built into this structure as we have seen, which had the effect (and perhaps the purpose) of assuring that the aristocratic leaders consulted with the lower orders prior to taking on risky foreign adventures. And these checks also restrained the overweening ambitions of some aristocrats, keeping them within the bounds of laws that had popular assent.

Later Romans came to see the common good less univocally – some thought of it as consisting in the preservation of a certain quality of public life (characterized by hard to define Roman values such as *libertas*, and so forth). Others might have thought that the common good consists in the production of the right kind of civic morality, steadfastness or patriotism. While Cicero and the younger Cato and the other late republicans could not envision completely new institutions, they began to revalorize the ones they had inherited, reinterpreting their purpose as being the defense of *libertas* and civic virtue.

Modern republicans like Rousseau made ethical considerations central to republican life. Rousseau saw the purpose as permitting people to live in freedom, which he defined as living under laws of their own making. Pettit, following Rousseau, places a kind of liberal egalitarian end in front – the reduction of domination – and urges that it play the central role in guiding institutional design. If ethical or moral considerations are the point of living in a republic, there is reason to devise quite a different kind of constitution than the Romans had exhibited. In particular it made sense to distinguish, as Rousseau had, between universal norms that can bind every person equally and specific norms that are directed to particular people or groups. The former, thought Rousseau, are properly the province of legislation whereas the latter belong to magistrates or courts. For this reason, republicans following Montesquieu and Locke have tended to endorse a functional separation of powers that tracks the universal–particular distinction. And those republicans who have endorsed a notion of checks and balances have advocated deploying checks to sustain institutionally separated powers.

On all these views, institutions play a more or less instrumental role relative to the common good, as they had in Polybius's theory. Others, like Cicero, have sometimes taken a less instrumental view of institutions, regarding the common good as more or less coextensive with the inherited institutions and practices of the republic. Madison is at pains to dismiss this view in the *Federalist* – saying that a constitution is made for the people and not the other way round – but we can certainly see many people today endorsing such a notion. I guess the expected constitutional prescription for this view would be to devise procedures that inhibit institutional change, such as requiring supermajorities or even providing consociational vetoes for various participants.

In addition to differing over the content of common interests, republicans have also disagreed as to what the interfering problem was that was preventing the attainment of those interests.[18] Throughout the republican period, Romans were especially worried about the possibility or reality of personal despotism or kingship and how to prevent it. Early on this threat mostly (although not always) arose externally; later in the republic the principal threats came from other Romans. The chief worry seems to have been about powerful men – with power bases in military prowess, popular appeal or access to great wealth, or all three – either capturing government or imposing their will in the face of a government too weak to stop them. Sometimes, faced with such threats, Romans took matters into their own hands and killed the usurper or drove him off, and they were often celebrated for it.

But, if patriotism cannot be counted on, people have sometimes crafted institutional devices to prevent the concentration of power in the hands of one person or a few, arranging the constitution to mitigate this threat. The Roman choice of a plural executive had this effect, as did term limits for high officials and prohibitions on repeated service. Moreover, the establishment of a Senate composed largely of former high executives, who could be counted on to watch jealously for usurpations, was continuously present in the Capital. Toward the end of the republic the frenetic constitutional innovations of the first century represent increasingly futile attempts to deal with the succession of warlords who controlled armies – sometimes privately levied – and threatened to overwhelm Roman public life and who eventually produced a circumstance of general civil war that lasted decades.

Renaissance republicans like Machiavelli and Harrington and Sidney had a similar but more specific set of worries about concentrated power, and they tried to devise institutional means to limit either monarchs or usurpers, seeing them as a threat to republican liberties. In England it seems that much of the resistance of monarchical absolutism took the form of efforts to establish independent judges or a role for the parliament in legislation. Again, the local concerns of modern republicans led them to functional power separations and efforts to build institutional walls around royal prerogative.

146

More recently, republican revivalists have worried about what seems a more abstract threat: liberalism, seen as a source of competing ideological claims about the appropriate role of government in public and private life and principally with its urge to protect individuals from state claims in ways that seem to discourage attention to common interests. In some ways the opposition to liberalism is similar to the ancient anxiety about the loss of civic virtue. The principal institutional implications of this concern seem to have been, first, an effort to limit excessive reliance on judicially enforceable rights and second, an effort to get judges to force Congress to provide reason-based justifications for legislative statutes. Obviously these two initiatives place quite different demands on judges – asking them on the one hand to be more passive or minimalist and, on the other, asking them to be more aggressive in reviewing statutes.

3. CONCLUSIONS

From a constitutional viewpoint it is not a surprise that classical and modern republicans endorsed different institutional "solutions" to the problem of government. The classical theory, because it rests on a particular hypothesis about the nature of the city – as structurally and stably divided into rich and poor classes that have distinct interests and concerns – is drawn to support a substantive theory of law, whereby the laws of the city are largely aimed at regulating the relations between the classes, and preventing the collapse of the regime into a tyranny. Such laws tend to be fundamental because the class interests are assumed to be stable, and hard to change without a fight, and as a consequence, tend to be relatively few and durable. Modern republicanism (and modern liberalism) in envisioning a society made up of individuals who have diverse and shifting interests, tends to accept a proceduralist theory of law that allows for rapid and flexible legal change and that doesn't sharply distinguish law from public policy. Law is whatever the legislature enacts (or courts enforce). Obviously there are important exceptions to this trend, so I don't mean to assert it as more than a tendency.[19]

At the constitutional level, classical and modern republicanism have supported different notions of power separation. Classical republicans wanted to separate institutions and offices to prevent the rule of a dominating class or the accretion of tyrannical powers in the hands of one man. They urged divided or plural executives and the representation of distinct social classes in separate councils. Modern republicans endorsed a

147

functional separation of the judicial from law-making and law-enforcing powers, insisting that law application and law-making be kept apart. Moreover, classical republicans thought that constitutional "checks and balances" would regulate relations among the social orders that make up society; modern republicans seem to see checks and balances as elements of (contrived) institutional design that can be arranged rationally to maintain functionally separate powers.

Both the classical and modern views capture important and enduring features of any society. Societies are made up of individuals, each of whom is a distinctive source of value; but the pattern of people's interests and opportunities are also structured, to a great extent, by relatively stable economic factors that tend to produce and stabilize a division of labor. Class interests are real structural facts in any society and tend to be relatively stable even in the modern world, even if they are only imperfectly organized or self-conscious. Of course a modern society is more fluid and diverse than most classical ones. But this pluralism does not eliminate the fact that the rich and powerful tend to have different interests and opportunities than others. I fear that modern republicanism has, in many ways, lost sight of this underlying fact – the resilient fact of class divisions – and has tended to evolve into a kind of quasi-liberal theory that is grounded on the kind of individualism on which liberalism is founded. This may be a good or bad thing; I do not know. But it is a loss of an aspect of republican thinking and it seems worthwhile to remark on its passage.

It is important to look at what has been lost in the transition. The Roman (classical) bargain, as I described it, amounted to giving, or better, yielding to the people (or to nonelites) control over the law in return for elite control over policy. Laws and law-making at Rome were therefore direct or popular, in the sense that the people had to agree directly to a new law in one of the assemblies. And the control of the agenda of these assemblies was competitive in the sense that the people's elected representatives had the same kind of control over agenda-setting as did elites. At least that was the case juridically. And these popular rights were taken as a matter of right, of power, and not meekly pleaded for. In an important sense, the Roman plebes (to use Pettit's language) looked their aristocrats in the eye, with unbended knee, and insisted on a constitution that recognized them and their interests. They thought that no ordinary individual had the power to do this by himself or herself – she needed to coordinate her demands with others like himself or herself. Of course this was a collective assertion of the kind that no longer satisfies.

148

In the modern setting, by contrast, nothing is done by the people directly. Elites make both policies and laws without any direct action of popular acceptance at all. And here is no sense in which the ordinary people have specifically accepted a law that governs them. Lacking any direct popular involvement in law-making, modern philosophers find it difficult to agree on the nature of political obligation. They find it necessary to ask whether ordinary people have a general obligation to obey the law, or whether obligation extends only to specific justified laws. Insofar as this question gets answered well, there is an abstract sense, provided by the philosophers, in which each person has constitutional dignity.

What was gained, however, was putting the individual in the center, as a source of value and a source of demand for justification. Liberal theories have characteristically recognized this centrality and have offered justifications of responsive, in principle, to this demand. But a shortfall of liberal theories is that they don't focus on chronic structural conflicts between the wealthy and powerful few, and the many, who are neither. Moreover, liberal theories do not really base their institutional structures on the power of the many, on the leverage they may have on the rich and powerful. For a liberal, institutions are to be arranged so that each person's rights are respected, no matter how weak and vulnerable he or she is. But of course, in modern society every particular individual is weak and in no position to demand rights or recognition. It seems to me that modern republicanism has gone a long way to accepting this description. Rights, in this posture, become a kind of gift of the constituent power – that fictionally is the people acting directly – but really they are mostly just a gift. But old time republicans don't ask for their rights to be given to them as suppliants to the state or the powerful; they demand respect and recognition on account of their powers and such concessions are plausible bases of dignity and pride.

REFERENCES

Ferejohn, J. and F. Rosenbluth (2005). "Republicanisms." Presented at a conference organized by Pasquale Pasquino with the support of the Olivetti Foundation, Rome.

Ferejohn, J. and F. Rosenbluth (2006). "Republican Liberalism." Presented at the Yale University Political Science Department.

Hansen, M. (1991). *Athenian Democracy in the Age of Demosthenes*. Oxford: Blackwell.

Lintott, A. (1999). *Violence in Republican Rome*, 2nd edn. Oxford: Oxford University Press.

Madison, J., A. Hamilton and J. Jay (1987). *The Federalist Papers*. Harmondsworth: Penguin.

Millar, F. (1998). *The Crowd in Rome in the Late Republic*. Ann Arbor: University of Michigan Press.

Nippel, W. (1995). *Public Order in Ancient Rome*. Cambridge: Cambridge University Press.

Pettit, P. (1997). *Republicanism*. Oxford: Oxford University Press.

Rousseau, J.-J. (1997). *The Social Contract and Other Later Political Writings*. Cambridge: Cambridge University Press.

Skowronek, S. (1982). *Building a New American State*. Cambridge: Cambridge University Press.

Sunstein, C. (1985). "Interest Groups in American Public Law." *Stanford Law Review* 38: 29–87.

Sunstein, C. (2009). "The Enlarged Republic – Then and Now." *New York Review of Books* 56 (March 28–April 8): 45–8.

Tocqueville, A. de (2000 [1840]). *Democracy in America*. Eds and trans. H. Mansfield and D. Winthrop, Chicago: University of Chicago Press.

Wood, G. (1991). *The Radicalism of the American Revolution*. New York: Vintage.

Notes

1. The body of citizens could be quite small, however, as it was in Venice after the citizenship was closed to newcomers. For that reason, some republics are hard to distinguish from oligarchies.

2. Pettit and Cass Sunstein may be taken as exemplary modern republicans. I do not claim that Pettit and Sunstein agree in their views of republicanism, democracy, or deliberation. Sunstein is perhaps a little more emphatic than Pettit in recognizing that Publius's writings in *Federalist* (mostly the papers of Madison and Hamilton) departed from the "classical" model associated with Montesquieu, who was mostly describing classical governments. A recent statement of Sunstein's views about republicanism is found in Sunstein 2009. This piece is largely drawn from his early law review article (Sunstein 1985) and does not seem to depart from it materially.

    Pettit generally places his own views within the "broad republican" current and so does not really emphasize any ruptures in that tradition. He may not actually deny that there have been some, however. He argues that the principal objective of a republican government is to reduce domination in society and to do that equally for everyone. In some respects his views have evolved since his first book on the subject (Pettit 1997). His remarks in this volume in fact make it clear that he does not think that dominance reduction is the only admissible task for government. Rather, he argues that people can and should deliberate as to what further ends they wish to pursue in common and that government ought to respond to the results of such processes.

3. In conversation and in his contribution to this volume, Pettit has resisted the notion that his theory is similar in some respects to Rousseau's. I believe, however, that their conceptions of freedom have something important in common. Rousseau sees a person as free insofar as he can be said to govern himself which, on his theory in *The Social Contract*, he can be regarded as doing. Law is the positive enactment of general will that is a part of each person's individual will and so being commanded by law is

being commanded by oneself. Pettit says that to be free or undominated is not to be subject to the arbitrary will of another. Thus, legal commands can dominate a person if their content is unrelated to that person's interest (widely defined to include interests in public goods). Only if law tracks public interests (in which each of us share) will it not be dominating in this way. So, as in Rousseau's theory, appropriate laws – in this case laws with appropriate content – enhance freedom.

Someone could argue that Rousseau's notion of freedom is positive in the sense that it requires that people actually enact the laws, whereas Pettit's freedom is negative and requires not that we make the laws ourselves but only that (for whatever reason) law tracks our interests. As far as I can see, however, the only sense of "positive" self-government in Rousseau's account is at the level of the collective actor: Positive law is made in the assembly under some kind of voting rule, so for a law to be validly enacted a (qualified) majority of voters must have voted for it. But no particular individual is required to vote for a law that binds him or her. Indeed it is possible that a person votes for the losing side (or abstains) on every vote – Rousseau would still say that he or she is self-governing and in that way free. So it seems to me that active law-making at the individual level is not required for a person to be free under (or through) law. The reason she is free is that a validly enacted law, for Rousseau, is almost certainly an expression of the general will and therefore tracks each person's interest no matter how he or she voted. There remains the (very slim) possibility, however, that a valid law does not in fact express the general will and such a law may permit some person or persons to be dominated (in Pettit's sense). I believe Rousseau would say that a person subject to such a command would not be free since he or she is not being governed by his or her genuine interest (which is the general will). And this seems to be exactly Pettit's view if I understand him.

4. This is a complicated area that is well discussed in chapter eleven of Lintott 1999. The thrust is that the rights to trial were very much matters of political contest in the late republic and were variously seen as fundamental republican rights and, at times, as justifiably derogated in the interest of preserving the republic. Cicero's use of the Senate as a special law court for trying the Catilinarian conspirators is one example. And at times, the Senatus *consultum ultimum* was understood to authorize a magistrate (or even a private person) to execute someone without a trial at all.

5. I develop my argument through a consideration of Roman institutions but more or less the same story could be told in Athens by focusing on the Solonic and then Cliesthenic reforms in the sixth century BCE. Josiah Ober argues, especially in the case of the latter, that the institution of Athenian democracy was not a constitutional "gift" of some framer (Cliesthenes was said to have joined the thetes, the working poor, to his friendship group or political coalition) but was wrested by force by the poor classes who essentially made Cliesthenes an offer that was hard for him to refuse: to include the thetes fully within the citizen body thereby making Athens a democracy. Democratization then continued through later pro-democratic reforms under Ephialtes and Pericles.

6. Steven Skowronek 1982 described an earlier era in America as the era of "courts and parties" and his book is an account of its eclipse by the modern administrative state. I agree with Skoronek that administrative rule is the central activity of the modern state but, at a foundational level, courts remain important as regulators of interactions between state organs and the people.

151

7. One may ask why I focus on a shift in social ontology rather than in sociology. In my view, the shift between the ancient and modern era is not so much a shift in actual social practices but in how social phenomena were commonly understood. This is of course a severe abstraction that could probably not be defended in detail.

8. I do not subscribe to any general analysis of "class" in this paper. Certainly the Romans made it easy to see an economic aspect of class by weighting votes by wealth in one of its two voting assemblies. But they also distinguished between patricians and plebes, and between traditional resident citizens of Rome and newcomers to the citizenship, and these classifications were somewhat separate from wealth, especially later in the republic. Still wealth had quite a lot to do with who held power and so the struggles to rebalance citizenship rights with economic power was interminable. As it is nowadays.

9. As plebes were admitted to high office some of them intermarried with patrician families and prospered economically eroding the social distinctions between them and the patriciate so that, by Cicero's time, people spoke of class conflict differently: as between the optimates and the people.

10. Millar's 1998 book is controversial because it asserts that after Sulla's fall, Rome became a democracy. I rely on it only for evidence that there was popular involvement in law-making in ad hoc meetings or "*contiones*" that were convened in the Forum by a magistrate seeking support for his proposal, as a prelude to voting in the *comitia*. Millar argues that the crowd, in a contio, was active and involved in deliberations that went beyond passive listening. He argued that the crowd expressed itself first by showing up and at the meeting and staying, and then by cheering, heckling and threatening, and sometimes even engaging in violent mob actions. Whether this makes Rome in that period democratic is a semantic matter.

11. I guess the real effects of these restraints were probably less than promised. The tribunes were regularly coopted or intimidated, and a plebeian aristocracy developed fairly rapidly whose interests were not sharply different than the old patrician elite. Moreover, the patrician class was not impermeable either. So usually vetos were probably not exercised often and when they were they were probably aimed at securing minor concessions or payoffs.

12. There were unconstitutional dictators much later when Sulla and then Caesar staged coups to claim the mantle and then asserted powers to change the constitution itself, which was never in the authority of a constitutional dictator. And with the failure of the dictatorship model, the Romans increasingly resorted to irregular commissions to do what dictators might have done before. But these were not plainly unconstitutional in the way that Sulla's and Caesar's actions were. Pompei's commission to eliminate piracy was an example that was agreed to in a formal law in 67 BCE.

13. Madison's views are stated very concisely in *Federalist* numbers 49 and 63. In the first he argues (against Jefferson's view) that there should not be frequent appeals to the people of constitutional questions. Such appeals would tend to undermine salubrious habits of obedience by removing from the Constitution the "veneration that time bestows on all things." In 63, he argues that the genius of the proposed constitution was in the fact that it permitted no role for the people at all in the government of the country. It is well to recall that the Constitution did not permit direct election of the Senate, which was in any case apportioned in a nonpopular way. And it did not

require that people vote, even directly, for the president either, although most states soon adopted this practice.

14. Things were more complicated of course. The triumphal return of the anti-federalists was as much a triumph of provincial elites over metropolitans as it was a replacement of patricians by a meaner sort of politician. And the new elites were often both slave-holders and popular like Andrew Jackson. Still, both Wood (1991) and Tocqueville (2000) saw the deeper and more popular strains as emblematic of what American democratic culture was to become and is still becoming.

15. *Federalist* No. 51.

16. Rousseau's assembly would have worked more or less like the Athenian process for making laws. After the Athenian laws were codified in 399, law-making took place in the Nomothetai, which was a special jury court drawn from the (randomly selected) pool of 6,000 jurors. As in other jury courts, law-making procedures were binary and adversarial, with some magistrates defending the existing laws against a new proposal. The two teams made presentations and then the court would decide by secret ballot whether to accept or reject the proposal (Hansen 1991).

17. In some ways, Rousseau's account is both original and peculiar. He accepted the modern or post-Hobbesian view that society is made up of individuals, and in that respect refused to recognize deep conflicts in society. He manages to do this by insisting on a two-stage contractualism where the people have to agree unanimously to form a state and only later agree, by some form of majority voting, on the laws that will bind everyone. This two-stage process allows him to assume that there are no deep internal divisions and that everyone shares common interests in the abstract norms that can be the basis for binding law. Once that is accepted, his institutional prescriptions for legislation appear to be persuasive. Most modern republicans have not accepted this maneuver preferring to deal, one way or another, with a diverse society with deep and perhaps irreconcilable conflicts.

18. Frances Rosenbluth and I have developed some of these ideas in two essays: Ferejohn and Rosenbluth 2005, 2006. Both papers argue that republicanism is diverse, as I argue here, and that the diversity can be explained negatively by characterizing what it is opposing: direct democracy, monarchy, liberalism, pluralism, and so forth.

19. See especially the antipositivism of Ronald Dworkin, John Rawls and Lon Fuller, all three of whom would probably be well characterized as republicans but whose conceptions of law are importantly substantive rather than procedural.

CHAPTER 6

A Kantian Republican Conception of Justice as Nondomination

Rainer Forst[1]

No one has done more to situate republicanism firmly within the contemporary landscape of political theory than Philip Pettit. His version of freedom as nondomination proves powerful and fruitful in a number of ways and contexts, including that of global political structures.[2] But my (long and not very elegant) title points to two questions about Pettit's approach and to two answers that I will suggest. To begin with the first: If republicanism is presented not just as a partial, but as a general theory of legitimate government, why does it not imply a notion of *justice* with respect to a basic social and political structure or to transnational relations and structures? I propose a certain hypothesis as to why this might be the case, and I also argue that a republican conception of justice is congenial to Pettit's approach and is called for in any case. This is because justice is, as Rawls (1999, 3) rightly argued, the first virtue of social institutions, and it is only on the basis of considerations of justice that one can justify the kinds of freedom, equality or other values participants in a context of justice owe one another.[3]

My second question delves further into the very basis of a republican conception of justice as nondomination and locates it within the principle of justification, which says that no one should be subject to norms or normative arrangements that cannot be properly justified to him or her as a free and equal agent of justification. I explain what it means to respect others as such agents of justification and to see them as having a basic right to justification in a Kantian sense by reference to the idea of persons as "ends in themselves" and as having a claim to be the authors and addressees of both moral and political norms, given different contexts of justification. I also believe that – at least on one reading – such an idea of autonomy and respect is implicit in Pettit's approach, but admittedly such a Kantian interpretation goes against the grain of his emphasis on a non-Kantian notion of freedom of choice and his general consequentialist understanding of his own theory.[4]

Further implications and differences follow from the alternative between my Kantian and Pettit's republicanism, especially with respect to democracy as an expression of political autonomy rather than as an arrangement of nondomination and for the very understanding of nondomination itself, which in my view requires the status of an active agent of justification and not primarily that of an agent secure in his or her freedom of choice against arbitrary interference. Thus, I interpret the notions of "arbitrariness" and "domination" in a discourse-theoretical way: Arbitrary rule or domination appears where persons are subjected to actions, norms or institutions without adequate justification, while the authority to determine what a "good" justification is rests with those subjected, given the principle of justification.[5] Kantian republicanism,[6] I argue, differs from Pettit's "negative republicanism," as I call it, which focuses on legally and politically secure freedom of choice, by being grounded on a discursive notion of agents, social relations, justice and freedom.

1. TWO PICTURES OF JUSTICE

I want to begin by arguing for a republican, political conception of justice as nondomination. And I do this by offering a certain hypothesis about the reasons why the discourse of republicanism and that of theories of justice often remain, unfortunately in my view, at some distance from one another. This is because both defenders of certain approaches of justice and their republican critics are often "held captive" by a one-sided and narrow understanding or "picture" of justice.

The understanding of "picture" on which I want to base my discussion I borrow from Ludwig Wittgenstein.[7] In *Philosophical Investigations*, Wittgenstein writes: "A *picture* held us captive. And we could not get outside it, for it lay in our language and language seemed to repeat it to us inexorably" (Wittgenstein 1978, 48e [§ 115]; emphasis in original). I believe that reflection on justice is all too often held captive by a specific, *unpolitical* picture that rests on a particular interpretation of the ancient principle "To each his own" (*suum cuique*). This principle, which has been central to our understanding of justice since Plato, is interpreted in such a way that the primary issue is what goods individuals receive or deserve as a matter of justice – in other words, the primary issue is who "gets" what. The search for answers leads either to comparisons between the collections of goods people possess and points to relative conclusions; or one asks whether individuals have "enough" of the goods that are vital for leading a good life or one befitting a human being, irrespective of comparisons. Granted, these goods-centered, distribution-centered, *recipient-oriented* points of view have their point, for distributive justice is, of course, a matter of allocating goods; nevertheless this picture conceals essential aspects of justice – in the first place, the question of how the goods to be distributed come "into the world," thus questions of production and its just organization. Second, and furthermore, this picture ignores the *political* question of who determines the structures of production and distribution and how, as though there could be a huge distribution machine that only needed to be programmed correctly.[8] Yet not only would such a machine be problematic, because it would mean that justice would no longer be understood as an accomplishment of the subjects themselves and would turn them instead into passive recipients, but this idea also neglects, third, the insight that justified claims to goods do not simply "exist" but can only be ascertained discursively through corresponding justification procedures in which – and this is the *fundamental requirement of justice* – all are *involved* as free and equal individuals.

Finally, in the fourth place, the goods-fixated view of justice also largely ignores the question of injustice; by concentrating on overcoming deficiencies of goods, it treats someone who is deprived of goods and resources as a result of a natural catastrophe as being equivalent to someone who experiences the same deprivation as a result of economic or political exploitation. It is true that assistance is appropriate in both cases but, as I understand the grammar of justice, in the one case it is required as an act of moral solidarity, whereas in the other as an act of justice conditioned by the nature of one's involvement in relations of exploitation and injustice[9] and the specific wrong in question. Ignoring this difference can lead one to mistake what is actually a requirement of justice for an act of generous "aid" (Forst 2005).

For the reasons cited, it is necessary, especially when dealing with questions of distributive justice, to recognize the *political* point of justice and to liberate oneself from a false and reified picture that is focused solely on quantities of goods. On the contrary, if we follow a second, more appropriate picture, justice should aim at *intersubjective relations and structures*, not at *subjective or supposedly objective states* of the provision of goods. Only by thus taking into consideration the *first question of justice* – namely, the justifiability of social relations and, correspondingly, of how much "justificatory power" individuals or groups have in a political context – does a radical, critical conception of justice become possible, one that gets at the roots of relations of injustice.

But what justifies us in speaking of a "false" as opposed to a more "appropriate" picture of justice? After all, the goods- or recipient-centered understanding can appeal to the time-honored principle *suum cuique*. Is there a more original, deeper meaning of justice than this? In my opinion there is, and it directs us to the heart of a republican conception of justice as nondomination. The general concept of justice possesses a core meaning to which the essential contrasting concept is that of *arbitrariness*,[10] understood in a social sense, whether it assumes the form of arbitrary rule by individuals or by part of the community (for example, a class) over others, or of the acceptance of social contingencies that lead to asymmetrical positions or relations of domination and are defended and accepted as an unalterable fate, even though they are nothing of the sort. Arbitrary rule is the rule of some people over others without legitimate reason, that is, *domination*, and where struggles are conducted against injustice they are first and foremost directed against forms of domination of this kind. The underlying impulse that opposes injustice is not primarily that of wanting something, or more of something, but of not wanting to be dominated, harassed or overruled any longer in one's *basic right to justification*. This right expresses the demand that no political or social relations should exist that cannot be adequately justified toward those involved – and, more specifically, that no person should be subjected to certain norms or normative arrangements that cannot reciprocally and generally be justified to those subjected. Herein resides the profoundly *political* essence of justice that the principle *suum cuique* not only fails to grasp but tends to conceal; for justice is a matter of *who determines who receives what* – thus the dimension that in Plato is represented by the idea of the Good or by the philosopher king. In my picture, the demand for justice is an emancipatory one; reflexively speaking, it rests on the claim to be respected as a subject of justification, that is, to be respected in one's dignity as a being who can provide and demand justifications. The person who *lacks* certain goods should not be regarded as the primary victim of injustice but the one who does not "*count*" in the production and allocation of goods. In other words, justice is primarily about status, not about goods.

One can cut different paths through contemporary discussions on justice. However, the one opened up by the question of the two pictures of justice is especially instructive, for from this perspective certain adversaries unexpectedly find themselves in the same boat. An example is provided by the recent debate concerning equality. By this is actually meant two points of discussion: On the one hand, the question *"Equality of what?"* – of resources, welfare, or capabilities[11] – and, on the other, the question *"Why equality at all?"* From the perspective of the difference between the two pictures of justice, however, it becomes apparent that both the advocates and the opponents of equality frequently operate with the same understanding, and this often finds expression in a specific image, that of the goddess Justitia as a mother who has to divide up a cake and asks herself how this should be done.[12] Egalitarians argue for the primacy of the equal distribution of goods, according to which other arguments for legitimate unequal distributions – for instance, ones based on need, merit or prior claims – then have to be treated as special reasons. Alternatively, an egalitarian calculus of need satisfaction – welfare – is posited that serves as the goal of distribution.[13] However, in the approaches the question of how the cake was produced and, even more important, who gets to play the role of the mother, remains largely unthematized. Yet that is the principal question of justice.

Analogous problems are found on the side of the critics of equality. In Harry Frankfurt's (1988, 1999) view, for example, the defenders of egalitarian conceptions of justice cannot be concerned with the value of equality at all; for if you ask them what is so bad about inequality, they respond by pointing to the negative consequences of living conditions in a society of inequality, in particular to the fact that certain people lack important goods for a satisfactory life.

So-called "sufficientarians" (Crisp 2003) have taken up these arguments and argue that "at least the especially important, elementary standards of justice are of a nonrelational kind" (Krebs 2000, 17f.) and that justice is concerned with creating "conditions of life befitting human beings" that can be measured according to "absolute standards of fulfilment," not according to what others have. On this view, a universal conception of the goods "necessary for a good life" should be produced with reference to particular lists of basic goods.[14]

These approaches are also open to serious objections. Thus Frankfurt's assertion that the pivotal issue is not how much others have but only whether I have "enough," is valid *only when* conditions of background

justice pertain, that is only when others have not previously taken advantage of me. Hence we must look for reasons for such background justice
elsewhere. But, in addition, the idea of "having enough" or "getting
enough" does not get at the essence of justice, that is, the prevention
of social domination. Justice is always a "relational" matter; it does not
first inquire into subjective or objective *states of affairs* but into *relations
between human beings* and what they owe to one another for what reasons.
In particular, we do not explain the requirements of justice on the model
of morally required aid in specific situations of want or need; instead they
come into play in situations where what is at stake are relations between
human beings that are fundamentally in need of justification, where
those involved are connected by social relations of cooperation in the
production and distribution of goods – or, as is mostly the case, by relations of "negative cooperation," of coercion or domination (whether by
legal, economic or political means). It makes a huge difference whether
someone is *deprived of* certain goods and opportunities unjustly and
without justification or whether he or she, for whatever reason, *lacks*
certain goods (for example, as a result of a natural catastrophe, as mentioned above). By losing sight of the former context, one misses or conceals the problem of justice as well as that of injustice. Justice requires that
those involved in a context of (positive or negative) cooperation should
be respected as equals. That means that they should enjoy equal rights to
take part in the social and political *order of justification* in which the conditions under which goods are produced and distributed are determined.

So here is the correct picture of justice: Justice is the human capacity
to oppose relations of arbitrary rule or domination. Domination is rule
"without justification" and it is assumed that a just social order is one
to which free and equal persons could give their assent – not just their
counterfactual assent but assent based on institutionalized justification
procedures. This is a *recursive* implication of the fact that what is at stake
in political and social justice is norms of an institutional basic structure
that claims reciprocal and universal validity. Thus a *supreme principle*
holds within such a framework, namely the *principle of general and reciprocal justification*, which states that every claim to rule as well as to goods,
rights or liberties must be justified in a reciprocal and general manner,
where one side may not simply project its reasons onto the other but has
to justify itself discursively.

This brings us to the central insight for the problem of political and
social justice, namely that *the first question of justice is the question of power*.

159

For justice is not only a matter of which goods, for which reasons and in what amounts should legitimately be allocated to whom, but concerns in particular *how* these goods come into the world in the first place, *who* decides on their allocation and *how* this allocation is made. Theories of a predominantly allocative-distributive kind are accordingly "oblivious to power" insofar as they conceive of justice exclusively from the "recipient side," and if necessary call for "redistributions," without emphasizing the political question of how the structures of production and allocation of goods are determined in the first place. The claim that the question of power is the first question of justice means that justice has its proper place where the central justifications for a social basic structure must be provided and the institutional ground rules are laid down that determine social life from the bottom up. Everything depends, if you will, on the relations of justification within a society. Power, understood as the effective "justificatory power" of individuals, is the higher-level good of justice.[15] It is the "discursive" power to demand and provide justifications and to challenge false legitimations. This amounts to an argument for a "political turn" in the debate concerning justice and calls for a *critical theory of justice as a critique of relations of justification* (Forst forthcoming).

A comprehensive theory of political and social justice should be constructed on this basis, something at which I can only hint here.[16] First we must make a conceptual distinction between *fundamental (minimal)* and *full (maximal)* justice. Whereas the task of fundamental justice is to construct a *basic structure of justification*, the task of full justice is to construct a *justified basic structure*. The former is necessary in order to pursue the latter, that is, a "putting-into-effect" of justification through constructive, discursive democratic procedures in which the "justificatory power" is distributed as evenly as possible among the citizens.[17] In spite of the appearance of paradox, this means that fundamental justice is a substantive starting point of procedural justice. Based on a moral right to justification, arguments are presented for the basic structure in which those who are part of it have real opportunities to codetermine the institutions of this structure in a reciprocal and general manner. Fundamental justice guarantees all citizens an effective status "as equals" in this sense.

2. Kantian vs. "negative" republicanism

These short remarks might suffice to indicate why I think that a kind of "Kantian republicanism" can fill in the right picture of justice properly.

I call it "Kantian" republicanism because the autonomy of persons to be both authors and addressees of the law, which holds in the moral realm as well as in the legal and political spheres, with proper modification, is the basic idea. Public justification then is the medium of that kind of autonomy in the political realm.

How does this approach relate to Philip Pettit's version of republicanism? According to him, republicanism essentially is a theory of legitimate government based on a particular idea of freedom as "nondomination," as "the social status of being relatively proof against arbitrary interference by others, and of being able to enjoy a sense of security and standing among them" (Pettit 1997a, viii). In contrast to freedom as mere "noninterference," nondomination is tied to being and seeing oneself as someone who is not at the mercy of others' arbitrary will, even if these others were to leave you alone most of the time. It is the *potential* of arbitrary interference against which the republican notion of self-respect and freedom is directed (Pettit 1997a, 5, 22f.); hence the importance of the rule of law and of a social status that protects persons against social and political vulnerability to the possibility of arbitrary interference. The notion of freedom here at work has as its counterpart the slave, the extreme version of a dominated person. Still, even though Pettit is right to stress the difference between freedom as noninterference and freedom as nondomination, the former, negative conception of liberty remains normatively essential in his view, for the argument for nondomination ultimately is in the service of securing the "negative" realm of freedom of choice of persons against arbitrary interference.[18] This is why I call it "negative" republicanism: The republican infrastructure is mainly a sheltering mechanism for individual liberty thus understood.

So how close or how different are my Kantian conception of republican justice as nondomination and Pettit's conception of republican freedom as nondomination? In that regard, I would like to claim three things. First, I want to argue that justice is the more basic term, and that Pettit's republicanism implicitly relies, at least on one reading, on an argument of justice rather than of freedom. But there are two possible reasons why this does not come to the fore: Pettit seems to be held captive by a goods-oriented picture of justice[19] and his focus on securing negative liberty might prevent him from fully embracing a political conception of social justice. Second, I want to argue for a Kantian republicanism that puts public justification and political autonomy at center stage, such that the two aspects of democracy that Pettit distinguishes – the electoral-authorial and the contestatory-editorial – can and ought to be combined under that heading. Third, I claim that a republican notion of justice needs to be broadened to cover areas of social life and institutions that a theory like Rawls's insists on being part of the basic structure.

(1) With respect to the first point, I regard the idea of freedom as non-domination as a very powerful one, yet I think its real force derives from a notion of justice that both grounds and defines it. It grounds it because the basic claim is not one of freedom generally, but one of freedom from *arbitrary* – that is unjust and unjustified – rule, that is domination; thus the claim is based on one's standing as a free and equal agent of justice and justification and it is a claim to a kind of liberty (and liberties) defined by what oneself and others can justifiably and justly ask from one another in a basic social structure. Justifiable rule is – as Pettit (2002) explains in his discussion of Quentin Skinner's view championing noninterference – not seen as domination, which compromises freedom, only *arbitrary* rule is, and that means *unjustifiable* rule over others, denying their standing as free and equal agents with (what I call) a "right to justification." To be denied that right leads to the "grievance … of having to live at the mercy of another," which Pettit (1997a, 4) isolates as the main social and political evil and given that interference or rule by others is not seen as an infringement of freedom if it is justifiable between equals,[20] the notion of *justice* referring to the quality of the relations between free and equal participants in a justifiable political structure is central.

This may seem to read a Kantian notion of freedom into Pettit's approach – but only if one overlooks the implications of his distinction between domination that compromises freedom and the nonarbitrary rule of law that does not; rather, it is seen as "conditioning" freedom (Pettit 2002, 342). This shows that the point of republican freedom is the "full standing of a person among persons" (Pettit 2002, 350) and with reference to Kant Pettit (2002, 351) goes on to explain: "The terrible evil brought about by domination, over and beyond the evil of restricting choice, and inducing a distinctive uncertainty is that it deprives a person of the ability to command attention and respect and so of his or her standing among persons." Pettit not only introduces a Kantian notion of respect here, he also gives it priority over mere freedom of choice because a "conditioning" of that freedom by reciprocally justifiable laws is not seen as an evil, while a huge space of freedom possibly granted by a mild dictator is. Thus the main evil is that of not being regarded as "a voice worth hearing and an ear worth addressing" (Pettit 2002, 350) – that is, in my words, as a person

162

with a right to justification. As Pettit (1997a, 91) formulates it: "To be a person is to be a voice that cannot properly be ignored, a voice which speaks to issues raised in common with others and which speaks with a certain authority: enough authority, certainly, for discord with that voice to give others reason to pause and think." Every person is to be respected as such a justificatory authority, and this is the essential meaning of freedom as autonomy: having a *categorical* right not to be subjected to norms that cannot reciprocally be justified. I do not see how – in Pettit's work as well as generally speaking – that kind of moral-political status can be explained in nondeontological terms. For can we imagine a value that could trump that kind of right and status?

At this point, we have gone quite a bit beyond a negative conception of freedom without at the same time adopting a controversial "positive" one. Thus it is freedom as autonomy, that is, freedom *from* unjustifiable subjection or coercion and freedom *as* a self-determining agent of (moral as well as political) justification that matters in a republican account of nondomination. Politically speaking, this means freedom within a just(ifiable) regime, and thus it is justice as justifiability that counts – not merely as an idea but as a real practice. Freedom as nondomination is only guaranteed where practices of justification exist that prevent some from dominating others.

(2) The emphasis on democratic practices of justification in Pettit's approach I see as reflecting a political picture of justice. In that respect, his stress on the notion of "contestation" rather than "consent" is important (Pettit 1997a, 63), yet I see *both* as different practices of democratic justification, being combined by the notion of fundamental justice, meaning that there can be no legitimate form of government that is not framed within a "basic structure of effective justification." Like Pettit (1997a, 114f.), I believe that the "power-ratio" of citizens in their relations to one another is essential for such a just basic structure. Hence a republican view of freedom is based on a republican notion of democratic justice, and at the heart of it lies the conception of the person as having a "right to justification," which demands the effective possibility of participating in practices of political justification.

It is, however, an important aspect of "negative republicanism" that it entails a certain critique of democracy, especially in its more "direct" and majoritarian forms and highlights the protective function of the rule of law and of a "depoliticized" practice of contestation (Pettit 2004).[21] Yet, any conception of the shared "civic control of the state" and of the law "tracking" the "avowable common interests" (Pettit 2002, 345) of citizens must be part of a democratic conception of justice as a practice of justification. For control must, to ensure nondomination, be collectively authorized, exercised and justified, and then public justification – or, rather, the institutional *force toward the better argument* – is the medium of that kind of control. "Contestation" means to identify and criticize policies or norms that cannot be reciprocally and generally justified and that kind of contestation has to take place in democratic debate rather than through depoliticized institutions (Pettit 2004), important a part of the democratic forum as they are – a "forum where the validity of the claim is assessed and a suitable response determined" (Pettit 1997a, 187). Contestation is an essential practice of democratic justification, and so "shared control" means, I believe, "control by justification," especially at the stage of law-making (Pettit 1997a, 191). Hence, I would argue that editorial and authorial control should be combined in thinking innovatively about the process of law-making itself. Practices of contestation by persons or groups whose legitimate claims have been overlooked should be incorporated into the political process rather than placed outside of it. Otherwise, the danger of contestatory paternalism looms, another possible source of domination.

(3) Classical republicanism was always primarily concerned with the political standing of free people, free also from the concerns of the *oikos*. Modern republicanism is to some extent striving to overcome this narrowing of the political, yet as Hannah Arendt's conception of political action shows, not always successfully. Pettit, on the contrary, is well aware of the fact that subjection to arbitrary rule or domination is not just a political issue in a narrow sense, for as examples of such domination he mentions a beaten wife, a fearful employee and a welfare dependent badly treated by a counter clerk (Pettit 1997a, 5). Still, if we understand nondomination to be a social aim in the broader sense, a theory of justice for a basic structure – from the family to the workplace – is required that is more comprehensive than Pettit's theory allows for, at least in its present form. His discussion of the inclusion of feminist and socialist concerns within the republican framework is important (Pettit 1997a, 138–43), yet for a basic structure that avoids domination in the most important social institutions we are in need of a general account of the justificatory practices and powers required in different social spheres. Again, I would argue that at that point the negative republican theory of freedom needs to be transformed into a theory of political and social justice, based

164

on the overarching principle of – or right to – justification. For only in a society that is just in this way can citizens be called "free" in the republican sense. This does not mean that distributive justice is instrumental to the exercise of republican self-determination; rather, it is its expression.

In line with Kantian republicanism we can formulate a discursive version of the Rawlsian difference principle according to which all social and economic arrangements have to be justifiable to all subjected to them as equal participants, which gives a qualified veto-right to the worst off in cases in which their basic standing as equals is violated. As Rawls (1999, 131) explains: "Taking equality as the basis of comparison, those who have gained more must do so on terms that are justifiable to those who have gained least." In that sense, "those who benefit least have, so to speak, a veto."

Let me conclude. Based on an analysis of what I consider to be the core of the concept of "justice," I have argued against a one-sided picture of it and for a fuller one that does not focus on the distribution of goods but rather on the relations between persons as relations of nondomination. With that background, I have argued that a modern republican view such as Pettit's in part relies on and in any case should fully adopt the picture of justice I have sketched and suggested that a Kantian interpretation of modern republicanism is more convincing than what I have called "negative republicanism," both from the standpoint of a theory of justice and from within Pettit's own view. If the latter – to some extent revisionary – interpretation proves untenable, however, then I fear that a wider gap between a Kantian conception of political and social justice and Pettit's republicanism results, to the detriment of the latter.

References

Ackerman, B. (1980). *Social Justice in the Liberal State*. New Haven: Yale University Press.

Anderson, E. (1999). "What is the Point of Equality?" *Ethics* 109: 287–337.

Arneson, R. (2001). "Luck and Equality." *Proceedings of the Aristotelian Society* suppl. vol.: 73–90.

Arneson, R. (2004). "Luck Egalitarianism: An Interpretation and Defense." *Philosophical Topics* 32: 1–20.

Berlin, I. (1981). "Equality." In: I. Berlin. *Concepts and Categories*. Ed. H. Hardy, Harmondsworth: Penguin: 81–102.

Bohman, J. (2007). *Democracy across Borders: From Demos to Demoi*. Cambridge, MA: MIT Press.

Cohen, G. (1993). "Equality of What? On Welfare, Goods, and Capabilities." In: *The*

Quality of Life. Eds M. Nussbaum and A. Sen, Oxford: Oxford University Press: 9–29.

Crisp, R. (2003). "Equality, Priority, and Compassion." *Ethics* 113: 745–63.

Forst, R. (2001). "Towards a Critical Theory of Transnational Justice." In: *Global Justice*. Ed. T. Pogge, Oxford: Blackwell: 169–87.

Forst, R. (2002). *Contexts of Justice: Political Philosophy beyond Liberalism and Communitarianism*. Berkeley/Los Angeles: University of California Press.

Forst, R. (2005). "A Dialectic of Morality." In: *Real World Justice*. Eds A. Follesdal and T. Pogge, Dordrecht: Springer: 27–36.

Forst, R. (2007). "Radical Justice: On Iris Marion Young's Critique of the 'Distributive Paradigm.'" *Constellations* 14: 260–5.

Forst, R. (2009). "Zwei Bilder der Gerechtigkeit." In: *Sozialphilosophie und Kritik*. Eds R. Forst, M. Hartmann, R. Jaeggi and M. Saar, Frankfurt: Suhrkamp: 205–28.

Forst, R. (2012). *The Right to Justification: Elements of a Constructivist Theory of Justice*. New York: Columbia University Press.

Forst, R. (forthcoming). *Justification and Critique*. Cambridge: Polity.

Frankfurt, H. (1988). "Equality as a Moral Ideal." In: H. Frankfurt. *The Importance of What we Care About*. Cambridge: Cambridge University Press: 143–58.

Frankfurt, H. (1999). "Equality and Respect." In: H. Frankfurt. *Necessity, Volition, and Love*. Cambridge: Cambridge University Press: 146–54.

Gosepath, S. (2004). *Gleiche Gerechtigkeit*. Frankfurt am Main: Suhrkamp.

Habermas, J. (2011). "'Reasonable' versus 'True,' or the Morality of Worldviews." In: *Habermas and Rawls: Disputing the Political*. Eds J. G. Finlayson and F. Freyenhagen, New York/London: Routledge: 110–31.

Hinsch, W. (2002). *Gerechtfertigte Ungleichheiten*. Berlin: de Gruyter.

Krebs, A. (2000). "Einleitung: Die neue Egalitarismuskritik im Überblick." In: *Gleichheit oder Gerechtigkeit*. Ed. A. Krebs, Frankfurt am Main: Suhrkamp: 7–37.

McCormick, J. (2011). *Machiavellian Democracy*. Cambridge: Cambridge University Press.

Nussbaum, M. (2006). *Frontiers of Justice: Disability, Nationality, Species Membership*. Cambridge, MA: Harvard University Press.

Pettit, P. (1997a). *Republicanism: A Theory of Freedom and Government*. Oxford: Oxford University Press.

Pettit, P. (1997b). "The Consequentialist Perspective." In: *Three Methods of Ethics*. Eds M. W. Baron, P. Pettit and M. Slote, Oxford: Blackwell: 92–174.

Pettit, P. (2002). "Keeping Republican Freedom Simple: On a Difference with Quentin Skinner." *Political Theory* 30: 339–56.

Pettit, P. (2004). "Depoliticizing Democracy." *Ratio Juris* 17: 52–65.

Pettit, P. (2010). "A Republican Law of Peoples." *European Journal of Political Theory* 9: 70–94.

Pettit, P. (2011). "The Instability of Freedom as Non-Interference: The Case of Isaiah Berlin." *Ethics*: 693–716.

Rawls, J. (1999). *A Theory of Justice*, rev. edn. Cambridge, MA: Harvard University Press.

Rawls, J. (2007). *Lectures on the History of Political Philosophy*. Ed. S. Freeman. Cambridge, MA: Harvard University Press.

Tugendhat, E. (1993). *Vorlesungen über Ethik*. Frankfurt am Main: Suhrkamp.

Wittgenstein, L. (1978). *Philosophical Investigations*. Trans. G. E. M. Anscombe, Oxford: Blackwell.

Young, I. M. (1990). *Justice and the Politics of Difference*. Princeton: Princeton University Press.

Notes

1. I have had the opportunity to discuss the ideas in this short paper with Philip Pettit and a number of colleagues on two occasions, and I am particularly grateful to Philip and to those colleagues for valuable suggestions and critique. These occasions were the panel on "Rawls, Civic Republicanism and the Power of the People" at the American Political Science Association's Annual Meeting in Boston in September 2008, organized by Miguel Vatter, and the Frankfurt conference on "Republicanism, the Rule of Law, and Democracy" in March 2009, organized by Matthias Lutz-Bachmann, Andreas Niederberger and Philipp Schink. Special thanks for their comments to those mentioned as well as Richard Bellamy, Jim Bohman, John Ferejohn, Jürgen Habermas, Steve Macedo and John McCormick. Thanks also to Ciaran Cronin and Erin Cooper for helping me to express myself in proper English.
2. See Pettit 2010 as well as the articles by Lena Halldenius, Duncan Ivison and Cécile Laborde in the same volume. James Bohman 2007 develops a conception of transnational democracy based on the idea of nondomination. For my own proposal of a conception of transnational justice, see Forst 2001 and forthcoming.
3. For this argument in general, see Forst 2002, 2012.
4. See especially Pettit's 1997b and 1997a, 97–109 discussion of consequentialism.
5. Obviously, I am indebted here to Jürgen Habermas's discourse theory and the concept of *herrschaftsfreier Diskurs*, that is, nondominated discourse. I cannot go into details about the function this idea plays in Habermas's theory and the many changes it underwent, but it remains a basic idea in his critical work. Bruce Ackerman 1980 has used it in a particular way as a basis for his liberal theory of justice.
6. The phrase is used, for example, by Habermas 2011 in his debate with Rawls, and he stresses the Kantian idea of moral autonomy as divided in legal and political contexts into the inseparable parts of public autonomy of "co-legislators" and the private autonomy of subjects of the law.
7. In the following, I rely on some parts of Forst 2009, English version in Forst (forthcoming).
8. For the first two points, see especially Young 1990 and Forst 2007.
9. Here a whole series of cases would have to be distinguished: direct participation in or (joint) causation of injustice; indirect participation in injustice by profiting from it, without oneself actively contributing to relations of exploitation; and the ("natural") duty to put an end to unjust relations, even if one does not profit from them but possesses the means to overcome them.
10. See also Rawls's 1999, 5 definition.
11. See, especially, Cohen 1993.
12. See, for example, Tugendhat 1993, 373f.; Hinsch 2002, 169f.; Gosepath 2004, 250ff. The cake example, although without the mother, can also be found in Berlin 1981, 84.
13. This is especially true of "luck egalitarianism." For a paradigmatic expression, see Arneson 2004, 2001. For a critique see Anderson 1999.

14. Nussbaum 2006 represents another example of such a goods- or in that case capability-oriented (although not sufficientarian) view.
15. Power is a kind of good that cannot be distributed like a material good, as Iris Young 1990, chap. 1 argued. But resources that help to generate power can be distributed, such as means of education and information and access to public communication; other such goods are social and political positions. I discuss the concept of power in my "Noumenal Power," Ms.
16. For a more detailed discussion see Forst 2012.
17. Bohman 2007, 45ff. presents a related argument for a "democratic minimum" that secures the "normative powers" required for deliberative democracy.
18. See especially Pettit 2002, 340; 2011; and his contribution to this volume, p. 172: "If you are to enjoy freedom as nondomination in certain choices, so the idea went, then you must not be subject to the will of others in how you make these choices. And that means that you must not be exposed to a power of interference on their part, even if they happen to like you and do not exercise that power."
19. In Pettit 1997a, 121, for example, he mentions "relief from misery or poverty, justice as fairness" as well as "freedom as non-interference" as "goods."
20. This is why, to add to the complication of squaring the notions of freedom and justice, Rawls in his discussion of Rousseau's political philosophy argues that Rousseau reflected on these social evils within a framework of equality: "Given our needs as persons and our natural indignation at being subject to the arbitrary power of others (a power that makes us do what they want, and not what we both can will as equals) the clear answer to the problem of inequality is equality at the highest level, as formulated in the social compact": Rawls 2007, 248.
21. For a historically based critique of republicanism because of these tendencies, see McCormick 2011, chap. 6. For a critique from the perspective of deliberative democracy, see Bohman 2007, 53f. *et passim*.

CHAPTER 7

Two Republican Traditions

Philip Pettit

Recent exercises in the renewal of republican theory have focused on the Italian–Atlantic tradition of republicanism and on its demise with the rise of classical liberalism in the early nineteenth century.[1] The focus on this tradition has been theoretically fruitful in generating a novel way of thinking about freedom and government in the contemporary world. But there is a distinct Franco–German tradition of republicanism, developed from the time of Rousseau and Kant, and it is important not to confuse this with the older way of thinking on which neo-republicans focus. My aim here is to reduce the risk of confusion by laying out the key differences between the two traditions and putting them in historical context. Inevitably I have to stylize the traditions I discuss but I hope that I do no serious injustice to the figures I address.

While Rousseau and Kant remained faithful to some core ideas in the Italian–Atlantic tradition of thinking – in particular, as we shall see, to the idea of freedom as nondomination – the way of thinking about citizens and the state that they ushered in was as inimical to the tradition as classical liberalism. Indeed, as liberalism came to displace traditional republican doctrine as the main ideology of the English-speaking world, the name "republicanism" came to designate the new Franco–German doctrine. It is primarily with this doctrine, rather than the Italian–Atlantic tradition, that critics of liberalism like Hannah Arendt (1958; 1973) and Michael Sandel (1996) identify, for example.[2] And it is this version of republicanism that is rejected, along with liberalism, in the work of Jürgen Habermas (1994; 1995).[3] Moreover, it is this doctrine that self-described liberals often focus on – certainly it is part of what they focus on – in arguing for the merits of their own approach (Brennan and Lomasky 2006).

My paper is in five sections. In the first, I review the story about classical republicanism that is broadly taken for granted among neo-republicans, distinguishing between the ideological ideal of equal freedom as nondomination that it hails and the twin institutional ideals of a mixed constitution and a contestatory citizenry; in the course of doing this, I also describe the classical liberal opposition that formed in response to Italian–Atlantic republicanism. In the second section I look at the way that Rousseau and Kant conceived of freedom, arguing that they remained faithful to the ideal of equal freedom as nondomination. The third section is an interlude in which I review the absolutist opposition in Bodin and Hobbes to the institutional ideals of republicanism, in particular that of the mixed constitution, since I believe that Rousseau and Kant were deeply influenced by these authors. Then in section four I look at the theory of the constitution in Rousseau and Kant, highlighting their opposition to the mixed constitution. And in section five I look at their view of the role of the citizenry, highlighting their opposition to the contestatory ideal. I use a brief conclusion to set up the contrast between the Franco–German, broadly communitarian version of republicanism, and the classical, Italian–Atlantic version that neo-republicans build on.

1. Republicanism and liberalism

The Italian–Atlantic tradition

Three ideas stand out as landmarks on the terrain of traditional republican thought. While the ideas received different interpretations and emphases in different periods and among different authors, they constitute points of reference that were recognized and authorized by almost everyone, down to the late eighteenth century, with a claim to belong to the tradition.

The first idea is that the equal freedom of its citizens, in particular their freedom as nondomination – the freedom that goes with not having to live under the power of another – is the primary concern of the state or republic. The second is that if the republic is to secure the freedom of its citizens then it must satisfy a range of constitutional constraints associated broadly with the mixed constitution. And the third idea is that if the citizens are to keep the republic to its proper business then they had better have the collective and individual virtue to track and, if necessary, contest public policies and initiatives: The price of liberty is eternal vigilance.

The mixed constitution was meant to guarantee a rule of law under which each citizen would be equal with others, a separation and sharing of powers that denied control to any one governing individual or body, and a degree of representation, whether by rotation or lottery or election, that gave each sector a presence in government. The contestatory citizenry was the civic complement to this constitutional ideal: It was to be a citizenry committed to interrogating the other elements of government and having its own say in the determination of law and policy. These institutional measures were taken to be essential for organizing a government that would promote the equal freedom of citizens without itself becoming a master in their lives – in other words, that would protect against private domination without perpetrating public.

Freedom as nondomination, the mixed constitution and the contestatory citizenry were all represented in Roman republican thought and practice, and they were articulated in different ways among the many writers who identified with Roman institutions (Wirszubski 1968). These authors included the Greek historian, Polybius, the orator and lawyer, Marcus Tullius Cicero, and the native Roman historian, Titus Livius or, as we know him, Livy. While they drew on earlier Greek sources, including Plato and Aristotle, they were united in the belief that it was Rome that first gave life and recognition to the key republican ideas.[4]

Leading thinkers in medieval and Renaissance Italy drew heavily on Polybius, Cicero and Livy when, more than a thousand years later, they reworked the republican ideas in seeking a political philosophy that would reflect the organization and experience of independent city-states like Florence and Venice (Skinner 1978). The neo-Roman framework of thought that they crafted in the course of this exercise – in particular the framework outlined in Nicolo Machiavelli's *Discourses on Livy* – served in turn to provide terms of political self-understanding for northern European countries that resisted or overthrew absolute monarchs. These included the Polish republic of the nobles in the sixteenth and seventeenth centuries, the seventeenth- and eighteenth-century Dutch republic and the English republic of the 1640s and 1650s.

While the English republic was the shortest lived of these regimes, it had the widest influence and the deepest impact. The republican ideas that emerged in the thought of defenders such as James Harrington, John Milton and Algernon Sidney, became a staple of political thought in eighteenth-century Britain and America, albeit often adapted to make room for a constitutional monarchy (Raab 1965). However differently interpreted or applied, the ideas were more or less common property to the Whig establishment in eighteenth-century Britain; to their Tory opposition, at least as that was formulated by the first Viscount Bolingbroke (Skinner 1974); to radical Whigs who were a constant sting in the side of every establishment (Robbins 1959); and of course to the American colonists, and their British apologists, who came to feel that the Westminster parliament ruled its colonies in a manner that betrayed the "commonwealthman" or republican heritage (Bailyn 1967; Reid 1988). Republican ideas provided the framework for the arguments made in support of the cause of American independence – including arguments made by English supporters such as Richard Price (1991) and Joseph Priestley (1993) – and for the arguments put forward in the constitutional debates between federalists and anti-federalists (Madison, Hamilton and Jay 1987; Ketcham 2003).

Among the three ideas associated with the republican tradition, the conception of freedom as nondomination is the most distinctive. If you are to enjoy freedom as nondomination in certain choices, so the idea went, then you must not be subject to the will of others in how you make those choices. And that means that you must not be exposed to a power of interference on their part, even if they happen to like you and do not exercise that power. The mere fact that I can interfere without serious cost in your choices if I want to do so – the mere fact that I can track the choices and intervene when I like – means that you depend for your ability to choose as you wish on my will remaining a goodwill. You are not *sui juris* – not your own person – in the expression from Roman law. You are unfree, as the eighteenth-century republican, Richard Price (1991, 26) explained, because your access to the options will depend on an "indulgence" or an "accidental mildness" on my part. To quote from a seventeenth-century republican, Algernon Sidney (1990, 17), freedom in this tradition requires "independency upon the will of another." Or, in an equivalent slogan from a popular eighteenth-century tract: "Liberty is, to live upon one's own terms; slavery is, to live at the mere mercy of another" (Trenchard and Gordon 1971, Vol. 2, 249–50).

In arguing that the state should be concerned in the first place with the equal freedom of its citizens, republicans held that citizens should each be assured of enjoying nondomination in a sphere of choice required for being able to function – (Sen 1985; Nussbaum 2006) – in the local society; this sphere might be described as that of "the basic liberties" (Pettit 2008a). They thought that a state organized under a mixed constitution, and disciplined by a contestatory citizenry, was the best hope of promoting this ideal.

The citizenry was traditionally restricted to mainstream, usually propertied, males and, under the republican vision, a citizen would be a *liber* or a free-man insofar as he enjoyed sufficient power and protection in the sphere of the basic liberties – and a corresponding normative status – to be able to walk tall among others and look any in the eye, without reason for fear or deference. John Milton (1953–82, Vol. 8, 424–5) captured the idea nicely in arguing that in a "free Commonwealth," "they who are greatest ... are not elevated above their brethren; live soberly in their families, walk the streets as other men, may be spoken to freely, familiarly, friendly, without adoration." In the vision of contemporary republicans, this ideal ought to be extended to an inclusive citizenry; freedom ought to be secured for all more or less permanent residents, independently of gender or property or religion.

The early liberal opposition

These remarks constitute the broadest of brush strokes but the pattern that they project onto the intellectual and institutional swirl of political history is not a capricious imposition; it is not like the figures that we may think we see in the snow or in the clouds or in the stars. The Italian–Atlantic tradition described constitutes a firm reality that endured across classical, medieval and modern times (Pocock 1975). The best sign of its independent importance is that the set of ideas described constituted a vivid and salient target of attack for those who espoused a rival way of thinking about liberty – a way of thinking that eventually gave rise to classical liberalism – in the later eighteenth century. The main figures here were utilitarians like Jeremy Bentham and William Paley (Pettit 1997, chap. 1).

Hobbes had already set himself against the republican way of thinking about freedom in the 1640s, offering a somewhat complex alternative – although not one that had a lasting influence – in its place (Pettit 2008b, chap. 8; Skinner 2008). Without explicitly drawing on that earlier precedent, Bentham reported in the 1770s "a kind of discovery I had made, that the idea of liberty, imported nothing in it that was positive: that it was merely a negative one: and ... accordingly I defined it "the absence of restraint"" (Bentham cited in Long 1977, 54). On this definition you are free in a given choice just insofar as others do not restrain the selection of any option: not the option you actually prefer, for sure, but also – at least on what came to be the standard reading (Berlin 1969, xxxix; Pettit 2011) – not any option you might have preferred but didn't. This conception makes the absence of interference enough for the freedom of a choice; it does not require the absence of a power of interference on the part of others. Even though you avoid interference only because of my being goodwilled and indulgent – even though you can choose as you wish only because I permit it – still, that will be enough to make you free.

Bentham and Paley and their ilk were reformers, committed to having the state cater for the freedom – and more generally for the utility or happiness – of the whole population, not just the freedom of mainstream, propertied males that government had traditionally protected. So why would they have weakened the ideal of freedom so that it is not compromised by having to live under the power of another, only by active interference? My own hunch is that it was more realistic to argue for universal freedom if freedom was something that a wife could enjoy at the hands of a kind husband, a worker under the rule of a tolerant employer, and did not require redressing the power imbalances allowed under contemporary family and master–slaver law, as a universalized freedom as nondomination would have required (Pettit 1997, chap. 1). It may be for this reason that Paley (1825, 168) described freedom as nondomination – an idea that "places liberty in security," in accord with "common discourse" (164–5) – as one of those versions of "civil freedom" that are "unattainable in experience, inflame expectations that can never be gratified, and disturb the public content with complaints, which no wisdom or benevolence of government can remove."

The rejection of freedom as nondomination raised a question about the linked ideas of a mixed constitution and a contestatory citizenry. Those devices were required on the traditional, republican way of viewing things because they were supposed to ensure that when the republic makes laws that protect its citizens against domination, it does not impose those laws in the dominating manner of an independent agent with an independent will. The idea was that if the interference imposed by the state is itself subject to the control of those on whom it is imposed, then it will not be dominating: It will not involve subjecting people to the will of a distinct, independent agent. It will be a nondominating – or, as it was often called, a nonarbitrary – form of interference. Once freedom came to be construed as noninterference, however, it was no longer clear why such constraints were necessary.

Every system of law coerces and penalizes its subjects – and every system of law presupposes taxation – so that there is no law without interference. If freedom means noninterference, therefore, then there is no freedom-based requirement to make the interference nondominating, as the mixed constitution and the contestatory citizenry promised to do. The best system will be that in which there is the least overall interference, public or private. And it may just be that the best system is one in which a benevolent despot coerces people so that they don't interfere with one another, yet keeps the coercion practiced to a minimum. William Paley, surely Bentham's most clear-headed associate, embraced the point when he noted as early as 1785 that the cause of liberty as noninterference might be as well served, in some circumstances, by "the edicts of a despotic prince, as by the resolutions of popular assembly." In such conditions, he said, "would an absolute form of government be no less free than the purest democracy" (Paley 1825, 166).[5] And, by his lights, no less free than the most classical republic.

While Bentham and Paley were mainly interested in advancing the utilitarian program, they shaped the way in which early nineteenth-century liberals thought about freedom and the requirements of freedom. We might define liberalism – somewhat tendentiously, in view of the many meanings given to the term – as any approach to government that makes freedom as noninterference paramount or central. And in that sense it contrasts quite sharply with the republican approach in which freedom as nondomination plays the central role. Liberalism in this sense may be right-of-center, as classical liberals or libertarians generally were, making freedom as noninterference into the only concern of government. Or it may be left-of-center, making freedom as noninterference into just one of government's goals: perhaps a goal derived from the broader concern with happiness, as in the case of utilitarians; perhaps a goal that is paired with a separate concern like equality, as in the case of John Rawls (1971; 1993; 2001), Ronald Dworkin (1978; 1986) and other egalitarians.[6]

No matter which form liberalism takes, it contrasts with republicanism on how to understand freedom, a value to which each approach gives a prominent place. On the republican construal, the real enemy of freedom is the power that some people may have over others, whereas on the liberal understanding, asymmetries in interpersonal power are not in themselves objectionable. Right-of-center liberalism is happy to tolerate such imbalances, so long as active interference is avoided. And left-of-center liberalism rejects them only insofar as they have unwelcome effects on equality or welfare or whatever other value is invoked to supplement the ideal of freedom.

But the conflict between republicanism and liberalism should not be overdrawn. For while Paley and others had seen that freedom as noninterference does not strictly require a mixed constitution or a contestatory citizenry, almost every form of liberalism has endorsed the main elements in the idea of the mixed constitution and given some recognition to the contestatory role of citizens. The rule of law, the separation of powers, and the liberties of speech and expression are reflections of those earlier institutional ideals. Republicanism differs from liberalism in espousing a more radical ideal of freedom, in arguing for a distinctive connection between freedom in that sense and its twin institutional ideals, and in giving a distinctive interpretation of those ideals, particularly that of a contestatory democracy. But nonetheless there are definite, discernible continuities between the traditions.

2. Rousseau and Kant on freedom

As mentioned earlier, this sketch of republicanism and liberalism summarizes the way of thinking about the two doctrines that is reflected in much contemporary work on neo-republicanism, my own contribution included. But the sketch says nothing about the republican way of thinking that was associated with Jean-Jacques Rousseau and to a somewhat lesser extent, Immanuel Kant.

I described Italian–Atlantic republicanism in terms of three ideas: freedom as nondomination, the mixed constitution and a contestatory citizenry. The Franco–German alternative was fostered in the first place, as we shall see, by a departure from the idea of the mixed constitution. But before commenting on that departure and on its affect on the other ideas, it is worth stressing that both Rousseau and Kant kept faith with the idea that the state should be founded in a concern for the equal liberty of its citizens and, in particular, that such freedom or liberty consists in not having to live under the will of another: that is, not being subjected to, or dominated by, another.

For Rousseau the un-freedom from which the ideal state should protect citizens equally is, as he suggests in a number of places, "personal dependence" or "individual dependence" (Rousseau 1997, 1.7.8; 2.11.1). While he may understand "dependence" more widely than subjection to the will of the other, such subjection is certainly the paradigm of dependence in

176

his view. And so the equal freedom that people are invited to expect – achievable only via reliance on the state – is clearly a variant of freedom as nondomination: It requires "that every citizen be perfectly independent of all the others" (2.12.3). Thus he says that that "which ought to be the end of every system of legislation is ... freedom and equality," where equality is valued "because freedom cannot subsist without it" (2.11.1).

The freedom that Rousseau has in mind here is "civil freedom," as he calls it, rather than "natural freedom." It consists in having a recognized and enforced right of choice in a closed domain as distinct from an unprotected right of choice in an open domain. As a parallel, Rousseau directs our attention to the way property consists in having a recognized and enforced right of ownership across a limited range of goods rather than a claim asserted on the basis of "force or the right of the first occupant" (1.8.3) to a more extensive range. He clearly thinks that civil freedom is better than natural, as ownership proper is better than uncertain possession.

Where Rousseau talks about civil as distinct from natural freedom, Kant talks of the "external freedom" that individuals can enjoy in relation to one another as distinct from the internal freedom of the will that each may achieve on their own. This external freedom, as he thinks of it, requires "independence from being constrained by another's power of choice" (Kant 1996, 393).[7] As Rousseau makes civil freedom the first concern of the state, so Kant represents external freedom as "the only original right belonging to every man by virtue of his humanity." As Rousseau links civil freedom with equality, so Kant says that external freedom is "not really distinct from ... equality; that is, independence from being bound by others to more than one can in turn bind them." And as Rousseau takes civil freedom to be established on the basis of law and right, so Kant holds that external freedom consists in a person's "being his own master (*sui juris*)" and in "being authorized" to act as he or she likes within certain limits: within a sphere of basic liberties that can be protected at once for all (Kant 1996, 393–4).

The line taken by Kant, even more clearly than that espoused by Rousseau, is perfectly consonant with the Italian–Atlantic conception of freedom. That is made especially clear in a passage written by Kant in his private notes on *The Social Contract*, where he demonizes precisely the sort of dependence on the will of another that all republicans had deplored.

177

> Find himself in what condition he will, the human being is dependent on many external things ... But what is harder and more unnatural than this yoke of necessity is the subjection of one human being under the will of another. No misfortune can be more terrifying to one who is accustomed to freedom.
>
> (Kant 2005, 11)

The right to freedom in the sense of nonsubjection to the will of another is, by many accounts, the fundamental idea in Kant's legal and political thought (Ripstein 2009).

While both of these thinkers sign on to the idea of freedom as non-domination, however, it is worth remarking that Rousseau promises to support a more radical interpretation of what it requires. On the face of it, freedom as nondomination is going to be undermined in the presence of poverty and economic inequality, since the poor are bound to be vulnerable to domination. Rousseau (1997, II.11.2) is clearly open to acknowledging this, as when he requires (in order to avoid "trafficking in public freedom") that "no citizen be so very rich that he can buy another, and none so poor that he is compelled to sell himself." He registers the same requirement when he says elsewhere that "the social state is advantageous for men only insofar as all have something and none has too much of anything" (I.9.8, fn). In making these remarks, and yet suggesting that the rich and poor should all be citizens, Rousseau may be taken to support a state that regulates wealth and perhaps redistributes it.[8]

Kant takes a different line on this issue. He allows that freedom requires that people be "all equal to one another as subjects," so that "no one of them can coerce any other except through public law." But he insists that "this thoroughgoing equality of individuals within a state, as its subjects, is quite consistent with the greatest inequality in terms of quantity and degree of possessions," and consistent therefore with dependency: It is possible that "the welfare of one is very much dependent upon the will of another (that of the poor on the rich)" (Kant 1996, 292). Thus the equality of all subjects does not entail their freedom, since freedom rules out the "subjection of one human being under the will of another." Should the state seek to ensure the independency and freedom of all subjects, making them worthy of citizenship proper? Kant thinks not, arguing that citizenship should only go to the relatively wealthy. "The quality requisite to this, apart from the natural one (of not being a child or a woman), is only that of being one's own master (*sui juris*), hence having some property (and any art, craft, fine art, or science can be counted as property)" (295). On this front – and, as we shall see, on others – Kant offers a more conservative interpretation of Franco–German republicanism than Rousseau.

But while Rousseau and Kant kept faith, in their different ways, with the republican conception of freedom as nondomination, and with the commitment to the equal freedom of citizens, they broke with that tradition on the two institutional ideals by which I characterized it. In place of the mixed constitution, they hailed the idea of a popular or representative sovereign. And in place of the contestatory citizenry, they installed the idea of a people whose primary job was to participate in the creation and sustenance of that sovereign assembly, to take Rousseau's version, or in Kant's more circumspect account, to elect the members of that body and then treat the body as a collective spokesperson that should have to brook no individual resistance.

These departures from the republican tradition are hardly going to be intelligible, however, except against the background of absolutist, institutional thinking in the sixteenth and seventeenth centuries. Jean Bodin, Thomas Hobbes and a number of other writers had attacked the institutional ideals of republicanism over that period, and I believe that they had an enormous influence on Rousseau's and Kant's attempts to explore the institutional implications of implementing equal freedom as nondomination. I outline their critique of republican ideals – in particular, their attack on the idea of the mixed constitution – in the following section and then return in sections four and five to the institutional ideals embraced by Rousseau and Kant.

3. BODIN AND HOBBES ON THE INSTITUTION OF THE STATE

Bodin

Bodin wrote his major anti-republican work, *The Six Books of the Republic*, just a few years after the St Bartholomew's Day massacre of Huguenots in 1572, at a time of great religious and civil strife in France. Hobbes wrote his equally anti-republican tracts in or about the 1640s – *The Elements of Law*, *De Cive* and *Leviathan* – in Parisian exile from an England beset by civil war. Goaded by the fear of civil strife, both argued vehemently that whatever individual or body held power – or at least the supreme power, as they saw it, of legislation – it had to operate as a unitary agent or agency, it had to carry the highest authority, and it could not embody separate, mutually checking elements within itself. Each believed that in the absence of such a unitary, absolute and indivisible sovereign, there was bound to be continuing dissension and, as Hobbes (1994b, 13.9) famously stated it, a relapse into a war of all against all: a state of nature in which no one owes any obligations to others and life is "solitary, poor, nasty, brutish and short."

Bodin begins from the assumption that among the functions of government, the making and giving of law is supreme, so that whoever has this power is in charge of other governing authorities: "All the other attributes and rights of sovereignty are included in this power of making and unmaking law" (Bodin 1967, I.10.44). His argument for the necessity of a unified sovereign derives from the further assumption that every law is a command, issuing from the will of the law-maker or sovereign: "Law is nothing else than the command of the sovereign in the exercise of his sovereign power" (I.8.35). The idea is that if the law is command, and so the expression of will, then there has to be a sovereign commander – a single or unitary agent, individual or corporate – such that law reflects that agent's will.

But why think that the sovereign, qua source of law, has absolute power? Bodin offers three observations that support this further claim. The first is that the sovereign cannot count as a commander if the effectiveness of sovereign commands is conditional on the agreement of another agency. "The first attribute of the sovereign prince therefore is the power to make law binding on all his subjects in general and on each in particular. But to avoid any ambiguity one must add that he does so without the consent of any superior, equal, or inferior being necessary" (I.10.43). The second observation is that the sovereign, as the source of law's commands, cannot be subject to those very commands: "[I]t is impossible to bind oneself in any matter which is the subject of one's own exercise of free will" (I.8.28). And the third is that while the sovereign ought ideally to conform to moral and sometimes even customary demands, the failure to do so should be taken as a sign of bad sovereignty, not nonsovereignty: "[T]he tyrant is a true sovereign for all that" (1.8.26; see too VI, 4).

The unitary, absolute sovereign for which Bodin argues can assume any of the three forms distinguished by Aristotle. It may be an individual king, as Bodin himself would prefer; or an elite, aristocratic committee; or a democratic committee-of-the-whole. "[T]here are only three states, or commonwealth, monarchy, aristocracy, and democracy" (II.1.51). Where sovereignty belongs to a multimember body, he explains, decisions should be made by majority voting among the members who choose to attend. No matter what the character of the sovereign, however, the sovereignty that characterizes a state should be distinguished in Bodin's novel view from the government of the state. "It is important that a clear distinction be made between the form of the state, and the form of the government, which is merely the machinery for policing the state, though no one has ever considered it in that light" (II.2.56). Thus, a monarchical sovereign may entrust government to the people as a whole, and a popular, democratic sovereign may entrust government to a monarch, and so on; in each case the sovereign will retain sovereignty to the extent that the delegation of power is reversible.

But not only does Bodin think that every proper state has to be organized around a unitary, absolute sovereign, he also maintains that this sovereign cannot contain conflicting, mutually checking components among which the sovereignty is divided. In his view, sovereignty is not just unitary and absolute, it is indivisible. This picture leads Bodin to oppose one single constitutional form with great vehemence: the mixed constitution, so beloved of the older republican tradition.

Under the mixed constitution some legislative powers may be separated, as when either of two or more bodies can make law, or they may be shared, as when two bodies are each required to endorse any bill that is to become law. Bodin opposes any such weakening of authority. The main ground he cites is that no one can be expected to be a law-giver in one respect, a law-taker in another. He asks how it is possible that "a prince, a ruling class, and the people, all have a part in" sovereignty. The answer, he thinks, is obvious. "The first attribute of sovereignty is the power to make law binding on the subject. But in such a case who will be the subjects that obey, if they also have a share in the law-making power?" (II.1.52). Weak though this consideration appears to be, Bodin takes it to undermine the very idea of a mixed constitution: "[N]one such has ever existed, and could never exist or even be clearly imagined" (II.1.55).

While often adopting the language of sovereignty that Bodin introduced, a number of commentators threw doubt on his rather weak case against the mixed constitution; they thought that a system that operated via different agencies – broadly, under a mixed constitution – may still have the status of a unified, absolute authority with a single will (Franklin 1991). Thus various German critics, anxious to make sense of the way the Emperor's powers were constrained by the different German "estates," pointed out that there were many ways in which law-making might be shared among different individuals or bodies, or divided out among them (Besold 1618, 279–80). But Bodin's critique of the mixed constitution did not wither away. And this, in great part, may be because of the further support that Thomas Hobbes provided for the critique.

Hobbes

Hobbes followed Bodin in making a case for a unitary, absolute, indivisible sovereign. The case he made was quite original in a number of respects – see Pettit (2008b, chap. 5) – but what marks it off most deeply from Bodin's is the novel framework for thinking about constitutional issues that he developed. This framework supported the case for thinking of the sovereign as unitary, absolute and indivisible. From our point of view it is important in particular for the way Hobbes used it to criticize and mock the mixed constitution.

Hobbes argued that we should think of the commonwealth, whatever form it assumes – monarchical, aristocratic or democratic – as a corporate body on the model of "a company of merchants" (Hobbes 1998, 5.10). In a monarchy – the constitutional form that he, like Bodin, prefers – the multitude of the people is incorporated into a body for which, by unanimous consent, the king or queen speaks. In an aristocracy or democracy, they are incorporated into a body for which, again by unanimous consent, an elite or popular assembly speaks. Prior to incorporation, according to Hobbes, the people in a country constitute just a multitude of dissonant voices: an "aggregate" or "heap" of agents (Hobbes 1994a, 21.11), "a disorganized crowd" (Hobbes 1998, 7.11), a "throng" (Hobbes 1994b, 6.37). After incorporation the people comes into existence as a proper agent. It forms a will and assumes the status of an agent or person via the single authorized voice of its spokesperson, whether that be the individual voice of a monarch or the majoritarian voice of an aristocratic or democratic assembly.

According to Hobbes, it is this spokesperson that constitutes the sovereign in any commonwealth. And because the sovereign plays a spokesperson role, it has to be a unitary, absolute and indivisible individual or body. In order to play that role, to take the first of these characteristics, the sovereign must operate as a single or unitary agent or agency; only a single person, after all, can speak with one voice. In Hobbes's view the sovereign has a unity that extends by courtesy to the multitude personated or represented within the state: "[I]t is the unity of the representer, not the unity of the represented, that maketh the person one ... and unity, cannot otherwise be understood in multitude" (Hobbes 1994b, 16.13).

But in order to play a spokesperson role, the sovereign also has to be given more or less absolute or unconstrained authority. According to Hobbes's view of the world, the individuals in a multitude must consent to being personated, forming a contract to establish a sovereign. They cannot make this contract with the sovereign collectively, since they must already have a sovereign – they must already be a corporate spokesperson – before they can do something like making a contract (Hobbes 1994b, 18.14). They have to contract with one another individually to recognize a sovereign, relying on that very sovereign to enforce the terms of the contract on each. But this means that the contract itself cannot contain any clause that limits the sovereign, for no sovereign could be expected to enforce such a self-denying ordinance. Subjects have no justiciable right to contest the sovereign.

> If any one or more of them pretend a breach of the covenant made by the sovereign at his institution, and others or one other of his subjects, or himself alone, pretend there was no such breach, there is in this case no judge to decide the controversy: it returns therefore to the sword again.
>
> (Hobbes 1994b, 18)

And so the contract they make will expose people to the power of the sovereign in the fullest measure to which they can rationally contract to be exposed. The sovereign will have more or less absolute authority in relation to subjects.

But not only is the Hobbesian sovereign unitary and absolute; using the same framework of thought, Hobbes argues that the sovereign must also be indivisible. Thus he sets himself squarely against the mixed constitution: "mixarchy," as he mischievously calls it (Hobbes 1990, 16). Hobbes's complaint is, predictably, that the mixed constitution authorizes a number of different spokespersons, thereby undermining the possibility of a commonwealth. It supports "not one independent commonwealth, but three independent factions; nor one representative person, but three" (Hobbes 1994b, 29.16; see too 1998, 7.4; 1994a, 20.15). His argument is straightforward: "[I]f the king bear the person of the people, and the general assembly bear also the person of the people, and another assembly bear the person of a part of the people, they are not one person, nor one sovereign, but three persons, and three sovereigns" (Hobbes 1994b, 29.16).

This critique of the mixed constitution, in full dress, relies on three distinct theses. First, the incorporation thesis, that the existence of a state or commonwealth requires the incorporation of the people. Second, the consent thesis, that incorporation involves the contractual acquiescence of its members in the identity of a group spokesperson, individual or otherwise. Third, and most crucially, the majoritarian thesis, that the only nonindividual spokesperson that a people might have is an assembly, aristocratic or democratic, that resolves issues by majority voting. If we go along with these claims, then it is very hard indeed to see how a state or commonwealth could operate under a mixed constitution.

I believe that even if we accept the incorporation and consent claims, we should reject the majoritarian. Groups that do not have an individual dictator may operate under many different modes of organization, not just via majority voting in an assembly. Ironically, indeed, it is demonstrable that they could not operate satisfactorily under majoritarian decision making; such an arrangement would be hostage to inconsistency in group judgments and policies (Pettit 2008b, chap. 5, appendix; List and Pettit 2011). In the present context, however, our interest is not in the flaw in Hobbes's argument but in the extent to which his claims, building on those of Bodin, affected the views of Rousseau and Kant.

4. Rousseau and Kant on the constitution

Rousseau

Rousseau follows Bodin and Hobbes in taking the legislative authority, rather than the executive or judicial, to be the sovereign, on the grounds that the work of any other agency is the "application of the law," not the making of law (Rousseau 1997, II.2.3). Following Bodin's novel distinction, however, he allows that there is a difference between sovereignty and administration, so that the people can be the sovereign without themselves constituting the administration or government (III.7.4). A regime in which the people served administratively as well as legislatively would count in his language as a democracy and, as we shall see, he rejects such a homogenous system in favor of a republic in which the sovereign is the people and the administration is delegated to appointed magistrates. Those magistrates may be divided among themselves and may constitute a "mixed government," a regime that is sometimes to be recommended (III.7.4). But this idea is very different from that of a mixed constitution.

184

Unlike the mixed constitution, mixed government is quite consistent with the indivisibility of the sovereign.

Rousseau joins Bodin and Hobbes in arguing for a single, absolute, indivisible sovereign. He inveighs against defenders of the mixed constitution who, failing to see that there has to be a single will at the origin of law, represent it as the work of independent bodies. Although he does not mention examples, he would have certainly rejected the English system – as represented in Montesquieu's (1977) *The Spirit of the Laws* – under which law is created by the king, the lords and the commons in combination. And equally he would have been opposed to the Roman system, as we understand it, under which a law might be created by the *Comitia Tributa*, for example, or by the *Comitia Centuriata*; he followed Bodin in denying that Rome had a mixed constitution, insisting that, at least when it lived up to its republican credentials, "the Roman people was genuinely sovereign both by right and fact" (Rousseau 1997, IV.4.21).[9] Perhaps he has these two sorts of mixed systems in mind when he complains about those who divide sovereignty between different partial bodies that "sometimes they mix up all these parts and sometimes they separate them" (IV.2.2). The English mix them up and, as we understand them today, the Romans separate them.

Asserting that sovereignty is indivisible, Rousseau deploys all his rhetorical skills against his opponents.

> [T]hey turn the Sovereign into a being that is fantastical and formed of disparate pieces; it is as if they were putting together man out of several bodies one of which had eyes, another arms, another feet, and nothing else. Japanese conjurors are said to carve up a child before the spectators' eyes, then, throwing all of its members into the air one after the other, they make the child fall back down alive all reassembled. That is more or less what our politicians' tricks are like; having dismembered the social body by a sleight-of-hand worthy of the fairground, they put the pieces back together no one knows how.
>
> (Rousseau 1997, II.2.2)

In developing this case against the mixed constitution it is fairly clear that Rousseau is following in the steps of Bodin and Hobbes. In particular, he goes along with all three of the claims invoked in Hobbes's argument: the claims I described as the incorporation, the consent, and the majoritarian theses.

Thus, to take the first thesis, the existence of a state, as distinct from enslavement to a despot (I.5.1), presupposes association or incorporation: "[T]his act of association produces a moral and collective body made up of as many members as the assembly has voices, and which receives by this same act its unity, its common *self*, its life and its will" (I.6.10; italics in the original). Moreover, as in Hobbes, this incorporation has to be supported by the consent of all: "There is only one law which by its nature requires unanimous consent. That is the social pact: for the civil association is the most voluntary act in the world" (IV.2.5). And, finally, the way for a group to make its decisions when it does not have an individual spokesperson is via majority voting: "Except for this primitive contract, the vote of the majority always obligates all the rest; this is a consequence of the contract itself" (IV.2.7).

The big break with Hobbes, and with Bodin, comes in Rousseau's claim that majority voting is the only legitimate way, not just one way among others, in which the people can make laws. There is no sovereign other than the popular sovereign that is given life within the assembly. Prior to publishing *Leviathan* in 1651, Hobbes suggests that when a state forms by explicit agreement or institution, a democracy will form at a first stage and then at a second stage one of two things will happen: either democracy will be upheld, with the assembled people retaining the role of sovereign, or, alternatively, that democratic sovereign will cede its sovereignty, giving itself over to the rule of an aristocratic body or a monarch (Hobbes 1994a, chap. 21; 1998, chap. 7). Rousseau probably did not know *Leviathan*, since it had not been translated in his time, and the argument in favor of popular, majoritarian sovereignty starts from this earlier suggestion.

Where Hobbes had envisaged the possibility of the popular or democratic sovereign transferring sovereignty to an aristocratic committee or to a monarch, Rousseau insists that sovereignty is inalienable, challenging Grotius rather than Hobbes on the point (Rousseau 1997, I.5.2). He argues that for any agent or agency "it is absurd for the will to shackle itself for the future," tying itself to what someone else "is going to will tomorrow;" this, he says, would be to deny its own nature as a will (II.1.3). And that premise leads him to his central anti-Hobbesian conclusion. "If, then, the people promises simply to obey, it dissolves itself by this very act, it loses its quality of being a people" (II.1.3; see too I.7.3). No individual man could give himself to another in this way and count still as being of sound mind. And thus neither could a whole, incorporated people.

> To say a man gives himself gratuitously is to say something absurd and inconceivable; such an act is illegitimate and null, for the simple reason that whoever does

so is not in his right mind. To say the same of a whole people is to assume a people of madmen; madness does not make right.

(Rousseau 1997, I.4.4)

We can see from this account of the linkages with Bodin and Hobbes that while Rousseau may have preserved the republican idea of freedom as nondomination, he totally betrayed the earlier tradition in espousing the idea of popular sovereignty. In Rousseau's idealized republic – a version of what Bodin and Hobbes called a democracy – individuals are confronted by the single powerful presence of "the public person," which "formerly assumed the name *City* and now assumes that of *Republic* or *body politic*" (I.6.10; italics in the original). While Rousseau envisages an ideal under which people are independent of one another as private persons, in line with the received conception of freedom, he thinks that this mutual independence is attainable only at the cost of a form of submission to the public person – specifically, to the general or corporate will of the public person – that would have been wholly at odds with Italian–Atlantic sentiments. While every citizen should "be perfectly independent of all the others," he says, this is only going to be possible insofar as each is "excessively dependent on the City" (II.12.3). The totally novel, consciously outrageous assumption introduced by Rousseau is that "each, by giving himself to all, gives himself to no one" (I.6.8).

It would be unfair to Rousseau, however, to suggest that he breaks with Bodin and Hobbes insofar only as he restricts legitimacy to a regime under which the assembled people make the law. For he reintroduces one element in the traditional idea of the mixed constitution by adding that the way the assembly should work is on the basis of a rule of law: as "an empire of laws, not of men," as James Harrington (1992, 8) had described it in the seventeenth century. In this image, the law-making assembly looks only to the good of citizens qua citizens and, being impartial in that sense, is not moved by the effect its decisions may have on this or that individual or faction as such; "the law considers the subjects in a body and their actions in the abstract, never any man as an individual or a particular action" (II.6.6).

This ideal means that if the people are to perform properly as a people – a body in which they all have equal standing – then they must each think as citizens, focused impartially on their common interest; they must vote, not out of personal or factional attachment, but on the impersonal basis that "it is advantageous to the State ... that this or that opinion

187

pass" (IV.1.6). The majority vote will reflect the general will properly only when such a condition is fulfilled: "[W]hat generalizes the will is not so much the number of voices, as it is the common interest which unites them" (II.4.7). Thus, the "more concord reigns in assemblies, that is to say the closer opinions come to unanimity, the more the general will also predominates; whereas long debates, dissensions, disturbances, signal the ascendancy of particular interests and the decline of the State" (IV.2.1). It is for this reason, indeed, that Rousseau rejects the idea that the people should serve both as sovereign law-maker and as executive authority, in what he calls a democracy. He argues that such an arrangement might corrupt members of the assembly into focusing on the personal or factional effects of the laws they implement, betraying rule-of-law impartiality (III.17.5).

Kant

Kant gives a greater role to the executive and judiciary than Rousseau.

> [T]he general united will consists of three persons: the sovereign authority (sovereignty) in the person of the legislator; the executive authority in the person of the ruler (in conformity to law); and the judicial authority (to award to each what is his in accordance with the law) in the person of the judge.
>
> (Kant 1996, 457)

But this is not because of any affection for "so-called mixed constitutions" (479). He treats the executive authority – and by implication the judicial – as "the organ of the sovereign" (462): the agent who gives the legislator a presence in the lives of people, promulgating and enforcing the law. In Kant's picture, it is as if the legislator is a silent, background power – a force akin to gravity – that becomes incarnate and visible only through the actions of its executive and judicial organs. More on this point later.[10]

Kant is quite explicit about the primacy of the law-maker in relation to other authorities, especially the executive: "[T]he ruler is subject to the law and so is put under obligation through the law by another, namely the sovereign" (460). Since the sovereign punishes offenders via the ruler, Kant says that the sovereign cannot punish the ruler as such: that is, while keeping the relevant individual or body in office. But this is scarcely a restriction, since the "sovereign can also take the ruler's authority away from him, depose him, or reform his administration" (460). For these reasons Kant praises Frederick II of Prussia for the fact that, acknowledging his subordination to the law, he "at least said that he was only the highest servant of the state" (325).

On this basic issue, then, the match between Kant and Rousseau is rather good. And it is reinforced by the fact that while treating the sovereign as the supreme and presumptively undivided authority in the state, he agrees with Rousseau that it is best that the persons of the sovereign and the executive be distinct (324–5). However, that common commitment still leaves room for a major divergence.

On our account of Rousseau's views, the general will has two conflicting aspects. On the one hand, it is the corporate will formed under majority voting by the only legitimate spokesperson he acknowledges: the assembled people. On the other hand, it is the impartial will that is formed by people who put aside their personal interests and make decisions impartially in light of the common good. When Rousseau refers to the general will of the people he sometimes appears to refer to their actual corporate will, however impartially or factionally formed, and sometimes to the will that they would form were they impartial. Kant registers this ambiguity, however implicitly, and uses it to build a variation on Rousseau's themes that preserves the indivisibility of the sovereign law-maker.

Kant follows Rousseau in thinking that the will that lies behind law has to be the will of the people, understood corporately, not the will of any individual or set of individuals: This is the will of the people "as a commonwealth," as he says, and not their will "as a mob" (300, fn). But taking this observation as his premise, he sticks with Hobbes rather than Rousseau in arguing that whenever a state exists, however imperfect in his or in Rousseau's terms, the will of the sovereign law-maker – or the will of the ruler or head of state qua "organ of the sovereign" (Kant 1996, 462) – represents the will of that incorporated people. Thus the people as individuals "cannot and may not judge otherwise than as the present head of state (*summus imperans*) wills it to" (462).

Kant supports this sacralization of the status quo on a distinctively Hobbesian ground. He says that if the people as an unincorporated set of individuals were entitled to challenge the sovereign or ruler on any public matter – on any matter where the people's will ought to rule – then the matter, as we put it earlier, would not be justiciable: There would be no one to judge between the competing sides, and no single will would be present. Or if there was to be someone to judge between the sides, than that person or body would count as the sovereign: the spokesperson for the incorporated people. Thus, speaking of the people as individuals, he holds that "in an already existing civil constitution the people's judgment to determine how the constitution should be administered is no longer valid" (298–9). His argument for that claim is as follows:

> [S]uppose that the people can so judge, and indeed contrary to the judgment of the actual head of state; who is to decide on which side the right is? No one can make the decision as judge in its own suit. Hence there would have to be another head above the head of state, that would decide between him and the people; and this is self-contradictory.
>
> (Kant 1996, 299)

While Kant is on Rousseau's side, then, in acknowledging that the law has to be backed by the corporate will of the people, he follows Hobbes in thinking that that will may be legitimately formed in any of a variety of ways, not just on the basis of assembly voting. But unlike Hobbes, he holds that the corporate will is ideally formed on a popular basis, not on the basis of an individual ruler's judgment. Thus he says that whereas the rule of the ideal sovereign is "absolutely rightful," the less than ideal sovereign only enjoys a "provisional right": a right that belongs to that sovereign, presumably, only provided there is nothing better in contention (481).

But what does the ideal of popular sovereignty mean for Kant? He thinks that it is impossible for all citizens – even on his narrow construal of the citizenry (294–5, 457–8) – to take part in legislation, and argues that a representative regime "is all that can be foreseen as attainable" (296). Thus he holds that "any true republic is and can only be a system representing the people" (481; see too 325). This breaks with Rousseau's ideal of a people that assembles and makes laws at regular intervals (Rousseau 1997, III.13–14) – an ideal under which it is axiomatic that "any law which the people has not ratified in person is null" (III.15.5). But the position is fully in line with the Bodin–Hobbes tradition to which they are each indebted. For Bodin and Hobbes the sovereign people may delegate government to an individual or an elite and there seems to be no deep reason why the government it authorizes should not have a legislative as well as an executive and judicial function. After all, in Kant's ideal republic the people would still have the power of being able to dismiss such a government and would remain sovereign in that traditional sense.

We have seen that while Kant thinks like Rousseau that there has to be a sovereign, indivisible will at the origin of the law in any society, this will may be legitimately formed in any manner, monarchical, aristocratic or popular; and that while popular will-formation is the ideal, as for Rousseau, in his view this supports a representative rather than a participatory system of decision making.

Notwithstanding these differences on the nature of the corporately formed will that shapes the law, Kant is absolutely on Rousseau's side in arguing that the will that shapes the law in that sense ought ideally to be impartial. The will expressed in law ought to be "the united will of a whole people" (Kant 1996, 296). Only such an impartial will, he says, could be expected to identify laws that would meet the demands of equal, universal freedom, giving each a freedom that "can coexist with the freedom of every other in accordance with universal law" (393).

How can Kant be relatively undemanding about the nature of the corporate will that is in actual charge of the law and yet very demanding about the need for it to be impartial? The reason, on reflection, is straightforward. He thinks, like Hobbes, that no matter what the form of sovereignty and government, the will that shapes the law always counts as the corporate will of the people. Thus he ignores or denies the distinction marked by Rousseau (1997, I.5.1) between "subjugating a multitude and ruling a society," where the individual who subjugates "remains nothing but a private individual" and realizes "neither public good, nor body politic." Given that the legislative will always counts as the will of the people, Kant's normative focus has to be on the content that that will assumes, not on how it is formed. What is important for him is that the legislative will, however it is formed, should have an appropriately impartial content.

How to identify a suitably impartial content? Here Kant invokes the idea of the social contract on which Rousseau and indeed Hobbes rely so heavily, but he gives it quite a different role from that which they envisage. Where they thought of the social contract, however implicit or virtual, as required for establishing the corporate people with a common will – Rousseau talked of it as "the act by which a people is a people" (Rousseau 1997, I.5.2) – Kant thinks of it as a theoretical device that serves to direct us to the content that the corporate will would have were it truly impartial.

The original contract is "only an idea of reason," he says, not something that has to be "presupposed as a fact" (296). The role it plays is to instruct the sovereign legislator on the content that the law ought to have. It binds "every legislator to give his laws in such a way that they *could* have arisen from the united will of a whole people" (296; italics in the original). It imposes an obligation on "the constituting authority to make the kind of government suited to the idea of the original contract" (480). What it provides, then, is not a template of how law ought to originate but "the touchstone of any public law's conformity to right" (297); "a rational principle for appraising any public rightful constitution" (301).

This reworking of Rousseauvian ideas means that every actual regime should aspire to the ideal republican form that might have been chosen in an original contract: "[E]ven if this cannot be done all at once, it is under obligation to change the kind of government gradually and continually so that it harmonizes *in its effect* with the only constitution that accords with right, that of a pure republic" (480; italics in the original). Such a self-improving regime may not actually become a pure republic, he suggests, but it should treat that republic at least as a regulative ideal, looking for the same effect – the same sort of law – that a republic would provide.

What institutional form would an ideal Kantian republic take? It ought to privilege institutions that are disposed, as Kant sees it, to encourage the formation of an impartial corporate will, giving all citizens equal freedom: that is, "independence from being bound by others to more than one can in turn bind them" (393–4). Kant singles out two institutional constraints in particular that a republic ought to satisfy. First, it ought to be a popular regime and so, on pain of infeasibility, a representative one (296); it ought to be a regime run "by all the citizens united and acting through their delegates (deputies)" (481; see too 325). And second it ought to separate out "the executive power (the government) from the legislative power" (324), avoiding the possibility of despotism that arises when the administration, inevitably focused on its particular policy objectives, doubles as sovereign and can formulate purportedly impartial law with an eye on achieving those ends.

The ideal of the mixed constitution fades just as effectively in this Kantian political theory as it does in Rousseau's. The popular sovereign that rules over people in the ideal republic, even the sovereign that rules over people in less than perfect regimes, has an unchallengeable authority to speak for the people in its corporate presence and to dictate what the constitution ought to be. And this sovereign is clearly meant to speak with a single voice, not to be the precipitate of rival, mutually checking powers, as under the mixed constitution.

While granting priority to the sovereign, as we saw earlier, Kant speaks as often of the ruler or head of state – "the organ of the sovereign" (462) – as he does of the sovereign power itself. This is because he tends to think of the sovereign, or at least the sovereign in the ideal republic, in abstract terms, as a power that "belongs not to human beings but to the laws" (491). He suggests that, shaped by impartial, rule-of-law constraints – shaped by the constraints of giving equal freedom to all – the legislature would generate law so inexorably that we can think of the law as an impersonal sovereign. Thus he says that at least in the ideal republic "the sovereign, which gives laws, is, as it were invisible; it is the personified law in itself, not its agent" (294, fn) – "law itself rules and depends on no particular person" (481).

5. Rousseau and Kant on the citizenry

Rousseau

Rousseau's allegiance to the tradition of Bodin and Hobbes not only leads him to break with the ideal of the mixed constitution, it pushes him into thinking of the citizenry in quite a novel, non-republican manner. In the Bodin–Hobbes picture, adopted by Rousseau and Kant, the indivisibility of the sovereign means a ruling out of the mixed constitution, as we have seen. And as we shall now see, the absolute power that the sovereign enjoys rules out a contestatory citizenry.

Rousseau explicitly invokes a Hobbesian style of argument for the absolute power of the sovereign – one that we have already seen Kant invoke – invoking the need for justiciability in support of denying the right of citizens to contest sovereign decisions. He claims that "if individuals were left some rights ... there would be no common superior who might adjudicate between them and the public" (I.6.7). The idea is that there has to be one, final spokesperson on what the law is and that if we allowed the people to contest the legislature's decisions, we would have to establish another body to rule between them. That being impossible, so the idea goes, the legislature has to have an absolute, incontestable standing in the lives of its subjects. Once the legislative assembly has spoken, then, it falls to individuals to comply, not complain.[11]

In the Rousseauvian representation of the members of a state, "they collectively assume the name of *people* and individually call themselves *citizens* as participants in the sovereign authority, and *subjects* as subjected to the laws of the state" (I.6.10; italics in the original). The crucial shift here is from the role of contestor to that of participant. Citizens are no longer invigilators of government, alert to any possible misdoing and ·

193

ready to challenge and contest the legislative, executive and judicial authorities. Rousseau's citizens are law-makers, not law-checkers, generators of law, not testers of law. They serve in the production of public decisions, not in controlling for the quality of those decisions.

As Rousseau elaborates on this new image of the role of citizens, emphasizing the need for majority decision making, the gestalt switch from the older model of republicanism is quite dramatic. Far from every law being a fair target for civic critique and challenge, each comes draped in an authority and majesty that brooks no individual opposition. Having been party to the creation of the popular sovereign no one as an individual retains the right of contesting decisions of the collectivity, even if those decisions were ones that the person argued against in assembly.

While it may seem incredible that individual people should be denied the right of contesting the decisions of the collective people, it makes some sense on the basis of an assumption, central to Rousseau's thought, that no law supported by the general impartial will "can be unjust, since no man can be unjust toward himself" (II.6.7). The idea is that the sovereign people, enacting a corporate or general will in the formation of which each citizen participates, cannot deal unjustly toward any member, although it can make mistakes and may need the guidance of a legislative counselor (II.7).

This jars deeply with the older republican way of thinking but is a faithful echo of Hobbes.

> [B]y this institution of a Commonwealth every particular man is author of all the sovereign doth; and consequently he that complaineth of injury from his sovereign complaineth of that whereof he himself is author, and therefore ought not to accuse any man but himself; no, nor himself of injury, because to do injury to oneself is impossible.[12]
>
> (Hobbes 1994b, 18.6)

Kant

Just as Rousseau casts the citizens of his ideal republic as participants in law-making, and denies them individual rights of contestation, so Kant enforces a similar line. He casts the citizens of his ideal republic as having a "colegislator" (Kant 1996, 294) status in virtue of their "right to vote" for legislative delegates (296). And on this basis he denies them any right of individually contesting what the legislative body formulates as law or what the executive – the ruler or head of state – does in promulgating or enforcing this law: "[A]ny resistance to the supreme legislative power, any incitement to have the subjects' dissatisfaction become active, any insurrection that breaks out in rebellion, is the highest and most punishable crime within a commonwealth, because it destroys its foundation" (298).

Why would allowing resistance of the kind envisaged – resistance, as Kant thinks of it, "in word or deed" (303) – destroy the foundation of the commonwealth? The telling consideration, as in Rousseau, is that the sovereign has to have an absolute status in deciding the law and the ruler or head of state – the organ of the sovereign – has to have an absolute standing in applying that law. Suppose that there is a complaint made by the citizens about the head of state. Who is "to decide the issue?" he asks. "Only he who possesses the supreme administration of public right can do so, and that is precisely the head of state; and no one within a commonwealth can, accordingly, have a right to contest his possession of it" (299).

Kant spells out his line of thinking more precisely when he argues elsewhere that it would be self-contradictory for the constitution to give the people the right to resist the sovereign or the sovereign's agents.

> For a people to be authorized to resist, there would have to be a public law permitting it to resist, that is, the highest legislation would have to contain a provision that … makes the people, as subject, by one and the same judgment sovereign over him to whom it is subject. This is self-contradictory and the contradiction is evident as soon as one asks who is to be the judge in this dispute between the people and sovereign.
>
> (Kant 1996, 463)

It may not be surprising to see Bodin and Hobbes argue in the France and England with which they were familiar that there could not be any arrangement that made the same people subject in one respect, sovereign in another. But it is surprising to see Kant argue a similar line in a period when he must have been aware of the mixed constitution that was successfully operating in contemporary Britain. He does comment on the "limited constitution" exemplified in Britain but takes this only to allow the people "by means of its representatives (in parliament)" – and parliament is presumably the sovereign, in his view – to refuse to accede to "every demand the government puts forth" (465). He insists, however, that "a so-called moderate constitution, as a constitution for the inner rights of a state, is an absurdity," maintaining that "a people cannot offer any resistance to the legislative head of a state which would be consistent with right" (463).

The position that Kant takes here may be explained, as in Rousseau, by his adherence to the Hobbesian view that the law cannot do wrong to the people insofar as it expresses the people's own will.

> [A] public law that determines for everyone what is to be rightfully permitted or forbidden him is the act of a public will, from which all right proceeds and which must therefore itself be incapable of doing wrong to anyone. But this is possible through no other will than that of the entire people (since all decide about all, hence each about himself); for it is only to oneself that one can never do wrong.
>
> (Kant 1996, 294–5)

The idea is that the people are identical with the legislative sovereign, at least when that sovereign is ideally formed, so that there is no room for the possibility of the people doing wrong by its members. Those members, therefore, need not worry about being wronged by the sovereign; if the sovereign represents the united will of the people, it cannot do them wrong.

This is as unpersuasive in its Kantian form as it is in the form it assumes in Hobbes and Rousseau. It may be axiomatic, even analytic, that an impartial will cannot do wrong to an individual in the sense in which doing wrong would mean not treating the person impartially. But it is hardly axiomatic that people cannot individually do wrong to themselves and it is certainly not axiomatic that people cannot corporately – that is, in their collective decision making – do wrong to themselves as individuals. Still, however unpersuasive, the argument may at least explain why Kant, like Rousseau, did not think it so objectionable that the citizenry should be denied the contestatory status accorded in the Italian–Atlantic tradition.

On Kant's view of the citizenry of the ideal republic, then, it is no part of their duty to challenge and contest what the sovereign and ruler decide, resisting their laws and decrees "in word or deed" (303). But neither in fairness is their role reduced just to that of voting for their legislative representatives. Kant insists in at least one context that "a citizen must have, with the approval of the ruler himself, the authorization to make known publicly his opinions about what it is in the ruler's arrangements that seems to him to be wrong against the commonwealth" on the grounds that the head of state might "err or be ignorant of something" (302). This "freedom of the pen … is the sole palladium of the people's rights" (302). The important difference between its exercise and a challenge to authority is that it is not designed to generate "unrest in the state," being offered in the manner of a loyal subject's advice: a form of counsel guided by "esteem and love for the constitution" (302).

This completes the account of how the citizens of a Kantian republic are meant to relate to the state – the sovereign and the government – and like the account in Rousseau, it makes clear that the citizenry of the Franco–German republic do not have the contestatory rights of their Italian–Atlantic counterparts. But in conclusion it is worth mentioning that Kant, in line with his view on constitutions in general, goes well beyond denying contestatory rights to the citizens of a well-ordered republic. He also thinks that the subjects of an oppressive regime lack such rights. In particular, they do not as individuals have the right to challenge and overthrow the authorities in power. Rousseau prudently ignored the issue of how the subjects of an oppressive regime are entitled to behave. Kant is bold enough to address the issue but is prudent enough to take a view that must have endeared him to the Prussian authorities under which he lived.

We saw that on Kant's view "any resistance to the supreme legislative power" in the ideal republic "is the highest and most punishable crime within a commonwealth." And we noted that this is because it would allegedly destroy the foundation of the commonwealth, putting in question the need for a single absolute authority to embody the people's will. But this injunction against resisting the legislative power is not meant by Kant to be restricted to the ideal republic. The "prohibition is unconditional," he says,

> so that even if that power of its agent, the head of state, has gone so far as to violate the original contract and has thereby, according to the subjects' concept, forfeited the right to be legislator inasmuch as he has empowered the government to proceed quite violently (tyrannically), a subject is still not permitted any resistance by way of counteracting force.

> (Kant 1996, 298)

Our earlier discussion of Kant's view of constitutions makes this position intelligible. He holds that in every state, no matter how imperfect, the people's corporate will is embodied in the sovereign – the sovereign law – and its agents. Assuming that there is such a will, as he thinks there always must be, then that is the obvious place for it to reside. And so he argues that the people cannot set themselves up as individuals against the sovereign or the ruler without giving the lie to that principle. For a people to challenge the sovereign or head of state in that way would be to presuppose "another head above the head of state, that would decide between him and the people; and this is self-contradictory" (299). Thus, if the people kill a head of state, as in the case of Charles I of England or

Louis XVI of France, then "it is as if the state commits suicide;" this, he notes, is "a crime from which the people cannot be absolved" (464, fn). The Hobbesian note is unmistakeable.

While Kant rails against revolution in this way, he is quite clear that many existing regimes are appalling. True, he maintains on the grounds just reviewed that "the people never has a coercive right against the head of state (insubordination in word or deed)" (301) and that "the sovereign has only rights against his subjects and no duties (that he can be coerced to fulfill)" (462). But equally he holds that "a people too has its inalienable rights against the head of state, although these cannot be coercive rights" (301). And of course he recognizes that there are many defective constitutions in which those rights are not satisfied. Where his constraints bite is in his insistence that while the imperfections of government always call for redress, this redress can only come by way of internal reform, not revolution from without. "A change in a (defective) constitution, which may certainly be necessary at times, can therefore be carried out only through reform by the sovereign itself, but not by the people, and therefore not by revolution" (465).

Kant's holds that when a revolution occurs "the previously existing constitution has been torn up by the people, while their organization into a new commonwealth has not yet taken place," giving rise to "the condition of anarchy" and its "horrors" (300, fn). But he is ready to admit that when the people get around to establishing a new constitution, then that new regime may be a great improvement on the old. And he freely acknowledges that whether or not it is an improvement, it is binding on the citizenry.

> [O]nce a revolution has succeeded and a new constitution has been established, the lack of legitimacy with which it began and has been implemented cannot release the subject from the obligation to comply with the new order of things as good citizens, and they cannot refuse honest obedience to the authority that now has the power.
>
> (Kant 1996, 465)

Kant can take this paradoxical viewpoint, because he is a nonconsequentialist about the duties of citizens, as he is a nonconsequentialist about duties in general. For citizens to rise up against a government is, in his view, to act against right – against "the concept of duty in its complete purity" – and that is quite consistent with acting in a way that happens to have excellent consequences, producing a better constitution and more overall "happiness" (287).

6. Conclusion

We have seen that while Rousseau and Kant remained broadly faithful to the Italian–Atlantic notion of freedom as nondomination, they transformed the earlier republican vision by dropping the institutional ideals of the mixed constitution and the contestatory citizenry. Rousseau put an ideal of popular sovereignty in place of the mixed constitution and an ideal of a participant, law-making citizenry in place of a contestatory citizenry. Kant hailed a similar ideal of popular sovereignty and linked it with a thinner, representative or electoral ideal of citizenship. According to each, individual contestation amounts to resistance or rebellion; such resistance is condemned unconditionally by Kant but not, presumptively, by Rousseau. And according to each there is a communitarian emphasis on the ideal of citizens in legislating for themselves, whether directly or indirectly, although the communitarianism is universalist in character, not particularistic. That emphasis replaces the older emphasis on the need to keep the state contestable – by virtue of a mixed constitution – and on the contestatory role of a vigilant citizenry.[13]

The different claims by those in the Italian–Atlantic tradition and by these two thinkers are mapped in the following table.

	Italian–Atlantic	Rousseau	Kant
Freedom	Nondomination	Nondomination	Nondomination
Constitution	Mixed constitution	Popular assembly	Representative assembly
Contestation OK?	Yes	Equals resistance	Equals resistance
Resistance OK?	With non-republic	With non-republic	Never

In the vulgar, primarily Rousseauvian form in which the communitarian set of ideas came to be represented, the conception of freedom as nondomination also disappeared. Benjamin Constant was probably the major figure in accomplishing this final step, although he did so as a critic, not a defender. Himself attracted to what was seen as a brand of liberalism – although one that in many respects kept close to the older republicanism – he gave a famous lecture in 1819 that described the supposedly ancient way of thinking about politics and freedom with which the liberal view has to compete (Constant 1988). According to this ancient way of thinking, he says, the people in a commonwealth constitute the sovereign, the role of citizens is to participate as officials or electors in sovereign decision making and – this is the alteration from the Rousseauvian and Kantian picture – freedom consists in nothing more or less than the right to participate in such communal self-determination: the right to live under a regime of law that one has a certain participatory or electoral role in creating.[14]

With this final twist, the followers of Rousseau and Kant became associated with a set of ideas that differ on every front from the defining ideas of the Italian–Atlantic tradition. This new communitarian ideology replaced freedom as nondomination with freedom as participation – the paradigm of Isaiah Berlin's (1969) positive liberty. It replaced the institutional ideal of the mixed constitution with that of a popular sovereign, whether participatory, as in the Rousseauvian version, or representative, as in the Kantian. And it replaced the ideal of a contestatory people with that of a legislative or elective citizenry who had no rights as individuals to contest community decisions.

It is important to recognize that despite their differences in other respects, Rousseauvians and Kantians are both exemplars of the new Franco–German republicanism. Frameworks of ideas that are characterized by abstract commitments of the kind rehearsed can assume very different shapes, and by keeping both Rousseau and Kant in the picture we highlight this inherent plasticity in the communitarian vision. Such plasticity is also found, of course, within the classical, Italian–Atlantic tradition, since representatives vary in how radically they construe the independence in which freedom is said to consist; in how mechanically they interpret the two institutional ideals; and in how far they give priority to one or other of those ideals or treat them more or less on a par. While the two forms of republicanism are distinct, they each exemplify a broad style of thinking, not a sharply defined, substantial set of commitments.[15]

REFERENCES

Arendt, H. (1958). *The Human Condition*. Chicago: University of Chicago Press.

Arendt. H. (1973). *On Revolution*. Harmondsworth: Pelican Books.

Bailyn. B. (1967). *The Ideological Origins of the American Revolution*. Cambridge, MA: Harvard University Press.

Berlin, I. (1969). *Four Essays on Liberty*. Oxford: Oxford University Press.

Besold, C. (1618). *Politicorum Libri duo*. Frankfurt: J. A. Cellii.

Bodin, J. (1967). *Six Books of the Commonwealth*. Ed. M. J. Tooley, Oxford: Blackwell.

Brennan, G. and L. Lomasky (2006). "Against Reviving Republicanism." *Politics, Philosophy and Economics* 5: 221–52.

Cohen, J. (2010). *Rousseau: A Free Community of Equals*. Oxford: Oxford University Press.

Constant, B. (1988). *Constant: Political Writings*. Cambridge: Cambridge University Press.

Dworkin, R. (1978). *Taking Rights Seriously*. London: Duckworth.

Dworkin, R. (1986). *Law's Empire*. Cambridge, MA: Harvard University Press.

Franklin, J. (1991). "Sovereignty and the Mixed Constitution: Bodin and his Critics." In: *The Cambridge History of Political Thought 1450–1700*. Eds J. H. Burns and M. Goldie, Cambridge: Cambridge University Press: 298–345.

Habermas, J. (1994). "Three Normative Models of Democracy." *Constellations* 1: 1–10.

Habermas, J. (1995). *Between Facts and Norms: Contributions to a Discourse Theory of Law and Democracy*. Cambridge, MA: MIT Press.

Harrington, J. (1992). *The Commonwealth of Oceana and a System of Politics*. Cambridge: Cambridge University Press.

Hobbes, T. (1990). *Behemoth or the Long Parliament*. Ed. F. Toennies, Chicago: University of Chicago Press.

Hobbes, T. (1994a). *Human Nature and De Corpore Politico: The Elements of Law, Natural and Politic*. Oxford: Oxford University Press.

Hobbes, T. (1994b). *Leviathan*. Ed. E. Curley, Indianapolis: Hackett.

Hobbes, T. (1998). *On the Citizen*. Ed. and trans. R. Tuck and M. Silverthorne, Cambridge: Cambridge University Press.

Holmes, S. (1995). *Passions and Constraint: On the Theory of Liberal Democracy*. Chicago: University of Chicago Press.

Kant, I. (1996). *Practical Philosophy*. Trans. M. J. Gregor, Cambridge: Cambridge University Press.

Kant, I. (2005). *Notes and Fragments*. Ed. P. Guyer, Cambridge: Cambridge University Press.

Ketcham, R. (ed.) (2003). *The Anti-Federalist Papers*. New York: Signet Classic.

Laborde, C. and J. Maynor (eds) (2008). *Republicanism and Political Theory*. Oxford: Blackwell.

List, C. and P. Pettit (2011). *Group Agency: The Possibility, Design and Status of Corporate Agents*. Oxford: Oxford University Press.

Long, D. C. (1977). *Bentham on Liberty*. Toronto: University of Toronto Press.

Lovett, F. and P. Pettit (2010). "Neorepublicanism: A Normative and Institutional Research Program." *Annual Review of Political Science* 12: 11–29.

Machiavelli, N. (1965). *The Complete Work and Others*. Durham, NC: Duke University Press.

Madison, J. A., A. Hamilton and J. Jay (1987). *The Federalist Papers*. Harmondsworth: Penguin.

Maynor, J. (2003). *Republicanism in the Modern World*. Cambridge: Polity Press.

Milton, J. (1953–82). *Complete Prose Works of John Milton*, Vols 1–8. New Haven: Yale University Press.

Montesquieu, Baron de (1977). *The Spirit of Laws*. Berkeley: University of California Press.

Nelson, E. (2004). *The Greek Tradition in Republican Thought*. Cambridge: Cambridge University Press.

Nozick, R. (1974). *Anarchy, State and Utopia*. Oxford: Blackwell.

Nussbaum. M. (2006). *Frontiers of Justice*. Cambridge, MA: Harvard University Press.

Ober, J. (1996). *The Athenian Revolution*. Princeton: Princeton University Press.

Paley, W. (1825). *The Principles of Moral and Political Philosophy*, Vol. 4, Collected Works. London: C. and J. Rivington.

Pettit, P. (1997). *Republicanism: A Theory of Freedom and Government*. Oxford: Oxford University Press.

Pettit, P. (1998). "Reworking Sandel's Republicanism." *Journal of Philosophy* 95: 73–96.

Pettit, P. (2001). "Non-consequentialism and Political Philosophy." In: *Robert Nozick*. Ed. D. Schmidtz, Cambridge: Cambridge University Press: 83–104.

Pettit, P. (2008a). "The Basic Liberties." In: *The Legacy of H. L. A. Hart. Legal, Political and Moral Philosophy*. Eds M. Kramer, C. Grant, B. Colburn and A. Hatzistavrou, Oxford: Oxford University Press: 201–24.

Pettit, P. (2008b). *Made with Words: Hobbes on Language, Mind and Politics*. Princeton: Princeton University Press.

Pettit, P. (2011). "The Instability of Freedom as Non-Interference: The Case of Isaiah Berlin." *Ethics* 121: 693–716.

Pettit, P. (2012). *On the People's Terms: A Republican Theory and Model of Democracy*. Cambridge: Cambridge University Press.

Pocock, J. (1975). *The Machiavellian Moment: Florentine Political Theory and the Atlantic Republican Tradition*. Princeton: Princeton University Press.

Price, R. (1991). *Political Writings*. Cambridge: Cambridge University Press.

Priestley, J. (1993). *Political Writings*. Cambridge: Cambridge University Press.

Raab, F. (1965). *The English Face of Machiavelli: A Changing Interpretation 1500–1700*. London: Routledge and Kegan Paul.

Rawls, J. (1971). *A Theory of Justice*. Oxford: Oxford University Press.

Rawls, J. (1993). *Political Liberalism*. New York: Columbia University Press.

Rawls, J. (2001). *Justice as Fairness: A Restatement*. Cambridge, MA: Harvard University Press.

Reid, J. P. (1988). *The Concept of Liberty in the Age of the American Revolution*. Chicago: University of Chicago Press.

Ripstein, A. (2009). *Force and Freedom: Kant's Legal and Political Philosophy*. Cambridge, MA: Harvard University Press.

Robbins, C. (1959). *The Eighteenth Century Commonwealthman*. Cambridge, MA: Harvard University Press.

Rousseau, J.-J. (1997). *Rousseau: "The Social Contract" and Other Later Political Writings*. Trans. V. Gourevitch, Cambridge: Cambridge University Press.

Sandel, M. (1996). *Democracy's Discontent: America in Search of a Public Philosophy*. Cambridge, MA: Harvard University Press.

Sen, Amartya (1985). *Commodities and Capabilities*. Amsterdam: North-Holland.

Sidney, A. (1990). *Discourses concerning Government*. Indianapolis: Liberty Classics.

Skinner, Q. (1978). *The Foundations of Modern Political Thought*. Cambridge: Cambridge University Press.

Skinner, Q. (1998). *Liberty before Liberalism*. Cambridge: Cambridge University Press.

Skinner, Q. (2008). *Hobbes and Republican Liberty*. Cambridge: Cambridge University Press.

Skinner, Q. M. (1974). "The Principles and Practice of Opposition: The Case of

Bolingbroke versus Walpole." In: *Historical Perspectives: Studies in English Thought and Society in Honor of J. H. Plumb*. Ed. N. McKendrick, London: Europa: 92–128.

Spitz, J.-F. (1995). "Le republicanism, une troisième voie entre liberalism et communautarianisme." *Le Banquet* 7 (2ème semester): 215–38.

Spitz, J.-F. (2010). *Philip Pettit: Le Republicanisme*. Paris: Michalon.

Trenchard, J. and T. Gordon (1971). *Cato's Letters*. New York: Da Capo.

Viroli, M. (2002). *Republicanism*. New York: Hill and Wang.

Weinstock, D. and C. Nadeau (eds) (2004). *Republicanism: History, Theory and Practice*. London: Frank Cass.

Wirszubski, C. (1968). *Libertas as a Political Ideal at Rome*. Oxford: Oxford University Press.

Notes

1. See, for example, Pettit 1997, 2012; Skinner 1998; Viroli 2002; Maynor 2003; Weinstock and Nadeau 2004; Laborde and Maynor 2008; Lovett and Pettit 2010. The first section draws heavily on Pettit 2012.

2. In discussing this conception of the republic in earlier work, in particular the conception as it appears in Sandel, I have sometimes described it as neo-Athenian (Pettit 1998). I regret that usage now, since as a matter of history – if not in later representations – Athens had many of the characteristics of a mixed constitution; it was not a city ruled by an assembly with Rousseauvian powers. See Ober 1996.

3. For the record, I think that Habermas's own views come close to counting as broadly republican in my sense.

4. Eric Nelson 2004 has identified a Greek tradition in later republican thought that coexisted with the neo-Roman tradition in which I am interested. I do not give attention to this tradition here.

5. Notoriously, this point is admitted in Isaiah Berlin's 1969, 130–1 claim that the "connection between democracy and individual liberty is a good deal more tenuous than it seemed to many advocates of both." For arguments to the effect that, under plausible empirical assumptions, negative liberty of this kind may make further constitutional demands, see Habermas 1995; Holmes1995.

6. A further distinction within liberal doctrines in this sense is that between those in which freedom is taken as a goal – as I think that freedom as nondomination should be taken as a goal; see Pettit 1997, chap. 3 – and those in which the rights associated with freedom are taken in non-consequentialist form as side-constraints; the best example of the latter approach is Nozick 1974. For a discussion of consequentialist and non-consequentialist approaches in political philosophy, see Pettit 2001.

7. In the translation by Mary J. Gregor that I reference, "Willkuer" is translated simply as "choice" rather than "power of choice." I think that the latter is more faithful to Kant's meaning.

8. Rousseau's radicalism in this respect may explain why republicans in nineteenth-century France often called for economic and workplace reform. I am grateful to Genevieve Rousseliere for drawing my attention to this connection.

9. It is also worth noting the contrast between the Rome of Machiavelli (1965) in which the adversarial relation between the rich and the poor was so important and the Rome

that Rousseau describes, where "even in the stormiest times, the people's plebiscites passed quietly and by a large majority, when the Senate did not interfere. The citizens, having a single interest, the people had but a single will": IV.2.2.

10. This aspect of Kant's picture may explain why he uses "such a variety of terms," as the translator, Mary Gregor, puts it (cited in Kant 1996, 457, n. h), for the authorities in the state. If the head of state or the ruler may be taken either as a physically embodied person or as the voicebox of the sovereign law, then context may often allow the expression now to refer to the legislative authority, now to the executive.

11. But how, Rousseau asks, "are the opponents both free and subject to laws to which they have not consented?" His response is "that the question is badly framed. The citizen consents to all the laws, even to those passed in spite of him, and even to those that punish him when he dares to violate any of them": IV.2.8.

12. As Rousseau allows that the sovereign may make mistakes – and should therefore seek the guidance of a legislative counselor – so Hobbes allows that the sovereign may deal with subjects in a way that conflicts with the laws of nature, laws that he conceives of as "dictates of self-interest": Hobbes 1994b, 15.41. But Hobbes 1994b, 18.6 insists that while "they that have sovereign power may commit iniquity," in this sense, they cannot commit "injustice, or injury in the proper signification." In this comparison I emphasize the assumption in Rousseau and in Hobbes – as I later emphasize it in Kant – that no one can do wrong to himself or herself. Note, however, that there is a separate assumption shared among these thinkers that might equally support their view about the justice of the sovereign: viz., that it is only the sovereign who can define what is just or unjust, strictly understood. If this is so, then there is a distinct reason why the sovereign can do nothing wrong or unjust to subjects.

13. Jean-Fabien Spitz has long cast traditional republicanism – a republicanism, however, that he sees as a continuing part of the French tradition – as an alternative to liberalism, on the one side, and communitarianism on the other. See Spitz 1995; 2010. Notice that while Joshua Cohen 2010, 21, 95 describes Rousseau's position as communitarian, he does so on somewhat different grounds from those invoked here.

14. Yiftah Elazar has persuaded me that while he may preserve other aspects of the Italian–Atlantic tradition, the eighteenth-century thinker, Richard Price (1991), had also begun to emphasize this self-legislative theme.

15. I am grateful for the very helpful comments I received on an earlier draft from Yiftah Elazar, Melissa Lane, Genevieve Rousseliere and Philipp Schink and from participants at a seminar where the paper was presented in Stanford University in March 2011. I am grateful also to Richard Tuck for many conversations on the influence of Hobbes on Rousseau; I had access to the manuscript of a forthcoming book on Rousseau.

CHAPTER 8

Freedom, Control and the State

Philipp Schink

The reasons for what is nowadays labeled the *republican revival* are certainly manifold. From reasons that lie in the dynamics of academic discourse up to reasons that are rooted in political controversies[1] the lasting interest (and correspondingly the expectation about the benefits of the republican political theory) in republicanism has various reasons. In what follows I will try to concentrate on one distinctive feature – or thesis – of republicanism that is more or less a unifying theme in the various strands of republican political theory. This "republican thesis" consists in the belief that freedom and a republican state are at least *compatible* or that freedom is even *constituted* by the republic.

The belief in the possibility of conceptualizing (and under certain circumstances even realizing) a form of an effective political order that is not per se based on a restriction of freedom becomes particularly attractive against the background of the experiences of the twentieth century. Up to the late 1970s political hope for a *free society* was closely connected with the state: While the national liberation movements of developing countries and colonies viewed the building of a national state as *the* way to end foreign domination, most progressive, social-democratic or socialist movements identified the state as *the* way for liberation from internal domination (mostly seen as being caused by an unequal control of the means of production). The reality of the post-colonial and socialist states led to a deep-going disillusionment, which nowadays has turned into fundamental skepticism about the relation between freedom and the state. This skepticism again fuelled a renewal of classic liberal political thought that culminated in the political movement of *neo-liberalism*.[2]

By "neo-liberalism" I generally understand a certain tradition of political thought that is based on a specific conception of negative freedom and in which the role of the state is reduced to protect a small set of pre-politically given liberty rights in order to safe-guard the voluntary interactions of its citizens. This line of thought is generally characterized by a deep-going skepticism towards the idea that societies can control their fate in an intentional and free manner. I understand republicanism as a tradition in which especially the idea of a political constitution of the society is at the center of attention. In this regard the socialist and social-democratic thought of the nineteenth and twentieth centuries clearly builds on this tradition. I believe that a diverging understanding of freedom is at the center of the controversy between neo-liberal and republican-socialist thought. Depending on the respective conception of freedom, there results a completely different understanding of the character of the state and the limits of political action.

In the face of the worldwide devastation that resulted from the progressive deregulation of the markets it seems particularly attractive to take up the tradition of republican-socialist thought. The (neo-liberal) skepticism against the idea of the political control and intentional shaping of societies ended in conditions in which private actors became the main source of unfreedom. It follows that the political movement of neo-liberalism has not led to a free global society, quite on the contrary. Therefore, it seems to be necessary to rethink the relation of the state and freedom and to avoid the conceptual mistakes of the republican-socialist tradition that have lent themselves to a justification of oppression by the state. So, my interest in the republican revival consists in verifying if it indeed offers the possibility to re-conceptualize the relation between freedom, politics and the state.

In what follows I will first outline the neo-liberal conception of the relation between freedom and the state. In a second step I will briefly depict the socialist-social-democratic criticism of the neo-liberal understanding of freedom. Finally, in a third step, I will address the neo-republicanism of Philip Pettit. It is my understanding that the neo-republican political theory is grounded in the attempt to put forward a convincing alternative to neo-liberal thought. Neo-republicanism takes up the "republican thesis" that under certain conditions freedom and a political order are not contradictory to each other and by starting from a radical reconceptualization of freedom tries to elaborate this thesis. Lastly, I will discuss to what extent the neo-republican approach is convincing. I will argue that in the end Pettit's conception of freedom as nondomination cannot provide the

206

basis for a refounding of the republican thesis – quite on the contrary: If one takes the analysis of nondomination seriously the obstacles to validate the thesis become even greater.

1. STATE AND FREEDOM IN NEO-LIBERAL POLITICAL THOUGHT

The philosophical roots of twentieth-century neo-liberal political thought are diverse and range from a rights-based defense of the minimalist state (Nozick 1999) to Hayek's criticism of the whole "positivist" approach to politics and the organization of society. While Nozick's libertarianism radically limits the legitimate scope of state action to securing a set of certain basic liberty rights, the liberalism of Hayek attacks the idea of *organizing a society intentionally*, that is, politically by means of the state. In Hayek's eyes this idea would inevitably lead to an activist state that while aiming to shape the society according to certain values (like equality of capabilities and a certain level of basic goods) would expand the realm of public law at the expense of private law. In doing so, the state would massively interfere in the (personal) freedom of its citizens since in shrinking the scope of private law it would limit the realm of interactions based on voluntariness.

Besides all differences, Nozick and Hayek agree that all actions of a government should be in strict accordance with the *rule of law*. Both argue that such a rule of law has to be understood as a set of principles by which the legitimacy of laws and regulations can be ascertained: "The rule of law, therefore, is also more than constitutionalism: it requires that all law conform to certain principles" (Hayek 1960, 205). The principles of the rule of law[3] – like nonretroactivity, generality, publicity and *nulla poena sine lege* – are not seen as mere criteria of *effectiveness* – so that the rule of law would embody principles that enable *any* government or ruler to rule according to *any* set of positive law in a rational way – but as representing criteria of universality. The reason why the idea of universalizability lies at the foundation of neo-liberal political thought[4] is based on the Kantian belief that only a formal conception of moral norms can be rationally justified. As such, moral norms – that are the foundation of claims to legitimacy – represent general rules (or as Kant says *laws*) that are valid for each and all, satisfy the principle of noncontradiction and hold invariantly. Universal moral norms are *absolute principles* that are independent of concrete circumstances, goals of specific persons or the character of the empirical world. As such they embody the conditions that are necessary and sufficient to be valid for rational beings – and the characteristic features of rationality hold independent of the goals and desires of empirical persons or of the empirical circumstances. Against this background a system of positive law can only be legitimate if it is in accordance with such a rule of law – and not if it furthers some particular substantial morality. While Hayek sees the universal principles of the rule of law emerge from the continuous as well as spontaneous interactions of individuals, Nozick defends a more foundationalist account in which certain compossible basic liberty rights represent everything that is rationally justifiable. Accordingly, a legitimate state has to be a state in which the scope of governmental and judicial activity is strictly limited to upholding the rule of law. This leads to a legal system in which the private law – understood as the realm of noncoercive voluntary interactions – clearly dominates over public law.

Now, for Nozick and Hayek all threads come together in grounding their respective liberal (or libertarian) theories in a certain understanding of freedom. If the central characteristic of human beings is their rationality and if a rationally justifiable system of principles and rules is thereby a universally valid system it follows that everything that goes beyond this realm is up to the single individuals themselves. Respecting persons in this way means respecting them in their separateness – and that again subsequently means to give them equal maximum freedom to pursue their particular conceptions of (a good) life. Against that background the role of the state consists in nothing other than upholding a system of universally justifiable rules and not to further particular and specific interests or moral beliefs. It is – so to speak – a strictly deontological and by no means teleological understanding of the rule of law and the function of state action.

The conception of freedom that underlies this line of reasoning has to be taken as essentially consisting in *noninterference*. Freedom as noninterference, as Berlin called this type of freedom,[5] is defined by the absence of intentional restrictions and is clearly distinguished from more "positive," ability-based concepts of freedom.[6] Now, the reasons to maintain an essentially negative understanding of freedom and to exclude abilities from a definition of freedom surely are manifold, but for Hayek and Nozick it is mainly one implication of ability-based concepts of freedom that render such definitions defective. If freedom is defined by having the ability to realize certain options or to do what one wants to do then the state would inevitably violate the rule of law. Nozick and Hayek argue that as the distribution of abilities is essentially an empirical and contingent matter no system of rights rooted in positive freedom could be compossible. To strive for, for example, an equality of ability would inevitably transform the role of the state fundamentally as the character of the state would shift from a *nomocracy* to a *telocracy*.[7] The implications of this shift are indeed far-reaching, since the way how laws guide state action and accordingly the process of their application and interpretation changes significantly. Hayek characterizes this difference as one between an *adjudicative* and *arbitrative* state: While in a system of adjudication the judge's judgment must be in accordance with and derived from the existing system of law and jurisprudence, the latitude of discretion is significantly and necessarily higher when the purpose of the state consists in furthering a certain goal (for example, equality of ability). As the distribution of abilities under empirical circumstances is completely contingent and redistributive policies usually have to take place under conditions of scarcity, for Hayek this is incompatible with a rationally justifiable political order. State action would become arbitrary and by becoming arbitrary it would violate freedom.

Now, apparently this understanding of freedom as noninterference does not imply that any intentional interference counts as a restriction of freedom but only arbitrary interference. This again implies in reverse that not any law, backed by coercive sanctions and not any state action are per se an impediment to freedom but only those laws that violate the criteria of universality. The reason for this lies in a certain understanding of unjustified coercion.[8] Forcing someone by threat into complying with rationally justified norms is not a restriction of this person's freedom in the neo-liberal's understanding as it does not violate criteria of generality and neutrality. Taking up the distinction between adjudication and arbitration, Hayek determines the evil of (unjustified) coercion in a Kantian fashion as using someone (solely) as a means to one's end.[9] In contrast to that, impersonal abstract rules do not represent such an instrumentalization of someone but: "When we obey laws, in the sense of general abstract rules laid down irrespective of their application to us, we are not subject to another man's will and are therefore free" (Hayek 1960, 153). Such laws backed by coercive power are in the neo-liberal's understanding necessary for reasons of protection, adjudication and predictability[10] and according to the noninterference-based definition of freedom by Nozick as well as Hayek the mere existence of political power is not per se an impediment to freedom. To be, as Hayek writes, subject to another person's will means that one is treated by commands that refer to specific actions of specific persons and specific circumstances and that serve the specific goals of the one who is in command. Nonarbitrary law instead means that the law's subjects are treated in a general, neutral and equal way and that state action as well as the adjudication ensues according to the rule of law.[11]

Of course, in political terms to enlarge the area of private and voluntary interaction means to establish a legal system of far-reaching property rights and consequently rights of transferral and acquisition. This again leads to a society that is essentially based on market relations. So the neo-liberal project is basically a defense of the free market. But it would be a misunderstanding of the neo-liberal perspective to limit the defense of private and voluntary interactions to the so-called economic sphere. As especially seen when discussing Hayek's idea of the spontaneous emergence of (universalistic) norms, neo-liberalism assumes that the whole reproduction of society can only be provided by "market-conform-relations-and-interactions." The role of a politico-legal order cannot (in any way) consist in intentionally shaping and creating a (however one understands this) "free society" (let alone that a free society consists in participation in political affairs) but has to be confined to protection and adjudication.

It is the limitation of the role of the state to safe-guard a particularly small set of supposedly rationally justifiable liberty rights that provoked massive criticism. Apart from "inner-philosophical" criticism that was aimed mainly at the consistency of the (neo-)liberal line of reasoning, the main thrust of the criticism focused on the thesis that a capitalist market society is a free society – independent of its way to distribute goods and control over resources. I can see primarily two alternative approaches that reject this thesis. Both ground their criticism in arguments based on a different understanding of freedom. The bottom-line of the criticism is that neo-liberalism's crucial mistake lies in a fundamentally unconvincing conception of freedom. The first criticism of neo-liberalism's conception of freedom argues that a merely negative understanding of freedom is far too austere. Too austere to explain why freedom is of central value in the history of political thought and in contemporary societies. Too austere in itself, as freedom is tightly connected to agency or even autonomy, and as both require certain means and abilities freedom has to be understood in a much more "demanding," that is "positive," way.[12] This understanding of freedom could be labeled as the classical social-democratic or socialist conception of freedom. In this perspective a market society could not be a free society (at least not without a "strong state on stand-by" that regulates market transaction and redistributes goods, opportunities and wealth) since it does not provide each and every one with the abilities required to lead a life according to one's wants, or a halfway decent life or even stronger an autonomous life.

The second criticism is that it aligns itself more with the neo-liberal's negative understanding of freedom when it comes to the role that abilities play in freedom but it joins in in the social-democratic rejection of the market society as a "no-matter-how-the-dices-fall-free-society-period." From the perspective of this second criticism the main deficiency associated with the neo-liberal understanding of freedom is that it focuses on interference as a necessary and sufficient element of unfreedom and that conversely freedom consists in noninterference. Against this position it is suggested that the freedom of an individual is already impeded if its choices and actions are under the control of other persons, groups or institutions. To be under the control of someone else does not mean that this other agent has to *exercise* his or her power. Actual interferences are not a necessary element of unfreedom.

This understanding of freedom is mainly developed by Philip Pettit who calls this understanding of freedom "nondomination," with "dominated" meaning under the control of other persons. This notion of freedom is consequently placed at the center of a whole normative approach that Pettit labels *neo-republican*. By reconceptualizing freedom in a particular way, neo-republicanism presents itself as a distinctive and encompassing alternative to neo-liberal as well as social-democratic or socialist thought. The implications of this notion of freedom and its differences to the social-democratic and neo-liberal understanding of freedom become manifest when relating them to the question of the relation between markets and freedom. As the neo-liberal only takes the intentional obstruction – that is coercion – of actions and options as a necessary element of unfreedom the so-called un-intended distribution of material goods by the market causes no restriction of freedom. Hayek argues laconicly: "Even if the threat of starvation to me and perhaps my family impels me to accept a distasteful job at a very low wage, even if I am 'at the mercy' of the only man willing to employ me, I am not coerced by him or anybody else" (Hayek 1960, 121) – and therefore free: The "effect" of the market-based distribution of goods, means and opportunities "on my freedom is not different from that of any natural calamity" (121). Against this a more "positive" understanding of freedom – as advocated by quite

211

a few social-democrats and socialists[13] – claims that the lack of certain goods or abilities is in itself a diminution of freedom, independent of its source and emergence. This implies that even the unintended effects of market-transactions would diminish the freedom of the persons that lose out or are negatively affected by the results – if the effects of the market transaction undermine their capacity for agency or to realize one's wants or aims, which, of course, markets do permanently (if not regulated ...). This criticism of neo-liberalism argues that markets are a bad device to provide each and every one with the necessary goods and opportunities for freedom.

In contrast to both positions the nub of the republican understanding of freedom – at least in my reading – consists in analyzing market transaction through the lens of domination or, to say it more precisely, relations of control. The difference to the approaches discussed above is striking as neither intentional interventions nor the mere lack of abilities is a necessary element of unfreedom. Instead, if transactions turn out to produce the result that persons have power over others the latter are unfree. So if market transactions lead to the existence of domination – no matter why – market transactions are inimical to freedom and if not, not. In contrast to both approaches above the (intentional or nonintentional) actual interference with other people's options is no necessary element of unfreedom; the crucial element is exactly what Hayek calls *to be at the mercy of someone*. This understanding of freedom differs from the social-democratic as well as the neo-liberal perspective as it focuses on *relations of power*. Or, to be more precise, on social or political relations in which one party has *power over* the other parties.

Now, from these different ways to conceptualize freedom three completely different perspectives on the character of the state follow. Basically, all three approaches concur therein that the normative role of the state consists in upholding the freedom of its citizens. But while – as already shown – for neo-liberalism this means a minimal state strictly confined in its powers and aims, socialists as well as neo-republicans rally for a state whose competences and powers are necessarily much greater. To take up a classification I made at the beginning, because of their conception of freedom the latter approaches tend to have a *telocratic* understanding of the state. This alone implies that the state has to have significantly more powers and competences to be able to fulfill its function than the envisaged neo-liberal state. So both alternative approaches to the relation between the state and freedom resemble at first appearance

212

very much the *nightmare of neo-liberalism*: an all too powerful state that in pursuing its goal of real freedom or nondomination permanently violates individual rights and massively interferes in exchanges and transaction based on voluntariness. Interestingly, Pettit's model of a republic based on freedom as nondomination concurs on the one hand with this perspective while claiming on the other hand that such a *telocratic* state does not necessarily violate the freedom of its citizens. The *neo-republican thesis* consists precisely in claiming the possibility of a political order in which the state has far more competencies and power than its neo-liberal counterpart without dominating its citizens. Pettit even goes one step further: Not only is it possible that freedom is compatible with the existence of a state, in fact, freedom is *constituted* by the (republican) state – that is, the existence of a certain political order is a necessary or at least an integral element of freedom. In doing so, Pettit interprets in a novel manner features that are connected with the concept of voluntariness and radically extends them in the sense of a "control-capacity." This is precisely why Pettit's conception of freedom demands high standards of a state. In contrast to the social-democratic understanding of the state, the relation between freedom and the state is not measured primarily in terms of "outcome" but incorporates strong elements of control. It is my understanding that therefore neo-republicanism presents itself as an alternative to the socialist outcome-oriented understanding of the state as well as to the proceduralism of neo-liberalism.

2. THE NEO-REPUBLICAN THESIS

In what follows I will outline the understanding of the relation between freedom and the state in neo-republicanism in a more formal way, first by contrasting it with two alternative ways of arguing for a compatibility-thesis. So, the central question still is under which conditions the existence of a legal order or a powerful state does not violate the freedom of its citizens that is that *freedom and the state are compatible*. Or, to put it differently, as law and the state in one way or the other always interfere with the actions and options of persons, the question is under which conditions interferences do not amount to unfreedom.

The first alternative consists in stating that a law or a state does not restrict the freedom of its citizens as long as it satisfies certain interests or wishes of the citizens. I will call this an *outcome-based defense of the compatibility-thesis*.

213

> An interference is no instance of unfreedom under the condition that it yields certain outcomes, for example given that a regime of positive law satisfies the basic interests of its citizens it constitutes no infringement on the freedom of its citizens.

The conception of freedom that underlies this position takes freedom to consist in the satisfaction of wants, desires or interests,[14] and when it comes to evaluate the freedom-friendliness of a certain state or regime of law the only relevant criterion is the above-mentioned satisfaction. The *modus operandi* under which a certain outcome is produced is in this perspective of no intrinsic relevance as long as the intended result is obtained.[15] I think that most social-democratic or socialist theories are prone to this understanding of political power and freedom.

In contrast to this, the second alternative focuses on procedural aspects. According to a *proceduralistic defense of the compatibility-thesis*:

> [A]n interference is no instance of unfreedom under the condition that it satisfies certain procedural aspects, for example, given that a regime of positive law is based on the consent of its citizens it constitutes no infringement on the freedom of its citizens.

The most influential procedural defense of the compatibility-thesis can be found in the tradition of contractualist political thinking or in the tradition of natural rights thought (from Locke up to Nozick). Here, an interference does not restrict the freedom of the interfered-with person if the latter explicitly consented to the interference – no matter if the interferences satisfies the interests, wants or desires of the respective person.

The difference between both alternative ways to defend the compatibility thesis is striking. While the outcome-based view determines the significance of interferences for the freedom of the interfered-with person solely by reference to the content of the interference, the procedural defense fully concentrates on the genesis of the interference. Obviously, both defenses of the compatibility-thesis are quite demanding, and it remains an open question how likely a free state or regime of laws is under the given empirical circumstances nowadays. But apart from this problem the reasons why Pettit does not follow one of these undertakings lie elsewhere. Especially in his latest writings (Pettit 2001b; 2008a; 2011) Pettit analyzes the notion of freedom as nondomination in terms of "control." In this way he highlights that the freedom of an agent cannot be defined independently from the character of the relations in which he or she stands to other agents. If being free with respect to certain political institutions or agents means that the respective *relations* have to be constituted in a particular manner then neither the outcome-based defense nor the procedural defense of the compatibility-thesis can satisfy this criterion – as I will point out below.

The outcome-based defense obviously is a "content-dependent" understanding of freedom.[16] As mentioned above, this means that the freedom of a person is exclusively defined by the interest or want satisfaction that again implies that, on the conceptual level, the conditions and circumstances due to which interferences are in accordance with the interests of the interfered-with person are of no definitional importance. This again means that this way of defending the compatibility-thesis strangely implies that only a contingent connection exists between the institutional structure of a state, the (material) character of the relations between state agents and citizens and the freedom of the citizens. If all that matters to determine if, for example, a certain ordering of political institutions restricts the freedom of its citizens is to check if they act in the interest of the citizens then the subjects of a tyrant are free if by coincidence the tyrant's interests happen to be the same as the interests of his or her subjects. Furthermore, as Pettit emphasizes (Pettit 2011), such an outcome-based understanding of freedom also has the deeply disturbing implication that people can become free by changing their interests. One only has to adopt one's wishes or interests to the set of options that are permitted by the tyrant to become free. And these implications surely make the outcome-based defense of the compatibility between freedom and a regime of law or the state quite unattractive and implausible.[17] Pettit himself draws the conclusion that a convincing concept of freedom must necessarily be "content-independent." This means that an agent is free in relation to other agents or institutions of the state if it does not depend on the content of his desires, wants or interests if they interfere with his choices or not. By introducing this criterion, Pettit tries to bypass the weakness of the outcome-based conceptions of positive freedom and points at the intrinsic connection between freedom and the character of the relations in which agents find themselves vis-à-vis others (be it individuals, groups or institutions). For Pettit – as I will show a little further down – the criterion of content-independence implies that interferences have to be controlled by the interfered-with person in order to not count as an instance of unfreedom.

Now, at first sight the concept of control itself is quite vague. To begin with it seems as if it directly leads to the proceduralist approach mentioned above – an impression that is not completely false. Standard proceduralism – against which Pettit argues – maintains that an interference does not count as an impediment to freedom if the affected person consented to it. And as consent in many ways can be the result of coercion the proceduralist approaches work with a built-in *caveat* of noncoercion. Pettit reformulates this type of "historical proceduralism" in interpreting the consent-condition in a dispositional fashion. Not the historical *datum* of the consent is decisive but the fact that the interferences are constantly consent-dependent. Drawing on arguments of Amartya Sen[18] in an original way, Pettit argues that for freedom it is not relevant if consent is given *before* the interference. Rather, it is decisive that if the consent had not *counterfactually* been given the interference would not have taken place. Pettit rejects the opinion that a one-time consent is sufficient for freedom and argues that consent is always an expression of wishes, interests, and so forth, so that these are decisive rather than the *datum* of the consent. Of course, if the basis of the consent changes, the character of the interferences changes, too. In other words, if "voluntariness" should be a relevant criterion it must be applicable in every single moment.[19] At the same time Pettit refutes the thesis that interferences in order to be compatible with freedom necessarily have to be based on explicit consent given in advance. Thus, he argues that as long as an interference would counterfactually not take place or would be aborted in case the interfered-with person wishes so the interference would not be an infringement of freedom. This reasoning leads Pettit to an understanding of freedom whereby a person is *primarily* free if his or her options are not under the control of other agents and *secondarily* if he himself or she herself controls the interferences of other agents.[20] The criterion of consent is replaced by the criterion of control with control being understood as a dispositional concept and not as an exercise concept.[21] By transforming the criterion of consent into the criterion of control Pettit complements his critique of outcome-based approaches to freedom in a decisive manner. Even if content-independence was applicable this alone would not say anything about the specific circumstances under which this independence exists. In the end interferences can have the content the interfered-with person desires because of the contingent inclinations of the interfering person or because of favorable political circumstances and so on.[22] Pettit finds fault with these implications, as he argues that freedom exists only under the condition that it is not up to other agents to decide if to interfere or not. A person is only free if his or her choices are also *independent of the will* of other agents.

3. Implications of nondomination

While discussing the political philosophy of neo-liberalism I pointed out that according to this approach an unintended and uncoerced (even radically) unequal distribution of economic goods (like money and means of production) via market transactions is seen as of no significance for freedom – and that the classic socialist and social-democratic criticism was motivated by this thesis. For the neo-liberal perspective, in turn, the socialist ability-based conception of freedom represented a nightmare: Relative to the variations in the empirical circumstances a socialist freedom-seeking state would necessarily have to continuously interfere in the outcome of the transactions and thereby dramatically restrict the realm of voluntary interactions (that is, the realm of private law). I think that this is, generally speaking, an accurate observation (although it does not represent a nightmare for me), which becomes even more dramatic in the case of a neo-republicanism based on nondomination: This is so as in contrast to the neo-liberal as well as socialist understanding of freedom actual interferences are not considered as a necessary criterion of unfreedom. And if the mere existence of a capacity of (uncontrolled) interference is already a criterion of unfreedom then, by implication, the *genesis* of the distribution of power is of no interest from the standpoint of freedom. What solely counts in this perspective is who commands which interference-options against whom. It follows that an unequal distribution of power (in the sense of *power over ...*[23]) is as a matter of principle highly problematic from the standpoint of neo-republican freedom – even if it came about by voluntary transactions of all involved and even if it still allows everyone to realize their wants and interests. This implication can be illustrated by drawing an analogy to Nozick's famous Wilt Chamberlain example:[24] Beginning with a monetary "starting-gate equality" all persons involved transfer some of their money to someone, who then performs a certain activity that all value highly. The outcome of the transaction is of course a concentration of money in the hands of this one particular person. Now, I understand money in this example as a currency in which to measure power, that is the more money someone owns the more power he or she has over other persons.[25] Transferred to the political level this implies that in neo-republicanism the state permanently has to interfere into market transactions to prevent the emergence of social relations of power and domination.

It is quite clear that for this purpose a strong state is required. Now, from the perspective of a socialist conception of freedom (which, again, also belongs to the broad church of freedom based on noninterference) a powerful state as such is not a problem. As long as the state actually concentrates on its function to guarantee (maximum) freedom the state in itself is not a source of unfreedom. But this, of course, does not hold in the case of the neo-republican understanding of freedom. Here, the strong state – required to provide "nondomination" – becomes a dominating agency precisely through its required plenitude of power. This paradoxical situation reminds one of the joke about Robin Hood who steals from the rich to give to the poor only to subsequently rob the poor since the latter has now become rich whereupon Robin realizes that now he himself is a rich person. In the context of this fairly silly joke the trivial solution consists, of course, in an equal distribution of wealth. It seems natural that in the case of freedom the solution would be that the state itself is subjected to the control of its citizens.

If this solution is sound then neo-republicanism indeed could do away with the nightmare of the neo-liberals since a type of *telocracy* would be imaginable that does *not* go along with a restriction of freedom and domination. Furthermore, because of its reconceptualization of the critique of the market the neo-republican conception of freedom becomes compatible with the socialist and social-democratic tradition or – after the historical experiences with the authoritarian state-centered socialisms – could even be an important element in its reorientation. So, the crucial question is how to conceive of a republican state that on the one side is powerful enough and equipped with sufficient competencies to guarantee at least a certain level of freedom to all of its citizens while on the other it should not have uncontrolled power at its command. It is important to keep in mind that for the power of the state to count as being controlled in the relevant sense it must be *effectively* controlled by those who are subjected to its power.

4. Interferences and control

In what follows I will discuss the "neo-republican thesis" that even a state's power and interferences can be controlled by its citizens. In order to do this I will first concentrate on analyzing what it means to have control over interferences. I will bring forward the argument that this idea – at least in Pettit's version – is only plausible at first sight but if you take a closer look, numerous problems and unresolved aspects become apparent.

To illustrate his arguments Pettit uses a certain set of examples, so in a first step I will concentrate on discussing them. I will argue that the examples point to a contradiction in Pettit's thoughts about freedom as the examples illustrate the possibility of *self*-binding, or to put it differently of *externalized self-control* – and I will argue that the problems of self-binding and self-control cannot be adapted to the problems of interpersonal, social or political control. But if these examples indeed show how Pettit conceives of the relation between freedom, control and interferences then neo-republicanism would in the end either boil down to the neo-liberal proceduralistic or to the social-democratic outcome-based understanding of freedom. Against this it seems to me much more plausible to stick to Pettit's definition of unfreedom and maintain the centrality of control thereby gaining a realistic assessment of the relation between freedom and the state. In fact I will argue that based on the understanding of freedom as nondomination the question of the compatibility between freedom and political order arises in a much more *radical* way than in the context of the various noninterference-based approaches.

5. Some thoughts on the concept of control

To begin with it is important to further analyze the concept of "control". In political philosophy the concept of control plays a pivotal role, but what it is supposed to mean exactly is rarely defined. I think it is not too exotic if I take control as a type of power, that is, as a capacity to intentionally bring about certain results. On this view, control is the capacity to "make something happen and to preclude it from happening" (Rescher 1969, 329) in an intended manner – a definition that is in line with Pettit's analysis of the conditions that must hold for an interference to not count as an instance of unfreedom.

Control, of course, is a gradual concept; that is, P can have full control over x or only the control over a sufficient or a necessary condition of x, and it is possible that several people have divided control over x. The higher the level of division of control the lower is the remaining control of each single agent. And if P has control over x if P has the capacity to intentionally bring about x or preclude x from happening, obviously to ascribe this capacity to a group of agents becomes problematic – at least from a certain number on. Imagine an electoral political system. Each person has a vote and in the end all votes are counted and a decision is reached by a (however sophisticated) principle of majority rule. At the first glance it seems plausible to say that all persons who are entitled to vote exercise full control over the decision collectively while each of them has partial control. But control exercised *in sensu composito* is only a figure of speech and is not the same as real control. To speak about control *in sensu diviso* implies that from a certain level of division partial control turns from weak control into influence.[26] The concept of control is also not just outcome-oriented but includes also the way in which the control is exercised or the outcome is brought about. This is especially of relevance for social or political relations of control: In this case, P's full control over A's x-ing consists not only in P's capacity to prompt A to x but also in P's capacity to determine the *modus operandi* in which A brings about x. A bank, for example, exercises control over its debtors by scheduling when the debts have to be cleared. But the control does not include the capacity to determine in which ways the debtors will clear their debts – if they do it by working overtime, by selling their property or by robbing a bank. In contrast to that, the godfather of a mafia clan can dictate the way in which a debtor has to settle his or her debts. Likewise, the International Monetary Fund (IMF) can link the deferral of a loan to "structural adjustments." It follows that full control is only applicable if it includes the control of the *modus operandi*. So control is always exercised (or potentially exercised) in relation to a certain agent (which is the only relevant context here), in a certain manner (divided or full, negative or positive, weak or strong, restricted to the outcome or including the *modus operandi* of the production of the outcome).

6. EXTERNALIZED CONTROL AND INTERFERENCES

As aforementioned, in the neo-republican view, interferences in the choices of a person are not restrictions of their freedom if the criteria of content- and will-independence are satisfied, that is, if the affected person has control over the interference. But it is not easy to understand what having control over interferences means exactly – and this has to do with the concept of "interference" as well as with the concept of "control".

Usually, Pettit illustrates the possibility of controlled interference by means of a particular example or a variation of it. Of course, the use of examples is often difficult in philosophy – even if it is indispensable in political philosophy. So, to motivate the criticism of an argument by

220

poking around in an example may seem to be silly. However, in the case of Pettit's reflections on the relation between freedom and the (republican) state, the plausibility of his arguments depends to a great extent on this example. Or, to put it differently, it seems to me that certain internal tensions between his analysis of freedom and his thoughts on the relation between freedom and the state fully become clear when taking a closer look at this particular example. The example is the famous "Ulysses and the Sirens" case, which is often referred to in the history of philosophy to illustrate the idea of (rational) *self-binding*.[27] The story is that Ulysses instructs his sailors to tie him to the mast so that he can hear the sirens' singing without falling prey to them (that is, to his passions). If the sailors do as they are told certain options would be taken away from Ulysses – according to Pettit – but this interference would be in accordance with his wishes and under his "check and control" (Pettit 2009b, 46). And since the criteria of will- and content-independence would hold, Ulysses would not be unfree in this situation.

> This scenario is classically portrayed in the story of Ulysses and the sirens, when Ulysses gives a power of interference to his sailors – they are allowed to keep him bound while the ship passes the island of the siren voices – and they exercise this power in accordance with his wishes. The interference practiced by the sailors is not arbitrary or uncontrolled. On the contrary it is a form of interference that is subject to the check or control of Ulysses himself. Thus the sailors are not his masters, and he does not operate under their power; rather they are his servants, the means by which he imposes his own will upon himself. The sailors operate as devices whereby B exercises self-control, enabling the reason with which he iden-tifies to triumph over the unwelcome passions that he expects the sirens to excite. The sailors are the conduits of that self-control, not the channels whereby an alien will might be given in his life.
>
> (Pettit 2009, 46)

If you compare the circumstances under which the binding of Ulysses takes place with a situation in which an agent decides for himself that he shall and how he shall interfere with other people's lives, the difference between both cases is intuitively striking. But is the difference really to be explained by reference to the concept of control? Or isn't the difference rather based on the fact that the binding takes place *according to Ulysses' wishes*? I want to raise doubts about the plausibility of this example and the underlying argument of Pettit in two respects. First, I will concentrate on the question of whether "externalized self-control" really deals with the same kind of "interferences" as in cases that are, say, not instances of self-binding or of self-control but of interpersonal or political control. In a second step I will call into question if the "autonomy-based" perspective that seems to me to be in the background of Pettit's example is actually suited to reconstructing the relation between freedom and the (republican) state. Finally, I will conclude that Pettit either has to substantiate the compatibility-thesis in a fundamentally different way, or even has to drop it completely, or he has to give up his conception of freedom on the basis of control.

In accordance with most conceptions of freedom, Pettit defines interferences as a *worsening* of things for the interfered-with person. If an option of a person is significantly changed by an intervention of another agent, so "that [the option] differs in regard to some feature that is valued" (Pettit 2008, 107), the intervention counts as an interference. Against the background of this definition it is a bit confusing to claim that an interference does not count as a restriction of freedom if it is controlled by the interfered-with person. How can we conceive of interferences as making things *worse* for the interfered-with person if they are under the control of the interfered-with person? The problematic matter is that it is a bit vague in which ways such controlled interferences differ from the ordinary choices of a person – being that ordinary choices are partly characterized by excluding other possible options, or by making things "worse," and so forth. Now, it is important to see that the neo-republican approach shares with a more traditional conception of negative freedom the assumption that freedom is an *irreflexive* notion. This means that no agent can make himself or herself unfree – an argument that is normally made in the context of the question about the freedom-related relevance of different sources of possible impediments to actions or options. Do natural obstacles count as a restriction on freedom or only obstacles that can be attributed to human agency? Can agents make themselves unfree (by, for example, acting irrationally) or not? Given the criterion of irreflexivity the argumentative power of the thesis that interferences do not restrict freedom if they are under the control of the interfered-with person becomes dubious – especially when this argument is made by reference to cases of external-ized *self-control*. Even proponents of noninterference-based conceptions of freedom can concede Pettit's argument – as long as they assume irreflexivity. If an "interference" happens in such a way that the interfering persons act as "devices" (46) of the interfered-with person then (given irreflexivity) such an intervention would not count as a restriction of freedom even from the standpoint of noninterference – the only difference left would be that such interventions wouldn't even be called "interference."

Against this background it seems as if Pettit's thesis – that the conceptual advantage of the neo-republican approach lies in making it possible to conceive of certain interferences as not inimical to freedom – rests on a terminological trick. It is my understanding that this is the case because Pettit uses the problem of self-binding and externalized self-control, a problem that is firmly rooted in the province of *positive freedom*. To discuss the issue of interpersonal freedom by analogy with problems of self-control is also highly problematic because of further difficulties. Self-control and self-binding is (in the case at hand) about externalizing the control that is necessary to yield a certain type of behavior. Other persons are authorized to exercise control to prevent oneself from acting in a certain manner. So the problem at hand is how agents can overcome "inner restraints," addictions, weakness of the will, and so forth, by binding themselves in a situation in which they are no longer capable of controlling themselves. Thus, the Ulysses-example is *not* about Ulysses *retaining* control when being bound by his sailors but about *transferring* the control to his sailors. And that in my understanding is the whole point of externalizing self-control. Once tied to the mast Ulysses does not exercise power over himself, but his sailors do – and that he regains control is no intrinsic feature of externalized self-control but is completely dependent on the type of behavior that is to be controlled.

Now, Pettit, as aforementioned, tries to avoid these implications of an "autonomy-based" interpretation of control by trying to integrate the standing capacity to stop interferences by other agents. And, if I am right, this standing capacity shall be provided by the republican state. This state functions as a "third party," which keeps the interfering agents "on track".[28] But this solution only shifts the problem since it can be asked how the third party must be constituted so that it only acts if the interfering agent does not interfere according to instructions. Another problem is how it can be avoided that this third party does not itself become a dominating agency, that is, that it still is under control. On the level of "face-to-face" interactions the first problem can be solved since these kinds of interactions open up the possibility of specifying allowed interferences in such a way that no bigger issues of interpretation arise. But obviously on the level of political and legal procedures and interferences it is hardly possible (let alone desirable) to specify interferences in such a way that the corresponding power of the interfering agency is in fact strictly restricted to fulfilling its purpose. Moreover, I think the analogy between interferences based on externalized self-binding or self-control and interferences by the state that are the result of political or democratic processes, falls into an imbalance since it is hardly possible in a democratic process to specify in advance exactly how the agencies of the state shall realize certain democratic decisions or legislative acts.[29] Of course, such a specification might be possible in the realm of private law, that is, in the case of contracts between consenting persons, but it is hardly possible nor even desirable in the realm of public law.[30] This point is linked to the argument about the irreflexivity of freedom I discussed in the previous passage. Either we can think of interferences by the state by analyzing them in analogy to the model of externalized self-control – and then – given that the criterion of irreflexivity holds – they cannot count as interferences any longer. Or we emphasize the disanalogies so that the interventions by the state in fact count as interferences but then – as I will argue in detail further below – it becomes questionable how we can conceive of them as not inimical to freedom (according to the conception of freedom as nondomination). It seems to me that when it comes to the relation between freedom and the state, Pettit either has to significantly change his understanding of control and domination or he has to significantly weaken his claim that one advantage of the neo-republican understanding of freedom consists in reconciling the existing of a (strong) state with the freedom of its citizens.

7. Domination, control and democracy

In the previous passage I argued that the example Pettit uses to explain what he means by the idea that interferences under certain conditions are not inimical to freedom are not only ill-suited but employ a different understanding of freedom than the one Pettit tries to develop. This led me into thinking that the neo-republican thesis of the compatibility of freedom and the state can only be validated by quietly substituting one conception of freedom through a different one. Of course, "control" plays a crucial role in a "rational self-control/autonomy" based understanding of freedom as well as in the nondomination approach. But it is understood in a completely different way: While in the first case content-independence is necessary and sufficient, in the latter both must hold: content- *and* will-independence. So it seems that what is in the end decisive for Pettit is that interferences take place according to one's wishes but not that the interfered-with person in fact exercises control over them. This suspicion is amplified when it comes to Pettit's reflections on the relation between control and interferences by the state. Here it seems as if in fact the notion of control changes its meaning in such a dramatic way that the neo-republican approach in the end boils down to either a proceduralist or an outcome-oriented understanding of freedom. And that would imply that the core definition of unfreedom and domination is abandoned in order to rescue the possibility of compatibility between "freedom" and interferences by the state.

I will explain my criticism by citing a passage in which Pettit outlines under what conditions interferences by the state are not inimical to the freedom of the individual citizens.

> An equal share in collective control will give each the highest possible level of control over the law, consistently with no one being given less than that level. Thus it will give members a level of control such that no one can complain of being treated in a way that neglects their will, as dominating overtures neglect their will. It will enable them each to think that in this less than perfect world – in this world of territorial scarcity – they have all the control over law that is required for them to regard the law as a form of interference that is non-arbitrary and un-dominating.
>
> (Pettit 2009b, 53)

Now, it is striking that Pettit modifies his definition of unfreedom or domination in this passage. Whereas before persons are not dominated, that is unfree, if they do not underlie the control of other agents or if they have control over interferences with their options, now Pettit defines domination as "being treated in a way that neglects their [that is, the interfered-with person's] will" (46). Obviously, this definition violates the criterion of *will-independency*; moreover, it is completely centered on the category of interference (and not on the existence of a capacity hereto). In my reading, Pettit tries to deal with this problem by conceding to each citizen an "equal share in collective control" (46) so that interferences by the state are not controlled by the will of a *single* or a *few* persons – and he concludes that under such conditions the control-criterion is satisfied. I have to admit that this line of reasoning (nonideal conditions or not) does not convince me at all – moreover, I have the impression that the normative problems of freedom and domination are trivialized so that this approach is finally not suited as an attractive alternative to both neo-liberal and social-democratic or socialist thinking (of course, only when it comes to the relation between freedom and the state).[31] My criticism is mainly motivated by the fact that the use of the notion of control somehow suggests that there would be a straightforward connection between the control that is required so that interferences do not count as an impediment to freedom and rights of political participation.

While discussing the concept of control in the digression above I have pointed out that control is essentially defined by the capacity to make something happen (or to preclude something from happening) in a planned and intentional way. And that relative to its level of division, control becomes weaker and weaker up to the point where it cannot be explained as control any longer. Of course, it is impossible to determine exactly from which point on partial or shared control is no longer control (but, for example, influence), but I would like to maintain that when it comes to contemporary large-scale democracies the criterion of control does certainly not hold anymore.[32] Since Pettit emphatically repudiates the "collectivist" tradition in political philosophy (in which a *free society* is not understood as a society in which each of its members is free but in which "society" is understood as some kind of "super-agent" (*Großsubjekt*)), the only relevant form of control is the level of control each single citizen has. But whereas the level of control that is required to guarantee that an interference on the interpersonal level is not an instance of unfreedom at least has to consist in the "negative" capacity to preclude interferences from happening, certainly, this capacity does not exist in the case of equally shared control in a democracy. The citizens of the neo-republic surely have control over their vote but measured against the possibility to control interferences by the state one has to concede that this "small scale power" is causally inefficacious. Plainly, a *dispersion of control* is no type of control since no *effective ability* corresponds on the side of the citizens.[33] And I think that this counterargument holds for all attempts in political philosophy to argue – because of an equal distribution of rights to political participation – for the compatibility between freedom and a politico-legal order by reference to an ability-based notion of freedom (and Pettit's conception of freedom is ability-based as far as the level of control is concerned), that is positive or real freedom. The neo-republican thesis of the compatibility of freedom and interferences by the state under conditions of "equally shared control" is not convincing – quite on the contrary. If one takes the shift from noninterference to nondomination seriously what is apparent is that the power of a state per se is a source of unfreedom. Furthermore, especially the neo-republican state has to have the power to establish relations of nondomination between its citizens under conditions of ever-changing empirical circumstances and constellations of power. And I cannot see how against the background of the neo-republican analytics of freedom this *standing capacity* cannot be charcterized as a dominating power. I can see why such a strong state might not be an infringement of freedom in the perspective of a telocratic social-democratic or socialist noninterference-based understanding of freedom, but I find it hardly reconcilable with the power and domination-centered view of freedom that Pettit develops so trenchantly. The relation between freedom and the state gets even more complicated since Pettit not only defends the thesis of compatibility but goes beyond it by claiming that the republican state *constitutes* freedom in the first place. It is my understanding that by claiming this Pettit is trying to point out that the conditions under which agents are free in relation to one another have to be a part of the definition of freedom. Someone is only free in relation to another agent if this freedom is not coincidental and bound to a specific moment but rather is noncontingent and continuous – and if I am right Pettit links these features to the existence of the state. So that the features of establishing stable and noncontingent relations between its citizens are ascribed to the state.[34] But, again, this much stronger thesis cannot be sustained if it was not that the power of the state is subjected to the control of its citizens – which, as shown, is not the case.

In a way contrary to what Pettit thinks about the relation between freedom and the neo-republican state, in my reading the conception of freedom as nondomination calls attention to the argument that the familiar separation between the "horizontal" and "vertical" dimensions of freedom cannot be maintained. According to the conception of nondomination, no free relations between citizens exist without freedom between each single citizen and the institutions of the state. It is only in this perspective that a nondominating state constitutes the freedom of its citizens.

My conclusion is primarily critical and negative: I pointed out why the neo-republican thesis, whereby freedom and the state are compatible, does not hold. To say that the state is under the control of its citizens is something that holds only in a very metaphorical sense. At the same time, I made it clear that the concept of nondomination, which the normative political theory of neo-republicanism is based on, requires a strong telocratic state – and that this exacerbates the problem of domination by the state. However, the neo-liberal option of a freedom-based argument for a minimum state cannot be an alternative. The concept of freedom as nondomination focuses on the nature of the relations between agents, thereby establishing a qualified critical perspective against the neo-liberal

227

apologia of the market. Thus, this concepts provides in fact a more profound and critical perspective than the outcome-oriented concept of freedom of the socialist or social-democratic tradition.

I feel that the conclusion of this article can be dealt with in two ways. We either have to broaden the normative basis of neo-republicanism. Instead of a monism of freedom, the republic would be justified on the level of plural values. The important question would then be which values would come into consideration and how they would relate to one another. Or, alternatively, the monistic perspective is maintained, but in this case it has to be transformed into a generally critical understanding of the state, which critically investigates the issue of domination, also in the context of (contestatory or "authorial") democracy. However, as to whether the answer to this can be found in the tradition of republicanism remains doubtful.

References

Barry, B. (1965). *Political Argument*. London: Routledge and Kegan Paul.

Berlin, I. (2002). "Two Concepts of Liberty." In: *Isaiah Berlin – Four Essays on Liberty*. Ed. Henry Hardy, Oxford: Oxford University Press: 166–217.

Brenkert, G.G. (1983). *Marx's Ethics of Freedom*. London: Routledge.

Brennan, G. and L. Lomasky (2006). "Against Reviving Republicanism." *Politics, Philosophy and Economics* 5: 221–52.

Brown, G. (2010). *Why the Right is Wrong*. London: Fabian Society.

Cohen, G. A. (2011). "Freedom and Money." In: *G. A. Cohen: On the Currency of Egalitarian Justice and other Essays in Political Philosophy*. Ed. M. Otsuka, Princeton: Princeton University Press: 166–92.

Elster, J. (1985). *Ulysses and the Sirens: Studies in Rationality and Irrationality*. Cambridge: Cambridge University Press.

Elster, J. (2000). *Ulysses Unbound: Studies in Rationality, Precommitment and Constraint*. Cambridge: Cambridge University Press.

Finnis, J. (1980). *Natural Law and Natural Rights*. Oxford: Clarendon Press.

Fuller, L. (1969). *The Morality of Law*. New Haven: Yale University Press.

Gaus, G. (2003). "Backward into the Future: Neorepublicanism as a Postsocialist Critique of Market Society." *Social Philosophy and Policy* 20/1: 59–91.

Geuss, R. (1981). *The Idea of Critical Theory: Habermas and the Frankfurt School*. Cambridge: Cambridge University Press.

Goodin, R. (2003). "Folie Republicaine." *Annual Review of Political Science* 6: 55–76.

Hayek, F. A. (1960). *The Constitution of Liberty*. London: Routledge and Kegan Paul.

Hirschmann, A. O. (1977). *The Passions and the Interests: Political Arguments for Capitalism before its Triumph*. Princeton: Princeton University Press.

Hirschmann, A. O. (1992). "The Concept of Interest: From Euphemism to Tautology." In: *Rival Views of Market Society*. A. O. Hirschmann, Cambridge, MA: Harvard University Press: 35–55.

Kramer, M. H. (2003). *The Quality of Freedom*. Oxford: Oxford University Press.

Kristjànsson, K. (1996). *Social Freedom: The Responsibility View*. Cambridge: Cambridge University Press.

Kristjànsson, K. (1998). "Is There Something Wrong with 'Free Action?'" *Journal of Theoretical Politics* 10/3: 259–73.

Lovett, F. and P. Pettit (2010). "Neo-Republicanism: A Normative and Institutional Research Program." *Annual Review of Political Science* 12: 11–29.

Lukes, S. (2005). *Power: A Radical View*. Basingstoke: Palgrave Macmillan.

Lyons, D. (1984). *Ethics and the Rule of Law*. Cambridge: Cambridge University Press.

Michelmann, F. (1988). "Law's Republic." *Yale Law Journal* 97/8: 1493–537.

Michelmann, F. (2010). "Foxy Freedom?" *Boston Law Review* 90: 949–74.

Morriss, P. (2002). *Power. A Philosophical Analysis*. Manchester: Manchester University Press

Nozick, R. (1999). *Anarchy, State and Utopia*. Oxford: Blackwell Publishing.

Oakeshott, M. J. (2006). *Lectures in the History of Political Thought*. Exeter: Imprint Academic.

Oppenheim, F. E. (1981). *Political Concepts: A Reconstruction*. Chicago: Chicago University Press.

Pettit, P. (1998). "Comment on Kristjánsson: Actions, Persons and Freedom as Nondomination." *Journal of Theoretical Politics* 10/3: 275–83.

Pettit, P. (1999). *Republicanism: A Theory of Freedom and Government*. Oxford: Oxford University Press.

Pettit, P. (2001a). *A Theory of Freedom: From the Psychology to the Politics of Agency*. Cambridge: Polity Press.

Pettit, P. (2001b). "Capability and Freedom: A Defence of Sen." *Economics and Philosophy* 1: 1–20.

Pettit, P. (2006). "The Determinacy of Republican Policy: A Reply to McMahon." *Philosophy and Public Affairs* 34/2: 275–83.

Pettit, P. (2007). "Joining the Dots." In: *Common Minds: Themes from the Philosophy of Philip Pettit*. Eds G. Brennan, R. Gooding, F. Jackson and M. Smith, Oxford: Oxford University Press: 215–344.

Pettit, P. (2008a). "Republican Freedom: Three Axioms, Four Theorems." In: *Republicanism and Political Theory*. Eds C. Laborde and J. Maynor, Malden, MA/Oxford: Blackwell: 102–30.

Pettit, P. (2008b). "The Basic Liberties." In: *The Legacy of H. L. A. Hart: Legal, Political, and Moral Philosophy*. Eds M. H. Kramer, C. Grant, B. Colburn and A. Hatzistavrou, Oxford: Oxford University Press: 201–21.

Pettit, P. (2009a). "Freedom in the Spirit of Sen." In: *Amartya Sen*. Ed. C. Morris, Cambridge: Cambridge University Press: 91–114.

Pettit, P. (2009b). "Law and Liberty." In: *Legal Republicanism: National and International Perspectives*. Eds S. Besson and J. L. Martí, Oxford: Oxford University Press: 39–59.

Pettit, P. (2011). "The Instability of Freedom as Noninterference: The Case of Isaiah Berlin." *Ethics* 121/4: 693–716.

Pettit, P. (2012). *On the People's Terms*. Cambridge: Cambridge University Press.

Plant, R. (2010). *The Neo-Liberal State*. Oxford: Oxford University Press.

Rescher, R. (1969). "The Concept of Control." In: N. Rescher. *Essays in Philosophical Analysis*. Pittsburgh: University of Pittsburgh Press: 327–53.

Schink, P. (forthcoming). *Eine Theorie sozialer Freiheit.*

Sen, Amartya (1982). "Liberty as Control: An Appraisal." *Midwest Studies in Philosophy* 7: 207–21.

Sen, Amartya (1985). "Well-Being, Agency and Freedom." *Journal of Philosophy* 82: 169–221.

Sen, Amartya (1992). *Inequality Reexamined.* Oxford: Oxford University Press.

Sen, Amartya (2009). "Responses." In: *Against Injustice: The New Economics of Amartya Sen.* Ed. R. Gotoh, Cambridge: Cambridge University Press: 297–309.

Sunstein, C. (1988). "Beyond the Republican Revival." *Yale Law Journal* 97/8: 1539–90.

Sunstein, C. (1993). "The Enduring Legacy of Republicanism." In: *A New Constitutionalism: Designing Political Institutions for a Good Society.* Eds S. Elkin and K. Soltan, Chicago: Chicago University Press: 174–206.

Tomkins, A. (2005). *Our Republican Constitution.* Oxford: Hart Publishing.

van Parijs, P. (2003). *Real Freedom for All – What (If Anything) Can Justify Capitalism?* Oxford: Oxford University Press.

Notes

1. Cf., for example, the ongoing controversy about the character, scope and limits of the US-American constitution (Michelmann 1988), (Sunstein 1988, 1993) or the debate about the pros and cons of a written constitution in the United Kingdom (Tomkins 2005).

2. For the neo-liberal conception of the state, see Raymond Plant 2010.

3. For a comprehensive list of the principles that constitute the rule of law, see Fuller 1969; Finnis 1980, 270–80; Lyons 1984.

4. At least when it comes to Nozick and Hayek.

5. See Berlin 2002.

6. "It is to this class of concepts that liberty belongs: it describes the absence of a particular obstacle – coercion by other men. It becomes positive only through what we make of it. It does not assure us of any particular opportunities but leaves it to us to decide what use we shall make of the circumstances in which we find ourselves" (Hayek 1960, 19).

7. The distinction between a nomocratic and a telocratic order stems from Michael Oakshott, a distinction which Hayek picked up. Raymond Plant defines both types of order in his masterful study on the neo-liberal state as follows: "a distinction between a *telocratic* order of society or a *telocracy* (an order devoted to the pursuit of some overall end, goal, or purpose) and a *nomocracy* (a rule governed order not devoted to the attainment of particular ends)" (Plant 2010, 6).

8. It is my understanding that Hayek (at least in *The Constitution of Liberty*) defines coercion in two different ways: first, as forcing someone to act not according to their own coherent plan of life, and second, as just forcing someone to act in a certain way – even if this way of acting is in accordance with a coherent life plan. Compare for the first understanding of coercion: "By 'coercion' we mean such control of the environment or circumstances of a person by another that, in order to avoid greater evil, he is forced to act not according to a coherent plan of his own but to service the ends of another" (Hayek 1960, 21). For the second understanding: "Coercion, however,

cannot be altogether avoided because the only way to prevent it is by the threat of coercion. Free society has met this problem by conferring the monopoly of coercion on the state and by attempting to limit this power of the state to instances where it is required to prevent coercion by private persons" (Hayek 1960, 21).

9. "Coercion is evil precisely because it thus eliminates an individual as a thinking and valued person and makes him a bare tool in the achievement of the evils of another" (Hayek 1960, 21).

10. Cf. Nozick 1999, 3–26.

11. "[B]ut what is it that makes the threatened coercion of the law non-arbitrary? The answer is purely its generality and its abstract nature. It is non-arbitrary in that it does not specify prohibitions and penalities for specified individuals; it is non-arbitrary in that it protects the private spheres of all equally; it does not prescribe a set of arbitrarily chosen ends, goals, purposes, or coherent plans of life giving these some kind of legal privilege" (Plant 2010, 68).

12. I take the negative–positive distinction to be largely a red herring. Essentially it is a distinction about what sort of "obstacles" count as interference: Does a lack of abilities per se count as interference? Do strong first order desires that someone does not identify with count as interference? All claims about "positive freedom" can be reformulated as claims about the *absence* of hindrances – so the dispute is about which kind of obstacles to what count as freedom-relevant.

13. Cf. Brown 2010; Brenkert 1983; Plant 2010.

14. For a helpful undertaking to define and distinguish both concepts cf. Geuss 1981; Hirschmann 1977, 1992; Barry 1965.

15. "When Isaiah Berlin talks of a 'man's, or a people's, liberty to choose to live as they desire', the point of direct reference is the ability to choose to live as one desires, rather than the mechanism of control. If people do desire a life without hunger or malaria, the elimination of these maladies through public policy does enhance their 'liberty to choose as they desire'. The fact that the levers of control are not in the hands of most people who are made more free in this respect does not compromise the importance of the enhancement of their effective freedom to live as they would choose" (Sen 1992, 67) .

16. For the discussion of the problems of content-dependent concepts of freedom see Pettit 2001b, 2009b, 2011.

17. For a dissenting view, see Sen 2009, 302f.

18. Cf. Sen 1982 and 1985.

19. "Whether a relationship sprang originally from a contract or not, whether or not it was consensual in origin, the fact that it gives one party the effective capacity to interfere more or less arbitrarily in some of the other's choices means that the one person dominates or subjugates the other" (Pettit 1999, 62).

20. Cf. Schink, forthcoming.

21. Cf. Peter Morriss 2002. Cf. especially Morris discussion of the *fallacy of exercise*, pp. 15–28.

22. Cf. Pettit 2011.

23. Cf. Morriss 2002, 32–5.

24. Cf. Nozick 1999, 160–4.

25. Considering that money regulates the command of material resources and that everyone by necessity has to have access to these resources, it becomes clear that a

close connection exists between the possession of money and the control over other persons.

26. Cf. Morriss 2002; Oppenheim 1981; Lukes 2005, 36; Pettit 1999, chap. 2.

27. Cf. Elster 1985, 2000.

28. "You will enjoy suitable protection in a particular choice just to the extent that other individuals or groups do not have access to means of non-deliberative control over that choice. Others may be able to deliberate with you on the basis of sincere, take-it-or-leave-it reasons and influence what you do. But they should not be allowed a power of interfering with the choice, without exposing themselves to an inhibiting risk of punishment; they should not be able to block, burden, or deceptively redirect the choice with any degree of impunity. In short, they should not have 'dominating control' over what you choose" (Pettit 2008b, 202). But see the controversy over the relation between domination/unfreedom and punishment between Kristjànsson 1998 and Pettit 1998.

29. To push the example of Ulysses and the sirens a little bit further: To act on Ulysses' desire to listen to the sirens without falling prey to them the sailors have to put wax in their ears, so that they can control him while he indulges in his passions. Now, assume that the sailors are a very cautious bunch and think that they should be 100 per cent sure that they are out of reach of the sirens' voices. To determine if that is the case they obviously can't rely on Ulysses' actions as he might act under the influence of the sirens. So they decide that they will collectively decide when to untie Ulysses. But they have a disagreement: Have the sirens already stopped singing? No sailor can check himself as then this would make him unreliable to the other sailors, as he could have fallen prey to the sirens' singing. I firmly believe that in politics and law most cases are much more like this situation than like the self-binding example Pettit uses.

30. This is also an implication of the telocratic character of the neo-republican state. Pettit clearly recognizes this problem and tries to deal with it by introducing the idea of "contestatory democracy" (Pettit 2007, 317ff.).

31. I do not want to go as far as Goodin 2003 or Brennan and Lomasky 2006 and reject the neo-republican project in its entirety – much to the contrary. But I think that the relation between freedom and the state must be reconstructed in a way that is much more critical of the possibility to establish a free society by means of a strong state.

32. Cf. for a similar argument (even if it aims at downgrading the role of control in freedom – an attempt with which I do not concur) Sen 1992, 2009.

33. Cf. van Parijs 2003, 8–17; Sen 2009, 302.

34. Cf. for example: "The key republican idea is that a person or citizen will be free to the extent that suitable choices are suitably protected and empowered ... And the suitable clause implies that it will not be enough for the person to have those choices protected by being enabled to appease or buy of would-be offenders, for example, to take evasive action, or to call on some mafia friends" (Pettit 2008b, 202).

CHAPTER 9

Legal Modes and Democratic Citizens in Republican Theory

Galya Benarieh Ruffer

If we think of a distinctly republican *rule of law* how would that alter common distinctions in republican theory made between "law's" citizenship and "democracy's" citizenship? Citizenship, in republican theory, seeks to express through a language of rights and a process of institutional engagements the ways in which we might actualize freedom of the individual through freedom from arbitrary interference or nondomination (Skinner 2008, Pettit 1997) when we come together in collective association. Its main concern, therefore, is with defining the commonwealth or civil association. Republican freedom represents a distinct conception of freedom as *nondomination* where freedom consists not in the noninterference of others as in negative liberty, nor as self-mastery as in positive liberty, but rather in agency, in that agents are free when they engage in *reflection and choice* and are, thereby, as actors and authors, freed of the possibility of arbitrary interference, or domination by others. In this understanding the constrained interference for the common good in the form of shared laws is nonarbitrary and, therefore, does not violate the republican principle of freedom. In what follows, I explore and evaluate three legal modes of democratic citizens that correspond to this understanding of freedom and analyze these modes in regards to the core concern of constituting civil association for the common good through equal participation. The ultimate focus of the examination is to consider how a rethinking of the *rule of law* through a republican lens may alter our understanding of the problematic of democratic citizenship today, and I argue that this *moment* of citizenship is best constituted as an activity of citizens in generating and maintaining the legal order through their reciprocal relationships, procedures, politics, and social relations.

The republican revival that began in the 1980s centered on a common set of assumptions regarding the conditions of law and democracy that began to take shape after World War II. Republican theorists offered a critique of rights-based liberalism that, they claimed, seeks to guarantee individual freedom through rights of noninterference that have not taken into account the underlying power structures and, in its emphasis on the individual, has devalued the activity of citizenship as a collective responsibility. The republican constitutionalist revival sought to redefine civil association in relation to authority in such a way as to secure freedom (nondomination). Republicanism seeks "the conceptual identification (although of course not outright identity or equivalence) of 'people' with 'laws,' which at the same time holds 'people' distinct from mere 'men'" (Michelman 1988, 1,502). Most republican theorists are looking to define a "process" of "jurisgenerative politics." Through the political process, "private-regarding 'men' become public-regarding citizens and thus members of a people" (Michelman 1988, 1502). The revival, according to Michelman, was not "some nostalgic republican revival, but rather American constitutionalism as we have all along thought it." It signifies "the sort of belief in jurisgenerative politics that it seems must play a role in any explanation of how the constitutionalist principles of self-rule and law-rule might coincide" (Michelman 1988, 1502). The tension a "jurisgenerative politics" resolves is that of the dual commitments of republican thought to the idea of the people acting politically as the sole source of law and guarantor of rights and to the idea of law, including rights, as the precondition of good politics. According to Michelman (1988, 1502), "Republican thought thus demands some way of understanding how laws and rights can be both the free creations of citizens and, at the same time, the normative givens that constitute and underwrite a political process capable of creating constitutive law."

The response of these concerns was to begin to conceptualize civil association as a jurisgenerative politics that could better connect "people" and "authority" through "rule of law" (that is, "citizenship"). In the next section I introduce three legal modes of democratic citizenship that capture this relationship of republican citizenship.

CITIZEN AGENTS, MANAGERS AND LEADERS

The question "What is democratic citizenship?" in republican theory is essentially a question of how to transform the "I" of "self-reflexive authority" into the "we" of civil association while maintaining the republican commitment to nondomination. *Rule of law* is a powerful concept in this transformation and creation of civil association in that it has the potential to offer an uncontested authority but only to the extent that its authority is consistent with the self-reflexive authorship. There are a number of ways in which law can claim an uncontested authority: (1) It can claim to represent universal morals; (2) It can claim to be the expression of a collective ethics; (3) It can claim to supply the "rules" and "boundaries" through which the many "I"s agree to follow in their contestation over their interests; or (4) It can claim to represent the authoritative "expression" of whatever the many "I"s have agreed to through their contestation.

These different positions regarding law's authority lead to different responses to the question of what is democratic citizenship. Specifically, because the different understandings of republican *authority* are based on different core beliefs regarding the overall project of civil association as between (1) universal morality vs. common ethics and (2) the capacity of humans in relation to public and private interests in this project. There are three distinct legal modes of democratic citizenship arising from these different positions of the relation between citizenship and authority of law in republicanism that I shall call "citizen agents," "citizen managers" and "citizen leaders."

1. Citizen agents

The mode of the *citizen agent* is premised on skepticism of universal morality and a realist belief that individuals serve their own personal interests. Grounded in a particular notion of *virtue* that derives from Cicero and Machiavelli, citizenship is fueled by competing passions. In this view, there are only private interests. One can only speak of a public interest as that position that *wins* or results out of contestation of private interests. Law in this position is the ongoing expression of contested private interests. It never rises to a moral or ethical expression of a common good that might come to dominate and infringe upon individual liberty. In this view, law is the "common asset" of contestation among citizens (Bellamy 2007, 82) and *rule of law* is the resulting product of contestation among equal citizens. There are no primary norms or agreed on general principles, but it is necessary to define the *status* of who are the citizens. Freedom from domination and arbitrary rule is achieved because those who share the status of citizenship compete equally in the democratic arena – democracy is instrumental and "rule of law simply is the democratic rule of persons" (Bellamy 2007, 83). In this view freedom is not so much the natural right of man as it is something gained through constitutional popular sovereignty. Laws and rights have no pre-political basis.

On the other hand, there must be someway to guarantee or secure equality. Therefore, a variation of the *citizen agent* position views law, not as a product, but as the *playing field* in the ongoing process of liberty. Laws structure the rules by which individual interests are expressed through contestation. Drawing upon Hobbes's early formulation of human nature as always "de-liberating" appetites and fears, there is no common good or public interest in this view. There are only private interests that interact on the playing field, and the expression of these private interests is what we call public deliberation. This position corresponds to Skinner's (2008, 34) characterization of Hobbes in his early writing where he said that "given that deliberation takes the form of 'alternate appetite; and not ratiocination', to speak of a rational will is nothing better than insignificant speech." In other words, individuals are only capable of private deliberation of their wants and fears. Public deliberation is the expression of private interests through the mediation of law. In this sense, it is a constitutional deliberation within a "proceduralist understanding of law." Habermas defines the procedural paradigm as such:

> In the proceduralist paradigm of law, the vacant places of the economic man or welfare-client are occupied by a public of citizens who participate in political communication in order to articulate their wants and needs, to give voice to their violated interests, and, above all, to clarify and settle the contested standards and criteria according to which equals are treated equally and unequals unequally. This move enlarges the perspective that previously restricted our view of the social functions of negative freedom and legally protected private autonomy.
>
> (Habermas 1996, 776)

Since the *citizen agent* position does not seek to define or agree upon universal moral principles or a common ethics, it remains open and capable of transformation in the ebb and flows of contestation of individual interests.

2. Citizen managers

A second position, which I have termed *citizen manager*, carves out separate public and private spheres of interests. The Platonic conception of *virtue* best describes citizens in this view in that when individuals fulfill their proper functions in both the public and private spheres, the result is a *virtuous* civil association. This position holds that individuals, although mainly concerned with their own private interests, are also essentially social beings who seek out the general good. Humans, in this view, deliberate within themselves and their *will* is the resolution they arrive at through this deliberation. In a separate act of deliberation they are capable of reason in regards to the common good. In this sense, they are not simply private agents, but also public managers (fiduciaries or trustees) of the common good. Representing a shift from the *citizen agent* position, law now defines and bounds the *playing field* with a set of common ethics to govern the game. As *virtuous* managers, individuals use their power of reason to deliberate the common ethics of civil association that then forms the boundaries in which they freely pursue and contest their private interests.

Theorists who espouse this view speak of a *jurisgenerative* politics of ongoing deliberation and transformation of the general laws that define and bound the public interest such that the political community remains inclusive (Michelman 1988, Sunstein 1988, Habermas 1996, 2006). Thus, a primary concern is how to arrive at the public interest as a common and vibrant ethics that is not in tension with private interests. Most theorists in this position look to a combination of the judiciary and democracy to resolve the tension between public and private interests. For example, Frank Michelman (1988, 1495) suggests the need for "normative tinkering" in which the "reconsideration of republicanism's deeper constitutional implications can remind us of how the renovation of political communities, by inclusion of those who have been excluded, enhances everyone's political freedom." Similar to Michelman, Michael Oakeshott (in *Talking About Politics*) outlines a vision of "civil association" where individuals are generally concerned with private interests, but can, at times, operate at a more general level. In this mode, citizens need "the independence of mind and judgment, the authenticity of voice, and – in some versions of republicanism – the diversity or 'plurality' of views that citizens bring to 'the debate of the commonwealth'" (Michelman 1988, 1505).

The *citizen manager* position relies on the *virtue* of individuals and relies on an optimistic view of human nature. In a slight variation, it is not *virtue* in the classical sense but rather *conditions* (Nussbaum 1996) that enable individuals to reason beyond their own personal needs. In this sense, republicanism is:

237

sensitive to both the dependence of good politics on social and economic conditions capable of sustaining 'an informed and active citizenry that would not permit
its government either to exploit or dominate one part of society or to become its
instrument,' and the dependence of such conditions, in turn, on the legal order.

(Michelman 1988, 1505)

Thus, the general ethics include rights that enable and promote action
beyond private interests such as free speech, property and privacy. In
this way the *citizen manager* position comes to resemble a liberal republicanism with liberal rights being brought in through the back door as
universal core principles that are necessary for individual and political
freedom (Sunstein 1988). Thus, there is a nonskeptical belief in the
possibility of settling at least some normative disputes with substantively
right answers. These *right answers*, however, are more of a common ethics
and not universal moral principles. Citizenship still remains an activity, manifesting itself in broadly guaranteed rights of participation. It's
the recognition that although citizenship "often occurs in nominally
private spheres, ... its primary importance is in governmental processes"
(Sunstein 1988, 1542).

Similar to the *citizen agent*, the deliberative process is one where private
interests are relevant inputs into politics; but they are not taken as pre-
political and exogenous and are instead the object of critical scrutiny
(Sunstein 1988). An essential core principle is, therefore, *equality* of
inputs and outputs in the deliberative process. Citizenship is something
that we can judge as to whether it exists in a desirable form by holding it
up to the norm of equality.

One key distinction between the *citizen agent* and *citizen manager* is
that the former conceives of citizenship as a *status* and individual freedom
as consisting in the implementation of ends that result from that status
while, for the latter, citizenship is a *function* of individual freedom and
the deliberate or reasoned selection of ends is the result of that function.
The *citizen manager* is assumed to be able to get outside of his or her
private interests, if but for a moment, in order to select a set of general
rules that recognize that sometimes private ends will be "distorted by
unjust social institutions, and the importance of increasing available
opportunities and information" (Sunstein 1988, 1557). Therefore, as
Sunstein (1988, 1579–80) points out, whereas the *Lochner* Court posited
the existence of a natural and prepolitical private sphere, one that served
as a brake on legislation, republicans believe in rights, understood as the
outcome of a well-functioning deliberative process; hence republicans

enthusiastically endorse the use of constitutionalism as a check on popular majorities.

As a jurisgenerative politics, the mode of the *citizen manager* relies on rights that will promote democratic engagement and a general set of rules of procedure in the case of disagreement, agreement and contested norms ("dialogical civic freedom"). Nondomination is secured because individuals, through their rights, are actively engaged in creating and recreating the general set of laws.

3. Citizen leaders

In a third position, which I have called *citizen leader*, law is a secular morality. It offers a *thicker* and more complex view of public *virtue* based in a common secular morality (Bickel 1975, Benhabib 2004). It is distinguishable from liberalism, however, since it is grounded in a neo-Kantian civil association and not universal rights. The type of *virtue* associated with this position is Aristotelian *moral virtue* based in friendship, participation in public life, and economic independence. Generally, this theory of government favors the pursuit of limited goals and respect for *rule of law* as the means for preserving the public order. In the *citizen leader* position, freedom consists in living within a system of common morality and, therefore, requires a certain level of homogeneity of ideas – a common history – but not ascriptive ethnic, religious, or cultural attributes (Benhabib 2004). In its Burkean version, *rule of law* exists alongside and reinforces *civility* – "manners and customs" – that makes public life possible. *Rule of Law* is the manifest constitution of structure and process. It is, thus, distinguishable from both the rights-based constitution of due process and equal protection and the metaphysical constitution of privileges and immunities. This view is republican in that the common morality is open to periodic review during "constitutional moments" (Ackerman 1993). In these constitutional moments we "[r]ecover the popular strain in republican theory" and "depart from our habitual scrutiny of the judiciary, and confront the noisy intolerance of popular participants" (Abrams 1988, 1608).

This version of the *citizen leader* promotes "institutional architects" (Abrams 1988, 1608) in addition to judicial advisers and is a distinctly Madisonian view of republican constitutionalism that distinguishes between the "Juridic Constitution" and the "Civic Constitution." John Finn (2001, 54) argues, "the Civic Constitution (as Ackerman has

239

observed but did little to advance in *We the People*), presupposes a citizenry with a sound grasp of the distinctive ideals that inspire its political practice." In distinguishing the juridic from the civic constitution, Finn is able to argue that the Civic Constitution is public while the Juridic Constitution becomes entrusted to professional and legal elites. Finn requires "thick" *citizen leaders* who know and care about the maintenance of the Constitution. He has an instrumental account of the Constitution "whose primary purpose is to constitute and enshrine a particular kind of polity; it aspires to be a public affirmation of the shared principles of national self-identity" (55).

CONSTITUTING CIVIL ASSOCIATION IN ACCORDANCE WITH THE COMMON GOOD AND EQUAL PARTICIPATION

In this section I examine the three citizen modes in terms of their position concerning how to constitute interests on behalf of the common good and guarantee equal participation in order to argue that, essential to a republican theory of *rule of law* is the view of law as (1) existing in reciprocal relationships, procedures, and politics and (2) an account of *rule of law* that enables interests to be heard, contested, translated into law and, after the laws are enacted, further contested by those who perceived their interests to have been violated.

1. Constituting interests on behalf of the common good

Each citizen mode differs in the way in which it provides for the common good because of their different understandings of the capacity of human reason and the ability of individuals to participate on behalf of public vs. private interests. Consider first the role of reason in each position. The *citizen leader* position is premised on the Hobbesian understanding that "it is Reason, not Authority, that is destructive of individuality" (Oakeshott 1962, 281–4). Hobbes, on this account, is a skeptic of the power of reasoning and, therefore, the capacity of individuals to deliberate. Therefore, the republican legal form that corresponds to this reading, offers an authority in the form of *rule of law* as secular morality, to secure freedom. It thus creates, as an authority, a public interest and, in this way, tries to resolve any tension that might arise between public and private interests by placing public interests outside of the contest.

For the *citizen agent* there are no public interests and therefore the problem regarding reason leads to the view that all we can hope for is a balance of power among competing private interests. As Bellamy (2007, 80; italics added) states: "[F]rom this perspective, the rule of law arises from a particular civic condition – one where all citizens enjoy an equal political *status* and have no domination over each other." In this view "justice emerges from a balance of power" (81) or, as Madison wrote in *Federalist* 10, pitting faction against faction. The tension between public and private interests is resolved by collapsing all interests into the private sphere. In this way, there is nothing *political* or, in the reverse, everything is *political*. Finally, the *citizen manager* position seeks to resolve the tension that arises between public and private interests due to the problems associated with human capacity to reason through the creation of common ethical rules that are renegotiated on an ongoing basis through civil association.

In all three modes law plays a role in negotiating the relationship of our public and private selves to secure the condition of equality necessary for participation. The distinction arises in the different focus in each position on how to make the addressees of a legal order equal and how to make them *authors* of the law to which they are subject. Whereas the *citizen manager* position creates an *ought* relationship of law to civil association in the form of a normative order of citizenship ("function"), for the *citizen agent* and *citizen leader* (in that it removes certain questions from public deliberation) *authority* of law in civil association *is* citizenship in fact (a "status").

This distinction has significant implications for the judicial analysis of whether legislative acts are valid expressions of the common good premised on equal participation. Consider, for example, Michelman's discussion of *Bowers vs. Hardwick*. According to Michelman, pluralists would strike down the Georgia morality-based justifications for the discriminatory sodomy law on the grounds that it denied homosexuals, as a group, a "fair shake" in the political process because of societal prejudice (that is, the *citizen agent* position or, in Bellamy's terms (Bellamy 2007), they were not part of the "contest" that made the law in the first place), whereas a republican conception of law may lead the Justices to uphold the Georgia law as an "expression of public values springing from the historically conditioned, normative persuasions of 'the people'" (1526). In this example, the former analysis is one of judging whether the *addresses* of the legal order were, in fact, citizens (which they were not because they lacked equality) while in the second analysis the judgment concerns whether they "ought" to be considered equal citizens in that they are part of the common ethics and, therefore, the remedy is their ongoing partici- pation in defining those ethics.

Thus, the solution, in the *citizen manager* "ought" position, is to guar- antee political autonomy through collective and open deliberation. Law, in this position, creates private autonomy so that individuals can freely debate. Private autonomy directly relates to and secures the guarantee of public autonomy and, in turn, public autonomy secures the conditions of private autonomy (Habermas 1996, 777). There is a mutual dependency or circular relationship:

> manifested in the genesis of valid law ... because legitimate law emerges from, and reproduces itself only in, the forms of a constitutionally regulated circulation of power, which should be nourished by the communications of an unsubverted public sphere of the lifeworld. Public sphere and civil society, the centerpiece of the new image, form the necessary context for the generation and reproduction of communicative power and legitimate law.
>
> (Habermas 1996, 777)

Consider the claim that welfare paternalism was an inadequate way to cure gender inequality because the overgeneralized/rationalized classifica- tions missed the real problem that resides in the existing institutional framework and context of a culture dominated and defined by men (Habermas 1996). The solution for all three citizen modes is to problema- tize the entire equation of gender before we will have a normative shift in regards to women. The difference is that the *citizen manager* position resolves this problem by having the affected parties themselves conduct public discourses in which they articulate the standards of comparison and justify the relevant aspects. Public autonomy is secured by promoting private autonomy (Habermas 1996, 783). Whereas the *citizen manager* uses public deliberation to secure against the use of law to promote social constructions that undermine freedom, it remains unclear how public deliberation of private interests result in law. Therefore, a variation of this position uses civil association to produce the general law that provides a critical space for learning and engaging the tensions between public and private interests (Oakeshott 1975a).

The difference in these two conceptions of public and private interests appears, in a different format, in Andreas Niederberger's work on neo- Roman republicanism and points to the way in which the relationship of public law to the framework within which we conceive of public and private interests hinges on whether we conceive of democracy as integral or merely instrumental to this framework. Niederberger (2012, 2) infers that "the republic is first of all the basic structure of public law" and "democracy is – as a more or less essential possibility to control or even steer this basic structure – one element among others of the republican rule of law." Democracy, he argues, is only instrumental in this version but can be brought into the theory as a foundational component of republican freedom. He argues that the way in which neo-Roman theory focuses on the "status" of actors ends up with no room for a "common democratic practice" since they posit that the relationship of individuals is always arbitrary. Even if we consider the contestation itself a "common democratic practice", the inability to have a common core of "interests" necessitates a "basic structure of the social space which would be comprehensive, universal or at least sufficiently general for a distinct society." In other words, the problem with all three citizen modes is that they seek to resolve the tension between public and private interests whereas, if we are to make democracy integral and a foundational component as Niederberger suggests, maintaining the tension between public and private autonomy is essential to securing freedom in civil association. In order to maintain and make use of the tension, we must conceptualize the authority of law and its relation to citizenship in such a way that equality is no longer a task of the law at all. What we need is an account of *rule of law* that enables interests to be heard, contested, and translated into law and, after the laws are enacted, further contested by those who have perceived their interests to have been violated. *Rule of Law* must be conceptualized as an activity of the citizen in maintaining the legal order and that, therefore, the moment of citizenship exists in the reciprocal relationships, procedures and politics through which law is constituted in social relations (Cicero, *On Duties* 1991).

2. Constituting equal participation

Law plays a central role in securing the conditions of either the process or the virtues of citizenship. A republican *rule of law* does not carve a private space to defend against the public, rather "a republican slant on the same issues produces a reoriented understanding: not only an appreciation of the active state's potential as an affirmative friend to effective liberty as political freedom, but an appreciation of privacy as a political right" (Michelman 1988, 1535). On the other hand, there is a tension concerning what role public law should play that revolves around whether one believes we should depend for the common good on the *virtue* of citizens or, in the alternative, assume that individuals will always pursue private interests and, thus, structure processes out of which these private interests will result in a common good.

For example, in Habermas's model of public deliberation, the *authority* of law does not depend on the actor's qualities, competences, or opportunities but instead on the forms of communication available. For Michelman, on the other hand, a process-based, republican-not-pluralist constitutional jurisprudence depends on perfectly "constituted" republican citizens who are able to engage in "a process of personal self-revision under social-dialogic stimulation" (1528). Although Michelman's analysis focuses exclusively on the courts, his theory of jurisgenerative politics places emphasis on all arenas in which citizens engage and does not focus only the most "visible" or "formal legislative assemblies" since:

> much of the country's normatively consequential dialogue occurs outside the major, formal channels of electoral and legislative politics, and that in modern society those formal channels cannot possibly provide for most citizens much direct experience of self-revisionary, dialogic engagement.
>
> (Michelman 1988, 1531)

Among the arenas he lists are "town meetings and local government agencies; civic and voluntary organizations; social and recreational clubs; schools public and private; managements, directorates and leadership groups of organizations of all kinds; workplaces and shop floors; public events and street life; and so on" (1531). It is through these arenas that "transformative dialogue" has the potential to occur. Michelman notes that "[s]uch a non-state centered notion of republican citizenship is, of course, both historically American and congenial to a characteristic strain in contemporary civic revivalism" (1532).

The common law tradition is particularly well-suited for the development of this understanding of republican law. Consider the writings of James Kent who, in his *Commentaries of American Law* discussed the proper role of Roman civil law in American Jurisprudence. Although he "expressed willingness to be guided by 'foreign jurists' in the absense of governing English law," he "drew a sharp line against such borrowing where the civil-law's treatment of 'the connexion between the government and the people' was at stake" (Morag-Levine 2006, 36). In other words, Kent saw a connection between the form of public law – common

244

or civil – and democratic citizenship and found common law more free spirited. In the late nineteenth century, "the question of codification inspired an extensive literature on the relative merits of the civil and common law traditions" and codes were viewed as "characteristic of states" which have "a despotic origin, or in which despotic power, absolute or qualified, is, or has been, predominant" (Morag-Levine 2006, 37). James C. Carter, for example, argued that "[i]n free, popular States, the law springs from, and is made by, the people," whereas codes are the instrument of a "sovereign [who] must be permitted at every step to say what shall be *the law*" (Morag-Levine 2006, 37; emphasis in original).

These tensions do not exist in isolation, but rather arise out of the specific historic context of the contested membership of citizenship today where the essential problem is how to account for ongoing transformation that can take into account diversity and constant flows of new members with conflicting and potentially mutually exclusive beliefs and moral. Through the analysis of these key tensions we can see that what remains unresolved in regards to the legal form of democratic citizenship in republican theory is a concept of civil association that maintains the tension between public interests and private interests in such a way that provides for a strong transformative capacity where democracy is a foundational component of freedom and does not depend on the *virtue* of citizens or on the *virtue* of civil association but rather on the *virtue* of an institutional process of public law conducive to the contestation and development of a common ethics. The next section explains this problem in greater detail, and the concluding section offers the outlines of a fourth mode of democratic citizenship consistent with republican theory.

The moment of citizenship today: *COURAGEOUS CITIZENS*

The question of citizenship today is essentially about transformative capacity and stems from two sets of concerns that are perceived to arise from conditions of global migration. The first set of concerns fall within the *limits of liberalism* debate and have to do with either (1) the claim that citizenship as "a bundle of rights" has failed to integrate newcomers even as it has protected their status or (2) the claim that citizenship as a "function" and as instrumental to democracy has been less than inclusive of disadvantaged groups. These core claims that pit *status* vs. *function* set

245

in motion a separate set of concerns that have to do with the impression that citizenship has been devalued.

The literature that emerged during the 1990s concerning democracy and immigration noted a friction between either (1) civic and cultural citizenship (Joppke 2000) or (2) civic and post-national citizenship (Soysal 1995, Rubio-Marin 2000, Jacobson 1997). "Civic," in each of these characterizations takes on different meanings. In the former, it is the civic understanding of the state as embedded within the liberal rights structure that serves as the opposing force to an ethnic impulse that would exclude those not deemed part of the national group and, in the latter, civic is understood as the exclusionary impulse as opposed to a human rights universal imperative for social and economic inclusion. Theorists who considered *civic* within an essentially *liberal* construct of universalized individual liberty against ethnic, organic, or communal impulses, were concerned with the split between permanent residents and full citizens. Much of this literature was concerned with this split – the idea that a constitutional democracy ought to not have a large group of people living within its borders that cannot vote or participate as *authors*, political beings in the Arendtian sense (Arendt 1973). The right of self-determination, in order to remain democratic, must provide a mechanism of naturalization of those within the territory who choose full membership. It was also concerned with what is owed to foreigners as strangers or outsiders as a civic culture committed to principles of good will and mutual aid (Walzer 1984). These theorists posited that the liberal understanding of civic tends toward inclusion and will, because of its own logic, ultimately be unable to maintain a position of exclusion toward migrants. In part because of the events of 9/11, their predictions were not born out and, instead, the rights of noncitizens were greatly curtailed.

The immigration debate, therefore, took a turn in the new millennium and has been concerned with the *value* of citizenship and the revaluation of *national* citizenship. The puzzle, however, is that the more that certain immigrants – Muslim, in particular – learned the common *liberal* rules of deliberation and accessed liberal rights, the more that the bar kept going up in terms of what a *shared* membership entailed. In other words, the more that certain immigrant groups began to *deliberate* or *contest* in the public sphere along the lines mentioned in the three citizenship modes discussed above, the more of a threat to the *liberal* state they seemed to pose. It began to seem clear that *parallel* societies were preferred as long as

246

they remained, indeed, *parallel* and did not lay any claim to the public or *civil association* in any real sense.

Certain claims to transform *civil association* are viewed as particularly threatening (for example, in France the veil in public schools) in that they have the potential to transform, through *democratic iterations*, the content of public institutions, if not their procedural forms. Certain claims on public space, which cannot be easily converted into the discourse of *interests* and *factions* but, at the same time, cannot be fully debated in public, are the greatest challenge we face in theorizing a legal form of democratic citizenship consistent with republican freedom.

All three of the legal modes of citizenship discussed above prove inadequate in terms of having the necessary capacity to constitute civil association on behalf of the common good and securing equal participation since, in each mode, law's *authority* is tied to the same "authors" who are themselves contested and possessing mutually exclusive moral-truth "world views" (Habermas 2006, 9–10). Law, therefore, must somehow play an ongoing, active, authoritative role in securing freedom from domination as the expression of shared laws. The activity of the citizen, therefore, must consist in the ongoing generation and maintenance of the legal order. Therefore, I introduce a fourth legal mode of democratic citizenship, *Courageous Citizen*, which draws upon the full potential of constitutionalism in incorporating new members in civil association as a process of "unconditional engagement of understanding" (Oakeshott 1975a, 8). New identities, in this mode, are not in need of assimilation or integration, but they rather obligate the already existing identities and the new identities to reaffirm their conditionality through the "going-on" of constitutional interrogation. The constitutional enterprise is one of making public law more intelligible not by judging identities in terms of the already existing "platforms of conditional understanding," as if these platforms are conclusive for membership in the polity, nor by:

> reidentifying them in a reconsideration of their component characteristics, nor by relating them more decisively to one another in terms of their features and of the circumstance of their occurrence, but by seeking to understand them in their postulates; that is, in terms of their conditions.
>
> (Oakeshott 1975a, 9)

In other words, the mode of *Courageous Citizens* requires a different sort of transformation than is envisioned in the other positions and better corresponds to the condition of plural societies today as one of mutually exclusive moral-truth "life-worlds" (Habermas 2006). Constitutionalism

247

is a moral position, but not in the sense of universal moral principles or values. Rather, the morality is of *rule of law* as the expression of self-disclosure and self-enactment in terms of the conditions of a noninstrumental 'practice' (Oakeshott 1975b). The mode of *courageous citizens* encourages an ongoing tension between public and private identities where multiple identities seek to understand a familiar constitutional platform in terms different from those in which it is already understood under the trust that the multiple new platforms that emerge will always, by virtue of the nature of the constitutional order itself, remain a bounded activity.

Alexander Bickel distinguished the liberal contractarian model of constitutionalism which rests on a "vision of individual rights that have a clearly defined, independent existence predating society and are derived from nature and from a natural, if imagined contract," (1975, 4) from the Whig model which "begins not with theoretical rights but with a real society" (1975, 4). He argued that the Whig model rests on a "mature skepticism" (1975, 4) but it is not value free. Thus, in this section I introduce a legal form of *courageous citizens* that stems from a "mature skepticism."

Mature skepticism takes into account that:

> [l]aw is more than just another opinion; not because it embodies all right values, or because the values it does embody tend from time to time to reflect those of a majority or plurality, but because it is the value of values. Law is the principal institution through which a society can assert its values.
>
> (1975, 5)

The values, in this account, are the expression of *moral* conduct in civil association. Although individuals come to civil association as beings possessing a moral-truth constellation, constitutionalism is an activity that requires public articulation of wants and needs. Tension between the divergent moral-truth constellations is assumed since society is plural but the various demands made in public based on needs and wants that derive from divergent moral-truth constellations must be articulated within the boundaries of the general language of the constitutional order.

In the mode of *courageous citizens*, constitutionalism is a union of public boundedness and private flexibility that generates a language of interaction between polity and mind. Whereas boundedness alone constitutes a static, repressive system, flexibility (private interests) by itself remains, in its constant flux, ultimately arbitrary. But through the ongoing tension and contestation of public and private interests we can come to see the common core that forms the boundaries of the polity. When viewed in this way, the articulations of public and private interests are variations on the common theme of the polity. In other words, just as I have shown three distinct republican forms that all fit within and are consistent with democratic citizenship, the constitutional order is a multidirectional process and has the potential to give birth to numerous realities because of the limited nature of its boundedness.

The *courageous citizen* mode is in line with Madisonian constitutionalism as espoused by John Finn, but also has significant differences. Finn's account of constitutionalism, mentioned above, that distinguishes between the "Juridic Constitution" and the "Civic Constitution" (2001, 54), argues: "The Civic Constitution (as Ackerman has observed but did little to advance in *We the People*), 'presupposes a citizenry with a sound grasp of the distinctive ideals that inspire its political practice.'" In distinguishing the juridic from the civic constitution, Finn is able to argue that the Civic Constitution is public while the Juridic Constitution becomes entrusted to professional and legal elites. Finn requires "thick" citizens who know and care about the maintenance of the Constitution. A mature skepticism, however, recognizes that even when we assume individuals can, at times, put aside their particular private interests, to reason over the common/public good, there will remain a tension between public and private interests. Thus, constitutionalism does not rely on "thick" citizens, and the goal is not to somehow arrive at a common moral or ethical constellation, but rather to understand that the ongoing public articulation of divergent moral and ethical claims when expressed through moral conduct (self-disclosure and self-enactment) produce multiple platforms and realities that correspond to the component characteristics and conditions – the boundary – of the constitutional order.

The question, then, is how to frame the process such that the following conditions are met: (1) deliberation over both public and private interests remains vibrant and (2) law does not operate in the service of one or the other. Seyla Benhabib has developed the concept of "democratic iterations" where, similar to the distinction between *moral conduct* and *moral-truth constellation* outlined above, Benhabib draws a distinction between *cultural integration* and *political integration*. She maintains that although both forms consist of "interpretation and reinterpretation, appropriation and subversion" (Benhabib 2004, 120), in:

> liberal democracies *conceptions of human and citizens' rights, constitutional traditions as well as democratic practices of election and representation*, are the *core* normative elements of political integration. It is toward them that citizens as well as

foreigners, nationals as well as resident aliens, have to show respect and loyalty, and not toward any specific cultural tradition.

(Benhabib 2004, 121–2)

At the same time, there is a "crucial interdependence of rights and identities, of political institutions and cultural communities" (Benhabib 2004, 127). To negotiate this interdependence she draws from Kant's formulation of generality and formal reciprocity to posit a postmetaphysical justification of the principle of right and says:

> instead of asking what each could will without self-contradiction to be a universal law for all, in discourse ethics we ask which norms and normative institutional arrangements would be considered valid by all those who would be affected if they were participants in special moral argumentations called discourses.
>
> (Benhabib 2004, 131–2)

These distinctions lead her to posit principles of membership that prohibit exclusion based on "the kind of being you are, your ascriptive and non-elective attributes such as your race, gender, religion, ethnicity, language community or sexuality" but permit exclusion based upon failure to show certain "qualifications, skills, and resources" deemed necessary for membership such as length of stay, language competence, civic literacy, material resources and marketable skills (Benhabib 2004, 138–9).

According to Benhabib, the grant of rights requires a bounded polity (the membership bounds in her terms are procedural not cultural) to enable the ongoing discussion, compromise and renegotiations that Benhabib says need to happen in order for integration to take place. Authority, in her theory, derives from closure and enables negotiation, compromise and constitutional growth. Moreover, she posits a dialectic between rights and identities in that "the exercise of rights themselves and the practice of political agency can change identities" (Benhabib 2004, 168). "Jurisgenerative politics" (Michelman 1988, 1502–3) as the "contestation around rights and legal institutions which themselves pave the way for *new* modes of political agency and interaction" (Benhabib 2004, 169; emphasis in original). Within this understanding of constitutionalism, "democratic iterations" – linguistic, legal, cultural, and political repetitions-in-transformation, invocations which are also revocations – change established understandings and allow for integration of new immigrant communities (Benhabib 2004, 180). Her theory, however, begs the question: In what way have constitutional rights in the

250

various contexts of Western liberal constitutionalism created the space for immigrant inclusion in a "jurisgenerative politics"?

CONCLUSION

We are now ready to return to the initial question that prompted this investigation: If we think of a distinctly republican *rule of law* how would that alter common distinctions in republican theory made between "law's" citizenship and "democracy's" citizenship? Throughout the essay I have drawn out the essential distinctions between "law's" functional citizenship that protects freedom and equality through a vision of the activity of citizenship as one of citizen managers or leaders who are responsible for the creation of a protective set of laws and "democracy's" status-centered citizenship that protects freedom and equality through a vision of the activity of citizenship one of citizen agents who are responsible to their own personal interests. How then would a distinctly republican rule of law alter these distinctions?

Although I have not yet fully developed the answer, I believe it begins with Cicero's understanding of rule of law and involves the activity of citizenship as essentialy one of reciprocal relationships engaged in the production of law. Constitutionalism is the ongoing activity of social and political relations through the medium of law. Unlike the jurisgenerative politics outlined by Benhabib, which is based on universal principles to define the terms of membership, a distinctly republican rule of law defines the terms of membership as the ongoing engagement in reciprocal relationships. Thus, a jurisgenerative politics of citizenship has a transformative capacity horizontally (immigrants, minorities, generations), vertically (governing institutions and civil society) and spatially across time (generations). The main problem is how to cope with the insecurity generated by the true nature of constitutionalism and, for this, we require *Courageous Citizens*.

REFERENCES

Abrams, K. (1988). "Law's Republicanism." *Yale Law Journal* 97: 1591–608.

Ackerman, B. (1993). *We the People, Vol. 1: Foundations*. Cambridge, MA: Harvard University Press.

Arendt, H. (1973). "The Decline of of the Nation and the End of the Rights of Man". In: *Origins of Totalitarianism*. New York: Harcourt, Brace.

Bellamy, R. (2007). *Political Constitutionalism*. Cambridge: Cambridge University Press.

Benhabib, S. (2004). *The Rights of Others: Aliens, Residents, and Citizens*. Cambridge: Cambridge University Press.

Bickel, A. (1975). *The Morality of Consent*. New Haven: Yale University Press.

Finn, J. E. (2001). "The Civic Constitution: Some Preliminaries." In: *Constitutional Politics*. Eds S. Barber and R. George, Princeton: Princeton University Press: 41–69.

Griffin, M. T. and E. M. Atkins (eds) (1991). *Cicero: On Duties*. Cambridge: Cambridge University Press.

Habermas, J. (1996). "Paradigms of Law." *Cardozo Law Review* 17: 771–84.

Habermas, J. (2006). "Religion in the Public Sphere." *European Journal of Philosophy* 14: 1–25.

Hobbes, T. (1997). *Leviathan: Authoritative Text, Backgrounds, Interpretations*, 1st edn. Eds R. E. Flathman and D. Johnston, New York: Norton & Co.

Jacobson, D. (1997). *Rights across Borders: Immigration and the Decline of Citizenship*. Baltimore: Johns Hopkins University Press.

Joppke, C. (2000). *Immigration and the Nation-State*. Oxford: Oxford University Press.

Michelman, F. I. (1988). "Law's Republic." *Yale Law Journal* 97: 1493–537.

Michelman, F. I. (1996). "Family Quarrel." *Cardozo Law Review* 17: 1163–77.

Morag-Levine, N. (2006). "Judges, Legislators, and Europe's Law: Common-Law Constitutionalism and Foreign Precedents." *Maryland Law Review* 65: 32–48.

Niederberger, A. (2012). "Republican Rule of Law and Democracy." Unpublished Manuscript.

Nussbaum, M. (1996). "Patriotism and Cosmopolitanism." In: *For Love of Country?* Ed. J. Cohen, Boston: Beacon Press: 3–17.

Oakeshott, M. (1962). "On Hobbes." In: M. Oakeshott. *Rationalism in Politics and Other Essays*, Indianapolis: Liberty Fund: 219–359.

Oakeshott, M. (1975a). *Hobbes on Civil Association*. Berkeley: University of California Press.

Oakeshott, M. (1975b). *On Human Conduct*. Oxford: Oxford University Press.

Pettit, P. (1997). *Republicanism: A Theory of Freedom and Government*. Oxford: Oxford University Press.

Pettit, P. (2008). *Made with Words: Hobbes on Language, Mind, and Politics*. Princeton: Princeton University Press.

Rubio-Marin, R. (2000). *Immigration as a Democratic Challenge: Citizenship and Inclusion in Germany and the United States*. Cambridge: Cambridge University Press.

Sheldon, G. W. and C. W. Hill, Jr. (2008). *The Liberal Republicanism of John Taylor of Caroline*. Madison: Fairleigh Dickenson University Press.

Skinner, Q. (2008). *Hobbes and Republican Liberty*. Cambridge: Cambridge University Press.

Soysal, Y. (1995). *Limits of Citizenship: Migrants and Postnational Membership in Europe*. Chicago: University of Chicago Press.

Sunstein, C. (1988). "Beyond the Republican Revival." *Yale Law Journal* 97: 1539–90.

Walzer, M. (1984). *Spheres of Justice: A Defense of Pluralism and Equality*. New York: Basic Books.

CHAPTER 10

Rights, Republicanism and Democracy
Richard Bellamy

INTRODUCTION

Rights are often seen as republicanism's Achilles' heel. Even certain friends of republican arguments fear its tendency to privilege democracy risks undermining respect for individual rights. As a result, they have suggested that we need to produce a marriage between liberalism and republicanism (for example, Dagger 1997, and in many respects Habermas 1996). Here I want to take a different tack and suggest that rights imply democracy rather than being a constraint upon it. By that I do not mean, as some have argued, that rights are implied by democracy – that all rights can be seen as somehow inherent components of a democratic process. Some, such as the right to vote, obviously are, but others, such as the right not to be tortured, have no intrinsic link to the democratic process (Jones 1994, 173–4). Rather, I wish to argue that rights claims can only be justified in democratic terms – as claims made under conditions of political equality. This understanding of rights is quite different to the deontological account standardly offered by liberal theories that hark back to the natural rights tradition. That account sits with a view of liberty as noninterference, which sees its main object as the restriction of law and government. By contrast, the democratic account of rights belongs to the republican view of freedom as nondomination. Here, rights reflect the common avowable interests of citizens and are both political in origin and in execution. On this account, the liberal view of a right against democracy appears both unjustifiable and incoherent.

The argument proceeds as follows. I start by showing how the very nature of a rights claim implies a democratic process in which citizens have the status of political equals when formulating collective decisions that are to apply equally to all. I then relate this democratic argument for rights to the republican conception of liberty as nondomination, rejecting along the way the liberal account of rights as trumps and its origins in a view of freedom as noninterference. Finally, I explore how this association of rights and democracy exists not simply at an ideal level but needs to be actualized within a real democratic process of a kind akin to the systems of actually existing democracies, with their combination of one person one vote, majority rule, and regular elections between competitive parties. Moreover, the normative and logical status of rights as intrinsically democratic in their mode of justification and application greatly circumscribes the legitimacy of using judicial and other non- or countermajoritarian mechanisms to uphold rights against democracy (Bellamy 2007).

Rights, political equality and democracy

Rights theorists working within the mainstream liberal tradition typically distinguish human and natural from institutional rights on the grounds that the former are in some sense prior to politics (Jones 1994, 73). That is to say, they are either moral entitlements that human beings could and ought to be granted even in a putative state of nature, such as freedom from physical assault, or – more demandingly – they encompass those basic interests of human beings that all political communities should seek to secure not just for their members but also for nonmembers. In other words, such rights should either exist outside of any polity, or be realized within and upheld by all polities. As such, they define the boundaries, foundations and to some extent the goals of politics (Jones 1994, 75–81).

So conceived, rights readily appear as constraints on democracy. Rights can be viewed as "trumping" those political decisions that curtail or fail to promote them. Yet, their apparent status as somehow prior to and above politics proves hard to sustain. Rights are sometimes presented as a two-term relation, whereby x has a right to some y. That gives rights a somewhat peremptory sounding character. However, rights are always a three-term relation, whereby x asks some z to recognize and respect his or her claim to y, with attendant costs and benefits to z who will wish x to likewise recognize either his or her similar claim to y, or to some other good such as v. That is true even of a Hohfeldian "liberty-right," whereby all that is being asked of others is that they have "no right" to prevent its exercise (see Jones 1994, 12–14, 17–22 for a discussion of Hohfeld's classification of rights and of liberty rights in particular). For such forbearance may itself be controversial, as in certain instances of someone exercising a liberty-right to do what might be commonly regarded as wrong (Waldron 1981). Therefore, x and z need to agree on rights and their respective correlative duties, or the lack of them, in given situations. It is this need for a collective agreement on which rights we possess, when and where, what their implications may be in a given case, how they interact with other rights, and which policies and procedures might be most suited to realizing them, that places rights within what Albert Weale and Jeremy Waldron have called the "circumstances of politics" (Weale 2007, 12–18; Waldron 1999, 107–13). For, these are all matters on which we may reasonably disagree yet need a common decision, producing the need for a political mechanism of some kind to resolve our disputes.

Theorists of natural and human rights have tended to assume away such disagreements. They have sought to ground their case for at least a set of basic rights on their "self-evident" character as dictates of reason, divine law, or essential elements of human well-being (Jones 1994, 96–7). Yet, self-evidence "is not a very promising foundation for rights" (Jones 1994, 97). What leads us to identify specific features of human beings or human sociability as "natural," "basic" or "divinely ordained" depends ultimately on the moral theories we hold for which the specified capacities prove important. The upshot is that appeals to human nature and other supposedly "objective" and "universal" foundations of rights reflect rival ontological claims for which no generally agreed epistemology exists with the capacity to mediate between them. Even where there is agreement on the rather abstract set of general rights found in International Human Rights Conventions or the domestic Bills of Rights, there can be disagreement about what they involve in practice with regard to a given case (Jones 1994, 224–5). These disagreements need not reflect self-interest or bad faith – although on occasion they clearly do so, as in the case of regimes whose reluctance to recognize rights results from their oppression of their subject populations. Rather, disagreements – such as one finds in most democratic countries – may simply issue from what Rawls has called "the burdens of judgement ... the many hazards involved in the correct (and conscientious) exercise of our powers of reason and judgement in the ordinary course of political life" (Rawls 1993, 55–6). On Rawls's account, these burdens range from the different life experiences people bring to the assessment of a situation, to the multiple normative considerations likely to be involved and the difficulties of relating them to the often complex empirical evidence. Although he believed that these "burdens" only applied to conceptions of the good, they clearly also produce different understandings of the right. People may reasonably hold differing views of not only the sources and substance of rights, but also their subjects and scope, and how they might best be secured (Bellamy 2001). Thus, Nozickian libertarians, Ricardian socialists, Rawlsean social democrats and Burkean conservatives all offer different accounts of the origins and extent of property rights and their relationship to other rights, which are expressed to different degrees, albeit usually in a less abstruse or sophisticated manner, in the everyday political debates of all mature democracies. At the level of principle, these disputes have not proved any more resolvable in the seminar rooms of philosophy departments than they have among policy-makers and citizens.

As I remarked, such reasonable ontological and epistemological disagreements about the nature of rights mean that the determination of which rights we have and how they should be upheld requires a political process. However, not just any kind of process will do if it is to be consistent with both the very idea of rights, as something possessed and claimable by all, and the reasonableness of these disagreements about them. The argument that best fits these two criteria would appear to be something like the fairness argument for democracy. According to this view, if the interests of individuals are equally affected by the overall decisions of the community to which they belong, and we follow J. S. Mill in regarding each individual as the best guardian of his or her own interest, then fairness dictates that they should all be able to play an equal part in the political process that makes those decisions (Jones 1994, 180). On the one hand, decisions about rights are ones in which those affected will have an equal stake over the long term and taking into account the full range of decisions. So we need a process that will treat all as political equals in reaching mutually acceptable agreements such as a system of majoritarian decision making on the basis of equal votes offers. On the other hand, majoritarian voting per se is not tied to any of the arguments – voters can vote for any position and for any reason. As such, it delivers a fair and neutral process for deciding which position can claim the most public support as being in the collective interest (May 1952).

So conceived, the choice of democracy is not purely pragmatic. It follows from the very idea of rights and certain structural features of any claim to a right and the disagreements that will surround it. First, although there are many different arguments for human rights, it is an intrinsic feature of all of them that since rights attach to human beings as such they apply equally to all. Second, and relatedly, although rights connect to individuals we have seen how they have a collective dimension. A right is not claimed solely for the individual in question but as a right that can be held and upheld equally by all other individuals – hence the need for a process to collectively agree on the right. Moreover, for the right to be collectively held and upheld requires not just each individual doing his or her bit according to some commonly agreed norm, but also common, publicly provided, structures – at a minimum a legal system and the means for law enforcement, such as a police force, courts, prisons. So secured, rights function in many ways like what Raz (1986, 198–9) has called an inherent public good: That is, they promote common benefits that we must collectively produce through our attitudes to others and in which we can all equally share – a point to which I return below. Finally, we have noted how rights also operate as claims against those in authority. They imply that certain things should not be done or should not be denied to any individual.

These three aspects of rights point toward a core claim that underpins all rights claims: namely, the claim by each individual to be treated as a political equal who owes and deserves equal concern and respect to and from every other individual in the shared arrangements that frame his or her social life, a claim that must also be acknowledged by the authorities charged with administering these arrangements. The intimate link between democracy and rights arises from this core claim. For, democracy offers the only forum where different rights claims can be made and the collective structures necessary for their realization can be provided in a way that is consistent with rights claimants recognizing their fellow citizens, with their potentially rival claims, as deserving of equal concern and respect, and ensuring that the public authorities are responsive to their collective disagreements and deliberations about rights. Democracy offers a means for making decisions in which all meet as political equals to make reciprocal claims on one another when framing common policies, and can hold governments to account when they fail to reflect their preferences. In this way, the democratic process grants what Hannah Arendt (1958, 296) termed the "right to have rights." I am not thereby implying that all rights are intrinsic to democracy. As I noted above, not all rights relate to the democratic process. What I am arguing is that all rights involve a democratic form of justification – they imply a spirit of political equality to be accorded equal concern and respect that can only be achieved through a democratic process.

RIGHTS AND INDIVIDUAL LIBERTY: LIBERAL AND REPUBLICAN PERSPECTIVES

Seeing rights as somehow intrinsically democratic might be thought to subvert their aforementioned "traditional political purpose," that of telling "those who wield political power what they may and may not do" (Jones 1994, 222). However, that perception arises from aligning that "traditional" understanding of the function of rights with the liberal conception of liberty as noninterference. By contrast, when that purpose is linked to the republican conception of liberty as nondomination – a view that more accurately accords with the nature of rights claims as delineated above – then democracy emerges as a necessary, even if not always sufficient, condition for its realization.

Liberalism, rights and freedom as non-interference

The liberal notion of freedom as noninterference seems to capture what many see as the central aspect of rights: namely, that there are certain things nobody should be allowed to do to another individual, such as torture, or prevent them from doing, such as exercising their freedom of speech. Given that such rights only require the forbearance of others, they ought to be compossible – able to be held by all others – by their very nature, and so be nonnegotiable because of their not requiring negotiation. Not all rights may be of this kind, but those that are offer some of the most important safeguards for individuals. On this account, there is no role for democracy to play in their formulation or maintenance – as noted above, they may even need to be exercised against democratic decisions.

Rights to noninterference seem the best candidates for being in some sense pre- and possibly antipolitical. Indeed, all law becomes inimical to rights in being a form of interference, albeit potentially necessary to render them secure. This approach offers the paradigm of the view of rights as trumps that are held by individuals against the collectivity. Such rights seek to drive a wedge between the right and any notion of the common good, offering preconditions for each and every individual to pursue his or her own good in his or her own way. Yet, even rights of this form cannot be isolated from the "circumstances of politics." For they will

258

not be immune from disputes as to their definition; from conflicts between the uses of these rights by different people as well as with other rights; or from the need for the intervention of public laws and collective structures to realize them. All these issues prove political in the broad sense noted above. For, they require a collective decision over the content and scope of these rights that will rest on value judgments concerning their purpose and nature – the public good or goods they serve – that allow for reasonable disagreement.

Thus, there may be agreement that no one should be tortured and all authorities and individuals should simply refrain from doing so, but interpretative disputes nevertheless exist as to whether certain punishments shade into torture or not – think of the arguments in the United States over whether the death penalty is per se "cruel and unusual" or only certain methods for delivering it. It might be countered that although the practical meaning and implementation of this right are political, the right itself is not – it is a moral right that attaches to individuals as something one simply should not do to any person – hence the aforementioned agreement that torture is wrong. As I noted above, however, the moral force of even the most basic human rights does not follow from our humanity per se but the moral theory we hold, and people can and do have different views about the morality of torture, not all of which are rights-based. These differences will always prove relevant because the circumstances in which even a right such as this arises is always political to the extent that the claim is made against other persons and requires institutions or at least an agreement to be reliably enforced among them. There is no right of the individual as such, but only of the social individual within a political and legal context (Bellamy 2010, 416–20). Indeed, the historical origins of a right not to be tortured lie not in an absolutist view that this right ought to be upheld whatever the consequences, but because it was regarded as ineffective as a means for extracting evidence and as corrupting of those who employed it. It was the general utility of torture as a means for upholding the rights of the public, rather than the right of an individual regardless of its affect on the public, that led to its abolition (Beccaria 1995). A political agreement on the public meaning and the good served by this right, as well as the best means to uphold it, are not additional to or potentially at odds with the nature of such a right: They are essential to its definition and justification.

Similar debates arise in the case of free speech and whether incitement or libel count as speech. Here, however, there is the additional issue of how a right the exercise of which appears to simply involve forbearance can nonetheless clash with its similar exercise by others. We regard rights as important not simply for a single individual but for all individuals. If a right to free speech is to be collectively exercised we will need rules of order so we do not always all speak at once so that nobody can be heard above the cacophony, and there may be uses of that right that subvert other rights of individuals, as is the case with slander, hate speech or the leaking of official secrets. Finally, such conflicts also mean that although many rights may appear simply to depend on an absence of interference, making them available to all will require intervention by public authorities to facilitate their use and guard against their abuse or subversion. It might be argued that we should simply seek to interfere as little as possible with the right in question so as to maximize its availability to all. Yet, what counts as interference is normatively laden (O'Neill 1979/80), as are the choices of what arrangements might maximally enhance a right in given circumstances. Some will regard certain omissions as well as acts as forms of interference, for example, or see threats and intimidation as potentially as inhibiting as physical force; others will not. Likewise, some may see an equal right as requiring no more than an equal chance to exercise it, such as may be achieved by a lottery, others that it be exercisable to an equal extent – with both views proving highly contestable even in their own terms, especially when it comes to establishing them in practice.

In collectively evaluating the nature and limits of rights and providing common means for their realization, as we have seen is necessary, the right comes to fall within, rather than being separate from, potentially opposed to and "trumping," the common or public good. For the rights that will be viewed as commanding the equal concern and respect of all citizens will be those that correspond to their commonly avowable interests and that therefore provide an equal benefit to all. Indeed, not to align rights with the public good in this way has the perverse effect of making rights seem like the privileges of particular individuals rather than the universal entitlements of all citizens – an aristocratic rather than a democratic view. As Raz has noted with regard to free speech (Raz 1994, 54), issues such as libel and slander make it implausible to see free speech as the right of each and every individual to say whatever he or she wants regardless of its more general effects on the rights of others. It also seems odd to suggest that we have an interest in this right for our own personal use as individuals in order to vent our frustrations in monologs delivered in front of the bathroom mirror – satisfying though this may be on occasion. It is also the case that few of us are likely to be opinion-formers or whistle-blowers either. So we do not necessarily have a personal interest in exercising this right ourselves. Rather, we all have an equal interest in the benefits of free debate and criticism of public policy by the comparatively small group of people with the time and expertise to participate in such – politicians, journalists, those with specialist knowledge in a given area and so on – and in the possibility of joining that group being equally open to all, including ourselves should we feel motivated to do so. An equal right to free speech is thus instrumental to securing a public good rather than distinct from any such good. Hence, the common rules and structures that we favor for regulating free speech are those that we believe best serve that public purpose – for, these are the rights all should and could have. Once such structures are in place, their role is to provide an equal and common benefit for all rather than a privilege for an individual to indiscriminately berate his or her neighbors or business rivals out of spite or for personal profit.

Republicanism, rights and freedom as nondomination

Rights, then, cannot be removed from politics. Instead, we need a form of politics that is consistent with their character. As we saw at the end of the first section, rights involve a core claim to be treated with equal concern and respect – both by one's fellow citizens in the shared arrangements that coordinate social life, and by the public authorities empowered to oversee them. Consequently, a political process for collectively claiming and deciding on rights will need to possess three key features. First, it must show equal respect for the different views of individuals as rights bearers. Second, it should also demonstrate equal concern for their capacity to employ their rights on the same terms as others. As such, it will need to be doubly collective – a process that involves all the public on an equal basis and promotes those rights and conceptions of rights that best reflect commonly avowed interests. Third, it will have to answer to the "traditional purpose" of rights as means for holding power to account and marking its limits.

Unlike the classic liberal view of freedom as noninterference, the republican notion of nondomination captures this core claim underlying rights by offering a normative basis for these three requirements of a justified rights generating political process. On this account, freedom and rights belong not to an asocial agent outside all social and institutional arrangements and able to do what he or she wants because of the lack of interference with or by others, but rather is a civic achievement of socially situated individuals whose relations are regulated by law. What gives these legal arrangements their liberty-preserving quality lies in them being formulated by free and equal citizens who are not bound to any master but rather negotiate their collective arrangements together as political equals in order to arrive at policies that serve the common good rather than the partial and potentially dominating interests of particular powerful individuals or factions. The rights that arise from these arrangements still reflect the ways in which citizens tell those in power what they may or may not do. Yet, citizens achieve that "traditional purpose" through claiming their rights through laws that apply equally to all – including their rulers – and which they ultimately control through a democratic process that shows each of them equal concern and respect as autonomous individuals.

Freedom as nondomination is not inimical to politics and law in the same way as freedom as noninterference (Pettit 1997, chap. 2). Its aim is to achieve freedom from the arbitrary rule of a master rather than freedom from any rule. Rights play a part in that achievement, but they are the rights of citizens not the natural rights of human beings that could be held either outside of any society, or as members of any society. Rather, they result from the laws that citizens give themselves as equal members of a polity.

The view of rights as existing outside and potentially against politics, and hence able to trump a democratic process, overlooks how rights are claims made by citizens on fellow citizens within a social and political setting. Two key errors flow from this oversight. First, it ignores the fact, explored above, that the rights claims of one individual affect those of other individuals. As we have seen, rights do not attach to human beings as such within a putative state of nature. They belong to and reflect a given social context and the public goods it provides for those who exist within and support it. An individual claiming a right is not the only person possessing trumps. All those he or she he is claiming against possess trumps, too. The trumping metaphor ceases to be useful in this context. At best, one can argue that there are some especially weighty claims that individuals may have that need to be weighed in the balance with the similarly weighty claims of other individuals. Second, these trumps have already been played in the democratic process where we decide what rights the legal system should enshrine within the relevant legislation (Waldron 1999, 12). Legislators and indirectly those who have elected them can all express their views on rights in framing legislation and seek to have protected their most basic interests and core views. All effectively play their trumps, but only on the same terms as everyone else. Therefore, in making a claim against a democratic decision, the rights claimer is illegitimately attempting to play his or her cards again, and in the process is failing to treat his or her fellow citizens with the equal concern and respect that rights demand.

What, however, do we do in the case of those who do not have access to any or to the relevant democratic institutions – who either live in non-democratic states or outside a given democratic state, be it as a stateless person or as a citizen of a different state – yet have a claim against the democratic decisions of a state that has adversely affected them? Surely, human rights claims often arise in their most powerful and urgent forms precisely in such situations, where either no democratic redress is available or democratic processes have ignored the interests of those excluded from them. Indeed, many established democratic systems have excluded certain members of the political community in the past – women, those without property, ethnic minorities, among other groups – and many continue to do so. All of this is undeniable. And yet, the claims such groups make can be seen primarily as claims for inclusion within the democratic community – to be treated as political equals.

Far from overlooking the claims of the excluded, the republican account has decided advantages over the liberal in this regard. For the liberal view can be used by the privileged to mandate such exclusions to prevent unjustified interferences with their entitlements – be it the property rights of the rich or the sovereignty of wealthy states. By contrast, the republican view mandates inclusion as a political equal within the decision-making processes of those powerful bodies capable of exercising domination over our lives. These may be public bodies – the state or its agencies – or private bodies, such as large corporations or financial institutions. The liberal language of human or natural rights leaves the unprivileged outside the city walls, as mere petitioners for redress by the privileged within, who may deploy these self-same rights to deny any civic responsibility for these others. The republican approach brings all rights-claimants within the city walls, giving them access to the political mechanisms required to offer them redress. Yet that brings the obligations as well as the privileges of citizenship – not least the duty to take the rights claims of others as seriously as they take their own. Unsurprisingly, the evidence shows that rights will only be reliably upheld where the democratic mechanisms exist for them to be claimed in this way, and that rights are just as reliably ignored and infringed where such mechanisms are absent (Christiano 2011). It is to the specific virtues of actually existing democracy that we now turn.

RIGHTS AND DEMOCRACY: REAL AND IDEAL

A number of theorists have acknowledged the democratic character of rights in framing their accounts in terms of an idealized democratic process – be it the rights that must be presupposed by free and equal dialog or discourse with another, or that would be agreed to, or could not be reasonably rejected in, circumstances where all participants are equally situated with regard to one another and none has power over another. This democratic argument for rights has been most explicitly stated by Jürgen Habermas (for example, 1998, chap. 10). Yet a parallel argument also informs John Rawls's *Political Liberalism*, where he characterizes his first principle of justice as reflecting an agreement between idealized citizens of a liberal democratic state as the necessary conditions for them to coexist as political equals (Rawls 1993, 3). However, this idealized argument of the foundations of rights does not necessarily entail a practical commitment to the use of real democratic systems to uphold them. First, both Habermas (1996, 304, 486) and Rawls (1993, 232–3) seek to distinguish constitutional from normal politics, regarding the more general and public debate they associate with the one as legitimately constraining and providing the norms underlying the other (for a critique see Bellamy 2007, chap. 3). Second, both see constitutional courts as exemplifying a more ideal form of democratic discourse than real democratic processes. Habermas (1996, 263, 278–9) argues that courts can review democratic decisions on procedural grounds to ensure they have issued from a duly democratic process, while Rawls (1993, 157, 161) maintains that they may review them on substantive grounds as well in order to ensure that certain non-democratic rights have not been infringed, thereby removing certain rights from politics altogether. Finally, and as a corollary of this last point, both see litigation as a form of democratic participation.

This section challenges and qualifies all three of these arguments. I shall argue that idealized, court-based democracy is no substitute for real democracy. If political equality is necessary for all to be treated with equal

264

concern and respect as both the claimers and the duty bearers of rights within the circumstances of politics, then no purely ideal account of democracy can substitute for the real democratic practices and participation. Such ideal theories risk being entirely circular, so construing the democratic process that it favors their preferred view of rights. Nor can any abstract theory be so specific as to incorporate all the features that figure within actual contexts – not least the very diverse life experiences and concerns of those involved.

I shall start by outlining the constitutional qualities of normal democratic politics. The superiority of real democratic systems over courts lies in their providing a mechanism for identifying the legislative embodiment of rights most likely to track the commonly avowed interests of citizens by treating them with equal concern and respect. It achieves that result through providing a means for citizens to reach agreements in conditions of political equality. On this account, so-called "normal politics" is constitutional politics, for it allows the ongoing legislative enactment of rights in the democratic terms required to justify and legitimately realize rights claims. I then turn to an examination of courts and argue that far from offering a more ideal version of this process, courts lack the fundamental democratic quality of allowing an equal input from all affected citizens – their "right" to author their rights. Nor can their interpretation of a constitutional document that may at some stage have had democratic legitimation in a referendum be regarded as offering a democratic basis for their judgments, isolated as these are from democratic views of the current citizenry. Meanwhile, the distinction between procedural and substantive review proves hard to sustain. Not only are the rights inherent to a democratic process as contentious as those that lie outside it, with the latter (as I noted) often more basic and important than the former, but also judgments on what counts as a due process turn to a considerable degree on views of the nature of an appropriate outcome. However, if the courts cannot provide a forum for what Pettit (2000, 116–17) terms "authorial" democracy, they can provide a venue for what he calls "editorial" or contestatory democracy for those groups that may not have had voice in the democratic determination of the right. Litigation can play a democratic role here. However, such "editorial" democracy is necessarily weaker than, and subordinate to, "authorial" democracy – it offers the basis for a weak form of judicial review that can be overridden by the legislature.

The authorial merits of real democracy

Democratic systems have undeniable defects and although they can be improved must always be expected to fall short of the ideal. However, much the same can be said of any human institution – including courts. So, in advocating courts as correctives for the mistakes of democratically elected and accountable executives and legislatures it is necessary to bear in mind the mistakes that they will also make. The key question has to be whether courts possess practical and normative qualities that render them more likely to uphold rights and to do so in more justified ways than democratic systems may. In posing this question, I do not wish to deny that courts and democratic mechanisms have various complementary qualities, with each being best supplemented by the other – a point I return to below. However, their complementarity per se is not at issue here. Rather, the central point is which should have constitutional supremacy in defining whether rights have been upheld or not. Political systems, such as the United States, which have strong rights-based judicial review, hand over that decision to a supreme or constitutional court that can disapply laws they believe infringe rights. But many other systems – such as the United Kingdom and Nordic countries like Finland and Norway – have traditionally had far weaker forms of judicial review and give more power on these matters to legislatures and special parliamentary committees. In what follows, I shall argue that the use of these legislative as opposed to judicial mechanisms for rights protection can be justified not just on pragmatic grounds but also for normative reasons to do with the democratic character of rights. For these normative arguments can never be embodied as fully in judicial practices as they are in legislative ones.

As I have argued elsewhere (Bellamy 2007, chap. 6), the key constitutional quality of actually existing democratic systems arises from their combining majority rule with a dynamic form of the balance of power that results from electoral competition between parties. This combination allows such systems to meet the requirement for political equality demanded of a republican notion of freedom as nondomination, thereby allowing rights to be considered in ways consistent with equal concern and respect, on the one side, and the blocking of arbitrary uses of power by those in government, on the other. Majority rule offers a fair decision procedure for resolving disagreements that gives all involved an equal voice, thereby satisfying the need for equal respect. Electoral competition in societies typified by cross-cutting cleavages, and where the main policy differences can be plotted on a left–right continuum, obliges voters indirectly and politicians vying for power directly to "hear the other side," thereby meeting the requirement for equal concern. For, to build a majority, parties – or coalitions of parties – must bring together the preferences of as many different groupings among the electorate as possible. The result is that the rival party blocks tend to converge on the median voter, which usually represents the Condorcet winner on a pair wise comparison of the various policy preferences of the electorate as a whole (Ordeshook 1986, 245–57). As research on the relationship of party manifestos to government policies has shown (Klingermann, Hofferbert and Budge 1994), within democracies that have these characteristics there is a reasonably high correlation between the electoral campaign and the legislative program of the successful parties. Moreover, governments in such systems inevitably operate under the shadow of the coming election, and so remain accountable to shifts in electoral opinion. They have an ever-present incentive to formulate polices that are non-arbitraty because they track public interests – those that will coincide with respecting the views of most citizens and addressing their common concerns as far as possible.

In this scenario, the prospects of any tyranny of the majority are low (McGann 2004). Those who lose consistently will be groups at the extremes of the political spectrum, who have failed to modify their views sufficiently to be able to link up with other sections of the electorate. It is not that their rights have been denied, for they have had the right to express their views on which rights ought to be available and in what ways (Tushnet 1999, 159). Their opinions about rights and the interests that lie behind them have been treated on an equal basis to everyone else's. However, they have not managed to convince their fellow citizens that their view of rights would treat all those affected by its implementation with equal concern and respect. And that failure largely results from not heeding the equally important rights claims of a sufficient number of their fellow citizens, so that the costs and benefits of any collective policy on rights can be shown to be fairly shared by all.

This argument will not satisfy a rights theorist who holds that rights attach to individuals outside of any social or political arrangements and should be respected regardless of their costs to others. However, the previous section showed this position to beself-defeating, since it involves a violation of rights itself. The justification of any rights claim needs to be on the grounds that it offers an equal recognition of the mutual rights claims of those others who will have the correlative duty to uphold it.

267

Given disagreement about rights, the best available way of mediating between rival claims is via a fair process in which each person's views is treated on a par with everyone else's and there is encouragement for all to accommodate the preferences of everyone else so far as they can. As we saw, such a process can be regarded as reflecting the democratic spirit that lies at the heart of any reasonable rights claim. It also provides a means for realizing freedom as nondomination, for it attempts to allow only those interferences that track common avowable interests – that is those interests that can be avowed politically as showing equal concern and respect to those involved in a shared social scheme through functioning as a public good in the sense mentioned earlier. What I have now argued is that actual democratic systems offer a realistic approximation to such a rights-promoting process.

Courts as unreal democracy

Nevertheless, there will certainly be occasions when democratic mechanisms – either inadvertently or otherwise – do not treat all interests equitably or do not accommodate certain key concerns sufficiently. Certain persons affected by collective decisions may be excluded from the decision-making process altogether, or may be ignored by others due to prejudice or because they are too small and dispersed a group to have any hope of being able to organize themselves so as to be electorally significant. Electorates may also act myopically or may be misinformed. In any democratic system there is also the possibility that certain constituencies may prove to have disproportionate influence or others none at all, with the result that electoral decisions may register false positives or false negatives. In these situations, many have thought that courts may offer a legitimate safeguard against democratic failures – not least because their processes can claim a certain democratic legitimacy of their own.

Two related claims are made in this regard. First, courts – especially constitutional courts – employ a form of public reasoning and deliberation that is more truly democratic than a standard electoral process. Judges are not only trained to apply the law impartially, so that it applies equally to all, but they also are bound to justify their arguments in terms of constitutional rights norms that themselves reflect the upshot of an ideal democratic process – the norms (roughly speaking, the main liberal civil and political and even certain socioeconomic rights) that anyone who accepted democracy would regard as necessary to secure participation as an equal within the public sphere broadly construed. The judiciary's independence from electoral pressures means they are less swayed by the need to pander to popular prejudices. Instead they can ask whether legislation could be regarded as consistent with a publically justified reading of these rights. As I noted, this argument may be interpreted in either a substantive manner, as relating to the outcome of democratic decisions (Rawls 1993, Lecture VI; Dworkin 1996, Introduction), or in a procedural manner, with regard to the processes by which democratic decisions are made (Ely 1980; Habermas 1996, chap. 6). Second, litigation is itself a form of participation. In particular, it allows legislation to be contested on the basis that it fails to meet the standards of equity and fairness inherent to democracy by giving those unable to get an adequate hearing in the regular political process a chance to voice their concerns (Kavanagh 2003).

Both these claims for courts to offer a better and more ideal democratic forum for the authorship of rights than real democracy can be challenged. For a start, we have seen that constitutional rights norms can be subject to reasonable disagreements, especially when applied to particular cases. Given that the decisions of multimember courts are often made on the basis of a majority vote, the judiciary can clearly disagree as much as the rest of the population. Yet, their disagreements need not be representative of, or responsive to, the electorate as a whole. That may be no bad thing if we had grounds for regarding their disagreements as somehow resulting from more "rights-responsive" reasons to those of the general public. But it is not obvious why that should be the case. The fact that they refer to rights in their reasoning does not of itself necessarily mean that their views of them are especially conscientious, better informed, or less biased than other people's. In fact, they may well be less so than politicians who precisely because they need to engage with the views of the electorate have to be aware of the affect of a particular way of interpreting and implementing rights on the lives and interests of those they represent. Each citizen's views may be partial, but the nature of the electoral contest makes politicians' views rather less so as they have to appeal across the board. By contrast, the danger is that the views of the judiciary are simply arbitrary from the public's perspective – they are merely the views of those individuals on the bench.

It will be objected that judicial reasoning is constrained by precedent and law. However, neither of these constraints per se can be regarded as necessarily producing a more objectively correct view of rights. If there was a clear methodology for arriving at the right answer on moral questions, then there would no longer be such disagreement about these issues – but no agreed method exists. At best, we have rival methods, each of which tends to exist in a circular relation to the view it wishes to promote. Meanwhile, not only is precedent a notoriously weak constraint – especially when dealing with hard or novel cases of the kinds that typically give rise to judicial review, but also it and legal reasoning more generally may in so far as they do apply be inappropriate constraints. If courts are tied by precedent, then that implies a status quo bias that hinders those cases that might rightly challenge previous decisions. Likewise, the only parties and considerations a court can consider are those that have legal standing in the case at hand. But when deciding public policy it is often necessary to consider the knock-on effects for a wide range of seemingly unrelated policies. Moreover, not all the relevant moral issues involved need be best articulated in terms of rights. Indeed exclusive focus on the way that a right has been legally defined may subvert a full discussion of the question at hand. Think of the distorting effect of arguments about the right to free speech that focus on whether a given form of expression can be characterized as "speech" or not.

Some theorists have argued that these difficulties can be overcome by a procedural approach to judicial review (Ely 1980). As Habermas (1996, 279) puts it, "a constitutional court guided by a proceduralist understanding of the constitution does not have to draw on its legitimation credit" – it can leave the substance of rights to a democratic process and confine its views to simply adjudicating on whether democratic decisions respect the "logic of argumentation." Yet, he defines valid procedures in terms of "the communicative presuppositions that allow the better arguments to come into play in various forms of deliberation" (Habermas 1996, 278–9). A "consistent proceduralist understanding of the constitution relies on the intrinsically rational character of a democratic process that grounds the presumption of rational outcomes" (Habermas 1996, 285). In other words, the test for judging the rationality and appropriateness of a given democratic procedure rests on whether it produces rational outcomes. This argument simply undermines the procedural–substantive distinction. As with other rights, rights related to the democratic process need to be claimed and reformed within existing, normal democratic politics. For example, it is through such mechanisms that the workers and women gained the right to vote in the United Kingdom, that forms of proportional representation were introduced in New Zealand and in the United

270

Kingdom for regional and European elections and so on. Compare these dramatic and progressive changes to the blocking of similar measures in the United States by successive judgments of the supreme court (for details see Bellamy 2007, 107–29).

What about the potential of litigation as an additional forum for democratic participation and contestation? Partly for related reasons, it may fail or be worse in this respect, too. Litigation will only be possible for those parties that the court views as having a case in law. So it is a restricted forum, the terms of which are controlled by the court. As we saw, these controls may be such as to hinder rather than facilitate new or hitherto excluded voices getting heard. Then there are the resource problems of going to court. Access to justice is costly and time consuming, and cases can take years to be heard. That can often favor those with deep pockets. Given that all citizens start with an equal vote, there is the danger that courts enable illegitimate double counting, with those who cannot muster sufficient popular support to win in politics shopping in an alternative forum that is less open and hence more favorable to the position of privileged minorities or sectional interests.

As a result of these defects courts, like legislatures, can register false negatives and positives as well as legislatures (Bellamy 2009). But this practical weakness is not entirely symmetrical to that found in political processes. Althoughthose who get to court may be treated equally with regard to the law, by contrast to the political system they cannot claim their rights to equal concern and respect on their own terms as political equals. The terms whereby they get access to the law are always the laws, and in these sorts of cases the tribunal they must address is not one of their peers but the judiciary who are set above them as those who determine the state of the law on the case in question. The difficulty lies in the very constraints needed to give individuals a fair trial under the law by impartial judges can make courts inappropriate forums for considering the public good aspects of rights and ensuring that they show equal concern and respect to all those not represented within them. The insistence on legality, on the one side, and independence from extraneous influences, on the other, aims to ensure that judges as far as possible make decisions free from personal bias and financial inducements and fear of reprisals from those sympathetic to one or other of the parties. Yet, the common good aspects of rights may involve considerations beyond the law in question and require responsiveness to the consequences for the public at large. Courts engaged in rights-based review typically deal with such questions under the heading of "proportionality." Yet unlike legislatures they lack the feedback mechanisms likely to ensure that such judgments are well-informed. Governments have to respond to the votes of millions of citizens and their assorted needs by presenting them with a program of government, and they have both the opposition and several hundred representatives seeking re-election from their diverse constituencies to remind them of that fact. For good reasons, courts are isolated from such pressures.

Courts and editorial democracy

It will be pointed out that not all litigants in human rights cases are tobacco companies contesting restrictions on advertising in the name of free speech or film stars protecting their ability to sell their wedding photos to the highest bidder in the name of privacy. There are also asylum seekers, prisoners, the mentally ill, immigrants and other minority groups, with limited if any access to the democratic sphere. Even if not all deserving cases get to court and not all those that do are decided well, there is at least the prospect that some of those individuals whose rights would otherwise go unregarded will get a hearing. For these cases, courts can offer a legitimate avenue of contestatory democracy. While the constraints typical of courts make them a poor authorial forum, they prove well-suited as supports for an editorial forum. Courts seek in their own proceedings to ensure that litigants are treated impartially with regard to the settled norms of the law. In doing so, they apply notions of equity and procedural fairness. As a result, they are highly attuned to adjudicating on the issue of whether a given party to a dispute has been given an adequate hearing or if the norms governing a case have been interpreted even-handedly to all parties. In cases where a litigant, such as an asylum seeker or a prisoner, could show that his or her position had failed to be treated equitably in either of these ways, then under contestation of the authorial decision seems legitimate with the courts and appropriate forum. The issue then becomes how strong can such contestation be before it merges into a less legitimate form of authorial democracy?

Some accounts of editorial democracy, such as Pettit's – at least in some formulations – see a written constitution and bill of rights as offering the authorial basis for such editorial contestation (Pettit 1999, 2000). However, that overlooks the fact that the electoral branch may have claimed to offer these as much attention as the judicial and sought

272

to legitimately reinterpret them so that they accorded more truly with the current views and interests of people with regard to certain issues. If a court is allowed, as under strong contestatory review, to strike down legislation or to read into it its own reading of its fit with constitutional norms, then it is in effect usurping the authorial function of electoral democracy. By contrast, a weak form of contestation allows courts merely to question the compatibility on the fairness grounds outlined above and to force reconsideration by the legislature. In many respects, the British Human Rights Act can be read in such terms as a form of "weak" contestatory judicial review (Bellamy 2011). Under this scheme, the rights enumerated under the Act remain an ordinary piece of legislation that the electoral branch can alter if it deems that necessary. However, in the meantime it seeks to ensure that its current legislation is compatible with such rights norms and to mark when it seeks, for reasons it deems legitimate, to depart from them. Yet courts can dispute whether it has done this sufficiently thoroughly and ask the legislature to reconsider – although how and when remains the prerogative of the authorial branch of democracy. Here democracy – real democracy – remains the authorial foundation for rights, with the courts offering a supplementary function as an editorial alarm bell.

CONCLUSION

Liberal accounts of rights view them as distinct from and potentially constraints upon politics. They are means for preventing illegitimate interferences with individual liberty. Democracy offers at best the most appropriate mechanism for upholding them. But that is only because of the empirical flaws of the alternatives and of our reasoning about rights, not due to the very nature of rights themselves. By contrast, I have argued that rights involve an implicit appeal to democratic forms of reasoning. Moreover, this inherently democratic character of rights follows from the republican view of liberty as nondomination. Nevertheless, this view can still capture "the traditional political purpose of natural or human or fundamental rights" (Jones 1994, 222) if this is seen as defending against arbitrary rule rather than any rule at all. Nor is this account simply an ideal view of the relations between rights and democracy, that itself has only a pragmatic relation to actually existing democratic processes. The only justifiable authorial foundation of rights must be some form of ongoing democratic decision making that allows rights to be claimed

273

under conditions of political equality. At best, courts provide the basis for a weak form of contestatory or "editorial" democracy that draws attention to neglected or otherwise unheard voices. However, the only legitimate final say on rights rests with the people themselves, among whom the benefits and burdens of rights must equally fall as commonly avowed goods that serve their shared interests.

References

Arendt, H. (1958). *The Origins of Totalitarianism*, new edn. Orlando, FL: Harcourt Brace.

Beccaria, C. (1995 [1764]). *On Crimes and Punishments*. Ed. Richard Bellamy, Cambridge: Cambridge University Press.

Bellamy, R. (2001). "Constitutive Citizenship vs. Constitutional Rights: Republican Reflections on the EU Charter and the Human Rights Act." In: *Sceptical Essays on Human Rights*. Eds T. Campbell, K. D. Ewing and A. Tomkins, Oxford: Oxford University Press: 15–39.

Bellamy, R. (2007). *Political Constitutionalism: A Republican Defence of the Constitutionality of Democracy*. Cambridge: Cambridge University Press.

Bellamy, R. (2009). "The Republic of Reasons: Public Reasoning, Depoliticisation and Non-Domination." In: *Legal Republicanism: National and International Perspectives*. Eds S. Besson and J. L. Martí, Oxford: Oxford University Press: 102–20.

Bellamy, R. (2010). "Dirty Hands and White Gloves: Liberal Ideals and Real Politics." *European Journal of Political Theory* 9: 412–30.

Bellamy, R. (2011). "Political Constitutionalism and the Human Rights Act." *International Journal of Constitutional Law* 9: 86–111.

Christiano, T. (2011). "An Instrumental Argument for a Human Right to Democracy." *Philosophy and Public Affairs* 39: 142–76.

Dagger, R. (1997). *Civic Virtues: Rights, Citizenship and Republican Liberalism*. Oxford: Oxford University Press.

Dworkin, R. (1996). *Freedom's Law: The Moral Reading of the American Constitution*. Oxford: Oxford University Press.

Ely, J. H. (1980). *Democracy and Distrust: A Theory of Judicial Review*. Cambridge, MA: Harvard University Press.

Habermas, J. (1996). *Between Facts and Norms*. Trans. W. Rehg, Cambridge: Polity Press.

Habermas, J. (1998). *The Inclusion of the Other*. Cambridge: Polity Press.

Jones, P. (1994). *Rights*. Basingstoke: Macmillan.

Kavanagh, A. (2003). "Participation and Judicial Review: A Reply to Jeremy Waldron." *Law and Philosophy* 22: 451–86.

Klingermann, H.-D., R. I. Hofferbert and I. Budge (1994). *Parties, Policies and Democracy*. Oxford: Westview Press.

May, K. (1952). "A Set of Independent, Necessary and Sufficient Conditions for Simple Majority Decision." *Econometrica* 10: 680–4.

McGann, A. J. (2004). "The Tyranny of the Supermajority: How Majority Rule Protects Minorities." *Journal of Theoretical Politics* 16: 53–77.

O'Neill, O. (1979/80). "The Most Extensive Liberty." *Proceedings of the Aristotelian Society* 80: 45–59.

Ordeshook, P. C. (1986). *Game Theory and Political Theory*. Cambridge: Cambridge University Press.

Pettit, P. (1997). *Republicanism: A Theory of Freedom and Government*. Oxford: Oxford University Press.

Pettit, P. (1999). "Republican Freedom and Contestatory Democratization." In: *Democracy's Value*. Eds I. Shapiro and C. Haker-Cordón, Cambridge: Cambridge University Press: 163–90.

Pettit, P. (2000). "Democracy: Electoral and Contestatory." In: *Designing Democratic Institutions*. Eds I. Shapiro and S. Macedo, New York: New York University Press: 105–44.

Rawls, J. (1993). *Political Liberalism*. New York: Columbia University Press.

Raz, J. (1986). *The Morality of Freedom*. Oxford: Clarendon Press.

Raz, J. (1994). *Ethics in the Public Domain*. Oxford: Clarendon Press.

Skinner, Q. 1998. *Liberty before Liberalism*. Cambridge: Cambridge University Press.

Tushnet, M. (1999). *Taking the Constitution Away from the Courts*. Princeton: Princeton University Press.

Waldron, J. (1981). "A Right to Do Wrong." *Ethics* 92: 21–39.

Waldron, J. (1999). *Law and Disagreement*. Oxford: Oxford University Press.

Weale, A. (2007). *Democracy*, 2nd edn. Basingstoke: Palgrave.

CHAPTER 11

Republicanism and Global Justice: A Sketch[1]

Cécile Laborde

Prima facie, republicanism has a blind spot about global justice. The republican tradition seems to have little to say about pressing international issues such as world poverty or global inequalities. According to the old, if apocryphal, adage: *extra rempublicam nulla justitia* (there is no justice outside the republic). Some may doubt that distributive justice (as opposed to freedom or citizenship) is the primary virtue of republican institutions; and at any rate most would agree that republican values have traditionally been realized in the *polis* not in the (oxymoronic) *cosmopolis*. In this paper, I sketch a republican account of global nondomination that suggests that duties of distributive justice are not necessarily bounded to the institutions of a single society. In particular, I argue that republicans have good reasons to seek to curb those global inequalities that underpin what I call *capability-denying domination*. Because my main purpose is to set out an agenda for research in a still largely unexplored area, I can only provide here a preliminary sketch of this republican argument for global justice. In fact, it is not part of my claim that republicanism offers a full, coherent account of global justice; nor that republicanism is a more attractive theory than existing liberal cosmopolitan theory. I merely attempt to conceptualize the distinctive features of a republican approach to global justice, leaving a full assessment of its merits for subsequent inquiry.

1. REPUBLICAN CITIZENSHIP AND JUSTICE: PRELIMINARY CLARIFICATIONS

The attempt to apply republican theory to issues of global distributive justice invites skepticism on two fronts: First, republicanism is only a theory of bounded citizenship and, second, republicanism is not a theory of distributive justice. Let me address these two doubts in turn.

Objection 1: republicanism is essentially a theory of bounded citizenship

There are three republican commitments (the three Vs) that at first sight make republicanism an unlikely candidate for the articulation of principles of global justice: voice, vernacular, and virtue. When combined, they underpin a particular understanding of freedom as citizenship in a bounded community. The first V is "voice", which sees freedom as a form of power, or (in Philip Pettit's [1996] term), antipower. On this view, freedom is essentially a political condition that involves not being subjected to arbitrary power. Traditionally, this was seen to be possible only through practices of self-government, or 'voice', in a bounded political community. Cosmopolitan republicanism, then, is an oxymoron because there is no global political community that would allow global citizens to govern themselves democratically. The second V is "vernacular", which sees freedom as a particular and contingent achievement. Republics are rooted in time and space; they are local, parochial and fragile achievements, maintained through specific institutional arrangements, historically associated with the stabilization of politics within nation-states. Insofar as cosmopolitanism seeks to invent new forms of political association, it is too utopian to be accommodated by republicanism. The third V is "virtue", which sees freedom as an inter-subjective bond. This emphasizes the psychological underpinnings of democratic governance: Republics rely not only on good laws but also on good mores, and are maintained through the mutual trust, civility and spirit of reciprocity exhibited by their citizens. Such virtues can hardly be replicated globally, as people have little psychological life in common with distant strangers. In sum, the traditional argument would conclude, republican cosmopolitanism is an oxymoron because, at the global level, it is not possible to reproduce the practices, institutions and virtue essential to founding and maintaining republics (see, for example, Miller 2000). At best, republicanism would generate a statist, or social liberal, theory of justice: Like Thomas Nagel (2005) or John Rawls (1999), it conceives of justice exclusively as a property of social relations among citizens of states.

I think that this appearance is misleading. The three Vs, if suitably interpreted, are not obstacles to theorizing global justice but, on the contrary, may be the foundation of a distinctive and attractive republican approach to it. Let me start with the first V, "voice." By contrast to advocates of positive liberty such as Jean-Jacques Rousseau, contemporary neo-Roman republicans do not advocate participatory self-government or direct democracy. Neo-Roman theory interprets the requirement of "voice" as implying nondomination or antipower: Citizens must be able to control or check the arbitrary or "alien" power exercised over them. The neo-Roman minimal understanding of democracy undeniably offers a useful paradigm for normative reflection on what James Bohman (2004, 338 passim) has called the new global circumstances of politics. These are characterized by complex new forms of unchecked arbitrary power exercised across national borders: More and more people are vulnerable to decisions made from afar, anonymously, and over which they have little control. Instead of relationships of 'cooperation' or 'interdependence', which would imply reciprocity and mutual benefit, the current international order is marked by one-sided and largely coerced domination and dependency (Forst 2001, 166). Just as republicans have historically pointed to the evils of arbitrary power in sub-state units such as the workplace and the family, they, similarly, can point to the evil of trans-national domination, be it by states, corporations or international organizations.

The second V, 'vernacular', can also be reinterpreted, as a methodological guideline. Thus, in the critical republicanism that I advocate, the conservative bias of 'politics in the vernacular' can be transformed into a praxis-oriented critical theory.[2] Critical republicans borrow from Frankfurt-style critical theory an interest in social critique and in social change: They start from existing institutions and relationships, identify their dominating and oppressive features, and advocate their transformation. Their primary concern with resistance to concrete forms of unjust power aligns them with conservative approaches such as Judith Shklar's (1998), whose "liberalism of fear" is a political not a philosophical doctrine aiming to "secure the political conditions that are necessary for the exercise of personal freedom", and to combat the bad rather than promote the good. Yet where critical republicanism is more radical than the liberalism of fear is that, in line with post-Marxist theory, it has a more expansive interpretation of what counts as a bad (or social evil), including not only state rule and the abuse of public power, but also more diffuse forms of social domination.

As for the third "V," "virtue", while it is clear that the republican values of mutual trust and reciprocity cannot be extended much beyond spheres of political citizenship, it is also undeniable that there is growing awareness that the actions of rich and powerful states, notably, contribute to affect and dominate the lives of others, be they distant strangers or future generations. The current global order exhibits sufficient levels of interdependence to motivate commitment to minimum standards, as movements such as the anti-debt Jubilee 2000, anti-war demonstrations, climate change lobbying and campaign for global labor standards amply reveal.[3] The international order does involve publicly recognized rules that all acknowledge – the discourse of human rights among them – and does provide a shared basis for the public justification of actions and the mutual socialization of international actors (Hurrell 2001, 43).[4] It is against this background of shared norms of basic justice that the gross inequalities that characterize the global order have come to be seen as iniquitous. As Stuart White (2003) has suggested, in reply to David Miller's (2000) skeptical comments about global citizenship, republicans are motivated by a sense of collective responsibility for the actions of their states (they are moved by such "honorific" sentiments as pride and shame) and they are committed to combating the evil of domination wherever it happens in the world. Thus civically minded citizens will be motivated to make sure that they – or their state – do not dominate others; that they are not dominated by others; and that others are not dominated by others. The difficult question of the psychological and moral foundations of such trans-national solidarity – whether and how cosmopolitan republican virtue can be motivated – can unfortunately not be pursued here (White 2003, Viroli 1995).

Objection 2: republicanism has no theory of distributive justice

While liberals such as Rawls argue that justice (and in particular social justice) is the first virtue of social institutions, it is unclear that republicans are similarly committed. Republicans are often suspected of disinterest for socioeconomic issues (Goodin 2003, Van Parijs 1999). Because what matters, for them, is the political status of citizenship, they are primarily concerned with questions of power, its justification, limitation, contestation and democratization. Thus, those republicans with cosmopolitan convictions have naturally turned their attention to procedural questions – the reform of international governance – rather than to substantive questions – the pursuit of global (distributive) justice. Topics such as nondomination and human rights, cosmopolitan citizenship, multilayered governance and a republican law of peoples, have been central to republican contributions to the expanding discipline of international normative theory.[5] This said, it would be a misinterpretation to assume that republicans have been silent about distributive justice. There are in fact two crucial ways in which, in republican theory, socioeconomic status cannot be separated from political nondomination. First, under an *optimal* regime of nondomination (typically, a democratic state or republic), individuals, relating to one another as citizens, collectively decide how best to equalize the particular resources and opportunities necessary for the enjoyment of citizenship in their state. Thus republics will typically ensure high levels of redistribution as well as high levels of social equality – but the substantive principles according to which specific resources will be fairly distributed in a given society can only be defined democratically. Optimal nondomination is the one that is realised in fully justified, collectively organized political entities such as states, where (as on a statist or "political" conception of justice (Nagel 2005, Sangiovanni 2007)), the density and quality of relationship between citizens justify that they collectively ensure that appropriate relations of social equality obtain between them.[6]

However, second, the accessibility of *basic* nondomination – the ability to set up a republic in the first place – has crucial socioeconomic pre-requisites. As Jean-Jacques Rousseau long pointed out, no republic can be founded if inequalities are too large, and the poor can be bought by the rich. Thus republicans have good reasons for seeking to address both absolute socioeconomic deprivation and large inequalities of wealth and power, as essential pre-requisites for citizenship. Note that on the interpretation I favor, the elimination of poverty and the reduction of gross inequalities refer not to the thick (optimal) principles of distributive justice that republics can permissibly implement – these will be defined democratically within optimal regime of nondomination such as democratic states – but, rather, to the thin (basic) principles of justice that must be in place for republics to be set up in the first place. This distinction – between basic and optimal nondomination – is particularly relevant to the application of republican distributive justice concerns to the global sphere.[7]

Why, then, should republicans worry about global inequality? Primarily for derivative, indirect reasons that do not appeal to the value of equality per se, but rather to the consequences of inequality for values that are distinct from equality itself.[8] On the traditional republican view, there are two such derivative reasons. The first is that large inequality leads to abuses of power and control of the poor by the rich. The second is that large inequality undermines the sense of dignity and self-respect of the poor, by fostering feelings of humiliation and envy. Such reasons appeal to values – the importance of control, on the one hand, and what Rawls would call the social bases of self-respect (1972, 178, 440, 534), on the other – which have traditionally been seen to apply exclusively to self-contained *polis*. Yet, I would suggest, they also apply, to some extent, to the new "circumstances of global politics." These, in Andrew Hurrell's (2001, 44) astute characterization, exhibit relations of high "density" and high "deformity", so that background inequalities between nations give rise to dramatic differences in bargaining power in international negotiations. In such organizations as the United Nations (UN), the World Bank, the International Monetary Fund (IMF) and the World Trade Organization (WTO), decisions are made that, given the levels of global interdependence, have great implications for developing countries but within which they have little say: They become utterly dependent on, and subservient to, rich and powerful states.

Furthermore, against those who, like David Miller (2007, 77–8), argue that comparisons of standing and status are only meaningful within small-scale, relatively homogenous communities, it can be pointed out that multifaceted processes of globalization have meant that the geographical and symbolic superimposition of extremes of wealth and destitution has created new forms of status anxiety and despair, as the global poor become aware of their permanent reject status from an inaccessible yet omnipresent rich world. The morally obscene gap between them and the Western rich is inconsistent with their sense of themselves as active agents, capable of effective conduct of their life. Large global inequalities thus bar mobility and breed despair and envy. In sum, republicans have grounds for extending their critique of large inequalities to the global realm, where such inequalities manifestly also have debilitating effects on mutual respect and self-respect, as well as on the capacity for minimum control and self-direction on the part of vulnerable groups and individuals.

Second, as indicated, republicans also have independent reasons for worrying about absolute levels of material destitution. The claim here is that there are absolute resource preconditions (nutrition, basic health care and education) that have to be met in order for individuals to function as citizens at all (Bertram 2005). This is a republican extension of the broader neo-Kantian point made by Onora O'Neill (1986), that the condition of extreme poverty and neediness is one of disempowerment, the

281

undermining of rational agency or autonomy. Deprivation makes people potentially vulnerable to domination: It is, in James Bohman's (2005a, 106) terms, "functionally equivalent to tyranny." For consider: If you lack basic education, you will be unable to articulate your views and interests in democratic forums, and you will be politically voiceless. If you can barely feed yourself and your family, you will be highly vulnerable to domination. If you lack the basic right of citizenship (for example, because you are a displaced refugee or a noncitizen resident in a state), your status and entitlements will be defined by others, with few possibilities of recourse on your part (Bohman 2005b). Among the basic capabilities that are essential for moral agency and democratic citizenship are a minimal ability for self-direction and autonomy, basic material resources (nutrition, shelter, health, sanitation) and some level of control over collective life (what Bohman calls the "democratic minimum" or the "right to have rights"). The republican critique of destitution and poverty may be sketchy and ultimately unsatisfactory: Important questions may be asked about the coherence of making the satisfaction of basic human interests derivative from the ideal of political citizenship. But for my purposes here, suffice it to say that republicans, insofar as they are committed to nondomination, have reasons to combat poverty and destitution.

Overall, it follows from this brief sketch that republicanism may have enough of a theory of distributive justice to worry about both global inequality and world poverty. People in poor and destitute states will be unable to set up republics if the inequalities of power and wealth that they suffer – both within their states and in the international sphere, as collectively organized entities – means that even basic nondomination is not within their reach. Thus, if we care about the universal good of nondomination, we have an obligation to assist others by reducing inequalities and alleviating poverty. The problem with this account of republican cosmopolitan duty is that it may be seen to rest on a thick view of republican cosmopolitan virtue – one that asks us positively to assist others in achieving basic nondomination for and within their states. Fortunately, there is another basis for grounding our cosmopolitan duties. Insofar as much global poverty can ultimately be *traced to* the dominating effect of global inequalities of power and resources, to that extent, it generates a political obligation on the part of citizens of rich and powerful states – the obligation to ensure that they (or rather, their institutions) do not dominate others.

2. DOMINATION AND GLOBAL INJUSTICE: LAYING THE FOUNDATIONS

At this point it is useful to say a bit more about the idea of domination. Domination refers to the relatively unrestrained and systematic (even if unexercised) ability of group or individuals to exert power over others in pursuit of their own interests at the expense of those subordinate to them.

Domination – in Philip Pettit's terms, the capacity arbitrarily to interfere in the affairs of others – is rooted in structural inequalities of power, and manifests itself in the denial of basic interests of the dominated. Several elements of this definition will need to be clarified but, on a preliminary reflection, consider how it intuitively captures a central aspect of global injustice. This is the widely accepted fact that, under the new conditions of globalization, rich and powerful countries set the rules of, and benefit from, the terms of global interaction, in ways that cause global poverty and deprivation (call this the "Pogge hypothesis" (Pogge 2002, 20)). I shall not attempt to defend the Pogge hypothesis here; I simply assume that it is both empirically verifiable and ethically compelling. I shall, in the following, put forward (and put to the test) a republican conceptualization of this global injustice.

The thought is that the most pressing form of global injustice today is the pervasiveness of capability-denying relations of domination between the rich and powerful and the poor and the weak. The enormous disparities in resources and powers between states are at the roots of global relationships of domination. While domination is always an evil for republicans (it denies a basic interest in minimum autonomy or "discursive control"), it is a tragedy when it results in the denial of basic human capabilities (such as subsistence). Therefore the priority of global justice should be to reduce those forms of global domination that grant one set of agents the potential to deny basic capabilities to others. Reducing domination means rectifying the inequalities that underpin it: in particular, restructuring institutional governance to give greater power and voice to poor countries in international organizations. The concept of domination, thus specified, is parsimonious enough to illuminate the concerns underpinning the Pogge hypothesis – notably the intimate connections between global inequalities of power and resources, institutional design and world poverty. Because a (critical) republicanism is best equipped to account for those connections, I would suggest that republicanism should be considered as a possible candidate alternative to cosmopolitan institutionalist theories of global injustice such as Pogge's.

Before I proceed to show how republican nondomination, as conceptualized notably by Pettit, can provide a compelling interpretation of the ideal of global justice, let me identify two ways in which my definition of global domination slightly modifies Pettit's account. On my view domination refers not only to inter-personal relationships but to basic, systemic power structures (clause A) that significantly threaten or deny basic capabilities (clause B). Clause B is narrower, and clause A broader, than Pettit's definition. Let me discuss these two points in turn. First, my definition is narrower than Pettit's in the sense that it connects global domination to the denial of a specific sub-set of human interests (basic capabilities). On my view, those forms of what Pettit (2007a) calls "alien control" that affect people's basic interests or capabilities are particularly problematic from a global point of view. How significant is this as a modification of the standard definition of domination? *Prima facie*, it would seem illegitimately to smuggle in a moralized and a substantive component into the definition: It tells us what people should be free to have access to (basic material resources or capabilities). It seems therefore twice removed from the negative and factual conception of freedom that Pettit adheres to. Yet I want to suggest that Pettit has left open the possibility that nondomination and basic capabilities might be intimately connected.

There are three plausible points of entry of substantive concerns (such as access to basic capabilities) into Pettit's conception of nondomination. The first, noted above, is that the presence of certain material resources is a precondition for people's enjoyment of nondomination. Notice that on this view, capabilities and nondomination remain definitionally distinct. As Pettit puts it, poverty and destitution do not compromise nondomination but merely condition it.[9] The second concession that Pettit can be said to make to the more substantive view that I defend follows from his point that "the free person will avoid alien control *in relevant choices* and on the right basis."[10] Thus it may not be alien control *tout court* that should be of concern to the normative republican, but specifically those forms of control that affect a subset of "relevant choices." Among these, we can presume, will figure basic liberties and rights; and among these, we can further presume, can figure socioeconomic capabilities.[11] There is, lastly, a third, more straightforward way in which substantive concerns might enter Pettit's definition of domination. In his 1997 book, Pettit (1997, 55) refers to domination as the capacity for interference that is arbitrary, that is, that does not track the "relevant ... interests and ideas

284

of the person suffering the interference." A nondominating power, then, tracks the "relevant interests" of persons. Critics have pointed out that this interest-based specification of nondomination is incompatible with a nonpositive and nonmoralized conception of freedom (Carter 2007, 64–6; McMahon 2005, 69; Waldron 2007). In response, Pettit (2005, 94) has insisted that the judgment that a particular interference is arbitrary (or freedom-infringing) is factual not normative; it is "fixed by the controls to which it is subject, not the ends that it happens to effect."[12] Whether Pettit can provide a nonmoralized definition of "control" – and whether, more generally, his theory of freedom is as immune to normative moralization as he claims – is a question I shall leave to one side here.

On the view that I favor, nondomination (like most plausible conceptions of liberty) is inevitably moralized: It is definitionally connected to particular human interests that we have reason to value. Minimally and uncontroversially, domination infringes our basic interest in maintaining control or "discursive autonomy" – it denies our agency as human beings (Dagger 2005; Laborde 2006). More complicated is the further specification of the more expansive and substantive "relevant interests" that dominating power fails to track. Pettit (2001a, 174; 2006) suggests that a nondominating state will track "common avowable interests," in a way that encourages individuals to map their subjective ideas about their interests onto a public criterion of nonarbitrariness. Does this mean that relevant interests can only be identified through the processes of deliberation, contestation and participation that characterize the republican nondominating state? Here we should distinguish between the identification and the protection of basic interests. Unambiguously, on a republican view, democratic processes should be not insulated from, and are instrumental to, the protection of basic interests. As Amartya Sen's (1982) work on famine has demonstrated, only democratic processes can secure the adequate protection of people's basic needs. Yet this does not necessarily mean that people's "relevant interests" can only be identified through democratic processes. The republican view, instead, points to a two-level approach to the identification of interests, one that sets out a core of basic, universal and objective human interests, but leaves the specification of further relevant interests to processes of democratic deliberation.

Once we connect in this way a thin theory of the human good with commitment to democratic processes, we can see how (a version of) the capabilities approach defended by Sen and Martha Nussbaum provides a natural foundation for a republican theory of global justice.[13] On the one hand, the content of *basic* capabilities can be specified independently of particular local and cultural contexts. Some human interests – to be free from starvation and from avoidable disease, to use obvious examples – are so essential that their absence indicates a "basic capability failure" – the inability of individuals and communities to choose valuable "doings and beings" that are basic to human life (Alkire 2005, 56). Here the capability theory is compatible with familiar accounts of the primary goods, basic interests or basic needs that underpin human rights claims. Yet, on the other hand, and beyond this sufficiency level, the concept of capability is useful from a republican point of view because of two crucial features.

First, there is a mutually supportive relationship between capabilities and democratic control: Minimum democratic control is one of the central capabilities (and it can be denied by either domestic or international domination), and the full content of the more specific capabilities can only be defined through democratic engagement with people's actual views and ideals about what constitutes well-being in their society Second, the distinction between capabilities and functionings is congenial to the view of freedom captured by nondomination, both in its "negative" dimension (people must be free to *choose* to exercise the capabilities) and in its "positive" dimension (people must have the freedom to pursue *valued* functionings). This account of the relationship between domination, human interests and capabilities is sketchy and begs many questions, but it is sufficient for the purposes of my argument here. Let me simply posit, then, that domination is capability-denying in two senses: Definitionally, it denies a basic interest in minimum control and autonomy on the part of individuals and the political communities they belong to; and normatively, those forms of domination that threaten access to basic socioeconomic capabilities such as subsistence and health are a matter of particular moral concern.

The second slight modification of Pettit's definition that I should like to propose is that, in line with sociological accounts of domination such as those of Karl Marx, Max Weber and Michel Foucault, we should direct our focus toward systemic power structures instead of exclusively to the inter-personal relationships of domination that they authorize. To see the point, consider two scenarios of domination. I can dominate you by virtue of my personal resources, such as my superior strength, intelligence, cunning or ambition (call this agent-relative domination) or I can dominate you by virtue of my location in a specific institutional system, such as as an IMF official, a police officer or a company director (call this systemic domination).[14] The political force of Pettit's ideal of nondomination was that it gave us an insight into systemic domination – as was powerfully brought out by the analogy between slavery and domination. Even kind and benign masters, who did not interfere with their slaves and bore them no ill will, could be said to dominate them (Pettit 1997, 32, 64). They did so, not in virtue of their personal, agent-relative resources, but in virtue of the systemic features of slavery as a deeply entrenched, institutionalized set of rules and conventions. The institution of slavery provided the resources and the background structure for the domination of slaves by their masters. The distinction between systemic and agent-relative domination is relevant in two respects.

First, it complements Pettit's discussion of global domination, which is exclusively focused on agent-relative rather than systemic domination. Thus Pettit analyzes the various ways in which collective entities such as strong states or multinational corporations can exercise alien control over weak states, but he spends less time accounting for the institutional framework – trade rules, global treaties, international law – that regulate international interaction. In other words, Pettit's "Republican Law of Peoples" (2010), much like Rawls's, is focused on inter-state, international relations (although, by contrast to Rawls, he is sensitive to the dominating power that nonstate actors such as trans-national corporations can have over weak states). Now, Pettit (2010) is right to suggest that the most serious and intractable forms of international domination are rooted in the inescapably unequal distribution of agent-relative resources such as "greater economic power, wider diplomatic clout, or the enjoyment of some strategic advantage." Yet he overlooks the fact that the global system is only in some respects analogous to an unregulated state of nature where relationships of (agent-relative) brute mastery obtain. It is in other respects a (structurally unfair) systemic order that authorizes and aggravates the pre-institutional subservience and dependency of weak states. This is true, notably, of the way in which processes of globalization and liberalization have been managed by international organizations such as the IMF, the WTO and the World Bank (Stiglitz 2006). For instance, the asymmetry, within the WTO, between the continued protectionism of rich states and the forced opening of third world markets, is a striking example of the way in which powerful countries have exploited their agent-relative dominant position by entrenching and institutionalizing it through iniquitous trade rules (Moellendorf 2005). This structural asymmetry cannot be accounted for in purely agent-relative terms.[15]

The second advantage of a systemic account of domination is that by shifting the focus away from the motives and actions of particular agents (such as trans-national corporations in the global market) toward the structures of domination within which they act (such as international trade rules), it points to our shared responsibility in upholding, and benefiting from, systems of domination. Thus, just as under the institution of slavery, not only exploitative but also benign slave-owners, who benefited from the system, could be said to be responsible for upholding the institution of slavery, similarly, in the new and evolving global economic order, citizens of rich and powerful states – in different degrees – can be said to be responsible for the maintenance of unjust international institutions and rules. Agents must work to ensure that the institutional structures that they collectively uphold do not dominate the poor in ways that make their access to basic goods insecure. Like all institutional accounts that focus on the pervasive impact of structural global systems of coercion on the global poor, the republican account emphasizes the shared responsibility of Western public officials, private corporations and individuals.[16] It suggests that there is a joint political responsibility to curb the dominating affect of existing global structures, as the best way of reducing the capability-denying effect of the unequal distribution of agent-relative resources among global actors. Having suggested two slight modifications of Pettit's account of global domination, I now move to highlight the advantages of republican nondomination as a global ideal.

3. Nondomination as a global ideal: building a case

The republican ideal of nondomination, I shall argue, has descriptively, ethically and strategically compelling features.

1. Descriptively: domination is a serious problem in contemporary world affairs

It is easy to show that the current world order is rife with domination. The growing inequalities of power and influence caused by globalization have meant that, under the "new circumstances of politics," the lives of ordinary people are deeply influenced by forces which neither they nor their governments can easily shape, control or even anticipate. The vulnerability they suffer as a consequence of their lack of resources is exacerbated and at times exploited by powerful agents, in particular rich Western states and multinational corporations. We live under a system of complex yet hierarchical interdependence: Powerful states, multinational corporations, international organizations such as the World Bank and the IMF enact rules and create institutions from which the global poor cannot realistically exit, and which causally contribute to the misery of much of the world's population. Participation is sufficiently involuntary and enforcement is sufficiently coercive to create relations of domination between members: As Bohman (2004, 340) puts it, "non-voluntary inclusion in indefinite cooperative schemes is ... a form of domination."[17]

More precisely, the concept of domination adequately captures four features of the current world order. First, as domination can obtain in the absence of actual interference, it adequately describes the diffuse, indirect, virtual and multifarious forms taken by globalized power. Thus domination describes a state of vulnerability on the part of poor and weak states, whereby offers are made to them on terms that they cannot refuse, and threats do not need to be carried out or even issued to be successful, all by virtue of the sheer inequality of power and resources between them and rich and powerful global actors. As Quentin Skinner (2007) and Pettit (2007a) have recently emphasized, the fact that the interference is *possible*, regardless of its actual *probability*, is of concern to republicans. This insight into the importance of the security of liberty and the predictability of the workings of power is extremely valuable in the context of globalization, which on many accounts is characterized by highly unpredictable and unaccountable forms of power.[18] The thought that poor and weak states are subjected to what Pettit calls virtual alien control by the rich and powerful (2007a) – they live under their thumb, they are dependent on their good will, even if they suffer no direct interference – is, I think, a fruitful intuition to develop in international normative theory.

Second, as domination can obtain in agent-relative as well as in systemic ways, it adequately captures a feature of the world order that exclusively systemic accounts of coercion tend to miss out. Consider, for example, the claim, made both by cosmopolitan and anticosmopolitan philosophers, that demands of distributive justice are triggered by the presence of institutionalized and rule-bound forms of coercion (call this the "systemic coercion" theory). Where cosmopolitans and their critics disagree is about the extent to which systemic forms of coercion obtain at the global level: Cosmopolitans such as Pogge think so (and I agree), and anticosmopolitans such as Nagel and Blake think not. But what they both underestimate is the normatively problematic nature of pre-institutional, lawless, agent-relative forms of power, such as the arbitrary power that rich states exercise over foreign citizens through border controls, or the largely unchecked power that trans-national corporations hold over developing countries in the liberalized global market. Dominant actors have a clear interest in ensuring that such coercive relationships are not regulated or subjected to scrutiny. Yet the "systemic coercion" theory perversely rewards them for preferring lawless coercion to institutionalized coercion. It thereby leaves the poor and weak in a double jeopardy: They are already disadvantaged by a lack of systemic coercion structures and find themselves further disadvantaged by the idea that without such coercion, worries about justice are inapplicable.[19] The republican theory of nondomination avoids such perverse consequences. Domination is worrisome from the point of view of justice whether it is lawless or law-bound, whether it is rooted in agent-relative or on systemic resources. Nondomination, in turn, can never be achieved outside the law: For republicans, freedom can only be achieved under institutionalized schemes setting fair (nondominating) terms of social cooperation.

This leads me to the third feature of domination that adequately captures a feature of global power: On the republican view, interference in itself need not be dominating, as long as it tracks "relevant interests." And because nondominating relations can only obtain in a civil, lawbound state, states are encouraged to leave the international "state of nature" and institutionalize their mutual relationships. Thus the ideal of nondomination, by contrast to those accounts that make the demand for justice conditional on the density of schemes of social interaction, does not provide reasons for rich states to disaffiliate from their existing relationships in order to exempt themselves from demands of justice. A republican world order demands high levels of "civil" interaction – economic, political, cultural – and direct interference in the affairs of other states – humanitarian, diplomatic, even military – as long as interference is non-alien, to use Pettit's phrase. International organizations, even if their membership is quasi-compulsory and their norms authoritative, need not dominate weak states: they can foster a culture of trust, accountability, publicity, "state socialization" and noncoercive compliance, and can be used to promote greater global justice.[20] They already provide "forums of interstate deliberation and exchange" and promote a "currency of common reasons" (Pettit 2010, 84).

2. Morally: the ideal of nondomination tallies with widespread moral intuitions

First, the theory advanced here captures the common view that what is morally shocking about the current world order is not so much global inequality per se, as the combination of the absolute destitution of the global poor with gross inequalities of power and resources between them and the better-off. The republican view provides coherence to these two intuitions, and gives us strong reasons both for lifting people out of absolute poverty (ensuring basic capabilities worldwide) and for reducing large inequalities (curbing or neutralizing the power of dominant states). Thus the republican view points to a sufficiency and a gap-reducing ideal of justice, without appealing to stronger (and less plausible) ideals of global equality as an end point.[21]

The second widely shared intuition that tallies with the republican view is that our primary duty is not to harm others, and insofar as our dominating others can be shown to constitute a clear form of harm (in particular if it denies basic capabilities), then we have a duty not to dominate others. This does not forbid the existence of positive duties to assist others in resisting domination by others – and therefore the republican view can also prescribe positive duties of assistance to burdened peoples – but, like Pogge's, the nondomination approach prioritizes the nonconsequentialist, deontological duty of abstention from harm.

The third advantage of the republican approach is that in its neo-Kantian critical dimension, it shares with dominant liberal approaches an emphasis on the need for justification. In fact, justificatory demands are built into the ideal of nondomination. An arbitrary or alien power, a dominating power, is a power that is not adequately justified to those who are subjected to it. Hence the republican emphasis on the right to have rights – which translates into a right to participation, contestation and/or justification. Part of what it means to be treated a human agent is not to be treated in a manner for which adequate reasons cannot be provided (Ivison 2010; Forst 2001).

Finally, the republican link between domination and deprivation echoes the popular "social" critique of globalization. This points out that even if globalization can be shown to have raised the absolute standards of living of the global poor (according to purely quantitative income-based metrics), it may still have reduced their quality of life or well-being, by depriving them of control over the parameters of their own lives. Thus to lose economic security and control over one's own labor, time allocation, reproductive freedom or occupational health for an absolute monetary gain might result in a net loss of well-being, if one includes in the metric of deprivation such qualitative factors as democratic capabilities.[22] There is more to well-being than access to material primary goods, and the nondomination account captures the more qualitative value of control, notably, although not exclusively, through political voice. Under globalization, non-democratic actors with truly global reach, capable of enacting norms and practices that have a determining impact on people's ability to lead a decent life, have proliferated without adequate checks. Thus republicans agree with advocates of cosmopolitan democracy who argue that "persons have a right to an institutional order under which those significantly and legitimately affected by a political decision have a roughly equal opportunity to influence the making of this decision" (Pogge 2002, 184).[23] And because, as we have seen, neo-Roman democracy is centered not on the ideal of equal influence on, and direct popular participation to, power, but on the possibility of its effective contestation, it is well-equipped to underpin the effective control of international organizations by states and peoples (Pettit 2010), and is, further, well-suited to the decentralized, multifarious, network-based nature of contemporary global power (Braithwaite 2007).

3. Tactically: the ideal of nondomination points to achievable political objectives

Republican global justice occupies an intermediate position between what David Miller (1988; 2000, 174) has called "weak cosmopolitanism," which aims to "respect the conditions that are universally necessary for human beings to lead minimally adequate lives," and "strong cosmopolitanism," which "takes inequalities as such between persons across borders to be a concern of justice." Republican global justice aims both to guarantee minimum conditions for leading nondominated lives, and to mitigate those global inequalities that have serious dominating effects on the worst-off. It is thus best equipped to conceptualize and tackle what has been called "radical inequality," whereby the worse-off are very badly off in absolute terms *and* in relative terms, and where such inequality is pervasive, impervious and avoidable.[24] This radical inequality is partly maintained and reproduced by an institutionalized system of domination of the global poor by affluent countries. To curb this domination, three (not mutually exclusive) strategies can be adopted. The first – call it the "liberal" strategy of distributive justice – aims to rectify the gross distributive inequities that underpin the global economic order through schemes of wealth redistribution from rich to poor countries.[25] The second – call it the "Realist" strategy of balance of power – aims to reinforce inter-state checks, either through the building of defensive coalitions between weak states, or through mutual neutralization between strong states (Pettit 2010). The third – call it the "critical" strategy of political empowerment – involves the reform of international organizations, to make them more representative and more accountable, in order to ensure that poor countries are better able to defend their interests and demand fairer terms of interaction.[26] While all are compatible with the republican approach, the latter directly addresses the concerns of this paper (and, as I shall suggest below, adequately expresses respect for the autonomy of states).

Greater regulation and accountability of the trans-national economic and political institutions whose workings affect ordinary citizens has been a central feature of republican cosmopolitan democracy (Bohman 2004). Yet republicans have somewhat neglected the effect of such democratization on the fight against world poverty. Cosmopolitan liberals, by contrast, have advocated the democratic reform of trans-national governance as a fairly reliable means of delivering fairer distributive outcomes for the global poor. Even though liberals such as Pogge and Caney (2006, 732–3) insist that the substantive goal of alleviating poverty should take priority over the procedural reform of modes of governance, and that democratic governance is instrumentally not intrinsically connected to distributive justice, it is remarkable how prominently institutional change features on their reform agenda.[27] Thus they would agree with Hurrell's (2001, 47) statement that "greater interstate justice is instrumentally necessary to achieve the sorts of outcomes desired by the moral cosmopolitan." This is easily explainable on a republican view, according to which the chief global evil is capability-denying domination. Unless and until the worst forms of domination generated by the global economic order are checked and constrained by appropriately accountable political institutions, universally fair access to basic capabilities cannot be institutionally secured. Another advantage of republican global justice, as I show in the last section, is that, while taking into account the dominating effects of new forms of global power, it respects the autonomy of collectively organized peoples (or states).

4. FREE STATES AND COLLECTIVE NONDOMINATION

One key feature of republican political theory is its emphasis on citizenship as membership in a self-determining political community. Such communities are valuable, I have suggested, because within them, citizens can collectively achieve a status of optimal nondomination. The idea cannot be fully elaborated here, but the thought is that within justified and comprehensive schemes of social cooperation, citizens positively engage in collective deliberations over more substantive principles of justice than the democratic minimum and the "basic capabilities" that are guaranteed universally. Once we reach the "democratic minimum" – in Bohman's (2005a, 104) terms, "the linchpin that makes it possible for the transformation of democracy itself to be the basis for more justice" – republicans put their trust in democratic deliberation as the guarantee of social equality. On a republican account, relations between co-citizens are *par excellence* equality-justifying relations. Of course, each society will have its own view of what optimal nondomination requires within it – which social goods, capabilities, rights and powers should be collectively guaranteed and distributed as a matter of justice. Some societies will opt for a welfare safety net and others for a basic income; some will tolerate large inequalities of income and wealth provided they benefit the worst-off while others (perhaps more republican-minded ones) will worry about the effects of material inequalities on the status of citizenship and political equality. Some will pursue economic growth at all costs, and others will focus on other goods. The point is, republicanism can easily account for such variations and, to this extent, agrees with critics of cosmopolitan global justice that *ceteris paribus*, inequalities between nations are a natural consequence of collective self-determination (Rawls 1999; Bertram 2005; Miller 1999b, 2007, 62–75).[28]

Yet on a critical republican view, the *ceteris paribus* clause is crucial. Critics of cosmopolitanism exaggerate the extent to which weak and poor states can be said to be responsible for the sorry state of their population, and underestimate the effects of external domination on states' ability to fulfill the basic rights of their citizens. If, for example, states are crippled by the service of an "Odious Debt" and by the operation of unfair international trade rules, their choices are largely dependent on factors outside of their control. To use the old republican saying: They are not free. A free state is not "moved to act by a will other than its own" (Skinner 1997, 27). On the revised account suggested by Pettit (2010), a free state does not necessarily enjoy full self-determination and complete sovereignty: It is a state that is not dominated by others, that is not dependent on the will of others or on alien forces that it cannot control. Thus the republican theory of international (inter-state) relations will demand something less than complete sovereignty of states and substantive equality between them. Free states, we could say, are states that are not denied a basic capability for minimum self-direction. Thus republican states can voluntarily decide to enter into binding agreements with other states and other forms of trans-national cooperation, but they may not surrender their nondominated status: They must retain the capability for minimum self-direction. Whichever arrangements they enter into must not leave them at the mercy of more powerful states.

The value of a free state, on the republican view, lies in the fact that its people can collectively control the power exercised over them. This connects to a long-standing republican worry about the way in which external domination by powerful states leads to internal domination. States that are subjected to outside domination are unlikely to be able to establish nondominating rule domestically. Such a worry underpins Pogge's (2002) discussion of the "international borrowing principle" and the "international resource principle," which provide incentives for corrupt third world elites who cooperate with powerful global players (Western governments, banks and companies) to exploit their countries' natural and human resources in order to increase their power and enrich themselves, with scant regard for democratic accountability (Forst 2001, 174). Both examples vindicate the republican thought that there can be no democracy at home while there is domination abroad.[29] Domestic and international reform must go hand-in-hand.

The question of which principles of international relations should follow from the account of republican nondomination is a complex one that I can only raise, but not address, here. Tricky questions, in particular, arise in relation to the legitimacy of outside interference in the internal affairs of a state. On a republican view, a state that exercises capability-denying domination over its citizens – a state, that is, that is both non-representative and that fails to meet the basic socioeconomic needs of its populace – can legitimately (we could say paradigmatically) be subjected to external interference, as it has forfeited its right to be treated as free and sovereign by others (think of Burma today). But imagine that the failures of the state in question can demonstrably be traced back to its dominated status within a system of global interaction where it is structurally dependent on those very states that now purport to intervene in its affairs. To what extent does this affect the legitimacy of external interference? How do we ensure that external interference is not itself dominating? And more generally, how is the "dual domination" suffered by the world's poor best addressed? Such questions cannot be answered here, but their urgency is obvious. Let me simply note, to conclude, that Pettit neglects this "dual domination" because – like Rawls – he endorses a form of explanatory nationalism that makes unrepresentative states solely responsible for the problems of "abuse, poverty and insecurity" that their populations may suffer. As a result, Pettit is only able to provide instrumental, consequentialist arguments for the relief of the global poor – arguments that are grounded in self-interested concerns regarding the causes of global terrorism, mass immigration and environmental damage. In this paper, I have suggested that a critical republican theory can provide stronger reasons for seeking to reduce global distributive inequalities, insofar as these can be traced to the capability-denying domination that rich and powerful states exercise over the global poor.

References

Abizadeh, A. (2007). "Cooperation, Pervasive Impact, and Coercion: On the Scope (not Site) of Distributive Justice." *Philosophy and Public Affairs* 35: 318–58.

Alkire, S. (2005). *Valuing Freedoms: Sen's Capability Approach and Poverty Reduction.* Oxford: Oxford University Press.

Anderson, E. (1999). "What is the Point of Equality?" *Ethics* 109: 287–337.

Beitz, C. (2001). "Does Global Inequality Matter?" *Metaphilosophy* 32: 95–112.

Bell, D. (2009). "Republican Imperialism: J. A. Froude and the Virtue of Empire." *History of Political Thought* 30: 166–91.

Bertram, C. (2005). "Global Justice, Moral Development and Democracy." In: *The Political Philosophy of Cosmopolitanism.* Eds G. Brock and H. Brighouse, Cambridge: Cambridge University Press: 75–90.

Besson, S. and J. L. Martí (eds) (2009). *Legal Republicanism: National and International.* Oxford: Oxford University Press.

Bohman, J. (1997). "The Public Spheres of the World Citizen." In: *Perpetual Peace: Essays on Kant's Cosmopolitan Ideal.* Eds J. Bohman and M. Lutz-Bachmann, Cambridge, MA: MIT Press: 179–200.

Bohman, J. (2004). "Republican Cosmopolitanism." *Journal of Political Philosophy* 12: 336–52.

Bohman, J. (2005a). "The Democratic Minimum: Is Democracy a Means to Global Justice?" *Ethics & International Affairs* 19: 101–16.

Bohman, J. (2005b). "Constituting Humanity: Democracy, Human Rights, and Political Community." *Canadian Journal of Philosophy* 31 (supplementary): 227–52.

Bohman, J. (2007). "Nondomination and Transnational Democracy." In: *Republicanism and Political Theory*. Eds C. Laborde and J. Maynor, Oxford: Blackwell: 190–216.

Braithwaite, J. (2007). "Contestatory Citizenship; Deliberative Denizenship." In: *Common Minds: Themes from the Philosophy of Philip Pettit*. Eds M. Smith, H. G. Brennan, R. E. Goodin and F. C. Jackson, Oxford: Oxford University Press: 161–81.

Caney, S. (2006). "Cosmopolitan Justice and Institutional Design: An Egalitarian Liberal Conception of Global Governance." *Social Theory and Practice* 32: 725–56.

Carter, I. (2007). "How are Power and Unfreedom Related?" In: *Republicanism and Political Theory*. Eds C. Laborde and J. Maynor, Oxford: Blackwell: 58–82.

Dagger, R. (2005). "Domination and the Republican Challenge to Liberalism." In: *Autonomy and the Challenges to Liberalism*. Eds J. Christman and J. Anderson, Cambridge: Cambridge University Press: 177–203.

Forst, R. (2001). "Towards a Critical Theory of Transnational Justice." *Metaphilosophy* 32: 160–79.

Goodin, R. (2003). "Folie Républicaine." *Annual Review of Political Science* 6: 55–76.

Haque, A. A. (2005). "Justice without Borders: A Reply to Nagel." Available at SSRN: http://ssrn.com/abstract=654941 (last accessed 17/12/12).

Held, D. (1995). *Democracy and the Global Order: From the Modern State to Cosmopolitan Governance*. Cambridge: Polity Press.

Hurrell, A. (2001). "Global Inequality and International Institutions." *Metaphilosophy* 32: 34–57.

Ivison, D. (2010). "Republican Human Rights?" *European Journal of Political Theory* 9: 31–47.

Laborde, C. (2006). "Female Autonomy, Education and the *Hijab*." *Critical Review of International Social and Political Philosophy* 9: 351–77.

Laborde, C. (2008). *Critical Republicanism: The Hijab Controversy and Political Philosophy*. Oxford: Oxford University Press.

McMahon, C. (2005). "The Indeterminacy of Republican Policy." *Philosophy and Public Affairs* 33: 67–93.

Miller, D. (1988). "The Ethical Significance of Nationality." *Ethics* 98: 647–62.

Miller, D. (1995). "Complex Equality." In: *Pluralism, Justice and Equality*. Eds D. Miller and M. Walzer, Oxford: Oxford University Press: 197–225.

Miller, D. (1999a). *Principles of Social Justice*. Cambridge, MA: Harvard University Press.

Miller, D. (1999b). "Justice and Inequality." In: *Inequality, Globalization and World Politics*. Eds A. Hurrell and N. Woods, Oxford: Oxford University Press: 248–72.

Miller, D. (2000). *Citizenship and National Identity*. Cambridge: Polity Press.

Miller, D. (2007). *National Responsibility and Global Justice*. Oxford: Oxford University Press.

Moellendorf, D. (2005). "The World Trade Organization and Egalitarian Justice." *Metaphilosophy* 36: 145–62.

Nagel, T. (2005). "The Problem of Global Justice." *Philosophy and Public Affairs* 33: 113–47.

O'Neill, Onora (1986). *Faces of Hunger: An Essay on Poverty, Development and Justice*. London. Allen and Unwin.

Pettit P. (1996). "Freedom as Antipower." *Ethics* 106: 576–604.

Pettit, P. (1997). *Republicanism: A Theory of Freedom and Government*. Oxford: Oxford University Press.

Pettit, P. (2001a). *A Theory of Freedom: From the Psychology to the Politics of Agency*. Cambridge: Polity Press.

Pettit, P. (2001b). "Capability and Freedom: A Defence of Sen." *Economics and Philosophy* 17: 1–20.

Pettit, P. (2003). "Agency-Freedom and Option-Freedom." *Journal of Theoretical Politics* 15: 387–403.

Pettit, P. (2005). "The Domination Complaint." In: *Political Exclusion and Domination. NOMOS XLVI.* Eds M. Williams and S. Macedo, New York: New York University Press: 87–117.

Pettit, P. (2006). "The Determinacy of Republican Policy: A Reply to McMahon." *Philosophy and Public Affairs* 34: 275–83.

Pettit, P. (2007a). "Republican Freedom: Three Axioms, Four Theorems." In: *Republicanism and Political Theory*. Eds C. Laborde and J. Maynor, Oxford: Blackwell: 102–31.

Pettit, P. (2007b). "Joining the Dots." In: *Common Minds: Themes from the Philosophy of Philip Pettit*. Eds M. Smith, H. G. Brennan, R. E. Goodin and F. C. Jackson, Oxford: Oxford University Press: 215–344.

Pettit, P. (2008). "The Basic Liberties." In: *The Legacy of H. L. A. Hart: Legal, Political and Moral Philosophy*. Eds M. Kramer, C. Grant, B. Colburn and A. Hatzistavrou, Oxford: Oxford University Press: 201–21.

Pettit, P. (2010). "A Republican Law of Peoples." *European Journal of Political Theory* 9: 70–94.

Pevnick, R. (2008). "Political Coercion and the Scope of Distributive Justice." *Political Studies* 56: 339–416.

Pogge, T. W. (2002). *World Poverty and Human Rights: Cosmopolitan Responsibilities and Reforms*. Cambridge: Polity Press.

Pogge, T. W. (2005). "Real World Justice." *The Journal of Ethics* 9: 29-53.

Pogge, T. W. (ed.) (2007). *Freedom from Poverty as a Human Right. Who Owes What to the Very Poor?* Oxford: Oxford University Press.

Quill, L. (1995) *Liberty after Liberalism. Civic Republicanism in a Global Age*. Basingtoke: Palgrave Macmillan.

Rawls, J. (1972) *A Theory of Justice*, rev. edn. Oxford: Oxford University Press.

Rawls, J. (1999). *The Law of Peoples*. Cambridge, MA: Harvard University Press.

Robeyns, I. (2006). "Assessing Global Poverty and Inequality." In: *Global Institutions and Responsibilities: Achieving Global Justice*. Eds C. Barry and T. Pogge, Malden, MA: Blackwell: 29–47.

Sangiovanni, A. (2007). "Global Justice, Reciprocity, and the State." *Philosophy and Public Affairs* 35, 3–39.

Sen, Amartya (1982). *Poverty and Famines: An Essay on Entitlements and Deprivation*. Oxford: Clarendon Press.

Shklar, J. N. (1998). "The Liberalism of Fear." In: J. N. Shklar. *Political Thought and Political Thinkers*. Eds S. Hoffmann and G. Kateb, Chicago: Chicago University Press: 3–20.

Skinner, Q. (1997). *Liberty before Liberalism*. Cambridge: Cambridge University Press.

Skinner, Q. (2007). "Freedom as the Absence of Arbitrary Power." In: *Republicanism and Political Theory*. Eds C. Laborde and J. Maynor, Oxford: Blackwell: 83–101.

Slaughter, S. (2005). *Liberty beyond Neoliberalism: A Republican Critique of Liberal Governance in a Globalising Age*. Basingstoke: Palgrave Press.
Stiglitz, J. (2006). *Making Globalization Work*. London: Penguin.
Van Parijs, P. (1999). "Contestatory Democracy versus Real Freedom for All." In: *Democracy's Value*. Eds I. Shapiro and C. Hacker-Cordon, Cambridge: Cambridge University Press: 191–8.
Viroli, M. (1995). *For Love of Country: An Essay on Patriotism and Nationalism*. Oxford: Oxford University Press.
Waldron, J. (2007). "Pettit's Molecule." In: *Common Minds: Themes from the Philosophy of Philip Pettit*. Eds M. Smith, H. G. Brennan, R. E. Goodin and F. C. Jackson, Oxford: Oxford University Press: 143–60.
White, S. (2003). "Republican Cosmopolitanism." In: *Forms of Justice: Critical Perspectives on David Miller's Political Philosophy*. Eds D. Bell and A. De-Shalit, Lanham, MD: Rowman and Littlefield: 251–68.
Young, I. M. (2004). "Responsibility and Global Labor Justice." *The Journal of Political Philosophy* 12: 365–88.

Notes

1. This paper was published in a special issue of the *European Journal of Political Theory* on 'Republicanism and International Relations', January 2010 vol. 9 no. 1 48–69. I am grateful to the editors for permission to reprint.
2. For an application of critical republicanism to issues of multicultural justice, see Laborde 2008.
3. On the new global politics of resistance, and "cosmorepublican liberty" see Quill 1995.
4. On global public opinion, see Bohman 1997.
5. See the other contributions to this volume, as well as Besson et al. 2009.
6. On social equality see Anderson 1999; Miller 1995; 1999a, 15–16, 240–1.
7. See, similarly, Rainer Forst's (2001, 172) distinction between maximal and minimal justice: "[M]aximal justice is the result of the justificatory discourses made possible by [the basic] structure, discourses about the details of economic production and distribution, of the legal system, the educational system, and so forth. Not all of this is covered by minimal justice, for this only establishes a threshold of political and social equality, making justificatory discourses possible in the first place."
8. For an insightful discussion, see Beitz 2001.
9. As he puts it, "ensuring your social freedom will require eliminating those material and related disadvantage that expose you to control by others. They don't compromise liberty in the manner of social control, but condition the range and ease with which liberty may be exercised – they reduce the worth of liberty": Pettit 2007b, 303, fn 43. In another paper, Pettit 2003 has suggested that poverty might indicate a lack of "option-freedom," while domination is a paradigmatic case of lack of "agency-freedom."
10. Pettit 2007a, 103; italics added. Cf. also Pettit 2006.
11. The thought is pursued in Pettit (2008). There, Pettit argues that free persons have a suitable degree of protection against alien control in the realm of certain choices that he describes as the basic liberties, and which would include basic capabilities.
12. See also Pettit 2006, 278–9; 2007a.

13. For suggestive links between freedom as nondomination and the capabilities approach, see Pettit 2001a, chap. 7; 2001b.

14. Pettit 1997, 59 provides a list of resources of domination, but he does not sufficiently distinguish between institutional and agent-relative resources.

15. Pettit does recognize that "representative states may be subject to the alien control of public, international bodies" but he sees the latter not as systemic structures of domination but, rather, as third parties endowed with their own agent-relative power. He also thinks that they tend to be "relatively accountable and non-arbitrary," which may be true of the majority of international organizations (IOs), and may be true of their dealings with Western representative states, but fails to account for the structurally dominating position that IOs such as the IMF, the World Bank or the WTO have over developing countries. Pettit concludes that only a "perverted sense of priority" would put the reform of IOs on the republican agenda. This is true only if what I have called the "Pogge hypothesis" is implausible.

16. On shared responsibility, see the chapters by Elizabeth Ashford and Simon Caney in Pogge 2007, and Young 2004. Like such accounts, the republican account is vulnerable to the critique that the shared responsibility is too vague to ground a clear duty to act on the part of specific agents. It is true that this vagueness is detrimental to a precise *legal* account of rights and duties, but it is not so detrimental to a more *political* account of civic responsibility, such as that favoured by republicans.

17. See also Haque 2005.

18. A strong republican theme is that economic globalization has been too depoliticized and left to the vagaries of seemingly natural market forces, which arbitrarily determine the fate of whole societies, denying their citizens minimal control over their collective destinies; see Slaughter 2005.

19. Here I draw on Pevnick 2008 and Abizadeh 2007.

20. For a concise survey of the empirical literature on how international institutions promote global justice, see Caney 2006.

21. For criticisms of such ideals, see Miller 2007, chap. 2.

22. For an identification of relevant metrics of poverty and inequality, see Robeyns 2006.

23. For a good discussion of the institutional implications of this demand, see Caney 2006.

24. For the relevance of radical inequality to thinking about "real world justice," see Pogge 2005; 2002, 198.

25. Proposals include: the Tobin tax, cancellation of Third World debt, and Pogge's idea of a Global Resource Dividend.

26. For concrete proposals (examples include: equalizing influence in such organizations as the IMF, the World Bank and WTO; facilitating the participation of vulnerable people; improving enforcement mechanisms; setting up international ombudsmen; and improving democratic accountability) see Caney 2006, 745–51. See also Held 1995.

27. Pogge 2002, 184 argues, in republican vein, that even when political choices are morally "closed" (for example, when they concern the protection of fundamental rights) "the primary and ultimate responsibility for their being made correctly should lie with the persons themselves," and he places what he calls a "human right to equal opportunity for political participation" at the heart of his cosmopolitan proposals. Caney 2006, 743 defends an instrumental view of democratic procedures, as the best

way to achieve a basic justice threshold, but beyond that threshold, argues that competing ideals of justice be mediated fairly in an "international area where all those bound by global rules and regulations have a chance to shape the construction of the rules."

28. Yet Miller rightly adds a crucial proviso: "[I]f *we could prevent the conversion of material advantage into political domination*, there would be nothing inherently reprehensible about some nations being richer than others" (italics added).

29. This is also true of imperial states that exercise unchecked domination over foreign peoples: They are liable to see *their* domestic liberties and rights undermined in the process. Witness the effects of the War on Terror today, and, more generally, Bohman 2007. For an alternative view of the relationship between republicanism, empire and liberty in nineteenth-century Victorian thought, see Bell 2009.

CHAPTER 12

Republicanism and Transnational Democracy

Andreas Niederberger

The past ten years have seen a host of new publications examining the significance of the republican tradition for international relations and a cosmopolitan political philosophy (for example, Bohman 2007; Deudney 2007; Onuf 1998; Pettit 2010a), a development that is paralleled by a renewed interest in republicanism among historians of ideas (for example, Skinner 1998; van Gelderen and Skinner 2002; Pocock 2003) and political philosophers (for example, Pettit 1997; Viroli 2002). It seems clear now that the problem of legitimate international organizations and, more generally, of legitimate transnational political arrangements must be defined as a tension between two claims. First, such institutions are necessary to ensure that states or nonstate international agents (such as multinational corporations or nongovernmental organizations) do not dominate other states or communities whose states cannot properly shield them from such encroachments. But second, international organizations and institutions in themselves also present a danger to freedom: this requires a response if we are not to be left with an infinite regress of yet more comprehensive institutions. This article argues that the premises of republican theory necessitate a rejection of common conceptions of a legitimate international order (such as a free association of individual states or a world state). A more precise understanding of these premises will enable us to formulate an alternative definition of a legitimate global order. This definition differentiates between states, federations of states, other organizations and political communities in which material rules or policies are established for a range of very different areas on the one hand, and, on the other, global or transnational institutions or bodies that ensure that states do not become internally or externally dominating, and that nonstate international agents, too, do not dominate others. Republican theory thus defends a conception of transnational democracy as the basic structure of a legitimate global order.

In what follows, I will first give a general characterization of republican political theory and show how it differs from other approaches (1). I will then examine the internal connection between republicanism and modern statehood (2). In a third step, I will show why reducing republicanism to individual states or attempting to "globalize" the single republican state are two alternatives that are at odds with fundamental republican principles (3). In a final step, I will elucidate the exact nature of the relationship between republicanism and different elements and levels of statehood. Against this backdrop, I will sketch a model of transnational democracy that departs from the single state model and in which these levels and elements can be realized on a global scale (4).

1. PRELIMINARY REMARKS: ON THE CHARACTER OF REPUBLICAN THEORY AND COMMON MICONCEPTIONS

Republican political theory examines the conditions under which a political commonwealth can exist as a *political commonwealth*. Alternative political theories usually do one of the following: either they examine the preconditions that allow us to define certain structures as ones of power or domination, that is, to identify them as prescribing collectively binding norms and rules; or they develop criteria of legitimacy for any kind of domination, either in ethical terms or in terms of a theory of justice. "Realistic" or so-called rational choice theories thus highlight the equilibrium or disequilibrium that can be expected to prevail under real conditions of power where actions are motivated by self-interest. "Liberal" theories of justice, on the other hand, distinguish between ideal and nonideal theories and, against this backdrop, identify general or common interests of all individuals, and then examine how such interests may be met under more or less adverse circumstances.

Republican theories[1] do not simply add a third variant to these two types of political theory. Instead, they doubt that these approaches provide an adequate account of one important aspect of their subject, namely the conditions and foundations of political order. The reason for this is that these approaches misconstrue methodological individualism as a kind of voluntarism or decisionism. The idea that the existence of an order directly relies on the motivations, will or rationality of its members is thus misguided, and it is not surprising that the two seemingly different forms of political theory see the concluding of, and adherence to, a contract as paradigmatic cases of the formation and maintenance of political order.[2]

Republican theories, in contrast, while not rejecting ontological or methodological individualism, stress the interdependence of agents as well as the necessity of assuming collective intentionality[3] in order to be able to understand and explain complex forms of interaction.[4] Agents desiring to act (that is, desiring to develop and exercise a will) will always be aware that others also act or want to act (at least if we assume "normal" goals of action that almost always refer to the actions of others in one way or another). Every "decision" to affect the actions and lives of others by one's own actions implies an understanding of the possibility of becoming the "victim" of someone else's decisions. One's actions are therefore determined by one's will only if others do not simultaneously have the possibility of acting in a way that prevents one from acting. Therefore, willing to be the origin of one's actions and their limits implies the will to live in an order where others cannot arbitrarily interfere with one's actions.[5]

Republican theories ask *which structures, institutions and procedures (that is, which order in the above-mentioned sense) are best suited for making the interest of the commonwealth's members, or whatever it is that enables such complex forms of interaction, a collectively binding norm.* The theories thereby combine important elements of the two alternative approaches. But in combining them, they also challenge some of their central premises by highlighting the mutual dependency of agents as well as of validity claims and possibilities of enforcement. It is necessary even for selfish agents (indeed sometimes especially for selfish ones) to place themselves in such relations of interdependency in order to be able to pursue their goals – for otherwise, they would not be able to envisage such goals in the first place. At the same time, a "moral point of view" in a theory of justice structurally falls short of its object since what is at stake are interactions between non- (or not necessarily) moral agents, or, in Kant's terminology, the interrelationship between "external freedoms" or "freedom of choice."[6] An adequate political theory can and must therefore refer to such shared relations of interdependency because social action would otherwise be inconceivable. It cannot and should not, however, conceive of this sharedness as something that is morally or rationally required but as something that would also apply to a "nation of devils" (Niesen 2001).[7]

304

In the history of ideas, republican thought is often depicted as emphasizing the general good and arguing for ways of strengthening its normative powers. This likens republicanism to communitarian or virtue ethical positions that highlight the significance of the community for practicing virtues, perfecting human existence or generally realizing interests that are always related to concrete social contexts.[8] This is certainly important for many republican theorists, and especially for Jean-Jacques Rousseau, who is often seen as the central advocate of republicanism in modern times. But such references to the common or general good must not be understood either as simply virtue ethical arguments for the value of certain virtues, nor as assumptions that communities are morally valuable in and of themselves. Rather, the point is to emphasize that shared conditions of action are indispensable and, sometimes, to recognize that the motivational power of such an understanding of their indispensability is limited, the idea being that this lack of motivation can be replaced or supplemented by ingraining the reference to the community through habitualization.[9] Emphasizing the value of the common good thus always also has the purpose of alluding to an ethical theory that addresses the problem of lacking or insufficient motivations for action.

Therefore, it is misleading to characterize republican theories as the most "idealistic" ones in virtue of their emphasis on the agents' common-good orientation.[10] Rather, such theories deduce this orientation from the necessity of shared social and political structures whose existence or possibility agents must assume even from a selfish point of view. The existence and maintenance of such structures therefore must constitute the real subject of political theory. Pointing to the common good orientation, then, is just one strategy among others of explaining why such structures exist and how they are maintained. At the same time, this strategy emphasizes that it is not concerned with a theory of reason of state but with an order that actually secures and promotes the freedom of every one of its citizens. In the following, I will introduce and discuss another important strategy that centers on the state and the rule of law and in some respects directly repudiates the emphasis on civic virtues; as such, it is characteristic of so-called neo-Roman republicanism[11] or neo-republicanism.[12]

2. REPUBLICANISM AND MODERN STATEHOOD

For a long time, it has seemed the case that because of their close association with the conditions for the validity and enforcement of legitimate
rule, only small political communities that are capable of governing
themselves democratically make legitimate or ideal republics. For only in
small or at least relatively homogenous polities does it seem possible that
that which is (equally) good or necessary for all can actually constitute,
through a shared exercise, procedure or structure of power, the community's main determining purpose. Many authors have therefore given
pride of place to civic republicanism and its emphasis on the development
and practice of communally oriented or political virtues, effectively identifying republicanism and communitarianism (Habermas 1998; Honohan
2002; Honohan and Jennings 2006). Republican theories thus appear as
approaches that depend on the social, historical and cultural conditions
for the emergence and existence of communities.[13]

In the past years, a variant of republicanism has emerged, first among
historians, and then among political theorists, that has freed republicanism
to a large extent from its communitarian elements while highlighting the
neo-Roman aspects of many modern republican positions.[14] Surprisingly,
however, this separation of republicanism and communitarianism has
not induced scholars of republicanism to seriously engage with space and
action beyond historically grown nation-states. True, states are no longer
seen as an expression of a common cultural or national "destiny." But
they are still the main and sometimes even exclusive point of reference
for republican conceptions of the rule of law and democracy. This focus
on state-based republicanism is not just a transitory phase of scholarship
to be superseded by a new understanding of the world in an age of globalization. In liberal approaches, the theoretical justification of individual
normative claims often precedes the question of their realization, or, to
put it another way, their justification is distinct in a way that it retains a
critical capacity even where the normative claims have seemingly been
put into practice: Their theoretical justification can thus never be fully
contained in their practical realization.[15] Such a standard of normative
claims may be applied to every basic structure or institution. This is why
liberal justifications of principles or of rights lend themselves so well to a
critical appraisal or evaluation of global structures and institutions. The
neo-Roman republican conception of legitimacy, by contrast, is closely
associated with the genesis and development of modern Western state-

306

hood, and not least because it wishes to avoid reducing republicanism to virtue ethics. For in this variant of republicanism, normative claims are inextricably linked to the way they are put into practice in structures or institutions. Thus, the way in which claims are realized is in itself essential when it comes to justifying claims.

Given this background, it may seem that there are only two options when discussing the problem of global republicanism: Either one assumes that republicanism must stay confined to individual states, since the conditions for republican statehood are "unglobalizable" (and then proceeds to develop more extensive global regulations or institutions for promoting bi- or multilateral contracts between individual states), or one develops a conception according to which statehood must be expanded on a continental or global level, as this is the only way of making republicanism viable on a global scale. Both options, however, are potentially at odds with some basic tenets of republican theory, rendering them unattractive or even unacceptable – which again is clearly an important reason why this question remains largely unexamined.

Not surprisingly, therefore, Nicholas Greenwood Onuf argues in *The Republican Legacy in International Thought* that republicanism's existence as an autonomous theory of order and political rule was confined to the premodern era. According to Onuf (1998, 31–84), republicanism consists of a conception of a (purely) political association or coordination and of a (purely) political control of social conditions of action (which is why the terms *politeia*, *civitas* and *res publica* are in his view pivotal to republican theory). With the advent of the modern state, however, order, rule and ultimately also the conditions of legitimacy must be construed in terms of the scope and activities that are characteristic of the entire state's institutions and procedures. According to this conception, in modern times societies primarily emerge because of powerful state institutions and procedures, and not so much because of a political mode of mutual association and coordination or because of a thus legitimated practice of coercion. The republican *legacy* in modern states (here, the idea of a purposeful reactivation of republican motifs is presented as an alternative to Pocock's (2003) idea of a "tradition" (as a continuation of republicanism)) thus consists of the vestiges or of a new form of a (purely) political formation of societies that can be found in democracies and that can partially control or even program the internal actions of states but without actually becoming a really state-defining element (Onuf 1998, 6–8).

With regard to the significance of antiquity for modern politics or to models of "radical democracy," it may seem sensible to characterize a seemingly ancient conception of republicanism as its "real" form and then contrast this, either as a corrective or as an alternative ideal, with a modern, state-centered conception of politics and the concomitant emergence of "liberal" subjective rights since at least the late eighteenth century. This approach, however, neglects the fact that what is interesting about the recent "revival" of republicanism (Sunstein 1988) is not its social philosophy angle. Rather, what is significant is the specific way in which politics, law and institutions are bound together, precisely in order to achieve an adequate understanding and normative justification of the modern and coinciding inevitability of state structures and individual rights. In this respect, and in contrast to Onuf, one must realize that it was only *with modern statehood* that republicanism and its incorporation of individual rights became an overarching and convincing concept.

Neo-republicanism takes five main premises as its starting point.[16]

(1) Individuals have a basic normative interest in (freedom as) nondomination, that is, in interpersonal relations where individuals are not subject to arbitrary interference by others (Pettit 1997, 51–79).

(2) In order to realize (freedom as) nondomination between individuals and to secure people against having someone else's arbitrary will imposed on them, institutions must be established that prevent individuals from arbitrarily interfering with one another's actions (Pettit 1997, 80–109).

(3) The establishment and functioning of institutions designed to implement freedom as nondomination among individuals does not assume a dominating function itself only if those institutions, too, cannot arbitrarily interfere with the actions of individuals (Pettit 1997, 171–205).

(4) In order to ensure that institutions do not themselves turn into agents of domination, they must be designed in a way that makes them necessarily and exclusively tied to the conditions for nonarbitrariness in individuals' dealings with one another.[17]

(5) The "conditions for the nonarbitrariness in inter-individual relations" cannot be construed in an exclusively "negative" manner. They must contain "positive" stipulations that lay down under which conditions it is permissible or even necessary that individuals mutually interfere with one another's actions or options and/or under which conditions these can or must be subject to interference from institutions. Without procedures and institutions that allow for political rule in the sense of governing and controlling reality, it would not be comprehensible why and how the republic is a precondition for the coordination of action.

On the basis of these premises one can show that a political order must fulfill three requirements in order to be legitimate, that is, to meet the standards stipulated by the basic premises. First, both the relations between individuals as well as those between individuals and institutions must be of a legal nature (a). Second, the law must emanate from a legislature that is chosen by all individuals that will be subject to its laws (b). Third, the relations between different institutions, and between institutions and the legislature, must be such that the institutions as well as those affected by them are mutually permitted or even forced to control the institutions' legality and prevent them from becoming independent to a degree that they cease to be revisable and controllable (c).

(a) Social conditions of action can only be nonarbitrary and independent of the arbitrary choices of all or some agents if all those affected (could) know what the social conditions of action (ought to) look like, and if they can be sure that this norm is the reason why completed actions are factually permissible/impermissible, and thus also the reason why interventions take place that prohibit impermissible actions and support permissible ones. This type of double knowledge (that is, knowledge of how things should be as well as of what will be done if this standard is not maintained) must consist of an ensemble of rules. In this ensemble, certain rules determine what is permissible and impermissible. Others decide that and how conflicts concerning the specific applicability of a rule may or will be resolved. These rules indicate how the possibly necessary implementation of a rule can be enforced and how the (possibly) illegitimate enforcement of a rule can be assessed and compensated for. The law is a paradigmatic case of such an ensemble of rules where different function levels correspond with bodies that authoritatively determine the applicability/nonapplicability of rules. Therefore, the legal nature of the relations between individuals and between individuals and institutions ensures, in a first basic respect, that these are not arbitrary in nature.

(b) Assuming, however, that the mere knowability of rules does not per se make them generally justifiable or acceptable, the condition sketched out above is only a necessary and formal one that ensures the nonarbitrariness of social circumstances of action. For as long as one cannot exclude the possibility that an uncontrolled or even uncontrollable legislator makes rules that are arbitrary in content,[18] even a nonarbitrary interpretation, application and enforcement of rules will be essentially arbitrary. It is therefore necessary to ensure that neither the *creation* nor the *confirmation* of legal rules and principles are arbitrary in nature. Under the conditions of a reasonable pluralism, this can only mean that all individuals living in social circumstances that are governed by rules and principles must themselves participate in their creation as well as in their administration and continuation. This means that a rule and principle making power is required that directly or indirectly includes those affected or at least enables them to participate if they get the impression that their relevant interests do not receive (adequate) consideration.[19] Only in terms of its conditions can one (partially) forego this direct appeal to such an inclusively construed legislature, for the legislature cannot, without becoming inconsistent, abrogate the conditions for its own legitimate position of primacy.[20]

(c) Including all persons affected in the legislative procedure and ensuring their permanent involvement creates the precondition for letting them shape and control the institutions that guarantee the legal nature of their dealings with one another. But this will only become binding if institutions *necessarily* require authorization through legislation or by the legislating power, or if their resources and possibilities depend on the persons involved or on other institutions to such an extent that without them they cannot exist or do not have certain relevant options. Institutions must therefore be sufficiently strong and well-endowed with resources for them to be able to guarantee the nonarbitrary validity of rules and principles. Strength and resources must not, however, have the consequence that these rules and principles are no longer the (exclusive) reason for the institutions' operations. These requirements become reconcilable with one another where institutions are differentiated functionally and in terms of their modes of acquiring and using resources, where political positions are combined with professionally chosen ones, and where there is legal and political accountability on different levels including the possibility of sanctions (unless the officials in question were explicitly relieved of any responsibility). Furthermore, courts must provide everyone with the possibility of enforcing the law by legal action, of controlling the institutions with regard to the law of the land, or of reviewing the admissibility of legislative acts in terms of the general conditions of the legitimacy of the political order.

It seems that especially with regard to the third and last requirement, the republican expectations of a legitimate political order can only be realized in the kind of state that emerged most of all, and perhaps even exclusively, in Europe and North America since approximately 1600.[21] By dint of functional differentiation and a professionalized administration, this type of statehood created an unprecedented power of steering and controlling society (that became particularly evident in the totalitarian manifestations of statehood in the twentieth century). At the same time the modern Western state developed, through a democratization and codification of statehood, important procedures and structures which those affected by the state's operations could use to control and influence it. Thereby, in the properly organized modern state there emerges at least the possibility of establishing general nonarbitrary social conditions of action while at the same time securing, through the medium of law and the underlying democratic procedures, that the nonarbitrariness is always an expression of the interests and decisions of the state's citizens (for example, Maus 2002).

3. REPUBLICAN ORDER BEYOND THE STATE? TWO UNCONVINCING ANSWERS

The above reconstruction of neo-republicanism's basic premises and the demands it makes on a legitimate political order clearly demonstrate that fulfilling republican expectations does not depend on conditions that are specific to a certain community. Communitarian conditions become significant only – and here Onuf has a point – when one examines how common projects emerge or which mutual concessions are made during the process of legislation in order to obtain results that are acceptable to the majority. At the same time it seems, however, as though republican conditions can only be fulfilled as a whole – for the three conditions set out above can in themselves only be considered necessary, but not sufficient. They must always imply the other conditions' validity, since without them one cannot exclude the possibility that, being only individually valid, they themselves contribute to an arbitrary state of affairs.[22] It remains unclear, however (at least with regard to the above), whether the democratic and law-governed state could, wholly or partially, serve as a starting point for constructing or reconstructing a republican order that transcends individual states. The modern system of individual states may be the result of a specific historical development; from a systematic point of view, however, it is hard to decide whether some of its levels or aspects are more fundamental than others[23] and could therefore serve as basic building blocks for forms of political order other than the state. Modern statehood is a particular constitution or form of the social sphere from which it would be hard to extract a substrate of general, normatively desirable social relations that ought to be aspired to before or beyond the state. Regarding the problem of whether the republican order can be expanded beyond the realm of individual states, we are faced with two questions: first, if and how it is possible to imagine the ideal of republicanism beyond the state, and second, what such an ideal could mean in the context of the present transformation or even transnationalization of social spheres of action and of statehood and its bodies of institutional steering and control.

A first obvious strategy when addressing the question of republicanism's "globalizability" would be to argue that coupling the republican political order with the model of the Western state or with a plurality of states in such a system is contingent in a way that makes the state necessary but does not engender the necessity of a *plurality* of individual states. Instead, the argument runs, the same considerations may directly serve as a justification of a single republican world state. This argument correctly emphasizes the fact that on the most general level of basic republican premises, as argued above, there is no reason for confining the state to any borders. One can certainly imagine a law-governed society, a shared legislature and functionally differentiated efficient institutions existing on a global scale, and such an idea may even be obvious when recalling, for example, James Madison's thoughts on the advantage of large political entities.[24] However, there are at least three counterarguments to be made: First, in terms of empirical evidence, it is not clear, and perhaps even disputable, whether properly functioning state or statelike institutions can indeed be established on a global or continental level. It remains to be shown that such institutions and structures are not merely abstract ideas. Otherwise, there is a risk that a philosophical theory will lend uncritical support to problematic structures and developments, or, at least, may not appreciate that the institutions, structures and procedures are genuinely novel ones. Second, where the legislature operates on a global scale, the content of legal rules and principles will be restricted in a way that will make it much more difficult to subject the social conditions of action to political decision making. Since a direct grasp on the common good is not available, and since laws can sometimes involve significant costs and burdens, depending on their scope and purpose, it is unlikely that laws are enacted that benefit "relatively few" people (because of the global frame of reference, this could still be a numerically significant group) while implying disadvantages to "relatively many" (for example, in the form of taxes).[25] One possibility would be that several minorities opt to form a majority by voting on or merging their different interests; but this is problematic in the sense that assessing different rules and principles in terms of their respective merits and weaknesses becomes more difficult or even "irrational" as a no-vote may entail grave consequences for those casting it. This is the reason why "package solutions" are often accepted (for example, in the case of European treaties but also when heterogeneous parties in individual states are forced to compromise), even though many of the package's individual aspects are actually considered nonsensical by the respective majorities.

Both these reservations partly depend on further considerations and assessments of the required institutions and of the formation of political interests and coalitions. Third, however, there is a systematic argument to be made against the perspective of a world state. According to this argument, republican theory must, since it stipulates that social conditions of action must not be arbitrary (both in terms of the relationship between individuals and between individuals and institutions) also imply the claim that this nonarbitrariness be guaranteed as widely and deeply as possible. What is interesting about the modern state is precisely its creation of a comprehensive new form of the social where many domains of interaction are, to an ever-increasing extent, no longer determined by individual arbitrary action.[26] The problem that the two goals of "width" and "depth" may sometimes be at odds with one another arises even where just one state is concerned; it will therefore be necessary to occasionally gauge their respective importance. It could, for example, be the case that in order to make conditions such that one is not in danger of being arbitrarily killed, one is forced to reduce people's options or to create opportunities of interfering without being able to present intrinsic, that is, in every case nonarbitrary reasons for doing so.[27] Arguing that the depth of securing certain fundamental claims is more important than widely securing other claims will often not be controversial; therefore, it is possible to make a generally acceptable and differentiated case for securing nonarbitrariness in depth and width within states and to provide an institutional guarantee to this end. (This effectively means providing an institutional safeguard that will always be controversial but with regard to which one would not dispute that an adequate balance could be established in principle.) However, a world state (conceived simply as a reproduction of the individual state on a global scale) presents us with a new dimension of the problem. For due to the global reach of institutions, the depth or width of nonarbitrariness is directly correlated with the institutions' potential for arbitrariness. In the last resort, therefore, individual spheres can no longer be weighed up; instead, the entire examination must assume the perspective of avoiding tyrannical institutions. Consequently, it becomes necessary to accept significant restrictions both in terms of depth and width. Bearing this in mind, the opportunities provided by an individual state are clearly more attractive than those of a world state – which is why practically no advocate of the world state model would assign it a function beyond that of securing basic human rights and controlling those forms of violence whose destructive potential could be global in reach.[28]

Having examined the difficulties of reconciling the desired depth and width in guaranteeing nonarbitrariness with the arbitrary potential of global institutions, we are led to a second possible republican option regarding the question of the desirability and possibility of a republican order beyond the individual state. According to this, such an order could not conceivably meet the requirements developed above (for example, Dahl 1999). The decidedly noncommunitarian argument supporting this claim is that in an overly extensive commonwealth, it is not possible simultaneously to realize *both* the interest in nonarbitrariness between agents *and* the interest in the nonarbitrary existence and operation of institutions. But if they cannot be realized simultaneously, one cannot define the goals and legitimacy of international institutions and structures on the basis of freedom as nondomination, for such a basis only makes sense if both perspectives can be brought together. Where there are no institutions, there cannot be nonarbitrariness between agents; but where the agents do not have the capacity to steer and control the institutions, nonarbitrariness cannot be realized either.

This argument may work "hermeneutically" in the sense of a state-internal reflection on the state's character and conditions of legitimacy. It is therefore possible to argue, as part of an internal reconstruction of a commonwealth, that when functions designed to secure the nonarbitrariness in certain areas in depth and in width are delegated to supranational institutions, this changes the type of obligation toward the institutions and may even nullify it. Philosophically, however, this argument is not convincing for at least two important reasons: First, one must take into account the factual global or continental interconnectedness of social spheres as well as the menaces and arbitrariness potentially inherent in inter-state relations. In view of this, it is necessary to reflect on the conditions of legitimate or desirable relations beyond and between states, even if one rejects the extensibility of the republican order. In light of the basic republican premises, it is not obvious why these relations should be sufficient even though they are arbitrary in nature. One would have to explain

314

why dealings between individual agents necessarily require a third authority to ensure nonarbitrariness while interstate relations do not require such
an authority. Alternatively, one would have to elucidate how, if such an
authority is indeed required, one could ensure its nonarbitrary character
without once again having to resort to the model of republican statehood.
Second, it is difficult to justify with respect to the basic premises why the
historical process by which individual states emerged should constitute
a sufficient reason for denying others the possibility of creating shared
legal and institutional safeguards of freedom. Republicanism's justification of laws and institutions is universal in nature and relies primarily
on methodological individualism. This may still imply that there are
limits as to the scope of the guarantee provided by this type of justification (and this is how the republican critique of a world state ought to be
understood); however, these limits in fact make it imperative to consider
possible alternatives. If alternatives cannot be found, then (freedom as)
nondomination could no longer serve as the *basic concept* of a theory of
legitimacy, for one could not exclude the possibility that as a consequence
of nondomination, some individuals are "legitimately" dominated in the
sense that they are denied the possibility of living under shared laws and
institutions, or in the sense that nondomination is established only for
some, thus enabling them to dominate others.[29]

4. THE REPUBLICAN MODEL OF A TRANSNATIONAL DEMOCRACY

Thus, the model of a uniform world state must be rejected because in
such a state, the simultaneous nonarbitrariness of inter-agent relations
as well as agent-institution relations can only be realized by minimizing
the depth and width of nonarbitrariness. In virtue of its minimalism, the
world state would necessarily significantly fall below the level of depth
and width that was achieved in certain states in the second half of the
twentieth century, a level that is regarded as essential for justice and
democracy in these states. At the same time, one must not unduly restrict
the implementation (or the requirement of implementation) of a republican state of affairs to individual states (that exist in a plurality of such
states). For such a restriction would not do justice to the universal claim
that freedom as nondomination be achieved – neither in terms of the
extent of nonarbitrariness, nor in terms of the number of those making
this claim. Therefore, we should not give up the level of nonarbitrariness

that has thus far been achieved (or could still be achieved) in some states; nor should we give up the goal of achieving nonarbitrary conditions of action as well as a nonarbitrary functioning of institutions in trans- and international areas that are still determined by arbitrary factors. However, in criticizing these "all too simple" answers to the question of the republican conditions for a legitimate order beyond the individual state, we may already see the outlines of a possible alternative strategy emerging: for modern statehood was never as simple and closed as implied by the two alleged options. In many cases, it combined unity with complex differentiation, gradation and on occasion even with a reflective negotiation and re-negotiation of institutions and procedures, thus increasing the degree to which social spheres became subject to a statelike organization and enabling the state's democratization. The model of a transnational democracy that I now wish to propose takes its cue from this complexity of modern statehood. The model demonstrates how republican premises and standards of a legitimate order may be achieved in a globally consistent, legal, political and institutional structure.

Thus, to develop an account of a legitimate global order, the critique of the "too simple" answers means that the basic premises developed in the beginning must be stated in more precise terms; moreover, more requirements must be added to the three laid out above. The first basic premise then ought to read:

> (1*) *All* Individuals have, *in equal measure*, a basic normative interest in (freedom as) nondomination, that is, in interpersonal relations where they are not subject to arbitrary interference by others.

These additions emphasize the universalist character of republicanism. They exclude the possibility that nondomination for some can be achieved in a manner that leads to the domination of others. And they make it clear that a republican theory must account for the claims of *all* individuals *worldwide*.

The other criteria of a legitimate political order that so far follow from the basic premises also require a more precise formulation and/or additional stipulations. They are (a) that human actions are governed by laws, (b) that there exists an inclusive legislature, and (c) that there are procedures for controlling and regulating the institutions designed to protect the law, as well as a generally accessible jurisdiction. The first criterion (a) must now be understood to mean that laws must govern the actions of *all* humans *globally*. This is the only way of making sure that all agents in every conceivable situation can expect other agents and institutions, to which they (may) find themselves exposed, to act (at least in principle) in a nonarbitrary manner. When trying to justify why legal regulations in certain areas are preferable to similar regulations elsewhere (as in saying that it is more important to regulate labor conditions within national borders than to regulate the conditions for overseas investment by companies), the reasons given usually consist of empirical assumptions concerning interests, conducts of life, and so forth, that often will not stand up to philosophical scrutiny. One must therefore assume *prima facie* that a demand for legal regulation does not allow for a fundamental distinction between areas with a graded necessity or desirability.[30]

The second requirement (b) must be rephrased to say that all laws and regulations must rely on inclusive legislation or on the conditions of inclusive legislation. This allows for the existence of different legal spheres and levels with corresponding different legislatures or bodies that determine the conditions that must obtain in order for inclusive legislatures to exist; indeed, it actually demands this in order to ensure that the "positive" conditions for the nonarbitrariness of legal content obtain. This re-phrasing of (b), together with the third requirement (c), entails the new requirement (d) that third parties affected by these structures and institutions, be they individuals or other systems and their structures and institutions, must be given the opportunity to assess the arbitrariness of these effects and apply the necessary remedies. The legitimate activities of partial structures and institutions thus end where third parties are affected that were not included in the legislative process that authorized or initiated these activities. In this case, nonarbitrary conditions of action only obtain where there are bodies capable of determining (non-)arbitrariness, and where these bodies are endowed with sufficient resources to put a stop to such arbitrariness.

The four requirements must be met, and must be met simultaneously, if an individual or a global order claims to be legitimate. A fifth requirement (e) must be added, to be construed as a regulative principle, according to which the (global) political order must maximize the width and depth of nonarbitrary conditions of action. Thus it may be necessary to create bodies or institutions that can determine what maximization should look like and what conceivable variants there are for balancing width and depth. The fifth requirement introduces a yardstick that may be used to resolve conflicts between political entities, for such bodies provide the possibility of collectively finding solutions that enable people to

317

pursue projects and goals (possibly not shared by a global majority) while taking third party concerns into account in a way that they do not feel dominated.

These additions to and specifications of the basic republican premises and the corresponding criteria of a legitimate order point us in the right direction when it comes to developing an account of the conditions of legitimate rule beyond the individual state. It emphasizes the fact that in a neo-republican perspective, searching for a "world ethos" or identifying a global civil society are not decisive preconditions. Rather, the central concern is to ensure the existence of nonarbitrary conditions of action on a global scale, while not making amends in terms of the depth and width of nonarbitrariness.

Revising the premises and requirements in this way does not directly pave the way to a specific form of the global political order – just as the path to statehood came in many different guises. However, some further considerations may show how the state-centered perspective of republican scholarship thus far will change as a result of this revision. Now, modern statehood can no longer constitute the exclusive and, in some respects, primary point of reference, for the violation of the requirement of global nondominating conditions as well as external domination are both characteristic of modern statehood, while the new requirements explicitly exclude these features. A global republican order, by contrast, should crucially distinguish between two types of political structures and institutions: On the one hand, individual political orders with structures and institutions are required that are capable of establishing nonarbitrary conditions of action in a way that successfully balances the depth and width of their reach and on the other, structures and institutions must be capable of making sure that single orders do not become dominating themselves and do not fail at their task of securing nonarbitrariness. In terms of models, one should think of the second set of structures and institutions as a *network structure* whose function is to guarantee that the first orders, as *network elements*, do not conflict with one another or do not become internally arbitrary.

For the first single orders, the modern state remains a suitable point of reference. It enables us to explain how different dimensions and degrees of the nonarbitrary establishment, shaping and control of social conditions of action may be balanced. However, other forms of organization and order should also be considered. The process of globalization has precipitated the emergence of structures and institutions that differ significantly

318

from the state model, be it in terms of the scope of their goals or of the limits of their operations. In such cases, it would not make sense to model them on state institutions and structures. For example, international organizations and institutions often pursue fairly narrow goals, but do so in a global manner, whereas nongovernmental forms of association such as trade unions, non-governmental organizations (NGOs), professional organizations and multinational corporations can certainly be construed as ensuring nonarbitrariness in certain areas while not taking the state as a model. Using the state as a point of reference may help to describe how institutions operate on a deep and wide-reaching level. It may also help us to understand the functional differentiation and controllability, or the limits of controllability, of institutions. And the state model is useful when it comes to normatively reconstructing coordination procedures and deliberations between people with divergent positive as well as negative interests. Because of the heterogeneity as well as the occasionally conflicting nature of interests and projects, the state model should be used with care. Its combination of functions, goals and so forth often turns out to be dysfunctional, both in terms of efficiency and, especially, in terms of freedom.

Therefore, the "network elements" are the primary guarantors of nonarbitrary social conditions of action. Characteristically, their legality and the way structures and institutions operate in them are crucially rooted in, or supported by, a shared legislature. Thus, nonarbitrariness in this context depends on the principle that all individuals are capable of determining, by means of an (at least potentially) shared legislation, the governing rules and principles as well as the depth and width to which their validity is guaranteed. Only a shared legislation ensures that those concerned may construe the operations of structures and institutions as originating in themselves and in the limits and possibilities of their relationships with other agents. There must also exist a corresponding judicial system that decides on the lawfulness of individual actions and institutional operations based on the inclusively enacted legislation (with some rare exceptions concerning the conditions of universal participation in the legislative process). At the same time it seems clear that structures and institutions will have forfeited their legitimacy if the shared legislative activity has the sole purpose of ensuring that the relevant structures and institutions do not or cannot employ their power in an arbitrary manner.

The second set of structures and institutions must be construed very

differently; these really only make sense as global bodies. They constitute the apex of a comprehensively nonarbitrary arrangement and thus
assume a subordinate function. They have the authority and capacity to
intervene in cases where states and other organizations are not sufficiently
powerful to ensure nonarbitrary conditions of action. Such cases usually
come in one of four different forms: first, when individual network elements fail to internally establish nonarbitrary conditions (as in the case of
human rights violations); second, when network elements dominate one
another by arbitrarily interfering with the options of other elements (for
example, by threatening violence or "externalizing" ecological damages);
third, when (individual) agents do not have the possibility of acting in
nonarbitrary conditions as provided by the first set of institutions and
structures (for example, people living in failed states or in civil war contexts); and fourth and finally, where the network elements are such that
their revision (even where no single element can be held responsible for
"actively" dominating others) could entail a significant maximization of
nonarbitrariness (for example, in areas where a costly administration is
maintained in many different locations). In cases of the first and second
type, global structures and institutions will assume a primarily negative
function. They must be capable of stopping structures and institutions in
individual network elements or within the relevant orders from dominating others. Those affected by the third type must also receive positive
support. This should not mean, however, that global structures and institutions themselves assume the form of a network element.

This last point is paramount: The individual orders must primarily be
construed as the expression of the collective legislative activity of those
affected. The bodies of the network structure, on the other hand, must
primarily (that is, in view of types one to three) be construed according
to the judicial model. In democracies the judiciary (ideally) is accorded
two functions: On the one hand, it gives everybody the opportunity of
determining in a nonarbitrary manner whether individual or institutional
actions were lawful or not. This function is decisive as it provides a
general guarantee of the lawfulness of the conditions of action. On the
other hand, the judiciary has the power of judicial review, meaning that
it must review all legislation and all executive measures that are enabled
by, or even become necessary on, this basis in terms of their compatibility with the principle of nonarbitrariness in collective legislation. The
network structure's functions must be construed accordingly. Its bodies
and institutions must enable individuals, groups and network elements to

320

review the nondominating character of decisions and modes of operation and modify them where necessary.

The bodies and institutions of the network structure must not even assume a subsidiary function where people are "stateless" and have no access to the legislation and related institutions of a political order. For even in a case like this, agents may demand to codetermine the social conditions of which they themselves are part. "Subsidiary" operations by global institutions, on the other hand, would entail the consequence of having to include all those affected by them, and this in turn would amount to circuitously creating a comprehensive world state after all. The same goes for the goal pursued by global institutions of maximizing the width and depth of nonarbitrariness. For this, too, should not be about merely doing away with the existing network elements but would rather mean changing the dynamics of the relationships between them as well as between those affected by them.

All this is, at first, very abstract. This is because the reflections above aim to explain how the claim to nondomination must be construed on a global scale. The two main dimensions of nondominating conditions, first not to be subject to arbitrariness by others, and second to be able to participate in the shaping of these conditions, cannot be reduced to one another. But such reductions are usually at the core of approaches that either argue for a strict hierarchical global order or reject every form of political integration beyond the individual state (or emphasize the problems inherent in this idea). In the first case, it is argued that the avoidance of arbitrariness can only be guaranteed on a global scale, while deferring the question of how participation in the further shaping of the conditions may be ensured. In the second case, it is assumed that individuals can only influence legislation and the appointment of executives to a maximum degree within the framework of individual states which is why possible dominating effects on third parties are disregarded. To continue the neo-republican perspective leads to a network model that is capable of doing justice to both dimensions of nondomination without giving priority to one of them.

5. TRANSNATIONAL DEMOCRACY – A PERSPECTIVE EVEN UNDER NONIDEAL CONDITIONS?

The above remarks have shown that the neo-republican theory presents an interesting perspective on questions with a global reach, both on a fundamental level as well as on the level of institutional conceptions. But as indicated above, it is still not clear whether the mere conceivableness of a republican "ideal" of global political order means that there is good reason to actually strive for this ideal under nonideal conditions (which could mean putting in jeopardy standards of nonarbitrariness that have already been achieved, or picking the wrong "battlefield"):[31] If, in the republican perspective, a factually existing nonarbitrary state of affairs ought not be given up in the light of a potentially more comprehensive nonarbitrary state of affairs (if, that is, an "ideal" helps to better understand reality and possibly criticize it but does not in itself lend legitimacy to "new" agents), then it would seem as if the above arguments do not get us much further.

The answer to this question can only be a complex one and would require much in terms of further reflection. This cannot be done here; instead, I will conclude by offering three short observations:

First, it cannot be justified, even under nonideal conditions, that the realization, deepening or broadening of nonarbitrariness, be it within a state or another form of political organization, should entail dominating, that is, arbitrary effects on others. In this respect, there is an obligation to create a nonarbitrary lawful state of affairs even in areas where none has existed thus far. This mainly means that states who see themselves as republican must put a stop to their arbitrary effects on third parties and must submit to international regimes whose purpose is precisely that.

Another difficulty is, second, that new lawful regimes beyond individual states may sometimes only be achieved under the condition that they do not have at their basis a shared inclusive legislature or at least the conditions for one, perhaps in individual states. During the past decades, many international treaties have succeeded in establishing a more lawful global state of affairs. But this has in fact made participatory legislation more difficult, one consequence being that courts have assumed powers of control and regulation previously held by parliaments. However, the potential arbitrariness inherent in the realm outside of individual states or of international institutions (or, to put it more precisely, individual states who feel empowered by their existence to act in an advocatory manner) makes increasing juridification in principle a (relatively) more important goal than establishing inclusive legislation or securing the relevant conditions for such legislation.

Third and finally, in spite of the relative precedence of juridifying international relations as well as those between nonstate agents, one must not lose sight of the fact that even under nonideal conditions there are several means that may help pave the way for realizing the ideal of transnational democracy. Presently, this includes above all efforts to promote the continental integration of individual states – the EU being the paradigmatic case here, its many difficulties notwithstanding – mobilizing resources for state building, and further consolidating international law, with its already existing principles and mechanisms of avoiding and eliminating dominating effects on others, especially in the area of human rights and collective security.

References

Bohman, J. (2007). *Democracy across Borders: From Dêmos to Dêmoi*. Cambridge, MA: MIT Press.

Buchanan, A. (2004). *Justice, Legitimacy, and Self-Determination: Moral Foundations for International Law*. Oxford: Oxford University Press.

Dahl, R. A. (1999). "Can International Organizations Be Democratic? A Skeptic's View." In: *Democracy's Edges*. Eds I. Shapiro and C. Hacker-Cordón, Cambridge: Cambridge University Press: 19–36.

Deudney, D. H. (2007). *Bounding Power: Republican Security Theory from the Polis to the Global Village*. Princeton, Oxford: Princeton University Press.

Geuna, M. (2002). "Republicanism and Commercial Society in the Scottish Enlightenment: The Case of Adam Ferguson." In: *Republicanism: A Shared European Heritage – Vol. II. The Values of Republicanism in Early Modern Europe*. Eds M. van Gelderen and Q. Skinner, Cambridge: Cambridge University Press: 177–95.

Goldsmith, J. L. and E. A. Posner (2005). *The Limits of International Law*. Oxford: Oxford University Press.

Habermas, J. (1998). "Three Normative Models of Democracy." In: J. Habermas. *The Inclusion of the Other*. Cambridge, MA: MIT Press: 239–52.

Hamilton, A., J. Madison, and J. Jay (1999). *The Federalist Papers*. Ed. C. Rossiter, New York: Mentor.

Honohan, I. (2002). *Civic Republicanism*. London: Routledge.

Honohan, I. and J. Jennings (eds) (2006). *Republicanism in Theory and Practice*. London: Routledge.

Kant, I. (1991). *The Metaphysics of Morals*. Trans. M. Gregor, Cambridge: Cambridge University Press.

Lovett, F. and P. Pettit (2009). "Neo-Republicanism: A Normative and Institutional Research Program." *Annual Review of Political Science* 12: 11–29.

Maus, I. (2002). "Vom Nationalstaat zum Globalstaat oder: Der Niedergang der Demokratie." In: *Weltstaat oder Staatenwelt? Für und wider die Idee einer Weltrepublik*. Eds M. Lutz-Bachmann and J. Bohman, Frankfurt am Main: Suhrkamp: 226–59.

Miller, D. (1999). *Principles of Social Justice*. Cambridge, MA/London: Harvard University Press.

Nagel, T. (2005). "The Problem of Global Justice." *Philosophy & Public Affairs* 33: 113–47.

Niederberger, A. (2008). "Konstitutionalismus und Globale Gerechtigkeit in der Theorie Transnationaler Demokratie." In: *Transnationale Verrechtlichung. Nationale Demokratien im Kontext globaler Politik*. Eds R. Kreide and A. Niederberger, Frankfurt am Main, New York: Campus: 183–206.

Niederberger, A. (2009). *Demokratie unter Bedingungen der Weltgesellschaft? Normative Grundlagen legitimer Herrschaft in einer globalen politischen Ordnung*. Berlin/New York: de Gruyter.

Niesen, P. (2001). "Volk-von-Teufeln-Republikanismus. Zur Frage nach den moralischen Ressourcen der liberalen Demokratie." In: *Die Öffentlichkeit der Vernunft und die Vernunft der Öffentlichkeit. Festschrift für Jürgen Habermas*. Eds L. Wingert and K. Günther, Frankfurt am Main: Suhrkamp: 568–604.

Onuf, N. G. (1998). *The Republican Legacy in International Thought*. Cambridge: Cambridge University Press.

Pettit, P. (1997). *Republicanism: A Theory of Freedom and Government*. Oxford: Oxford University Press.

Pettit, P. (1999). "Republican Freedom and Contestatory Democratization." In: *Democracy's Value*. Eds I. Shapiro and C. Hacker-Cordón, Cambridge: Cambridge University Press: 163–90.

Pettit, P. (2004). "Depoliticizing Democracy." *Ratio Juris* 17: 52–65.

Pettit, P. (2008). "Three Conceptions of Democratic Control." *Constellations* 15: 46–55.

Pettit, P. (2010a). "Legitimate International Institutions: A Neo-Republican Perspective." In: *The Philosophy of International Law*. Eds S. Besson and J. Tasioulas, Oxford: Oxford University Press: 139–60.

Pettit, P. (2010b). "A Republican Law of Peoples." *European Journal of Political Theory* 9: 70–94.

Pocock, J. G. A. (1995). "The Ideal of Citizenship since Classical Times." In: *Theorizing Citizenship*. Ed. R. Beiner, Albany: State University of New York Press: 29–52.

Pocock, J. G. A. (2003). *The Machiavellian Moment: Florentine Political Thought and the Atlantic Republican Tradition*, 2nd edn. Princeton/Oxford: Princeton University Press.

Reinhard, W. (2002). *Geschichte der Staatsgewalt. Eine vergleichende Verfassungsgeschichte Europas von den Anfängen bis zur Gegenwart*, 3rd edn. München: Beck.

Richardson, H. S. (2002). *Democratic Autonomy: Public Reasoning about the Ends of Policy*. Oxford: Oxford University Press.

Richter, E. (2004). *Republikanische Politik: Demokratische Öffentlichkeit und politische Moralität*. Reinbek bei Hamburg: Rowohlt.

Sandel, M. J. (1996). *Democracy's Discontent: America in Search of a Public Philosophy*. Cambridge, MA/London: Harvard University Press.

Scanlon, T. (1998). *What We Owe to Each Other*. Cambridge, MA/London: Harvard University Press.

Searle, J. R. (1995). *The Construction of Social Reality*. New York: Free Press.

Skinner, Q. (1998). *Liberty before Liberalism*. Cambridge: Cambridge University Press.

Sunstein, C. (1988). "Beyond the Republican Revival." *The Yale Law Journal* 97: 1539–90.

Viroli, M. (2002). *Republicanism*. New York: Hill and Wang.

van Gelderen, M. and Q. Skinner (eds) (2002). *Republicanism: A Shared European Heritage*, 2 vols. Cambridge: Cambridge University Press.

Walzer, M. (1983). *Spheres of Justice: A Defense of Pluralism and Equality*. New York: Basic.

NOTES

1. The terms "republicanism", "realism" and "liberalism" do not refer to schools of thought but more to a certain type of argument. According to these definitions, historical authors such as Locke, Montesquieu and Kant clearly made republican, not liberal, arguments. Other important arguments for the republican examination of politics may be found in the works of David Hume and James Madison.

2. The decisionist streak is evident, for example, in Goldsmith's and Posner's 2005 analysis of the limited validity of international law, an analysis that is situated somewhere between realism and rational choice theory. See also the account of the relevance of understanding and rejecting (or deliberately accepting) principles for the social contract in Scanlon 1998, 189–247.

3. In this context, "collective intentionality" does not refer to the intentionality of ontologically independent collectives; rather, it denotes the joint intentions or we-intentions, or, as the case may be, the shared interpretations of a situation and the normative expectations without which one could not conceive of the many social actions which render individual actions meaningful as part of a cooperative and coordinated action. For this concept of collective intentionality see Richardson 2002, 162–76.

4. For the interdependence argument, see Deudney 2007, 33–41; for the meaning of collective intentionality for social action see Searle 1995, 31–57 as well as Niederberger 2009, 172–91.

5. Cf. Kant's argument for the necessity of leaving the realm of private law and entering the realm of public law in Kant 1991, 68–122 (§§1–42).

6. "Right is therefore the sum of the conditions under which the choice of one can be united with the choice of another in accordance with a universal law of freedom" (Kant 1991, 56).

7. Cf. also the following statement: "We cannot assume that Leviathan will come to our aid in a genuine crisis; on the contrary, we are in a state of nature all the time, but the state of nature is precisely one in which people do in fact accept systems of constitutive rules, at least nearly all the time" (Searle 1995, 91).

8. For this kind of republicanism see, for example, Sandel 1996. For a discussion of these issues see also Richter 2004.

9. In this context, see for example the examination of the significance of the early modern militia for many republicans such as Adam Ferguson in Geuna 2002.

10. Such an account would characterize realism and its radical self-interest as the most "realist" theory, followed by rational choice theory with its concession of egotistically grounded cooperation and coordination. Liberal theories would then deny the necessity of individual selfishness and allow for motives of equality and justice among individuals, while republicanism finally assumes that actions are fully motivated by what is best for all and thus for the coexistence in a polity.

11. The ideal typical distinction between neo-Roman and neo-Athenian republican approaches refers to the difference between Athens as a republic in which the affairs of the polity were determined through collective discussion and action on the agora, and Rome as a republic in which the legally secured status of citizens and the corresponding legally codified practice of elections, assumption of offices and procedures is seen as characteristic. See, among others, Pocock 1995. Other authors prefer to distinguish between Atlantic and continental republicanism, for example, Onuf 1998, 38–57.

325

12. The term "neo-republicanism" tries to circumvent the difficulties of using Rome as a reference while still emphasizing its difference from especially Rousseauian republicanism (Lovett and Pettit 2009).

13. Compare also the "republican" theories of justice as developed by Miller 1999 and Walzer 1983.

14. See the references at the beginning of this article.

15. For this, see the approach in Buchanan 2004. Buchanan begins by drawing up a moral-philosophical list of ten basic human rights (128–30) and then proceeds to evaluate the legitimacy of particular agents on this basis (233–60).

16. For an extensive account of the following see Niederberger 2009, 191–231.

17. If, in order to solve the problem implicit in assumption (3), one were to introduce another assumption in the manner of (2), an infinite regress would ensue. One must therefore find a way to guarantee the nondominating character of institutions that differs from the way nondomination among individuals is guaranteed.

18. And this arbitrariness would remain even if the judiciary had the power not to apply arbitrarily enacted laws. This would merely amount to a confrontation between two arbitrary powers.

19. It is important here to note that this second requirement assumes that the first requirement is realized. For the fact that everybody may participate in legislating can guarantee non-arbitrary social circumstances only if the laws enacted determine the basic legality of social circumstances.

20. This justification of universal participation in the procedures and institutions of legislation is also designed to counter Pettit's position that democracy ought to be confined to contestation; see Pettit 1999, 2004, 2008. Contestation is indeed an interesting way of addressing problems of representation and of the direct influencing of legislatures. However, it does not replace the inclusionary mechanisms of the legislature but merely complements them.

21. See the overview in Reinhard 2002.

22. One could, for example, imagine an order where those concerned are excluded from the legislative process or where institutions are not subject to control and political decision-making by those affected but where society is nevertheless governed by laws. This would be a case of an "administrative dictatorship" or an ideological concealment of arbitrary power. A comprehensive legislature where society is not governed by laws, or where institutions are not controlled by this legislature, is impotent or may even generate false obligations. Finally, where powerful and controllable institutions exist but society is not governed by laws and legislation is not organized inclusively, this could easily amount to a form of tyranny.

23. It is not clear, for example, whether the legal form of social relations is such a high priority that different institutions can have the purpose of safeguarding it. On the other hand, it is not obvious that the existence of an institutionally established monopoly of violence has precedence over the rule of law.

24. See Madison's *Federalist* No. 10, in Hamilton, Madison and Jay 1999, 45–52.

25. One possibility of addressing this danger of reducing political regulation to the lowest common denominator would be to define the default option in terms of a theory of justice. One would then have to assume that a relatively large redistribution of goods is the normal state of affairs where the burden of proof does not lie with the advocates of redistribution but with those who reject the idea. However, first, it is not clear why

there should not be a large majority against redistribution, and second, in view of the plurality of justifications provided by theories of justice, it is not clear what a transition from one such justification to a specific and comprehensive default redistribution would look like.

26. The increasing number of lawsuits that investigate matters seemingly pertaining to the private sphere or the realm of civil society are a case in point, both in terms of extent and intensity.

27. For this see the discussion of intensity vs. extent in Pettit 1997, 103–6.

28. This is the republican perspective in Deudney 2007. Going beyond the arguments presented above, there are good reasons against a simple world state, both in terms of freedom and democracy, for in a world state there are considerably fewer opportunities for positively exercising freedom than in existing individual states. These reasons, however, go beyond the basic framework of republican conditions for a legitimate political order as set out above; therefore, they do not play an important role in the present argument. For a more detailed account see Niederberger 2008.

29. For this argument see also Bohman 2007, 101–34.

30. Thomas Nagel 2005, by contrast, argues that the necessity of shared legal institutions depends on the potential or actual exercise of coercion.

31. For an alternative view of the neo-republican ideal and its function cf. Pettit 2010b, 89–90.

Index